THE CAMBRIDGE COMPANIO
MERLEAU-PONTY

Maurice Merleau-Ponty (1908–1961) was described by Paul
Ricoeur as "the greatest of the French phenomenologists."
The new essays in this volume examine the full scope of
Merleau-Ponty's philosophy, from his central and abiding
concern with the nature of perception and the bodily constitution of intentionality to his reflections on science, nature,
art, history, and politics. The authors explore the historical
origins and context of his thought as well as its continuing
relevance to contemporary work in phenomenology, philosophy of mind, cognitive science, biology, art criticism, and
political and social theory.

What emerges is a fresh image of Merleau-Ponty as a deep
and original thinker whose philosophical importance has
been underestimated, in part owing to the influence of intellectual movements such as existentialism and structuralism, into which his work could not be easily assimilated.

New readers will find this the most convenient and accessible guide to Merleau-Ponty currently available. Advanced
students and specialists will find a conspectus of recent developments in the interpretation of Merleau-Ponty.

Taylor Carman is Associate Professor of Philosophy at
Barnard College, Columbia University.

Mark B. N. Hansen is Associate Professor of English at
Princeton University.

The Cambridge Companion to

MERLEAU-PONTY

Edited by

Taylor Carman
Barnard College, Columbia University

Mark B. N. Hansen
Princeton University

CAMBRIDGE UNIVERSITY PRESS
Cambridge, New York, Melbourne, Madrid, Cape Town, Singapore,
São Paulo

Cambridge University Press
40 West 20th Street, New York, NY 10011-4211, USA

www.cambridge.org
Information on this title: www.cambridge.org/9780521809894

First published 2005
Reprinted 2006

Printed in the United States of America

A catalog record for this publication is available from the British Library.

Library of Congress Cataloging in Publication Data

The Cambridge companion to Merleau-Ponty / edited by Taylor Carman
and Mark B. N. Hansen.
    p.   cm. – (Cambridge companions to philosophy)
Includes bibliographical references and index.
ISBN 0-521-80989-4 – ISBN 0-521-00777-1 (pbk.)
1. Merleau-Ponty, Maurice, 1908–1961.   I. Carman, Taylor, 1965-
II. Hansen, Mark B. N.   III. Series.
B2430.M3764C36   2004
194 – dc22   2003069683

ISBN-13   978-0-521-80989-4 hardback
ISBN-10   0-521-80989-4 hardback

ISBN-13   978-0-521-00777-1 paperback
ISBN-10   0-521-00777-1 paperback

CONTENTS

v

RENAUD BARBARAS is Professor of Contemporary Philosophy at the University of Paris-I Panthéon–Sorbonne. He is the author of *De l'être du phénomène: Sur l'ontologie de Merleau-Ponty* (1991, 2001), *La perception: Essai sur le sensible* (1994), *Le Tournant de l'expérience: Recherches sur la philosophie de Merleau-Ponty* (1998), and *Le désir et la distance: Introduction à une phénoménologie de la perception* (1999). *De l'être du phénomène* and *Le désir et la distance* are both forthcoming in English translation.

JUDITH BUTLER is Maxine Elliot Professor in the Departments of Rhetoric and Comparative Literature at the University of California, Berkeley. She is the author of *Gender Trouble: Feminism and the Subversion of Identity* (1990), *Bodies That Matter: On the Discursive Limits of "Sex"* (1993), *The Psychic Life of Power: Theories of Subjection* (1997), *Antigone's Claim: Kinship between Life and Death* (2000), and numerous articles and contributions to philosophy and feminist and queer theory.

TAYLOR CARMAN is Associate Professor of Philosophy at Barnard College, Columbia University. He has written articles on topics in phenomenology and is the author of *Heidegger's Analytic: Interpretation, Discourse, and Authenticity in "Being and Time"* (2003). He is currently writing a book on Merleau-Ponty.

HUBERT L. DREYFUS is Professor of Philosophy in the Graduate School at the University of California, Berkeley. He is the author of *Michel Foucault: Beyond Structuralism and Hermeneutics* (with Paul Rabinow) (1983), *Mind over Machine* (with Stuart Dreyfus)

vii

(1986), *Being-in-the-World: A Commentary on Heidegger's "Being and Time," Division I* (1991), *What Computers (Still) Can't Do* (1992), and *On the Internet* (2001).

JONATHAN GILMORE is Assistant Professor of Philosophy at Yale University. He has written articles in the philosophy of art, art history, and legal theory. He is the author of *The Life of a Style: Beginnings and Endings in the Narrative History of Art* (2000).

LYDIA GOEHR is Professor of Philosophy at Columbia University. She is the author of *The Imaginary Museum of Musical Works: An Essay in the Philosophy of Music* (1992) and *The Quest for Voice: Music, Politics, and the Limits of Philosophy* (1998). She is currently working on music and critical theory, one example of which appears in *The Cambridge Companion to Adorno* (2004).

MARK B. N. HANSEN is Associate Professor of English at Princeton University. He is the author of *Embodying Technesis: Technology beyond Writing* (2000), *New Philosophy for New Media* (2004), *Bodies in Code: Interfaces with New Media* (forthcoming); and essays on cultural theory.

SEAN DORRANCE KELLY is Assistant Professor of Philosophy and Jonathan Edwards Bicentennial Preceptor at Princeton University. His principal interests lie at the intersection of phenomenology, philosophy of mind, and cognitive neuroscience. He was recently awarded a Guggenheim Fellowship in recognition of his work in these areas.

CLAUDE LEFORT teaches social and political theory at the École des Hautes Études en Sciences Sociales in Paris. His work has appeared in English translation under the titles *The Political Forms of Modern Society: Bureaucracy, Democracy, Totalitarianism* (1986), *Democracy and Political Theory* (1988), and *Writing: The Political Test* (2000).

JOSEPH ROUSE is Hedding Professor of Moral Science and Chair of the Science in Society Program at Wesleyan University. He is the author of *Engaging Science: How to Think about Its Practices*

Philosophically (1996), *Knowledge and Power: Toward a Political Philosophy of Science* (1987), and *How Scientific Practices Matter: Reclaiming Philosophical Naturalism* (2002).

RICHARD SHUSTERMAN is Professor of Philosophy at Temple University, Philadelphia, and the Collège International de Philosophie, Paris. He is the author of *Pragmatist Aesthetics: Living Beauty, Rethinking Art* (2d ed., 2000), *Practicing Philosophy: Pragmatism and the Philosophical Life* (1997), *Performing Live: Aesthetic Alternatives for the Ends of Art* (2000), and *Surface and Depth: Dialectics of Criticism and Culture* (2002). He is also the editor of *Bourdieu: A Critical Reader* (1999).

CHARLES TAYLOR is Professor Emeritus of Philosophy at McGill University, Montreal. He is the author of *The Explanation of Behaviour* (1964); two volumes of collected essays, *Human Agency and Language* and *Philosophy and the Human Sciences* (1985); *Sources of the Self* (1989); *The Ethics of Authenticity* (1991); *Philosophical Arguments* (1995); and *Varieties of Religion Today: William James Revisited* (2002).

MARK A. WRATHALL is Associate Professor of Philosophy at Brigham Young University. He has published articles on topics in the history of philosophy and philosophy of language and mind, drawing on both the analytic and continental traditions in philosophy. He recently edited *Religion after Metaphysics* (2003) and coedited *Heidegger Reexamined* (2002), *Heidegger, Authenticity, and Modernity* (2000), *Heidegger, Coping, and Cognitive Science* (2000), and *Appropriating Heidegger* (2000).

Introduction

Maurice Merleau-Ponty was one of the most original and important philosophers of the past century. Yet in many ways the full scope of his contribution is becoming clear only now, more than forty years after his death. His impact on philosophy, psychology, and criticism has been enormous, although his intellectual reputation was initially somewhat overshadowed – first by the greater notoriety of his friend Jean-Paul Sartre and then by structuralism and poststructuralism in the latter half of the century. As a result, in part due to his premature death, Merleau-Ponty's presence in contemporary intellectual life has remained strangely elusive. His influence has cut across disciplinary boundaries, yet it has tended to move beneath the surface of mainstream scholarly and popular intellectual discourse.

As a result, perhaps understandably, academic and nonacademic readers alike have been slow to appreciate the real depth and significance of Merleau-Ponty's thought, which cannot be neatly pigeonholed in familiar conceptual or historical categories. He was a phenomenologist above all, yet he differed in fundamental ways from the three other major phenomenologists, Husserl, Heidegger, and Sartre. Unlike these philosophers, Merleau-Ponty availed himself of empirical data and theoretical insights drawn from the biological and social sciences, although he was not a psychologist, a linguist, or an anthropologist. He could fairly be called an existentialist, although that label has come to seem less and less informative in hindsight, embracing as it did such a disparate array of literary and intellectual figures. Merleau-Ponty was not himself a structuralist, although he saw sooner and more deeply than his contemporaries the importance of Saussurian linguistics and the structural anthropology of Claude Lévi-Strauss, who remained a close friend throughout his life.

I

It was a life as private and discreet as Sartre's was public and spectacular. Merleau-Ponty was born 14 March 1908 and raised as a Catholic in Paris by his mother following the death of his father. His early career followed the typical path of a French academic: he attended the Lycée Louis-le-Grand and then, with his friends Lévi-Strauss and Simone de Beauvoir, the École Normale Supérieure, graduating in 1930 and passing the *agrégation* in his early twenties. (Merleau-Ponty appears in Beauvoir's *Memoirs of a Dutiful Daughter* under the pseudonym "Pradelle.") In 1933, while teaching at a lycée in Beauvais, he submitted his first scholarly work, two research proposals on the nature of perception, to the Caisse Nationale des Sciences. Two years later, he returned to Paris as an *agrégé répétiteur* (junior member) of the École Normale. It was around this time that he attended Aron Gurwitsch's lectures on Gestalt psychology, and, in 1938, he completed his first major philosophical work, *The Structure of Behavior*, submitted as his *thèse complémentaire* for the *doctorat d'état* but not published until 1942. In 1939, Merleau-Ponty enlisted in the French army, serving as a lieutenant in the infantry; following demobilization, he returned to teaching at the École Normale and began work on what would be his major work, *Phenomenology of Perception* (1945).

The end of the war saw Merleau-Ponty in a new position at the University of Lyon, where he lectured on child psychology, aesthetics, and the mind–body problem and joined his fellow intellectuals – Sartre, Beauvoir, Michel Leiris, Raymond Aron, and others – in the editing and publication of the influential and still-prominent periodical *Les Temps modernes*. During this time, Merleau-Ponty discovered the structural linguistics of Ferdinand de Saussure, which he began teaching and integrating into his phenomenological account of perception as an embodied experience of being in the world. He published two books in 1948: *Humanism and Terror*, a volume of essays on philosophy and politics, and *Sense and Non-Sense*, a collection devoted to aesthetics, metaphysics, and psychology. With his reputation firmly established, Merleau-Ponty joined the faculty of the Sorbonne in 1949 as professor of psychology and pedagogy at the Institute of Psychology, where he concentrated on theoretical issues related to developmental psychology, including experimental work by Jean Piaget, Henri Wallon, Wolfgang Köhler, and Melanie Klein.

In 1952, Merleau-Ponty was appointed to the chair of philosophy at the Collège de France, a position once occupied by Henri Bergson and similar to those later held by Roland Barthes and Michel Foucault. Merleau-Ponty was instrumental in securing Lévi-Strauss's election to the Collège in 1959, and, in 1962, Lévi-Strauss dedicated his book *The Savage Mind* to the memory of his deceased friend. Merleau-Ponty's inaugural lecture at the Collège, "In Praise of Philosophy," both marked his debt to the work of Bergson and indicated the limitations of this eminent forebear. Elevation to the most prestigious academic position in philosophy in France triggered a period of intense work on Merleau-Ponty's part, much of it devoted to the philosophy of language, history, and politics. The following years witnessed a break with Sartre, in the wake of increasingly sharp political and philosophical differences. As Lydia Goehr argues in her essay in this volume, the two had radically different conceptions of the nature of political commitment and the relative autonomy of philosophical reflection. Although the break occurred in 1953 and led to his resignation from the editorial board of *Les Temps modernes*, Merleau-Ponty made it official in 1955 with the publication of *Adventures of the Dialectic*, a skeptical assessment of Marxist theory as a guide to political practice and the catalyst of Sartre's own *Critique of Dialectical Reason*. Claude Lefort's essay offers a rich account of the sophistication of Merleau-Ponty's political thought and his increasing awareness of the essential indeterminacy of human actions and events, an indeterminacy less alien to Marx himself than to the scientific pretensions of subsequent Marxist orthodoxy.

In the late 1950s Merleau-Ponty began to devote more time to his professional responsibilities. He edited *Les Philosophes célèbres*, a massive compendium of essays by important academic philosophers of the day, including Jean Beaufret, Roger Caillois, Jean Starobinski, Karl Löwith, Gilles Deleuze, and Alphonse de Waelhens. Many of Merleau-Ponty's own contributions to this anthology, introductions to the various sections of the book, appear in *Signs* (1960). During his nine years as professor of philosophy at the Collège de France, Merleau-Ponty devoted lecture cycles to a vast array of topics, including important courses on the concept of nature (1956–60). All the while he was at work on two major philosophical undertakings: one provisionally titled *Vérité et existence*, the other *The Prose of the World*. The former may well have been part of the work later titled

The Visible and the Invisible, which, despite its unfinished state and posthumous publication, constitutes his final major philosophical contribution. Merleau-Ponty's brilliant philosophical career, in full bloom, indeed still clearly in ascent, was abruptly cut short on 3 May 1961 when he died of a heart attack at the age of fifty-three.

Recently, renewed efforts to come to grips with Merleau-Ponty's philosophical achievement have been gaining some momentum in the English-speaking world. As part of this trend, the essays in this volume attempt to spell out the substance of his central insights and highlight the enduring legacy of his ideas in such diverse fields as epistemology and the philosophy of mind, psychology and cognitive science, biology and the philosophy of nature, aesthetics, and the philosophy of history and politics. What characterizes Merleau-Ponty's work in all these domains is his unique combination of penetrating insight into the phenomena, his perspicuous view of the origin and organization of knowledge, and his command of a wide range of literary and artistic references to render his arguments vivid and culturally relevant.

Admittedly, the style that emerges from Merleau-Ponty's unique blend of interests and abilities is at times eclectic. His arguments are not systematically organized; his prose is often lush, occasionally hyperbolic; and he delivers few memorable bon mots or resonant slogans by which to identify and recall his considered views. Indeed, he rarely asserts those views in the form of discrete, conspicuous propositions. Instead, his approach is more often interrogative, suggestive, elliptical, conciliatory, yet in the end persistent and unmistakable. Merleau-Ponty cultivates a deliberately nonadversarial dialectical strategy that is bound to seem alien, even disconcerting, to anyone educated in the explicit theoretical assertions and blunt argumentative techniques of contemporary analytic philosophy. He often avoids stating a thesis directly by way of staking out a position in contrast to competing views, or else he does so only obliquely, after extended preliminary discussion, exploration, and imaginative unfolding of the problem at hand. More frequently, and more confusingly, he will often try to imagine himself into the philosophical perspectives of the thinkers and ideas he is critically examining, borrow their insights, appropriate their terminology for his own purposes, and only then make a clean break by pronouncing a negative verdict in favor of his own (often radically different) position. What might initially sound like cautious doubts, tentative objections, and subtle reformulations in Merleau-Ponty's prose often prove, on closer inspection, to signal fundamental disagreements, deep shifts in perspective, and startlingly original insights. In view of these potential stylistic and substantive stumbling blocks, it is worth trying to get a preliminary overview of Merleau-Ponty's work, its sources, its characteristic features, and its continuing relevance to contemporary philosophy, psychology, and criticism.

The chief inspiration behind Merleau-Ponty's thought as a whole was the phenomenology that emerged in Germany in the early decades of the twentieth century. In the 1930s, he and Sartre both, although separately and in different ways, discovered the works of Edmund Husserl, Martin Heidegger, and Max Scheler, introduced them to a French audience, and began to make their own original contributions to the field. Phenomenology was the chief formative influence on Merleau-Ponty, and yet, as we shall see, his own approach differed crucially from that of any of its other major figures, Sartre in particular.[1]

Husserl, the founder of the movement, had in effect inaugurated a new way of doing philosophy, and with it a novel conception of the nature and purpose of philosophical reflection. Having abandoned his own early effort to analyze the fundamental concepts of arithmetic in psychological terms, and moreover breaking with the indirect theory of perception espoused by his mentor, Franz Brentano, Husserl developed a detailed account of what Brentano called the "intentionality" of consciousness, that is to say, its object-directedness, its of-ness, or "aboutness." Husserl's theory of intentionality marks a watershed in the history of late modern philosophy because, although Brentano was responsible for importing the term into our technical vocabulary, it was Husserl who effectively put the concept to work against many of the guiding assumptions that had dominated psychology and the philosophy of mind since Descartes.

It is not, of course, as if no one before Brentano or Husserl knew that consciousness is (typically) consciousness of something, that our mental attitudes are directed toward objects and states of affairs in the world. And yet, astonishingly, that humble fact had managed to slip through the cracks of Cartesian and Lockean epistemology, perhaps precisely owing to its seeming obviousness. According to the indirect representationalist theory of ideas in Descartes and Locke, by contrast, what we are directly aware of is, strictly speaking, not external objects, but our own mental states, which (presumably) both respond to and represent those objects. Representationalism thus sought to analyze, and perhaps explain, the directedness of consciousness by positing inner mental tokens whose function it was to depict or describe things out in the world. Ideas, or in Kantian jargon "representations" (*Vorstellungen*), thus formed a kind of bridge, both causal and experiential, between the inner and the outer and were thus made to serve both a rational and a mechanical function simultaneously: ideas were at once supposed to be *effects* produced in us by the external world and to contain or *express* our knowledge of that world. If we could grasp the peculiar nature and operation of those representational intermediaries, it was assumed, we would understand the relation between the mind and the world. Intentionality would then reveal itself not as a primitive feature of experience, but as an emergent, derived phenomenon – perhaps even an illusion, as Berkeley in effect argued.

Yet even supposing that intentionality is a kind of illusion, the question remains what our awareness *of* our own ideas consists in, for ideas are themselves objects of awareness. Indeed, that's just what "ideas" were meant to be: objects of awareness. But this just shows that the attempt to dissolve intentionality in the theory of ideas was incoherent from the outset, because that theory took the notion of our awareness of our own ideas for granted as self-evident, and hence unworthy of critical consideration in its own right. The very notion of an indirect representationalist theory of perception thus presupposes intentionality in the way it conceives of our epistemic relation to our own ideas, and yet it disallows itself any recognition of that relation as an essential aspect of thought or perception.

Husserl's phenomenology was groundbreaking in its rejection of this epistemological picture, which it managed to do in part by distinguishing between the *objects* and the *contents* of consciousness.[2] There is a difference, that is, between the things we are aware of and the contents of our awareness of them. This distinction allows us to conceive of intentionality as something different from and irreducible to the causal connections between external objects and internal psychological states, for the objects of my awareness are not (ordinarily) the contents of my mind; rather, those inner contents constitute my awareness *of* outer objects. Intentional content is not (ordinarily) *what* I am aware of; it is rather the *of*-ness, the directedness of my awareness. As Wilfrid Sellars would later argue, traditional epistemology tried to draw both the rational and the causal dimensions of perception onto the same map, as it were, thus generating the hybrid, arguably incoherent, concept of "ideas" as all-purpose intermediaries between mind and world.[3]

Husserl, by contrast, like Sellars, and, more recently, John McDowell, insists on a distinction between the normative and the nonnormative, between the "ideal" (abstract) and the "real" (concrete) aspects of mental phenomena, between the intentional content of experience and the causal conditions in the world (and in our brains) that allow it to have that content. The ideal, normatively defined, timeless content of an intentional state is what Husserl calls its *noema*, in contrast to its *noesis*, the token psychological episode occurring in time. Husserl's phenomenological method thus involves two coordinated abstractions, or "reductions," that serve to zero in on the noema, or pure intentional content as such. The first, the "transcendental reduction," or *epochê*, consists in directing one's attention away from the "transcendent" (perspectivally given) world back to the "immanent" (epistemically transparent) contents of consciousness. This reduction takes us from the external world, broadly speaking, to the inner domain of the mental. The second, the "eidetic reduction," points upward, as it were, toward the ideal, normative aspects of mental content, away from its real temporal and causal properties. This reduction moves us away from factual psychological reality toward atemporal conceptual and semantic content, from facts to essences.

What inspired more than one generation of phenomenologists in all this was Husserl's insistence on simply describing intentionality adequately at the outset, prior to any construction of theories, which tend more often to obscure than illuminate what he called "the things themselves" (*die Sachen selbst*). Philosophical explanations frequently go wrong precisely by beginning with impoverished or distorted descriptions of the phenomena they set out to analyze. To understand Merleau-Ponty's work at all, one must appreciate his abiding commitment to Husserl's conception of phenomenological description as an antidote to abstract theorizing, conceptual system building, and reductive philosophical explanation.

Contrary to the impression he often gives, however, Merleau-Ponty was and remained deeply dissatisfied with the letter of Husserl's doctrines, however enthusiastically he embraced the spirit of the enterprise as a whole. To begin with, he could never accept Husserl's distinction between the immanence of consciousness and the transcendence of the external world, or between the mere psychological facts of perceptual experience and the pure essences that alone supposedly constitute its intentionality. Like Heidegger and Sartre, Merleau-Ponty rejected the transcendental and eidetic reductions as illegitimate abstractions from the concrete worldly conditions of experience that render it intelligible to itself. In the preface to *Phenomenology of Perception*, for example, Merleau-Ponty writes, as Husserl never could, "The greatest lesson of the reduction is the impossibility of a complete reduction" (*PP* viii/xiv/xv).

Heidegger had already attacked the phenomenological reductions, both implicitly in *Being and Time* and explicitly in his lectures of the 1920s. Heidegger rejected what he called the "worldless" subject of Cartesianism,[4] which he saw reaffirmed in Husserl's conception of a "transcendental ego" conceptually distinct from, although metaphysically identical to, the concrete psychophysical human being. Once I perform the reductions, Husserl insisted, strictly speaking, "I am then not a human I."[5] But surely it is precisely as a human being that I am able to reflect on my experience and understand myself as intentionally opened onto a world; this is just what calls for phenomenological description. Husserl's studied disregard of concrete existence was thus anathema to Heidegger, who insisted that intentionality be ascribed to embodied human agents, not worldless transcendental subjects: "Transcendental constitution is a central possibility of existence of the factical self."[6] We understand ourselves precisely as existing beings, defined as much by the *that* of our existence as by the *what* of our nature or identity; indeed, "if there were an entity *whose what is precisely to be and nothing but to be*, then this ideative contemplation of such an entity would ... amount to a fundamental misunderstanding."[7] As far as Heidegger was concerned, Husserl's phenomenological reductions amounted to an abstract, theory-driven distortion of the phenomena. In *Being and Time* he therefore advanced his own alternative account not of some preconceived domain of "pure" consciousness, or transcendental subjectivity, but of what he called our everyday "being-in-the-world" (*In-der-Welt-sein*).[8]

The difference between Husserl and Heidegger, then, is striking, at least in retrospect. Unfortunately, Merleau-Ponty's naturally conciliatory hermeneutic approach to the texts and thinkers he admired often led him to conflate the two. For example, Merleau-Ponty seems to read Husserl's theory of essential or eidetic intuition into Heidegger's conception of human existence as being-in-the-world. In the preface to the *Phenomenology*, he writes,

The need to proceed by way of essences does not mean that philosophy takes them as its object, but on the contrary that our existence is too tightly held (*prise*) in the world to be able to know itself as such at the moment of its involvement, and that it requires the field of ideality in order to become acquainted with and to prevail over its own facticity. (*PP* ix/xiv–xv/xvi)

But this is a hybrid. Taking essences as objects was precisely the point of the eidetic reduction. Moreover, Heidegger's notions of existence and facticity were precisely what Husserl insisted phenomenology must remain indifferent to, just as mathematicians must remain indifferent to the contingent properties of drawings or models of geometric figures: "a phenomenological doctrine of essence is no more interested in the methods by which the phenomenologist might ascertain the *existence* of some experiences," he writes, "than geometry is interested in how the existence of figures on the board or models on the shelf might be methodically confirmed."[9] This abstraction from human existence as the site of intentional phenomena thus marks a sharp and irreconcilable difference between Husserl's eidetic phenomenology and Heidegger's "existential analytic," which Sartre and Merleau-Ponty both followed, although in different ways and with different results.[10]

Like all philosophers inspired by phenomenology, what Merleau-Ponty learned from Husserl was the need for faithful description of phenomena, as opposed to metaphysical speculation and philosophical system building. What he learned from Heidegger, by contrast, was that "the things themselves" lend little support to the categories and distinctions on which Husserl based his method of phenomenological reduction and description. Far from revealing a realm of pure transcendental subjectivity separated from the external world by what Husserl deems "a veritable abyss,"[11] or for that matter a do-main of ideal essences distinct in principle from all factual reality, phenomenological inquiry instead finds embodied agents immersed in worldly situations in virtue of perceptual and affective attitudes whose contents are themselves often conceptually indeterminate.

Indeed, notwithstanding his enormous debt to Heidegger, Merleau-Ponty arguably goes farther in acknowledging the mutual interdependence of the normative contents of our attitudes and the factical worldly conditions in which those attitudes are enmeshed. For although Heidegger dismissed Husserl's still all-too-Cartesian conception of human beings as "worldless" subjects, along with his "ontologically obscure separation of the real and the ideal,"[12] he drew a firm distinction of his own between the "ontological" and the merely "ontic," that is, between the intelligibility of be-ing and contingent facts about entities. Insisting on this "ontologi-cal difference" between being and entities, as Heidegger does, in ef-fect prevents him from drawing close connections between general structural dimensions of intelligibility and the fine details of con-crete phenomena, above all those pertaining to perception and the body. Remarkably, in all of *Being and Time*, Heidegger says virtually nothing about perception and mentions the body only to exclude it from the existential analytic proper: "corporeity" (*Leiblichkeit*), he says, "contains a problematic of its own, not to be dealt with here."[13] For Merleau-Ponty, by contrast, perception and the body together constitute *the* phenomenon most crucial to an under-standing of what he, too, calls our "being in the world" (*être au monde*). As several of the essays in this volume make clear, in partic-ular those by Charles Taylor, Richard Shusterman, and Judith Butler, Merleau-Ponty's account of the bodily nature of perception, of the perceptual bedrock of human existence, remains his most profound and original contribution to philosophy.

It should be no surprise, then, that Gestalt psychology was an almost equally important source of inspiration for him. Merleau-Ponty learned about Gestalt theory from Aron Gurwitsch's lectures at the Institute d'Histoire des Sciences in Paris in the 1930s.[14] Max Wertheimer, Wolfgang Köhler, and Kurt Koffka, the central figures of the movement, attacked the atomistic and mechanistic assump-tions that had dominated psychology for centuries. Indeed, it is one of the enduring legacies of the Gestalt school to have thoroughly discredited the theory of ideas that held sway in one form or another since Descartes and Locke. Rather than conceiving of sensory experience as a kind of mosaic of sensations, each correlative to a discrete stimulus, the Gestalt theorists insisted that perception is organized around configurations or ensembles of mutually reinforcing components, which often fail to correspond to individual stimuli in any direct or isomorphic way. Meaningful forms or constellations of this kind are the truly primitive elements in perception, and grasping them is neither the mere passive registration of meaningless input nor unconscious conceptual judgment, but a kind of perceptual intelligence or insight that underlies the application of concepts and inferential reasoning. The holistic structure of experience, which is a function neither of sensation nor of judgment, is evident, for instance, in the context-sensitivity of our perceptions of color and size constancy: seeing or hearing isolated colors and shapes is possible only (if at all) as an abstraction from our ordinary perceptions of natural objects, artifacts, the empty spaces between them, relations, situations, persons, and events. To suppose that we piece such things together from more immediately evident bits of sensory input is to mistake theoretical abstractions for concrete phenomena.

Yet while acknowledging that the meaningful intentional structure of sensory experience has profound philosophical implications, Merleau-Ponty believed the Gestaltists generally failed to appreciate them. There is, he insists, "an entire philosophy implicit in the critique of the 'constancy hypothesis'" (*PP* 62n/50n/58n) – but *only* implicit. For such a philosophy calls for a radical reconceptualization of perception itself as an aspect not of this or that mental function or capacity, but of our very being. The Gestalt school tried to spell out wholly general laws of perceptual form and, moreover, anticipated the eventual reduction of those laws to causal mechanisms in the brain. Yet our relation to the world, like our relation to ourselves, is not merely causal but intelligible, indeed practical, and no purely theoretical account of general laws can capture what we understand intuitively in our prereflective self-understanding.

Merleau-Ponty consequently found some confirmation of his dissatisfaction with the psychological literature in the work of the neurologist Kurt Goldstein. In collaboration with the Gestalt theorist Adhémar Gelb, Goldstein conducted important studies of aphasia in brain-damaged patients and thought deeply about the philosophical

foundations of biological knowledge. Contrary to all reductive impulses toward mechanism and modularity in the philosophy of psychology, impulses that remain powerful to this day, Goldstein insisted that medicine and physiology be attentive to the essential
unity of organisms and the global and subtle intermingling of seemingly discrete organs and functions. Goldstein distanced himself
from Gestalt theory,[15] but he shared with it an emphasis on the holistic character of experience and the idea that animals have a natural
tendency to integrate their behaviors, to minimize perceptual distur-
bances, and to maintain a kind of equilibrium in their sensorimotor
orientation. The idea common to Goldstein and the Gestaltists –
namely, that ordinary perception and behavior are always organized
around a *normative* notion of rightness or equilibrium – is, as the essays by Hubert Dreyfus and Sean Kelly demonstrate, one of the most
important insights at work in Merleau-Ponty's own phenomenology.

Merleau-Ponty thus sought to rescue our understanding of perception from the conceptual oblivion to which traditional psychology
and epistemology had consigned it. Perception, as Taylor Carman
and Mark Wrathall each point out in their essays, is neither brute
sensation nor rational thought, but an aspect of the body's intentional grip on its physical and social environment. Most philosophers today readily dismiss the empiricist notion of brute "sense
data" as symptomatic of a more general failure to appreciate the intentionality of perception. Far less widely acknowledged, however,
is the distinction Merleau-Ponty also draws between perception and
cognition, the dominant assumption today being rather that the notions of sensation and cognition pose an exclusive dilemma for theories of perception and that there is no intermediate phenomenon
between the two. Indeed, since Merleau-Ponty wrote on the subject, what was once called "intellectualism" (roughly equivalent to
what we now call "cognitivism") has received renewed impetus both
from the cognitive revolution in linguistics and psychology and from
the various forms of linguistic or pragmatic rationalism inspired by
Sellars.[16] According to Sellars, our understanding of the contents of
our own thoughts and experiences is as linguistically constructed,
hence theory-laden, as our understanding of the composition and
behavior of physical objects. The mind is not incorrigibly present
to itself; rather, we posit "inner episodes" in psychology just as
we posit unobservable particles and forces in physics. For Sellars,

"*impressions* are theoretical entities." Moreover, our positing of impressions is inextricably bound up in theory with ascriptions of propositional attitudes, so that "seeing is a *cognitive* episode which involves the framework of thoughts." Perception is no mere brute confrontation with sensory particulars, Sellars argues, but is conceptually and linguistically constituted, even in the mere recognition of things under aspects: "instead of coming to have a concept of something because we have noticed that sort of thing, to have the ability to notice a sort of thing is already to have the concept of that sort of thing, and cannot account for it."[17]

Philosophers such as Gareth Evans and Christopher Peacocke have maintained, on the contrary, that perceptual experience has content that is intentional, but *not* conceptually articulated. Drawing on Charles Taylor – who was in turn, not accidentally, drawing on Merleau-Ponty – Evans first drew the attention of analytic philosophers to the nonconceptual content underlying and informing our judgments about the world, for example, the content of the information states that allow animals to sense their own bodily position and orientation.[18] Replying to John McDowell's influential critique of Evans,[19] Peacocke has defended the notion of nonconceptual content on the grounds that concepts are either too crude or too refined to capture the qualities presented to us in perception. For whereas a concept such as *red* is too coarse-grained to specify precisely what I see when I see something red, a demonstrative concept such as *this shade of red* imports a notion of *shade* that need not play any role in my sensory experience as such.[20] Sean Kelly, relying explicitly on Merleau-Ponty, has argued alternatively that the nonconceptual content of perception is due both to the context-dependence of the sensory appearance of objects and to the object-dependence of the sensory appearance of qualities. The same things look different in different situations, just as generically similar properties differ phenomenally depending on the kinds of objects of which they are properties.[21] As Sartre says, and as Merleau-Ponty reiterates, when Matisse paints a red carpet, he manages to evoke the color not as an abstract property, but as a concrete feature of a genuinely tactile object: what he paints is not just *red*, but "a *woolly* red."[22] Remarkably, Merleau-Ponty's arguments on this point are only now managing to be heard in the analytical debate, some sixty years after the fact.[23]

Merleau-Ponty's insights into perception and embodiment were not limited to phenomenology and psychology, but extended to themes in the arts, literature, history, and politics. It was inevitable that he should pursue multiple approaches to the phenomena, for their significance was for him global. As he saw it, no corner of human life is unmarked by the fact of our situated bodily perspective on the world. Perception therefore cannot be merely a topic of specialized concern for the biological and social sciences, for it touches all aspects of the human condition.

Jonathan Gilmore's essay in this volume explores Merleau-Ponty's fascination with painting, both for what it can teach us about vision and visibility and for the way it embodies primitive elements of all human behavior: gesture, expression, style. What does painting tell us about the visible as such? Representational art is at once like and unlike its objects, and its peculiar proximity to and distance from the world it depicts is a source of persistent, if subtle, confusion. On one hand, great paintings are not just objects or artifacts. Rather, as Heidegger said, a work of art is capable of disclosing an entire world by creating a space of meaning in which entities can first emerge into the light of day, sink into obscurity, or both.[24] Works of art are not of a piece with mundane reality, then, but stand apart by concentrating and focusing in some explicit way the tacit, inarticulate understanding we already have prior to any overt expression or reflection. Works of art open onto a world we already inhabit and understand, however dimly. Painting in particular serves as a window onto the very visibility of the visible, Merleau-Ponty suggests, allowing us literally to *see* what it is to see.

At the same time, looking at a painting is utterly unlike looking at any other object, not least of all the object it represents (if it does). Contrary to our naive tendency to assimilate representations to their objects, and contrary to the realistic prejudices of popular aesthetic sensibilities, paintings relate to the worlds they disclose in profoundly artificial and conventionalized ways. The invention of linear perspective was not the discovery of a uniquely correct way of depicting three-dimensional scenes in two dimensions. Rather, pre-Renaissance artists simply projected images onto flat surfaces in different ways and for different reasons. In ancient and medieval art, for example, figures often appeared large or small depending on their allegorical importance, rather than their distance from the implied viewer. There is no one right way to paint spatially extended forms, any more than there is one right way to express an emotion in music. No matter how closely they seem to duplicate three-dimensional visual stimuli, no matter how realistic they seem, paintings are always essentially discontinuous and incommensurable with the real perceptual world, just as the sounds of words are incommensurable with the concepts and objects they signify.

Indeed, like music and poetry, painting is an expressive exercise. Its philosophical significance is therefore not limited to its effects and qualities, but extends to its mode of production in the work of the artist. Paintings are not just finished products, but echoes of human effort, human perceptions of the world, human lives. We can no more regard a painting as a mere object than we can hear articulate speech as mere noise. Even if we don't understand the language, what we hear is someone speaking, not just sounds. So, too, like voices addressing us, works of art are living extensions of flesh-and-blood persons, and they manifest the human condition in much the same way our bodies do: by realizing in gesture a particular coherent *style*, an understanding, a sensitivity, a way of being in the world. Style characterizes great art, but it is also an essential aspect of ordinary perception and action. Over and beyond the objective movements of a person's body, what we see when we see the person – in particular, when we *really* see him, by *recognizing* him – is his *character*, the style of his comportments. What is enigmatic about style, apart from its sheer conceptual elusiveness, is its ubiquity; it is not an isolated property, but manifests itself globally in handwriting, in typical behaviors, in voice and speech.[25] Only by drawing direct connections between what we learn from the exemplary expressive power of artists and what we already know of ourselves and each other by knowing our characters, Merleau-Ponty believed, will we come to appreciate the philosophical significance of perception and the body, as phenomenologists and psychologists have begun to describe them.

It is important to remember that the "structure" in the title of Merleau-Ponty's first book, *The Structure of Behavior*, referred to the form, configuration, or ensemble posited by Gestalt psychology to describe the immediately felt, intelligible meanings available to us in perceptual experience. As his work proceeded, however, another notion of structure began to attract his philosophical attention, namely, that posited by the linguist Ferdinand de Saussure and by anthropologists and ethnographers such as Lévi-Strauss. The phonetic and symbolic structures they described were not phenomenal forms, but objective, impersonal systems of rules allegedly operating unconsciously beneath, or outside, the bounds of ordinary experience. Merleau-Ponty did not make the mistake of identifying the structuralists' structures with the Gestaltists' gestalts, and yet from early on he saw such emerging theoretical developments as both a challenge and an opportunity.

One would expect Merleau-Ponty's early enthusiastic engagement with structural linguistics and anthropology to have opened a fruitful dialogue between philosophy in the grand tradition and the newly evolving human sciences. And for a time it did, for several reasons. First, Merleau-Ponty himself played an instrumental role in disseminating much of that new scientific work. As François Dosse's interviews attest, Merleau-Ponty was instrumental in psychoanalyst Jacques Lacan's discovery of Saussure, just as his effort to develop a philosophy of history from Saussure's work in turn inspired the structuralist linguist Algirdas Julien Greimas. Merleau-Ponty's role is perhaps best summarized by philosopher Jean-Marie Benoist, for whom "Merleau-Ponty acted like a precursor phase conditioning the reception of the richness of the structuralist labor."[26]

More substantially, the structuralist paradigm provided a rich source of material that would aid him in his ongoing critique of Sartre's dualism of being and nothingness. From Saussure Merleau-Ponty acquired the tools for a philosophy of history that would mesh with his phenomenology of perception. In his inaugural lecture at the Collège de France, Merleau-Ponty entertains the possibility that "The theory of signs, as developed in linguistics, perhaps implies a conception of historical meaning which gets beyond the opposition of *things* versus *consciousness*....Saussure, the modern linguist, could have sketched a new philosophy of history" (*EP* 56/54–5). If the phenomenology of perception brings about a displacement of the *cogito*, from the personal "I" to the prepersonal "one" (*l'on*), it likewise opens up a space of collective social existence between the first- and the third-person points of view, between what Sartre called our "transcendence" as subjects and our "facticity" as mere objects for one another. As Merleau-Ponty sees it, this shared social space is what makes philosophy of history possible, and its ground lies in the impersonal symbolic domain that places meaning *outside* individual consciousnesses.

In structuralist anthropology and ethnography, Merleau-Ponty found an implicit critique of Western reason that seemed to res- onate with his own concerns. In a 1959 essay he quite strikingly points up the affinities tying his own philosophical project to the work of Lévi-Strauss: "Thus our task is to broaden our reasoning to make it capable of grasping what, in ourselves and in others, pre- cedes and exceeds reason" (*S* 154/122). Whereas the subject–object dichotomy dominating Sartre's philosophy meant that all meaning must originate with human beings, linguistic and social structures furnished mechanisms for "the generalized meaning which works in these historical forms and in the whole of history, which is not the thought of any one mind but which appeals to all" (*EP* 55/54).

On both counts, however, as Vincent Descombes and others have pointed out, Merleau-Ponty's interpretations underestimate the extent of the structuralist break with the philosophy of the subject.[27] Whereas, for Merleau-Ponty, Saussurian linguistics fur- nished a model for the impersonal dimension of history, for the struc- tural linguists, psychoanalysts, and literary critics of the day, it re- ferred to a process operating in the absence of subjectivity altogether. Likewise, structuralist anthropology announced a thoroughgoing cri- tique of Western reason far more radical than Merleau-Ponty's inter- nal challenge to philosophy to broaden itself by encompassing the irrational.

Thus, we arrive at the paradox of Merleau-Ponty's influence: precisely by embracing Saussurian linguistics and structural an- thropology as allies in the battle against Sartrean subjectivism and voluntarism and by calling for a philosophy of history based on their principles, Merleau-Ponty effectively undermined his own effort to bring phenomenology into productive conversation with the human sciences. Ironically, then, the very figure who opened the French in- tellectual world to these new developments was in effect left behind as they coalesced into what, after his death in 1961, came to be called simply "structuralism." This paradox presents one of the most ur- gent reasons for revisiting Merleau-Ponty's thought today, namely, as a missed opportunity in the history of philosophy. For a genuine encounter between phenomenology and structuralism points to an alternative to poststructuralist antihumanism and its shadow, the politics of identity, which have all but dominated intellectual life in the humanities for the last thirty years.

To grasp Merleau-Ponty's contemporary relevance, we must return to the paradox mentioned earlier. Why was one of the figures most responsible for fostering the growth of structuralism eventually left behind in its wake? One reason, surely the most obvious, is the fact of Merleau-Ponty's premature death, which left his legacy in doubt. Subsequent neglect of Merleau-Ponty, however, also seems to have been the result of circumstances of intellectual history that in effect ensured the demise of his moderate position urging the opening of philosophy to other disciplines while retaining its longstanding privilege as the queen of the sciences. Descombes, for instance, suggests that Merleau-Ponty's "philosophical project was bound to fail for a very simple reason. The scholarly disciplines were already active in their own conceptual development and did not need Merleau-Ponty or any other philosopher to interpret their discoveries. They were all already at work on both levels."[28] If we bear in mind that the generation immediately succeeding Merleau-Ponty was the generation of 1968, this picture of disciplinary self-sufficiency gets filled out with the specter of radicalism which, in a zeal to supplant all that had come before, found it convenient to lump Merleau-Ponty together with many of the philosophers he had criticized most sharply, notably Husserl and Sartre.

Adding to the paradox, there is a bitter irony at work, for Merleau-Ponty's final philosophical project, left unfinished at the time of his death, resonates in many ways with the antisubjectivism common to the generation of '68. As the essays in this volume by Renaud Barbaras and Mark Hansen point out, Merleau-Ponty's final work marks a major departure from his earlier phenomenology of perception. If the global significance of this departure was a passage from phenomenology to ontology, its orienting point was nothing other than a thoroughgoing criticism of the residual subjectivism informing his *Phenomenology of Perception*. In one of the working notes collected in *The Visible and the Invisible*, Merleau-Ponty starkly underlines the inadequacy of his earlier work: "The problems posed in *Ph.P.* are insoluble because I start there from the 'consciousness'–'object' distinction" (*VI* 253/200). The turn to what he called an "ontology of the flesh (*chair*)" must be understood as an effort to overcome the impasse of dualism that, as he now understood, threatens the phenomenological project itself, with its defining motifs of intentionality and subjectivity.

This resonance of Merleau-Ponty's final work with poststructuralist French philosophy has gone largely unrecognized. One striking exception is the philosopher Gilles Deleuze, who enthusiastically cites Merleau-Ponty's concept of the flesh as the key to understanding what he calls the "being of sensation":

The being of sensation, the bloc of percept and affect, which appear as the unity or reversibility of feeling and felt, their intimate intermingling like hands clasped together: it is the *flesh* that, at the same time, is freed from the living body, the perceived world, and the intentionality of one toward the other that is still too tied to experience; whereas the flesh gives us the being of sensation ... flesh of the world and flesh of the body that are exchanged as correlates, ideal coincidence. A curious Fleshism inspires this final avatar of phenomenology and plunges it into the mystery of incarnation.[29]

Regrettably, this endorsement was virtually unique among the philosophers of the '68 generation, and one Deleuze offered only late in his career.[30] Indeed, one might compare it to Michel Foucault's deployment of Merleau-Ponty as a foil to Deleuze, a deployment that at once typifies Merleau-Ponty's reception in that milieu and reveals how the very name "Merleau-Ponty" had by 1970 come to signify something outmoded:

The Logic of Sense can be read as the most alien book imaginable from *The Phenomenology of Perception*. In this latter text, the body-organism is linked to the world through a network of primal significations which arise from the perception of things, while, according to Deleuze, phantasms form the impenetrable and incorporeal surface of bodies; and from this process, simultaneously topological and cruel, something is shaped that falsely presents itself as a centered organism and distributes at its periphery the increasing remoteness of things.[31]

If Dosse is to be believed, Merleau-Ponty's project of a philosophy of history was dealt a decisive blow by Foucault's growing antipathy for phenomenology in the years following his first book, *Madness and Civilization*. Foucault's work during this time testified to an increasing sense of the incompatibility of empirical research and the privileged transcendental position claimed for philosophy. Indeed, Foucault's archaeological studies of the early 1970s, most notably *The Order of Things* and *The Archaeology of Knowledge*, did perhaps more than any other work of the period to legitimize conceiving of processes without subjects. Accordingly, Foucault articulated his antihumanist program in those works in terms of the failure of phenomenology and the residual links between subjectivism and anthropology: "It is probably impossible to give empirical contents transcendental value, or to displace them in the direction of a constituent subjectivity, without giving rise, at least silently, to an anthropology."[32]

Even if one were to acknowledge the force of this argument tying the philosophy of the subject to an outmoded humanism, it is a striking fact that Foucault makes no mention of Merleau-Ponty's criticisms of Husserl and Sartre on precisely this point. Indeed, in his introduction to Georges Canguilhem's *The Normal and the Pathological*, when he sketches a bipartite genealogy of the reception of phenomenology in France, Foucault places Merleau-Ponty, alongside Sartre, squarely on the side of the philosophy of the subject. This was possible only because of his failure to recognize Merleau-Ponty's deep and ongoing interest in the empirical sciences of his day, not to mention his late effort to move beyond the transcendental impasse of the subject and subjectivity. In his sketch Foucault distinguishes between

a philosophy of experience, of sense and of subject and a philosophy of knowledge, of rationality and of concept. On the one hand, one network is that of Sartre and Merleau-Ponty; and then another is that of Cavaillès, Bachelard and Canguilhem. In other words, we are dealing with two modalities according to which phenomenology was taken up in France. . . . Whatever they may have been after shifts, ramifications, interactions, even rapprochements, these two forms of thought in France have constituted two philosophical directions which have remained profoundly heterogeneous.[33]

Merleau-Ponty would seem to be an ideal candidate to bridge the gap separating these allegedly heterogeneous directions. For what is at stake in Merleau-Ponty's assimilation of Husserl other than a more robustly intuitive account of knowledge, one not predicated on the prior existence of the subject, but rather productive of its very phenomenal appearance?

A similar critique of phenomenology for its supposed fidelity to humanist subjectivism can be found in other major philosophical figures of the period, including the structuralist psychoanalyst Jacques Lacan and the deconstructive philosopher and critic Jacques Derrida. For Lacan, whose early influential paper on the mirror stage enlisted support from phenomenology in its resistance to biological reductionism, Merleau-Ponty's phenomenology – including its alteration and complication in *The Visible and the Invisible* – remains too much caught up in the "mineness" of the perceptual field. In Lacan's jargon, it fails to grasp the inhuman dimension of "the gaze," which is, as Freud suggests, constitutive of the subject as a *lack* in its being:

> it is not between the invisible and the visible that we have to pass. The split that concerns us is not the distance that derives from the fact that there are forms imposed by the world towards which the intentionality of phenomenological experience directs us – hence the limits that we encounter in the experience of the visible. The gaze is presented to us only in the form of a strange contingency, symbolic of what we find on the horizon, as the thrust of our experience, namely, the lack that constitutes castration anxiety.[34]

Here Merleau-Ponty's alleged subjectivism is attributed to his philosophical perspective, which, in remaining focused on the conditions of perception, overlooks what Lacan takes to be the more fundamental question of the very constitution of the human being as a subject.

Derrida's project, rooted as it is in a return to Husserl, articulates another version of the same basic criticism of Merleau-Ponty. In his introduction to Husserl's *Origin of Geometry*, Derrida shows that the project of a phenomenology of history, Merleau-Ponty's legacy to the structuralists, is at its core impossible. Derrida's strategy is to return to the foundation of such a project, the origin of truth, to demonstrate, through a critique of Husserl's concept of intuition, that truth does not give itself in the form of an *inaugural fact* to which we can return at any (later) time. Rather, the need for tradition to find support in artificial memory aids undermines the phenomenological equation between meaning and being. His early engagement with Husserl, and obliquely with Merleau-Ponty, led to Derrida's deconstruction of the living voice in *Speech and Phenomena*, together with the correlated distinctions between impression and memory, indication and expression, and to his now famous deconstructive critiques of the texts of Western metaphysics. If Merleau-Ponty's own works never figure as objects of deconstruction themselves, that would seem to be owing to Derrida's assimilation of Merleau-Ponty with Husserl, an assimilation that informs his entire enterprise. When Derrida does discuss Merleau-Ponty directly in his early work, in his *Introduction to "The Origin of Geometry,"* he does so by way of defending Husserl against the charge that the "eidetic of history cannot dispense with historical investigation" and that philosophy "must begin by understanding all experiences."[35] Like Foucault and Lacan, that is, Derrida tends to view Merleau-Ponty entirely in the shadow of Husserl's essentializing transcendental project.

This systematic – but philosophically disastrous – assimilation to Husserl defines the common pattern for the reception and dismissal of Merleau-Ponty among the philosophical generation immediately following his own. What might be gained by a return to Merleau-Ponty now, at least in the context of recent French intellectual history and its American reception, is a turn away from the antihumanist radicalization of ontology and the cultivation of new ways of exploring the ontological correlation of human beings and the world that has been of renewed interest to scholars, for instance the late neuroscientist Francisco Varela, whose work sought to bridge the humanities and the sciences, and feminist scholars like Luce Irigaray and Elizabeth Grosz, who have attempted in different ways to reconceive the connection between woman and body. If the work of these scholars can be carried on in other areas of the humanities, perhaps Merleau-Ponty's unique vision will be granted the full attention and respect that it continues to deserve.

What Merleau-Ponty introduced to philosophy and the human sciences was in effect a new concept of perception and its embodied relation to the world. At the very least, he managed to realign our understanding of perception and the body with the phenomena we are always already familiar with before we fit them into conceptual categories, pose questions about them, and formulate theories. His contribution lies neither in pure analytical argument nor in empirical discovery, but in the realm of philosophical innovation. We learn anew from his work something we already understood, if only tacitly, about perception, the body, painting, history, politics – something we could never have acquired from mere logical analysis or empirical inquiry. Merleau-Ponty's work thus performs the recollective function that Plato ascribed to philosophy generally: reminding us in a flash of insight what we feel we must already have known but had forgotten owing to our unreflective immersion in the visible world.

NOTES

1. Sartre later recalled, with characteristic insight, that in German phenomenology and existentialism he and Merleau-Ponty had "discovered our real concern. Too individualist to ever pool our research, we became reciprocal while remaining separate. Alone, each of us was too easily persuaded of having understood the idea of phenomenology. Together, we were, for each other, the incarnation of its ambiguity. Each of us viewed the work being done by the other as an unexpected, and sometimes hostile deviation from his own. Husserl became our bond and our division, at one and the same time." Sartre, *Situations*, 159; Stewart, *The Debate between Sartre and Merleau-Ponty*, 568.

2. Husserl's distinction is roughly analogous to Frege's distinction between linguistic sense (*Sinn*) and reference (*Bedeutung*). See Føllesdal, "Husserl's Notion of *Noema*." It is doubtful that Frege influenced Husserl on this point, however, for other philosophers familiar to Husserl, such as Bernard Bolzano and John Stuart Mill, had already drawn roughly equivalent distinctions prior to Frege.

3. Sellars, "Empiricism and the Philosophy of Mind," in *Science, Perception and Reality*.

4. Heidegger, *Being and Time*, 211.

5. Husserl, from *Psychological and Transcendental Phenomenology and the Confrontation with Heidegger (1927–1931)*, 130.

6. *Confrontation with Heidegger*, 138.

7. Heidegger, *History of the Concept of Time*, 152.

8. For a detailed account of Heidegger's critique of Husserl, see Carman, *Heidegger's Analytic*, Chapter 2.

9. Husserl, *Ideas I*, 153.

10. It can only have been wishful thinking on Merleau-Ponty's part, then, to insist, as he did, that "Husserl's essences are destined to bring back all the living relationships of experience, as the fisherman's net draws up from the depths of the ocean quivering fish and seaweed. J. Wahl is therefore wrong to say that 'Husserl separates essences from existence'" (*PP* x/xv/xvii). Later in the text, Merleau-Ponty acknowledges the "dilemma" generated by his own existentialized reading of Husserl: "either [transcendental] constitution renders the world transparent, in which case it is not clear why reflection should have to pass through the

world of experience, or else it retains something and never rids the world of its opacity" (*PP* 419n/365n/425n). Merleau-Ponty attempts, rather unconvincingly, to ease the contradiction by positing a "second period of Husserlian phenomenology, a transition from the eidetic method or logicism of the early phase to the existentialism of the final period" (*PP* 317n/274n/320n). For more on their differences concerning perception and subjectivity, see Carman, "The Body in Husserl and Merleau-Ponty."

11. Husserl, *Ideas I*, 93.
12. Heidegger, *Being and Time*, 217.
13. *Being and Time*, 108.
14. See Gurwitsch's 1936 essay "Some Aspects and Developments of Gestalt Psychology," which was based on his lectures of 1933–4 and which he thanks Merleau-Ponty in a footnote for having read prior to its publication. *Studies in Phenomenology and Psychology*, 3n. Merleau-Ponty never gave him proper credit for it, but it is clear that Gurwitsch was the original source of his acquaintance with Gestalt theory and the work of Gelb and Goldstein.
15. See Goldstein, *The Organism*, Chapter 8.
16. See, for instance, Robert Brandom, who characterizes his view variously as "rationalist pragmatism," "linguistic pragmatism," and "linguistic rationalism." *Articulating Reasons*, 11–12, 14, 89.
17. Sellars, "Empiricism and the Philosophy of Mind," §§61, 45; *Science, Perception and Reality*, 192, 191, 176 (emphasis omitted).
18. Evans, *Varieties of Reference*, 227, 156. Evans quotes Taylor's essay, "The Validity of Transcendental Arguments."
19. McDowell, *Mind and World*, Lecture 3.
20. Peacocke, "Perceptual Content."
21. Kelly, "The Non-Conceptual Content of Perceptual Experience."
22. Sartre, *The Imaginary*, 364–5/190. Merleau-Ponty, *PP* 10/4–5/5; for "woolly blue," see *PP* 361/313/365.
23. For more on the contemporary debate, see the papers collected in Gunther, *Essays on Nonconceptual Content*.
24. See Heidegger, "The Origin of the Work of Art."
25. By his own admission, Pierre Bourdieu owed an enormous debt to Merleau-Ponty's account of the ubiquity of style in human behavior and cultural practices. Bourdieu's notion of *habitus*, for instance, is a direct descendent of Merleau-Ponty's concepts of motor intentionality and the global coherence of bodily and artistic styles.
26. Dosse, *History of Structuralism*, vol. I: 41.
27. Descombes, *Modern French Philosophy*, 69–74.
28. Descombes, quoted in Dosse, *History of Structuralism*, vol. I: 40.

29. Deleuze and Guattari, *What Is Philosophy?*, 178.
30. An exception must perhaps be made here for Jean-François Lyotard, whose work, from his 1954 *Phenomenology* to his important study of 1971, *Discours, Figure*, bore a consistent allegiance to Merleau-Ponty's brand of phenomenology.
31. Foucault, "Theatrum Philosophicum," *Aesthetics, Method, and Epistemology*, 347.
32. Foucault, *The Order of Things*, 248.
33. Foucault, Introduction to Georges Canguilhem, *The Normal and the Pathological*, 8–9.
34. Lacan, *The Four Fundamental Concepts of Psychoanalysis*, 72–3.
35. Merleau-Ponty, "Phenomenology and the Sciences of Man," *The Primacy of Perception*, 92; quoted in Derrida, *Edmund Husserl's "Origin of Geometry": An Introduction*, 112 (translation modified).

1 Merleau-Ponty and the Epistemological Picture

Ein Bild *hielt uns gefangen.*
                    Wittgenstein[1]

Se demander si le monde est réel, c'est ne pas entendre ce qu'on dit.

                    Merleau-Ponty[2]

I

The second saying, by Merleau-Ponty, represents the culmination of an argument whose effect was to undo the state of thraldom described in the first saying, taken from the *Philosophical Investigations* of Wittgenstein.

The picture that held us captive was that of a mediational epistemology. I mean by that an understanding of the place of mind in a world such that our only knowledge of reality comes through the representations we have formed of it within ourselves. The initial statement of this structuring picture is found in Descartes, who at one point declares himself "certain that I can have no knowledge of what is outside me except by means of the ideas I have within me" (*assuré que je ne puis avoir aucune connaissance de ce qui est hors de moi, que par l'entremise des idées que j'en ai eues en moi*).[3] This picture sets up a certain distinction between inside and outside (we can call it the I/O picture), which continues to reverberate through the tradition. The basic idea of a mediational epistemology is expressed by the preposition "through" (*par l'intermédiaire de,* in this Cartesian formulation). We grasp the world through something, what is outside through something inner.

26

What is remarkable is that this structure goes on influencing much of our thought and other elements of our culture, even though many of its elements are changed. Descartes is not in fashion these days. He is rejected as a dualist, as too rationalist, as clinging to an outmoded psychology, and for many other reasons. Yet even though his terms are repudiated, we frequently find the basic structure remaining in place.

Take the inner representations through which we know the outer world. Descartes saw these as particulate mental content, which he called "ideas." These hovered between little objects in the mind that could be seen as copies of external reality (a modern analogy would be photographs) and claims that something is the case, entities one could only describe in *that* clauses.

These intramental quasi-objects have been swept off the stage for some time now, and in more than one way. For some, all this was too dualistic, idealistic, too much accepting of nonmaterial mind-stuff. The whole mediational theory has to undergo a "drastic internalization," in Quine's expression. So instead of ideas, we should speak of "surface irritations," the affecting of nerve ends. From another point of view, Descartes's philosophy suffers from not having taken the linguistic turn. Instead of talking of ideas, we should talk of sentences held true. This at least has the advantage of disambiguating the original "idea" idea: it was now clearly seen as claim and not just as inert object.

Again, from a quite different direction, Kant transformed the mediational element. Instead of being seen as a unit of information, it is reconceptualized as the categorial form in which all units of information must obligatorily be cast. Only through the conceptual forms imposed by the mind does intuition acquire sight.

What goes marching on through all these changes is the basic mediational structure. Knowledge of things outside the mind/agent/organism only comes about through certain surface conditions, mental images, or conceptual schemes within the mind/agent/organism. The input is combined, computed over, or structured by the mind to construct a view of what lies outside.

The point of Wittgenstein's statement above is to stress how deeply this picture dominated our thinking. It wasn't just a particulate opinion that people happened to hold in great numbers. It was a structuring framework understanding that guided their questioning and reasoning about these matters. Precisely because of its framework status, it was rarely consciously focused on; it just went on shaping the thoughts that were in the foreground, without our really being aware of its action. Or put another way, qua framework it felt obvious, unchallengeable, the necessary irreplaceable context for all thinking about these matters, hence not something one would ever need to examine. In this way, it worked insidiously and powerfully.

It follows that it is not enough to escape its captivity just to declare that one has changed one's opinion on these questions. One may, for instance, repudiate the idea of a representation, claim that one has no truck with this, that nothing lies between us and the world we know, and still be laboring within the picture. A striking example comes from the work of Donald Davidson. At the end of his article against conceptual schemes, Davidson explicitly rejects the representational view: "In giving up the dualism of scheme and world, we do not give up the world, but reestablish unmediated touch with the familiar objects whose antics make our sentences and opinions true or false."[4] Yet one can see it operating in his work, for instance, in his theory of truth as reconciling coherence and correspondence.

Now the crucial point about the mediational picture is that it sees our knowledge of the outside coming through certain elements, call them "representations," on the inside. These elements have varied greatly in the tradition, but in the form in which Davidson takes them up, they are seen as beliefs. To buy into the picture is to hold that our knowledge is grounded exclusively in representations and that our reasoning involves manipulating representations. To speak the language of Sellars and McDowell, it is to hold that the only inhabitants of the space of reasons are beliefs.

In this sense, Davidson is still profoundly within the mediational picture. Thus Davidson says, "What distinguishes a coherence theory is simply the claim that nothing can count as a reason for holding a belief except another belief."[5] He makes it clear that in this sense he wants to endorse a coherence theory, albeit claiming that it is compatible with what is true in a correspondence theory. In the same passage, Davidson quotes Rorty approvingly: "nothing counts as justification unless by reference to what we already accept, and there is no way to get outside our beliefs and our language so as to find some test other than coherence."[6] The two seem to be in agreement on this.[7]

This is clearly a representationalist view. Beliefs are the only accepted denizens of the space of reasons. But I want to note something more here. This view is not put forward as a surprising finding. It is articulated as a truism. *Of course* nothing can justify a belief except another one. Why is this so obvious? Because, they insist, the only way you could find an alternative would be to "get outside our beliefs and language," in Rorty's formulation. Davidson makes the same point in talking of the possible alternative of confronting our beliefs "with the tribunal of experience. No such confrontation makes sense, for of course we can't get outside our skins to find out what is causing the internal happenings of which we are aware."[8]

What I want to bring out here is the way that both philosophers lean on the basic lineaments of the mediational picture to show their thesis to be obvious. We can't get outside. This is the basic image of the I/O. We are contained within our own representations and can't stand somehow beyond them to compare them with "reality." This is the standard picture, one that by its through-structure attributes an ineradicable place to the role of representation, in some form or other (here, belief). That this is seen as related like a representation to something outside itself emerges clearly in the suggestion that we might be tempted to step outside of language and compare. Why would this temptation even come to mind unless beliefs were about things? Here, paradoxically, we find the picture invoked within an argument that is meant to repudiate that very picture. This is what it means to be held captive.

To show how this coherentist claim is so far from obvious as to be plain false, we need to step outside the mediational picture and think in terms of the kind of embedded knowing that Heidegger and Merleau-Ponty have thematized. Of course, we check our claims against reality. "Johnny, go into the room and tell me whether the picture is crooked." Johnny does as he is told. He doesn't check the (problematized) belief that the picture is crooked against his own belief. He emerges from the room with a view of the matter, but checking isn't comparing the problematized belief with his view of the matter; checking is forming a belief about the matter, in this case, by going and looking. What is assumed when we give the order is that Johnny knows, as most of us do, how to form a reliable view of this kind of matter. He knows how to go and stand at the right distance and in the right orientation to get what Merleau-Ponty calls a "maximum grip" or "hold" (*prise*) on the object. What justifies Johnny's belief is his knowing how to do this, his being able to deal with objects in this way, which is, of course, inseparable from the other ways he is able to use, manipulate, get around among them, and so on. When he goes and checks, he uses this multiple ability to cope; his sense of his ability to cope gives him confidence in his judgment as he reports it to us. And rightly so, if he is competent. About some things, he isn't competent: "Is the picture a Renoir?" But about this, he is. Nor should we go off into the intellectualist regress of saying that Johnny believes that his view-forming here is reliable. This may never have been raised. He believes this no more than he believes that the world didn't start five minutes ago or that everybody else isn't a robot.

This shows how in certain contexts we can make perfectly good sense of checking our beliefs against the facts without swinging off into absurd scenarios about jumping out of our skins. The Davidson–Rorty truism is false. It also shows, I hope, how a picture can hold us captive, even when we think we are escaping it. It holds us by enframing our thought, so that the arguments we proffer and accept are conditioned by it; and we don't even notice because, in the nature of frames, it is invisible as long as we're operating within it.

II

I have already started on my main task, which is to show how Merleau-Ponty, following Heidegger, helped to break the thrall of the mediational picture. They didn't just deny it, they worked their way out of it, which meant that they articulated it and showed it to be wrong, to need replacing by another picture.

They started by taking seriously a point that Kant makes, his holism. The earliest form of mediational theory, Cartesian–Lockean foundationalism, breaks down because the certainty-producing argument would have to proceed from establishing elements (whatever else is true, I'm *sure* that *red here now*) to grounding wholes. But you can't isolate elements in the way you would have to for this to work.

In other words, a certain holism gets in the way. Here a confusion can arise. There are, in fact, a number of doctrines that take the name "holism." The idea I'm invoking here is *not* the Quine–Davidson holism. That is a holism of verification, first of all; it reflects the fact that propositions or claims can't be verified singly. It is only derivatively a holism about meaning, insofar as the attributions of meaning to terms in the observed agent's speech amount to claims that, like most others, can't be verified singly, but only in packages with other claims. In other words, Quinean holism is a thesis that applies even after accepting the classical Cartesian–empiricist doctrine of the atomism of the input, as Quinean talk of "surface irritations" and "occasion sentences" makes clear. The holism I'm invoking is more radical. It undercuts completely the atomism of the input because the nature of any given element is determined by its "meaning" (*Sinn, sens*), which can only be defined by placing it in a larger whole; and even worse, because the larger whole isn't just an aggregation of such elements.

To make this second point slightly clearer: the "elements" that could figure in a foundationalist reconstruction of knowledge are bits of explicit information – *red here now*, or "there's a rabbit" ("gavagai"). But the whole that allows these to have the sense they have is a "world," a locus of shared understanding organized by social practice. I notice the rabbit, because I pick it out against the stable background of those trees and this open space before them. Without having found my feet in the place, there could be no rabbit sighting. If the whole stage on which the rabbit darts out were uncertain, say, swirling around as it is when I am about to faint, there could be no registering of this explicit bit of information. My having found my feet in this locus, however, is not a matter of my having extra bits of explicit information – that is, it can never just consist in this, although other bits may be playing a role. It is an exercise of my ability to cope, something I have acquired as this bodily being brought up in this culture.

What is involved in this ability to cope? It can be seen as incorporating an overall sense of ourselves and our world, which sense includes and is carried by a spectrum of rather different abilities: at one end, beliefs that we hold, which may or may not be "in our minds" at the moment; at the other, abilities to get around and deal intelligently with things. Intellectualism has made us see these as very different sites, but philosophy in our day has shown how closely akin they are, and how interlinked.

Heidegger has taught us to speak of our ability to get around as a kind of "understanding" of our world, and indeed, drawing a sharp line between this implicit grasp on things and our formulated, explicit understanding is impossible. It is not only that any frontier is porous, that things explicitly formulated and understood can "sink down" into unarticulated know-how, in the way that Hubert and Stuart Dreyfus have shown us with learning,[9] that our grasp on things can move as well in the other direction, as we articulate what was previously just lived out. It is also that any particular understanding of our situation blends explicit knowledge and unarticulated know-how.

I am informed that a tiger has escaped from the local zoo, and now as I walk through the wood behind my house, the recesses of the forest stand out for me differently, they take on a new valence; my environment now is traversed by new lines of force, in which the vectors of possible attack have an important place. My sense of this environment takes on a new shape, thanks to this new bit of information.

So the whole in which particular things are understood, bits of information taken in, is a sense of my world, carried in a plurality of media: formulated thoughts, things never even raised as a question, but taken as a framework in which the formulated thoughts have the sense they do (for example, the never-questioned, overall shape of things, which keeps me from even entertaining such weird conjectures as that the world suddenly stops beyond my door), the understanding implicit in various abilities to cope. As in the multimedia world of our culture, although some parts of our grasp of things clearly fit one medium rather than others (my knowing Weber's theory of capitalism, my being able to ride a bicycle), the boundaries between media are fuzzy, and many of the most important understandings are multimedia events, as when I stroll through the potentially tiger-infested wood. Moreover, in virtue of the holism that reigns here, every bit of my understanding draws on the whole and is, in this indirect way, multimedia.

Now this picture of the background rules out what one might call a representational or mediational picture of our grasp of the world. There are many versions of this theory, but the central idea in this picture, as we have seen, is that all our understanding of the world is ultimatcly mediated knowledge. That is, it is knowledge that comes through something "inner," within ourselves or produced by the mind. This means we can understand our grasp of the world as something that is, in principle, separable from what it is a grasp of.

This separation was obviously central to the original Cartesian thrust that we are all trying to turn back and deconstruct. On one side, there were the bits of putative information in the mind – ideas, impressions, sense data. On the other, there was the "outside world" of which these claimed to inform us. The dualism can later take other, more sophisticated forms. As I said earlier, representations will later be reconceived no longer as "ideas," but as sentences, in keeping with the linguistic turn, as we see with Quine. Or the dualism itself can be fundamentally reconceptualized, as with Kant. Instead of being defined in terms of original and copy, it is seen on the model of form and content, mold and filling. In whatever form, mediational theories posit something that can be defined as inner, as our contribution to knowing and which can be distinguished from what is out there.

We can see now the connection between mediationalism and the continuing force of skeptical questions, or their transforms: maybe the world doesn't really conform to the representation? Or maybe we will come across others whose molds are irreducibly different from ours, with whom we shall therefore be unable to establish any common standards of truth? This thought underlies much facile relativism in our day.

A reflection on our whole multimedia grasp of things ought to put paid to this dualism once and for all. If we stare at the medium of explicit belief, then the separation can seem plausible. My beliefs about the moon can be held, even actualized, in my present thinking even if the moon isn't now visible – perhaps even though it doesn't exist, if it turns out to be a fiction. The grasp of things involved in my ability to move around and manipulate objects can't be divided up like that, however, because unlike moon-beliefs, this ability can't be actualized in the absence of the objects it operates on. My ability to throw baseballs can't be exercised in the absence of baseballs. My ability to get around this city, this house, comes out only in getting around this city and house.

We might be tempted to say that it doesn't exist in my mind, like my theoretical beliefs, in my "head," but in the ability to move that I have in my whole body. That understates the embedding. The locus here is the ability to move-in-this-environment. It exists not just in my body, but in my body-walking-the-streets. Similarly, my ability to be charming or seductive exists not in my body and voice, but in body-voice-in-conversation-with-interlocutor.

A strong temptation to place these abilities just in the body comes from the supposition that a proper neurophysiological account of the capacities can be given that would place them there. This is one source of that weird, post-Cartesian philosophical dream, the brain in a vat. Once one really escapes Cartesian dualism, it ceases to be self-evident that this even makes sense. Unfortunately, I haven't the space to go into that here.

Living with things involves a certain kind of understanding, which we might also call "preunderstanding." That is, things figure for us in their meaning or relevance for our purposes, desires, activities. As I navigate my way along the path up the hill, my mind totally absorbed anticipating the difficult conversation I'm going to have at my destination, I treat the different features of the terrain as obstacles, supports, openings, invitations to tread more warily or run freely, and so on. Even when I'm not thinking of them, these things have those relevances for me; I know my way about among them.

This is nonconceptual; put another way, language isn't playing any direct role. Through language, we have the capacity to focus on things, to pick an *x* out *as* an *x*; we pick it out as something that (correctly) bears a description "*x*," and this puts our identification in the domain of potential critique. (Is this really an *x*? Is the vocabulary to which "*x*" belongs the appropriate one for this domain or purpose?) At some point, because of some breakdown, or just through intrinsic interest, I may come to focus on some aspects of this navigational know-how. I may begin to classify things as "obstacles" or "facilitations," and this will change the way I live in the world. Yet in all sorts of ways, I live in the world and deal with it, without having done this.

Ordinary coping isn't conceptual, but at the same time, it can't be understood in just inanimate-causal terms. This denial can be understood in two ways. Maximally, it runs athwart a common ambition of much cognitive psychology, for example, which aims precisely to give one day a reductive account in machine terms. I would also bet my money that the denial will turn out right in this strong sense, and that the reductive ambition is ultimately a fantasy. For our purposes though, we just need to focus on a minimal sense – namely, that in the absence of this promised but far-distant mechanistic account, our only way of making sense of animals, and of our own preconceptual goings-on, is through something like preunderstanding. That is, we have to see the world impinging on these beings in relevance terms; alternatively put, we see them as agents.

We find it impossible not to extend this courtesy to animals, as I have just indicated. In our case, however, the reasons are stronger. When we focus on some feature of our dealing with the world and bring it to speech, it doesn't come across as a discovery of some unsuspected fact, like for example the change in landscape at a turn in the road or being informed that what we do bears some fancy technical name (Monsieur Jourdain in Molière's *Bourgeois gentilhomme* speaking prose). When I finally allow myself to recognize that what has been making me uncomfortable in this conversation is that I'm feeling jealous, I feel that in a sense I wasn't totally ignorant of this before. I knew it without knowing it. It has a kind of intermediate status between known and quite unknown. It was a kind of protoknowledge, an environment propitious for the transformation that conceptual focus brings, even though there may also have been resistances.

I have thus far been drawing on Heidegger, as well as Merleau-Ponty. We find in both this idea that our conceptual thinking is "embedded" in everyday coping. The point of this image can be taken in two bites, as it were. The first is that coping is prior and pervasive (*"zunächst und zumeist"*). We start off as coping infants and only later are inducted into speech. Even as adults, much of our lives consists in this coping. This couldn't be otherwise. To focus on something, we have to keep going – as I was on the path, while thinking of the difficult conversation; or as the person is in the laboratory, walking around, picking up the report, while thinking hard about the theoretical issues (or maybe about what's for lunch).

The second bite goes deeper. It's the point usually expressed with the term "background." The mass of coping is an essential support to the episodes of conceptual focus in our lives, not just in the infrastructural sense that something has to be carrying our mind around from library to laboratory and back. More fundamentally, the background understanding we need to make the sense we do of the pieces of thinking we engage in resides in our ordinary coping.

I walk up the path and enter the field and notice that the goldenrod is out. This is a particulate take on the world, rather of the kind that boundary events are supposed to be on the I/O, except that under the pressure of foundationalism, they sometimes are forced to be more basic – *yellow here now* – and only build up to goldenrod as a later inference. One of the errors of classical epistemology was to see in this kind of take the building blocks of our knowledge of the world. We put it together bit by bit out of such pieces. So foundationalism had to believe.

One of the reasons that Kant is a crucial figure in the (oh so laborious) overcoming of the I/O – even though he also created his own version of it – is that he put paid to this picture. We can't build our view of the world out of percepts such as "the goldenrod is out," or even "yellow here now," because nothing would count as such a percept unless it already had its place in a world. Minimally, nothing could be a *percept* without a surrounding sense of myself as perceiving agent, moving in some surroundings, of which this bit of yellow is a feature. If we try to think all this orientation away, then we get something that is close to unthinkable as an experience, "less even than a dream," as Kant puts it.[10] What would it be like just to experience yellow, never mind whether it's somewhere in the world out there or just in my head? A very dissociated experience, and not a very promising building block for a worldview.

So our understanding of the world is holistic from the start, in a sense different from the Quinean one. There is no such thing as the single, independent percept. Something has this status only within a wider context that is understood, taken for granted, but for the most part not focused on. Moreover, it couldn't all be focused on, not just because it is very widely ramifying, but because it doesn't consist of some definite number of pieces. We can bring this out by reflecting that the number of ways in which the taken-for-granted background could in specific circumstances fail is not delimitable.

Invoking this undelimitable background was the favorite argumentative gambit of Wittgenstein in both *Philosophical Investigations* and *On Certainty*. He shows, for instance, that understanding an ostensive definition is not just a matter of fixing a particular; there is a whole surrounding understanding of what kind of thing is being discussed (the shape or the color), of this being a way of teaching meaning, and the like. In our ordinary investigations, we take for granted a continuing world, so that our whole proceedings would be radically undercut by the "discovery," if one could make it, that the universe started five minutes ago. Yet that can't be taken to mean that there is a definite list of things that we have ruled out, including among others that the universe started five minutes ago.

Now this indefinitely extending background understanding is sustained and evolved through our ordinary coping. My recognition that the goldenrod is out is sustained by a context being in place, for example, that I'm now entering a field, and it's August. I'm not focusing on all this. I know where I am because I walked here, and when I am because I've been living this summer, but these are not reflective inferences; they are just part of the understanding I have in everyday coping. I might indeed take in certain geographic locations of the earth's surface in a certain season, and so on, just as I might lay out the environment I normally walk about in by drawing a map. This wouldn't end the embedding of reflective knowledge in ordinary coping. The map becomes useless, indeed ceases to be a map in any meaningful sense for me, unless I can use it to help me get around. Theoretical knowledge has to be situated in relation to everyday coping to be the knowledge that it is.

In this way, embedding is inescapable; in the stronger sense, all exercises of reflective, conceptual thought only have the content they have situated in a context of background understanding that underlies and is generated in everyday coping.

This is where the description of our predicament in Heidegger and Merleau-Ponty, the analyses of *In-der-Welt-sein* and *être au monde*, connect to the powerful critique of dualist epistemology mounted by John McDowell.[11] The dualism McDowell attacks, following Sellars, is the sharp demarcation between the space of reasons and the space of causes. The accounts of *In-der-Welt-sein* and *être au monde* also have no place for this boundary. They are meant to explain, as McDowell's also attempts to do, how it can be that the places at which our view is shaped by the world in perception are not just causal impingings, but sites of the persuasive acquisition of belief.

The phenomenological writers go beyond McDowell, however, in holding that we are only able to form conceptual beliefs guided by our surroundings because we live in a preconceptual engagement with these surroundings, which involves understanding. Transactions in this space are not causal processes among neutral elements, but the sensing of and response to relevance. The very idea of an inner zone with an external boundary can't get started here, because our living things in a certain relevance can't be situated "within" the agent; it is in the interaction itself. The understanding and know-how by which I climb the path and continue to know where I am is not "within" me in a kind of picture. That fate awaits it if and when I make the step to map drawing. Now, however, it resides in my negotiating the path. The understanding is in the interaction; it can't be drawn on outside of this in the absence of the relevant surroundings. To think it can be detached is to construe it on the model of explicit, conceptual, language- or map-based knowledge, which is of course what the whole I/O tradition, from Descartes through Locke to contemporary artificial-intelligence modelers, has been intent on doing. Just this is the move that recreates the boundary and makes the process of perceptual knowledge unintelligible, however.

III

This ought to ruin altogether the representational construal. Our grasp of things is not something that is in us, over against the world; it lies in the way we are in contact with the world. This is why a global doubt about the existence of things, which can seem quite sensible on the representational construal, shows itself as incoherent once you have taken the antifoundational turn. I can wonder whether some of my ways of dealing with the world distort things for me: my distance perception is skewed, my too great involvement with this issue or group is blinding me to the bigger picture, my obsession with my image is keeping me from seeing what's really important. All these doubts can only arise against the background of the world as the all-englobing locus of my involvements. I can't seriously doubt this without dissolving the very definition of my original worry, which only made sense against this background.

We can see this if we look at the whole complex of issues around realism and antirealism. The mediational view provides the context in which these questions make sense. They lose this sense if you escape from this construal, as Heidegger and Merleau-Ponty have done. Or perhaps better put, one awakes to an unproblematic realism, no longer a daring philosophical "thesis."

It has often been noticed how representationalism leads, by recoil, to skepticism, relativism, and various forms of nonrealism. Once the foundationalist arguments for establishing truth are seen to fail, we are left with the image of the self-enclosed subject, out of contact with the transcendent world. This easily generates theses of the unknowable, of the privacy of thought, or of relativism. More particularly in this last case, the picture of each mind acceding to the world from behind the screen of its own percepts, or grasping it in molds of its own making, seems to offer no way of rational arbitration of disputes. How can the protagonists base their arguments on commonly available elements when each is encased within her own picture?

From skepticism or relativism, the move is obvious, and it is tempting to adopt some mode of antirealism. If these questions can't be rationally arbitrated, then why accept that they are real questions? Why agree that there is a fact of the matter here about which one can be right or wrong? If we can never know whether our language, or ideas, or categories correspond to the reality out there, the things in themselves, then what warrant have we to talk about this transcendent reality in the first place? We have to deny it the status of the "real."

The crucial move in these nonrealisms is to deny some common-sense distinction between reality and our picture of it: the world as it is versus the world as we see it, what is really morally right versus what we think right, and so on. The irony is that this denies distinctions that were first erected into dichotomies by the representational construal.

Now it is obvious that foundationalism is in a sense in the same dialectical universe as nonrealism, that set up by mediational theories. These raise the fear that our representations might be just in the mind, out of touch with reality (even that we might be the victims of a *malin génie*). Foundationalism is an answer to such fears. This is why there is often such an indignant reaction in our scientific-philosophical community to various relativist or nonrealist theories: the whole culture is in the grip of a mediationalist perspective and therefore can entertain the nightmare of being irremediably out of touch with the real. Science, however, seems to depend on our not being so out of touch; so whoever flirts with such theories is against science, giving aid and comfort to the enemy, destroying our civilization, and so on.

The conception of the knowing agent at grips with the world opens quite different possibilities. There may be (and obviously are) differences, alternative takes on and construals of reality, which may even be systematic and far reaching. Some of these will be, all may be wrong; but any such take or construal is within the context of a basic engagement with or understanding of the world, a contact with it which cannot be broken off short of death. It is impossible to be totally wrong. Even if, after climbing the path, I think myself to be in the wrong field, I have situated myself in the right county, I know the way back home, and so on. The reality of contact with the real world is the inescapable fact of human (or animal) life and can only be imagined away by erroneous philosophical argument. As Merleau-Ponty put it, "To ask whether the world is real is not to know what one is saying" (*Se demander si le monde est réel, c'est ne pas entendre ce qu'on dit*). It is in virtue of this contact with a common world that we always have something to say to each other, something to point to in disputes about reality.

So the view of the agent as being-in-the-world has room for a distinction between reality and our grasp of it; we invoke this distinction every time we knowingly correct our view of things. It can distinguish between different, mutually untranslatable cultural "takes" on reality, but it cannot allow that these are insurmountable or inescapable.

IV

My thesis, relating the two quotes at the head of this essay, has been that the picture that "held us captive," which I have identified as mediational epistemology, can ultimately be overcome or escaped through a deeper understanding of the background of our thinking, which has been provided in the work of Heidegger and Merleau-Ponty. Further light can be cast on why this is so, if we consider some of the motivations underlying this dominant epistemology from its inception.

I want to concentrate on the recurring structural element in all mediational theories, that through which knowledge of the world takes place, be it conceived as idea, sentence, form of understanding, stimulation of nerve ends, or whatever. The positing of this element, be it impression, or sense datum, or minimal input, is overdetermined.

On one hand, it is encouraged by a picture of the subject as one item in a disenchanted nature, understood by post-Galilean science. This is the condition, at least of the subject's body. But the interaction with outside reality that we call experience must occur in this realm; it happens between the things that surround us and the body, hence it must be understood in terms of naturalistic laws. If you trace through the process whereby, say, light impinges on the eye, you come naturally to posit an end point where the resulting input enters the "mind" (dualist version) or becomes available for computation (updated materialist version). This transition point defines the particulate item of information "through" which the world is known. We could call this the "ontological" motive.

This structural element was also generated by the demands of the foundationalist enterprise. Myles Burnyeat has, I believe, an interesting point about the novelty of Descartes's invocation of skepticism in the First Meditation, in relation to his ancient sources.[12] Through it, Descartes manages to parlay a doubt about our everyday certainties into a certainty about the nature of doubt. Instead of remaining in the incurable uncertainty that rehearsing the sources of error was meant to bring on, the solvent of doubt is made to hit one irreducible kernel, namely, our experience of the world. Perhaps I am not really sitting before the fire, clothed, but it is clear that I think that I am so situated. The nature of this item of experience is quite clear and indubitable. Modern phenomenology has argued that Descartes didn't have the right to help himself to this clear delimitation of doubt, but the rights and wrongs are not to my purpose here. What is relevant is the role of this distinctly demarcated "adventitious idea" (idée adventice) in Descartes's foundationalist strategy.

Doubt reaches its limit at the existence of a mental item that purports to be about the external world and presents a determinate content. The issue of skepticism can therefore be exactly stated; we can be certain about the nature of doubt. The issue is, do these purported contents really hold of the external world, or do these ideas lie? A case in which the latter unhappy condition might hold would be one in which a malign spirit had set out to fool us. But now this, and any other such systematic cause of error, can be ruled out by our demonstrating that we are the product of a benign, veracious Creator.

How convincing the argument is doesn't concern me; what is important is that the foundationalist argument required the stabilization of doubt in a clearly defined issue. We can't be left reeling under the cumulative effect of all the possible sources of error, where the ancients abandon us with the injunction to cease the fruitless quest for certain knowledge. The reasons for doubt have to be shown to come down to a single clear issue, which we can then hope to handle. This requires the invention of the strange boundary event, the dual nature of which causes the trouble that I have been discussing here.

On one hand, it has to be about the world, present a unit of information, be a small item of knowledge, and hence belong to the space of reasons. On the other, it has to be prior to all interpretation; its having the content it has must be a brute fact, not in any way the result of thought or reasoning activity on our part. This latter feature emerges in the argument in the Sixth Meditation about possible sources of error, like the round tower that looks square in the distance. In order that this mistake, though the result of a general feature of appearances at a distance, not be laid at God's door, thus refuting the thesis of his goodness and veracity, we have to argue that the erroneous conclusion here results from some (in this case sloppy, unfocused) inference on our part. For this we are responsible, and we ought to have been more careful. What God stands surety for are the genuine cases of interpretation-free appearance. The system starts from these.

I have been discussing the motives for believing in this notion of a brute input within Descartes's philosophy, but it is clear that we can detach it from his idiosyncratic arguments and see how it has to figure in all foundationalist epistemologies. The aim of foundationalism is to peel back all the layers of inference and interpretation and get back to something genuinely prior to them all, a brute Given – then to build back up, checking all the links in the interpretive chain. Foundationalism involves the double move, stripping down to the unchallengeable, and building back up. Unless at some point we hit bedrock, if indeed interpretation goes on forever ("all the way down," in Dreyfus's apt expression), the foundationalist project is ruined.

My thesis is that an important motive behind the I/O picture, which generates all the aporiai of the sense datum, is the foundationalist project itself. It is not just that the picture of the mind in disenchanted nature generates the notion of the brute input, a site for insoluble philosophical problems, as an unfortunate side effect. I think this is true; that is indeed one motive. But it is also true that the foundationalist drive generates this unfortunate notion for its own purposes.

What takes place is a kind of ontologizing of proper method. The right way to deal with puzzles and build a reliable body of knowledge is to break down the issue into subquestions, identify the chains of inference, dig down to an inference-free starting point, and then build by a reliable method. Once this comes to seem the all-purpose nostrum for thinking, one has an overwhelming motivation to believe that this is how the mind actually works in taking in the world. Because if it isn't, one has to draw the devastating conclusion that the only reliable method is inapplicable in the most important context of all, in which we build our knowledge of the world.

Hence the notion of the brute input, under different names, goes marching on. Locke argues for something of this sort in his metaphor of building materials. We start with simple ideas, as builders start with their given materials. Construction is not an activity that can go on "all the way down." It has to start somewhere with things we just find lying around. So must it be with knowledge.

Again, the vogue in cognitive psychology for AI-inspired models of the mind was powered by the same double set of motives: on one hand, ontological – the mind is set in disenchanted nature, it is a product of the brain which is itself a piece of this nature, therefore it must work fundamentally like a machine; on the other hand, methodological – what is thinking, anyway? It is building chains of inference from minimal starting points. These starting points are givens. So that's how the mind must work.

V

In the light of this, we can see how theories of this range generate the classical dilemmas, puzzles, and aporiai, some of which have been mentioned earlier in the chapter. On one hand, the picture of our having access to the world *through* something inevitably suggests various skeptical or antirealist moves. At a first stage, we can wonder whether we are right to put confidence in our belief in "transcendent" objects, when all we have to go on are immanent ideas. Descartes's heroic proof via God's veracity couldn't go on convincing everyone, particularly as belief in a Providential order began to be shaken. But then the skeptical question in turn suggests another twist: if we can't say anything for certain about this realm of the transcendent, why are we talking about it at all; can we not just restrict ourselves to appearances, or sense data, or what seems right to us?

At the same time, mediational epistemology seemed to make experience problematic. We reason, argue, make inferences, and arrive at an understanding of the world. Yet our framework understanding, which most of these theories try to retain, is that we also learn from the world; we take things in, come to know things, on the basis of which we reason. It was this dual source of our knowledge that mediational epistemologies were meant to capture in their basic structure: receptivity produces the basic elements of input, and then reasoning processes these into science.

Yet the very boundary set up by the mediational element seemed to make it hard to conceive how these two sources could work together. What seemed like obvious solutions just enhanced the first problem, that of skepticism and nonrealism. These would amount to the idea that receptivity is to be understood in purely causal terms, that it just delivers certain results that we can't get behind; reason then does what it can to make sense of these.

Beyond this, the very idea of a boundary can be made to seem highly problematic. Critical reasoning is something we do, an activity, in the realm of spontaneity and freedom. As far as knowledge of the world is concerned, however, it is meant to be responsive to the way things are. Spontaneity has to be merged somehow with receptivity, but it is hard to see how this can be if we conceive of spontaneity as a kind of limitless freedom, which at the point of contact has to hit a world under adamantine, post-Galilean "laws of nature." The schizophrenic nature of boundary events, inexplicably partaking of both nature and freedom, is an inevitable consequence of this way of seeing things.

Indeed, the very idea of a boundary event, between a realm of causes and a realm of reasons, begins to seem problematic. This event would have to be in a sense amphibious, belonging to both. Yet are their natures not contradictory – on one hand an object, or a factual state of affairs, the causal upshot in our receptors of outside stimulation; on the other hand certain *claims*, to the effect that so-and-so, which could figure as reasons to adopt some broader view or other? This is the consideration that has led some philosophers to denounce the myth of the purely given, the brute, uninterpreted fact.[13]

The problem has been to account for experience, in the sense of a taking in of information from the world. In a sense, we have to receive this information; we are the passive party. In another, we have to know how to "grasp" it; we are active. How do these two combine? This has been the notorious problem of the tradition of modern philosophy, which has been defined by modern epistemology. In certain well-known classical writers, the absence of any plausible theory of experience was patent. Leibniz in the end denied it altogether and saw a picture of the world as present in its entirety within the monad. Hume seemed to go to the other extreme and allow that all our knowledge comes to us through experience, hence the vaunted title "empiricist." This was at the cost of denying the active dimension altogether, so that the deliverances of experience were unconnected bits of information, and what seem to ordinary people to be the undeniable connections were denounced as projections of the mind. Even the self disappears in this caricatural passivism. Kant notoriously tried to unite both Hume and Leibniz. At least he saw the problem, how to combine spontaneity and receptivity. Nevertheless, he was still too caught up in the mediationalist structure to propound a believable solution.[14]

VI

We can now see better what is needed to resolve these aporiai and escape from the picture:

(1) To breach the hard boundary between the spaces of causes and reasons, we need to allow for a kind of understanding that is preconceptual, on the basis of which concepts can be predicated of things;

something, in other words, that functions in the space of reasons below concepts.

(2) For this, we need to see this understanding as that of an engaged agent, determining the significances (*sens, Sinne*) of things from out of its aims, needs, purposes, desires. These significances arise out of a combination of spontaneity and receptivity, constraint and striving; they are the ways the world must be taken in for a being defined by certain goals or needs to make sense of it. They are thus in one way imposed on us by reality; what happens is a victory or a defeat, success or failure, fulfillment or frustration; we cannot (beyond certain limits) just choose to deny or alter this meaning. At the same time, this significance is only disclosed through our striving to make sense of our surroundings.

(3) The original, inescapable locus of this constrained, preconceptual sense making, however, is our bodily commerce with our world. This is where Merleau-Ponty's contribution, enlarged and developed more recently by Samuel Todes, has been so crucial. The most primordial and unavoidable significances of things are, or are connected to, those involved in our bodily existence in the world: our field is shaped in terms of up and down, near and far, easily accessible and out of reach, graspable, avoidable, and so on.

(4) Our humanity also consists, however, in our ability to decenter ourselves from this original engaged mode; to learn to see things in a disengaged fashion, in universal terms, or from an alien point of view; to achieve, at least notionally, a "view from nowhere." Only we have to see that this disengaged mode is in an important sense derivative. The engaged one is prior and pervasive, as I mentioned earlier. We always start off in it, and we always need it as the base from which we, from time to time, disengage.

A four-step view of this kind can enable us to overcome the Myth of the Given and get beyond the paradoxical boundary of mediational theories. But it also dissolves the temptations to antirealism, and this particularly in virtue of Step 3. If we see that our grasp of things is primordially one of bodily engagement with them, then we can see that we are in contact with the reality that surrounds us at a deeper level than any description or significance-attribution we might make of it. These descriptions and attributions may be wrong, but what must remain is the world within which the questions arose to which they were the wrong answers, the world from which I cannot escape because I nccd it in a host of ways, in the final analysis even to know who I am and what I'm about[15] – even if what I'm about is renouncing the world to go into the desert. My first understanding of reality is not a picture I am forming of it, but the sense given to a continuing transaction with it. I can be confused about it, but its inseparable presence is undeniable. That is why, as Merleau-Ponty says, even to frame the denial, I have to have lost touch with what the words really mean.

VII

This doesn't mean that words can't trip us up. I have been trying to give an account of Merleau-Ponty's rejection of antirealism, but this latter term, and others I have used, are my own and find their place in the contemporary philosophical debate. This doesn't mean that he used the same terms, and from this can arise possible confusion.

Thus when Merleau-Ponty says, in his discussion of the *cogito* in *Phenomenology of Perception*, "there is no question of justifying realism, and there is an element of final truth in the Cartesian return of things and ideas to myself" (*il n'est pas question de donner raison au réalisme et il y a une vérité définitive dans le retour cartésien des choses et des idées au moi*) (*PP* 423/369/430), is he relapsing into a species of idealism? To see that this is not so, we have to understand that "realism" for him designates the view according to which everything, including human thought and perception, can be explained in terms of objective, third-person processes. This reductive view, exemplified by various mechanistic accounts of human action and thinking, but also by certain accounts of reasoning in terms of ideal essences, is what he has been arguing against throughout the book. Indeed, he holds that it shares with idealism the inability to think the kind of opening to the world exemplified by our embodied agency.

"Realism" is to be rejected, then, because we would never be able to understand our experience of things if we tried to explain it in terms of such objective entities. The point here is similar to Heidegger's when he refuses to understand Dasein on the model of occurrent entities. The human agent doesn't just exist alongside entities; it has an understanding of its world, and this is something that can never be simply equated with any objective processes of exchange between agent and surroundings. Moreover, this understanding is never complete, or absolute. That is, there is always more to be grasped, and even what we have grasped depends on modes of understanding whose bases we can never fully render transparent to ourselves.

Thus, in the rest of this chapter on the *cogito*, Merleau-Ponty tries to define this kind of opening to the world. He vigorously combats the idea that we could ever define an inner zone of mental contents of whose nature we might be certain, independently of how they relate to the reality beyond them. This inability to fix a boundary between the indubitable inner and the unproblematic outer is argued not only for the case of perception, but also in relation to feelings like love, and even in the case of "pure thought" (*pensée pure*), as with geometrical reasoning (*PP* 439/383/446ff). The inner and the outer can't be separated in this way: "The world is wholly inside and I am wholly outside myself" (*Le monde est tout au dedans et je suis tout hors de moi*) (*PP* 467/407/474).

"The tacit *cogito*," that is, the fundamental dimension of our experience, which the *cogito* as explicit argument tries to articulate, is "myself experienced by myself" (*une épreuve de moi par moi*), "the presence of oneself to oneself" (*la présence de soi à soi*) (*PP* 462/403–4/469–70). It is, indeed, independent of any particular thought, but it is also in its unformulated state not really a bit of knowledge. To become this, it must be put into words. "The tacit *cogito* is a *cogito* only when it has found expression for itself" (*Le* Cogito *tacite n'est* Cogito *que lorsqu'il s'est exprimé lui-même*) (*PP* 463/404/470).

This predicament rules out absolute, that is, complete and self-evidently incorrigible knowledge. The nature of our opening to the world, of our contact with it, makes this impossible. But this contact also rules out total error. It can turn out that our grasp on things was wrong in this or that respect. Yet it cannot be entirely wrong, and for the same reason that it can't ever be guaranteed to be totally right. The inseparability of inner and outer means that there is no realm of inner certainty, but it also means that perceiving, thinking, feeling cannot be totally severed from the reality it bears on.

Consciousness, if it is not absolute truth or *a-lêtheia*, at least rules out all absolute falsity. . . . The truth is that neither error nor doubt ever cuts us off from the truth, because they are surrounded by a world horizon in which the teleology of consciousness summons us to an effort at resolving them. (*La conscience, si elle ne'est pas vérité ou a-létheia absolue, exclut du moins toute fausseté absolue. . . . Ce qui est vrai, c'est que l'erreur ni le doute ne nous coupent jamais de la vérité, parce qu'ils sont entourés d'un horizon de monde où la téléologie de la conscience nous invite à en chercher la résolution.)* (PP 456/398/463)

It is this inexpungeable contact with the world that sweeps away forever the myriad forms of antirealism engendered in the thraldom of the mediational picture.

NOTES

1. "A *picture* held us captive." *Philosophical Investigations*, §115.
2. "To ask whether the world is real is not to know what one is saying" (PP 396/344/401).
3. Letter to Gibieuf, 19 January 1642. *The Philosophical Writings of Descartes*, Vol. III; AT III 474.
4. Davidson, "On the Very Idea of a Conceptual Scheme," 198.
5. Davidson, "A Coherence Theory of Truth and Knowledge," 141.
6. Rorty, *Philosophy and the Mirror of Nature*, 178.
7. See also Robert Brandom, *Rorty and His Critics*, Introduction, xiv.
8. Davidson, "A Coherence Theory," 312.
9. H. L. Dreyfus and S. E. Dreyfus, *Mind over Machine*.
10. Kant, *Critique of Pure Reason*, A112.
11. McDowell, *Mind and World*.
12. Burnyeat, "Idealism and Greek Philosophy: What Descartes Saw and Berkeley Missed."
13. See McDowell, *Mind and World*, Lecture 1.
14. I have drawn on the extremely insightful work of Samuel Todes, whose doctoral dissertation has recently been published, many years after, as *Body and World*.
15. See the illuminating discussion in *Body and World*, Chapter 4.

2 Sensation, Judgment, and the Phenomenal Field

Merleau-Ponty's interconnected critiques of empiricism and intellectualism run like a double helix through the pages of *Phenomenology of Perception*.[1] In the decades since its publication in 1945, philosophical and psychological theories of perception have continued to take for granted empiricist and intellectualist models and metaphors, although their respective claims to preeminence have tended to swing to and fro in unpredictable ways. As a result, although the current state of play in the philosophy of mind for us today differs widely from what it was for Merleau-Ponty in the middle of the last century, neither would he find it altogether unrecognizable. His objection to the empiricist concept of sensation (or "sense data" or "qualia"), for example, is likely to strike contemporary readers as familiar and plausible, thanks in part to arguments advanced in a roughly kindred spirit by philosophers such as Ludwig Wittgenstein, J. L. Austin, Gilbert Ryle, Wilfrid Sellars, and Thomas Kuhn. To launch an attack on intellectualism as Merleau-Ponty does, by contrast, might look more like tilting at windmills, or beating a dead rationalist horse, or perhaps just failing, understandably enough, to anticipate the cognitive revolution in linguistics and psychology that took place after his death in 1961.

Yet while cognitive science has undeniably had a profound impact on contemporary thought, its enduring importance, like that of many research programs that have come and gone before it, may in the end prove largely negative. For cognitivist theories of perception and intentionality derive much of their apparent plausibility from little more than the implausibility of competing empiricist and behaviorist accounts and are in this sense of a piece with more traditional forms of rationalism. As Merleau-Ponty says, "intellectualism thrives on the refutation of empiricism" (*PP* 40/32/37). Deprived of its dialectical foil, cognitivism has less speaking clearly in its favor, and its weaknesses are often precisely those of the intellectualism Merleau-Ponty knew well and criticized in the 1940s. The critique of intellectualism advanced in *Phenomenology of Perception* thus remains highly relevant to contemporary theories of perception and cognition.

What follows in this essay is an account of Merleau-Ponty's criticism of empiricism and intellectualism, which is to say his rejection of the concept of sensations or qualia as primitive building blocks of perceptual experience on one hand and his equally emphatic denial that perception is constituted by or reducible to thought or judgment on the other. What emerges from that negative assessment of the two dialectical poles framing traditional debates about perception and the mind is a positive and original conception of perception as our most basic bodily mode of access to the world, prior to the kinds of reflection and abstraction that motivate the idea of discrete passive qualitative states of consciousness and spontaneous acts of cognition. What Merleau-Ponty calls the "phenomenal field" is neither a representation nor a locus of representations, but a dimension of our bodily embeddedness in a perceptually coherent environment, a primitive aspect of our openness onto the world.

I. SENSATION

Phenomenology of Perception commences with a critique of the concept of sensation. As Merleau-Ponty remarks, the word "sensation" is perfectly at home in ordinary language, and the notion at first "seems immediate and obvious." On closer inspection, however, it turns out that "nothing could in fact be more confused" (*PP* 9/3/3). Indeed, in theoretical contexts, the concept systematically obscures our understanding of perceptual experience: "Once introduced, the notion of sensation distorts any analysis of perception" (*PP* 20/13/15). What is wrong with this ordinary notion once we enlist it in the service of a theory of perception?

The first point to observe is a purely phenomenological one, namely, that notwithstanding the ordinariness of the word "sensation," what we find in ordinary perceptual experience is *not* internal sensations, but external things: objects, people, places, events. The concept of sensation "corresponds to nothing in our experience" (*PP* 9/3/3–4). Nowhere in our perceptual awareness do we come across discrete qualitative bits of experience fully abstracted from the external, perceptually coherent environment. Occasionally we might see an afterimage or hear a ringing in our ears, but typically we see objects and hear noises made by things and events. This is in part just to say that perceptual experience is *intentional*, that it is *of* something, whereas impressions, sensations, and sense data are supposed to be the nonintentional stuff from which the mind somehow extracts or constructs an experience of something. The *of* in "sensation of pain," however, is not the *of* in "sensation of red," for the latter is intentional while the former is not. In the latter case, we can draw a distinction in principle between the red thing and our sensation of it, whereas a sensation of pain just *is* the pain. Further, even pains are not just feelings that we associate with parts of our bodies; rather, my pain *is* my leg, my hand, my head *hurting*. Perception is essentially interwoven with the world we perceive, and each feature of the perceptual field is interwoven with others:

Each part arouses the expectation of more than it contains, and this elementary perception is therefore already charged with a *meaning*. . . . The perceptual "something" is always in the middle of something else, it always forms part of a "field." . . . The pure impression is therefore not just undiscoverable, but imperceptible and thus inconceivable as a moment of perception. (*PP* 9–10/4/4)

The concept of sensation in philosophy and psychology thus finds virtually no support in our actual experience, however firmly planted the word may be in ordinary discourse. Merleau-Ponty also offers a phenomenological diagnosis of our tendency to recur to talk of sensations, as if they really did occur in the normal course of perception. When the concept arises, he suggests, "it is because instead of attending to the experience of perception, we overlook it in favor of the object perceived" (*PP* 10/4/4). We are naturally focused on or "at grips with" (*en prise sur*) the environment, so that when we turn our attention to perception itself, we tend to project onto it the qualities of the objects we perceive:

we transpose these objects into consciousness. We commit what psychologists call the "experience error," which means that what we know to be in things themselves we immediately take to be in our consciousness of them. We make perception out of things perceived. And since perceived things themselves are obviously accessible only through perception, we end by understanding neither. (*PP* 11/5/5)[2]

The language of sensation is thus tainted by, and so parasitic on, the language with which we refer to the objects of perception: "When I say that I have before me a red patch, the meaning of the word 'patch' is provided by previous experiences that have taught me the use of the word" (*PP* 21/14/17).

Putting the point this way, in terms of the specifically linguistic conditions of our ability to identify and describe many of the qualitative aspects of our experience, brings Merleau-Ponty into close company with Wittgenstein and Sellars. In *Zettel*, for example, Wittgenstein insists that the language of perceptual appearance, or mere seeming, is parasitic on a language descriptive of external things:

To begin by teaching someone "That looks red" makes no sense. For that is what he must say spontaneously once he has learned what "red" means.... Why doesn't one teach a child the language-game "It looks red to me" from the outset? Because it is not yet able to understand the more refined distinction between seeming and being?[3]

It is not as if children are simply not observant or clever enough to notice that seeming is more basic than being; rather, the meaning of a term purporting to describe a mere appearance must already have acquired a normal use in describing the way things *are*. In much the same vein, Heidegger writes in *Being and Time*, "appearance is only possible *on the basis of* something showing itself," which is to say *being* some way or other.[4] Similarly, in his critique of what he calls the "Myth of the Given," Sellars distinguishes between merely *sensing* sense contents and *knowing* noninferentially that, say, something is red; "the classical concept of a sense datum," he insists, is a "mongrel," a confused hybrid blending features of inner sensory episodes and noninferential knowings. Yet there is no primitive layer of brute sensory knowledge by acquaintance; instead, "basic word-world associations hold ... between 'red' and red *physical objects*, rather than between 'red' and a supposed class of private red particulars."[5] It is a mistake, these philosophers agree, to construe the qualities of things in the perceptual environment as qualities of experience itself, and then suppose that we have an immediate epistemic acquaintance with those inner qualities on the basis of which we must infer or construct our knowledge of the world.

Another error, Merleau-Ponty observes, is to suppose that objects are given to us in perception "fully developed and determinate" (*PP* 11/5/6). The two errors are distinct, but they go hand in hand, for the notion that things are given to us with perfectly crisp and sharply delineated features provides covert support to the idea that perception involves some kind of inner awareness of the determinate qualities of experience itself, qualities perhaps even incorrigibly present to the mind. Experience rarely exhibits such sharply defined features, however, and no analysis of perception into discrete attitudes with crisply defined contents intending isolated qualities can capture the peculiar "perceptual milieu" (*PP* 58/47/54), always at once a "behavioral milieu" (*PP* 94/79/91), in which things show up for us under meaningful aspects. Suppose, Merleau-Ponty writes, that perception were merely the effect of a discrete stimulus.

We ought, then, to perceive a segment of the world precisely delimited, surrounded by a zone of blackness, packed full of qualities with no interval between them, held together by definite relationships of size similar to those lying on the retina. The fact is that experience offers nothing like this, and we shall never, using the world as our starting point, understand what a *field of vision* is. (*PP* 11/5/6)

The edges of my visual field are nothing like the edges of a canvas or a movie screen, for they are in principle not objects I can look at, but the horizons of my looking: "The region surrounding the visual field is not easy to describe, but what is certain is that it is neither black nor gray." Moreover, it is not as if things that fall just outside my visual field simply lapse into perceptual oblivion. Instead, "what is behind my back is not without some element of visual presence" (*PP* 12/6/6), for it still has a kind of perceptual availability as something there to be seen when I turn to look at it. The perceptual field thus cannot be equated with that range of objects directly affecting my sense organs at a given time.

"There is no physiological definition of sensation" (*PP* 16/9/11), yet it is tempting to try to define sensations in terms of the stimuli that cause them. Indeed, philosophical intuitions about the real character of our sensations, abstracted from the distorting effects of judgment, are regularly driven by assumptions concerning the external causes of our experience. If the Müller–Lyer illusion (Fig. 1) involves

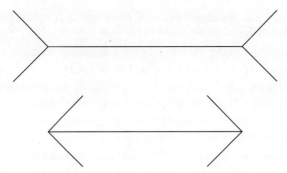

Figure 1 The Müller–Lyer illusion

a mistaken judgment about the relative lengths of the two lines, it is tempting to suppose that the underlying sensations must be sensations of lines of equal length. The lines themselves are the same length, after all, and surely our sensations do no more than register the effects of those causal sources of our experience. This "constancy hypothesis,"[6] which stipulates a strict correlation between stimulus and sensation, immediately confronts a plethora of counterexamples, however. Small patches of yellow and black side by side look green, and red and green patches together look gray. Motion pictures create an effect of movement by presenting the eye with a series of discrete still pictures in rapid succession. The gray areas in Figure 2 look strikingly different, but are in fact the same shade.[7] So, although it is tempting to define sensations in terms of stimuli, the fact is that there is no isomorphism between the contents and the causes of perception. And even if there were, the concept of sensation would be no better off, for the ordinary notion of sensation is meant to capture

Figure 2 White's illusion

how things look. Because stimuli turn out not to line up in any neat way with how things look, the concept of sensation that they motivate could at best stand only in a dubious relation to the phenomenology it was originally meant to describe.

The constancy hypothesis thus stands in need of auxiliary hypotheses to save it from sheer implausibility, and Merleau-Ponty first considers the classic empiricist response, namely, that sensations, having initially been fixed by the stimuli, subsequently undergo modification by the effects of association and memory. Ad hoc appeals to such cognitive operations are doomed to both obscurity and circularity, however – obscurity because these notions tell us only *that* some sensations elicit others, not *how* they manage to do so, that is, in virtue of what features or powers; circularity because the concepts of association and memory themselves presuppose the very perceptual significance they were supposed to explain.

The sensation of one segment or path in the figure of a circle, for example, may trigger an association by resembling another, "but this resemblance means no more than that one path makes one think of the other," so that our knowledge of objects "appears as a system of substitutions in which one impression announces others without ever justifying the announcement." The introduction of association and memory in the analysis, that is, sheds no light on the putative transition from discrete atoms of sensation to a perceptually coherent gestalt. Instead, for empiricism, "the significance of the perceived is nothing but a cluster of images that begin to reappear without reason" (*PP* 22/15/17).

Worse yet, the empiricist principle of the "association of ideas" takes for granted precisely the kind of perceptual coherence it is intended to explain. For what we in fact associate or group together, when we do, are things and the meaningful features of things, not sensations or atomic qualities, and a thing is a coherent whole, an ensemble, not a collection of discrete parts: "The parts of a thing are not bound together by a merely external association" (*PP* 23/15/18). Rather, the inner coherence of the things we perceive is what enables us to abstract aspects or features we can then associate with one another:

It is not indifferent data that set about combining into a thing because de facto contiguities or resemblances cause them to associate; it is, on the

contrary, because we perceive a grouping as a thing that the analytical attitude can then discern resemblances and contiguities. (*PP* 23/16/18–19)

As an attempt to save the concept of sensation, then, the empiricist
principle of association reverses the true order of explanation, mis-
taking an effect of perceptual significance for its cause. The principle
of association thus begs the question of perceptual meaning, for "the
unity of the thing in perception is not constructed by association,
but is a condition of association" (*PP* 24/17/19–20).

In addition to this negative point, Merleau-Ponty adds a positive
phenomenological account of the emergence of perceptual coherence
as an alternative to the crudely mechanistic theory of the association
of ideas. Perception, he suggests, involves the organism in a constant
fluctuation between states of tension and equilibrium, and the very
unity of a perceived object amounts to a kind of solution, or anticipated solution, to a problem we register not intellectually, but "in
the form of a vague uneasiness" (*PP* 25/17/20). I adjust my body, for
example, by turning my head and moving my eyes, squinting or cup-
ping a hand around my ear, leaning forward, standing up, reaching,
trying all the while to achieve a "best grip" (*meilleure prise*) on the
world (*PP* 309/267/311). Eventually, things come into focus, and my
environment strikes me as organized and coherent; my surroundings
make sense to me, and I can find my way about. Only then do I recognize things and establish "associations" among them. An impression
can arouse another impression, Merleau-Ponty remarks, "only provided that it is already *understood* in the light of the past experience
in which it coexisted with those we are concerned to arouse" (*PP*
25/17/20).

Appealing to memory as a way of salvaging the constancy hypothesis is subject to the same objections. For memory, like association,
is possible only against a background of perceptual coherence and
cannot, on pain of circularity, be invoked to explain it. Memory cannot "fill in" the gaps in the sensations that must, on the constancy
hypothesis, result from the poverty of our retinal images, for "in order to fill out perception, memories need to have been made possible
by the character (*physionomie*) of what is given." What is capable of
evoking a memory is not a decontextualized sense datum, but something one perceives and recognizes as familiar and meaningful under
an aspect. Like association, then,

the appeal to memory presupposes what it is supposed to explain: the patterning of data, the imposition of meaning on a chaos of sensation. At the moment the evocation of memories is made possible, it becomes superfluous, since the work we put it to is already done. (*PP* 27/19/23)

My present experience must already have some definite character or aspect, after all, to evoke *this* particular memory and not some other. In the end, Merleau-Ponty concludes, reference to the mind's unconscious "projection of memories" as a constitutive principle at work in all perceptual experience is a "bad metaphor" that obscures the true phenomenological structure of perception and memory alike (*PP* 28/20/23).

The distinctions between figure and ground, things and the empty spaces between them, past and present are not rooted in sensation, but are "structures of consciousness irreducible to the qualities that appear in them" (*PP* 30/22/26). Merleau-Ponty knows that he has no knockdown a priori argument against the atomism of empiricist epistemology, but it is enough to show that the concept of sensation lacks the phenomenological support and the explanatory force that would have to speak in its favor to vindicate it. The atomistic level of description will seem to be providing a more accurate picture of reality, he says, "as long as we keep trying to construct the shape of the world, life, perception, the mind, instead of recognizing as the immanent source and as the final authority of our knowledge of such things, the *experience* we have of them" (*PP* 31/23/27).

The concept of sensation is incoherent, then, because it is meant to serve two incompatible functions: first, to capture the actual content of perceptual experience; second, to explain how that experience is brought about by causal impingements on our sensory surfaces. The concept fails in the first effort precisely because of its service to the second, and vice versa. For when it describes the phenomena adequately, it explains nothing, and when it is subsequently invoked, along with auxiliary hypotheses concerning association and memory, to explain away the manifest phenomena, it no longer describes them as they are.

II. JUDGMENT

Because perceptual phenomena so clearly depart from what the concepts of sensation, association, and memory seem to demand, it is natural to suppose that the actual order of appearance must lie buried beneath a layer of cognition that actively restructures it, either wholly or in part. This is what Merleau-Ponty calls the "intellectualist antithesis" of empiricism, which lies at the heart of Cartesian and Kantian epistemology and continues to inform cognitivist theories of perception today. Descartes was perhaps an extreme case, insisting as he did that perception is not strictly speaking a bodily process at all, but the activity of an incorporeal mind. Yet contemporary physicalists like Daniel Dennett are no less adamant than their rationalist predecessors that perception must be organized by, indeed that it just *is*, thought or judgment. For Descartes and Kant, the very fact that it is *things* we see, as opposed to mere clusters of qualities, is due to our application of the concept of substance to the manifold of intuition provided passively by the senses.[8]

As we have seen, the constancy hypothesis assumes an isomorphism between stimulus and perception. One might suppose that that assumption is peculiar to empiricism, but as Merleau-Ponty points out, intellectualist theories rely on it as much or more, precisely to demonstrate that perceptual awareness is a product of active cognition, not of passive receptivity. Sensations, if they exist at all, are perfectly determinate but lie buried beneath the threshold of conscious awareness; then the spotlight of attention shines on them and brings them to consciousness. Thus, in the Second Meditation Descartes insists that objects are strictly speaking "perceived by the mind alone," not by the senses. Perception of a piece of wax melting, changing its qualities, and yet remaining one and the same piece of wax is a "purely *mental* scrutiny; and this can be imperfect and confused, as it was before, or clear and distinct as it is now, depending on how carefully I *concentrate* on what the wax consists in."[9] For Descartes, then, imperfect or confused perception is not a matter of having defective or obscure material available for mental scrutiny, but of *scrutinizing* it imperfectly or confusedly. What is given is given by God and cannot be imperfect; error and illusion flow from our own willful misconstructions. So, for the intellectualist, as Merleau-Ponty says, "The moon on the horizon is not, and is not seen to be, bigger than at its zenith: if we look at it attentively, for example, through a cardboard tube or a telescope, we see that its apparent diameter remains constant" (*PP* 35/27/32). What is literally given in perception, then, the intellectualist and the empiricist agree, is fixed by the stimulus.

But this means that attention and judgment can effect no change from perceptual obscurity to clarity after all because there was no confusion in the sensations themselves to begin with, only in the vagaries of intellect or will. Consequently, as Merleau-Ponty observes, "attention remains an abstract and ineffective power, because it has no work to perform." It is not as if our experience is a muddle and then the mind operates on it and sorts it out; rather, perceptual indistinctness is always only a matter of failing to attend carefully and judge correctly. "What intellectualism lacks is contingency in the occasions of thought" (PP 36/28/32). In this way, empiricism and intellectualism are two sides of a coin, the former rendering the transition from experience to judgment inexplicable, the latter taking it for granted by building thought into the very definition of perceptual objectivity: "Empiricism cannot see that we need to know what we are looking for, otherwise we would not be looking for it, and intellectualism fails to see that we need to be ignorant of what we are looking for, or equally again we should not be searching." In both, "the indeterminate does not enter into the definition of the mind" (PP 36/28/33).

More recent cognitivist theories of perception have dispensed with this problem concerning the relation between experience and judgment by dispensing with the very idea that anything is given in experience at all, prior to or independent of our judgment about it. Dennett, for example, radicalizing Sellars's attack on the Myth of the Given, insists that there can be no difference between the way things *seem* to us and the way we *think* they seem. What he calls his "*first-person operationalism* . . . denies the possibility in principle of consciousness of a stimulus in the absence of the subject's belief in that consciousness."[10] For Dennett, then, as for Descartes, experience is cognition "all the way down." Indeed, Dennett is an even more extreme intellectualist than Descartes, for whereas Descartes's characterization of all mental phenomena as modes of "thought" is largely a terminological idiosyncrasy, Dennett maintains that every conscious experience, even the most visceral and concrete, is literally a kind of judgment or supposition that something is the case.[11]

To make this point, Dennett refers to the "phi phenomenon," first so called by the Gestalt psychologist Max Wertheimer. Phi movement is the apparent movement perceived in such things as the flashing lights in the headline "Zipper" in Times Square or the rapid sequence of still photographs that make up a motion picture. Quite apart from whether anything in the world is really moving, the relevant phenomenological question is whether we *really see* (apparent) movement or merely *think* we see it.[12] From enough of a distance, it seems obvious that we really do *seem to see* movement, but as we get closer, it is not clear whether we are literally seeing movement or merely *judging that* what we are seeing looks as if it's moving. More specifically, ask yourself if you (seem to) see the letters on the zipper or the figures in the movie flowing *continuously*? Since it is impossible at any given moment to see into the future, must you not, in fact, be registering each successive image and then inferring back to an intermediate position between it and the one preceding it, an intermediate position that was not in fact visually present to you? Does this not amount to constructing a mere belief that you are seeing continuous motion, as opposed to literally seeing it in some nonepistemic sense?[13]

The conclusion Dennett draws from psychological experiments involving these kinds of nearly instantaneous perceptual effects and the reports subjects give of them is not just that there are peculiar borderline cases midway between attitudes about perceptions and perceptions themselves, but the much more radical thesis that, although we ordinarily suppose things are *given* in perception, and that we then form judgments about them, there is in fact no difference in principle between a perceptual experience and a judgment about a perceptual experience. To be sure, peculiar borderline cases are not confined to the psychology laboratory. If you are looking for Pierre in a café, you may have false sightings if isolated characteristic features jump out at you and catch your eye. The moment you think you see him, it may be perfectly indeterminate whether you *really* see a resemblance or merely *think* you see one. Are you responding to a genuinely present but misleading visual cue or simply jumping to a conclusion based on no good visual evidence at all? Foreign speech sounds like a continuous stream of sounds, but your own language sounds like discrete words. Do you literally *hear* the breaks between the words or merely insert them in thought? Indeterminate perceptual phenomena like these are neither passively registered nor spontaneously constructed in thought, but seem to be given with their perceptual significance already involuntarily integrated into our bodily response to them.

Rather than extend his phenomenology to include a positive account of this kind of perceptual ambiguity, however, Dennett flattens the field by simply reducing perception to cognition. For him, quite literally, seeing is believing: to lack a belief about a perceptual experience is to lack the experience altogether. But why should we suppose that the borderline cases threaten the very distinction between experience and judgment? To say that there is only a gradual difference between the two, rather than a sharp boundary, is in no way to deny that there are unambiguous instances of each. I perceive the book on my desk without any commitment of judgment at all, just as I judge that it must be about two o'clock without the faintest glimmer of qualitative feeling. As Merleau-Ponty says,

Ordinary experience draws a perfectly clear distinction between sense experience and judgment. It sees judgment as the taking of a stand, as an effort to know something valid for me at every moment of my life, and for other minds, actual or possible; sense experience, on the contrary, is taking appearance at its face value ... This distinction disappears in intellectualism, because judgment is everywhere pure sensation is not, which is to say everywhere. The testimony of phenomena will therefore everywhere be impugned. (PP 43/34/39)

One could almost believe Merleau-Ponty had Dennett in mind when he wrote those words. Indeed, Dennett does not so much impugn the testimony of phenomena as silence it: "*There seems to be phenomenology,*" he concedes. "But it does *not* follow from this undeniable, universally attested fact that *there really is* phenomenology."[14] We *seem* to have experience underlying and supporting our judgments about it, but that seeming is itself just a false judgment. On Dennett's view, the phenomena themselves testify to nothing because it is always only our judgments speaking in their stead. Ordinary experience, it seems, could hardly be more drastically mistaken about its own phenomenal character.

Yet the ironic effect of Dennett's intellectualism is a reinstatement of one of the prejudices of the Cartesian conception of the mind that materialists like him are otherwise so eager to discredit, namely, the idea that we are incorrigible about our own mental states. For if my consciousness and my beliefs about my consciousness collapse into a single effect, it will be impossible for my beliefs to be wrong *about* my experience. More precisely, although one of my beliefs may be false about another, I will have at least one incorrigible belief, one belief that cannot be false with respect to my experience, namely, the belief that constitutes that experience. If Dennett wants to preserve the fallibility of such beliefs, he can do so only by denying that they are about what they seem to be about, namely, conscious experience. I may be mistaken if my judgment is really a judgment about the physical state of my brain or if it lacks an object altogether, but if the judgment at once *constitutes* and is *about* my experience, then there will be no room for it to be false. Intellectualism entails a doctrine of incorrigibility, and Merleau-Ponty saw this: "if we see what we judge, how can we distinguish between true and false perception? How will we then be able to say that the *halluciné* or the madman 'think they see what they do not see'? What will be the difference between 'seeing' and 'thinking one sees'?" (*PP* 44/34–5/40). There is a difference between seeing and thinking one sees, not because "see" is a success verb, but because (success aside) things do not always *really* appear to me the way I *think* they appear, and intellectualism can make no sense of that distinction.

It is important to acknowledge, then, that when intellectualists insist that perceptions are constituted by judgments, they are in effect advocating a radical transformation of ordinary understanding and ordinary language. Perhaps they are simply instituting a new and different concept of judgment, which we ought not to confuse with the ordinary notion. But of course philosophers can say anything they like, if they allow themselves the freedom to cut new concepts out of whole cloth and tailor them to fit their theories. Besides, too much of what intellectualism says about judgment and its role in perception feeds on the ordinary notion for such a wholesale redefinition of the concept to carry any conviction. The awkwardness of the intellectualist position is evident in the awkwardness of Kant's concept of the manifold of intuition, which must be given for the imagination and the understanding to have something to work on, yet which cannot be given prior to having already been synthesized by those very faculties. Kant began in the first edition of the first *Critique* with a more robust notion of sensory appearance as distinct from the synthesized content of objective experience, but he had to banish that

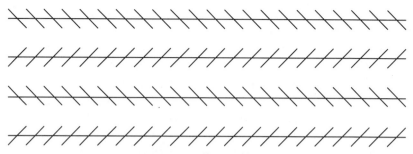

Figure 3 Zöllner's illusion

notion and leave it in limbo once he decided that subjects can be conscious of appearances themselves only thanks to the objectivity imposed by judgment. Intellectualism thus begs the questions, At *what* are the operations of the intellect directed? and How do minds *orient* themselves at the outset vis-à-vis their objects? Trying to answer these questions simply by positing more and more judgments, deeper and deeper layers of cognitive activity, "unconscious inferences" à la Helmholtz, or "micro-takings" à la Dennett,[15] is either to defer an inevitable question indefinitely or else to be forced into an arbitrary redefinition of terms.

Consider a concrete example. In Zöllner's illusion (Fig. 3), the horizontal lines are in fact parallel but seem to converge. "Intellectualism," Merleau-Ponty observes, "reduces the phenomenon to a simple mistake." But the mistake remains inexplicable. "The question ought to arise: how does it come about that it is so difficult in Zöllner's illusion to compare in isolation the very lines that have to be compared in the given task? Why do they refuse in this way to be separated from the auxiliary lines?" (PP 44/35/40–1). The erroneous judgment that is supposed to explain the perceptual appearance in this case begs a question that can only be answered by further phenomenological description of the recalcitrant appearance itself. If I judge falsely, it is because my judgment is motivated by an appearance that is not itself a judgment, but rather "the spontaneous organization and the particular configuration of the phenomena." The auxiliary lines break up the parallelism, "But why do they break it up?" (PP 45/36/41–2). Is that, too, the effect of a mistaken judgment? But why do I continue to make the mistake? Our ordinary concept of such intellectual errors presumes at least the possibility of some account of the perceptual source of the mistakes, but intellectualism cannot in principle acknowledge that presumption, since it denies the availability, if not the very existence, of phenomenal appearances underlying the judgments we make about them.

What intellectualist theories of perception fail to acknowledge, according to Merleau-Ponty, is the embodiment and situatedness of experience, for they reduce perceptual content to the free-floating cognition of a disembodied subject:

> Perception is thus thought about perceiving. Its incarnation furnishes no positive characteristic that has to be accounted for, and its hæcceity is simply its own ignorance of itself. Reflective analysis becomes a purely regressive doctrine, according to which every perception is just confused intellection, every determination a negation. It thus does away with all problems except one: that of its own beginning. The finitude of a perception, which gives me, as Spinoza put it, "conclusions without premises," the inherence of consciousness in a point of view, all this reduces to my ignorance of myself, to my negative power of not reflecting. But that ignorance, how is it itself possible? (PP 47–8/38/44)

Intellectualism is not just a phenomenological distortion, then, but an incoherent doctrine pretending to explain perceptual appearances the very accessibility or even existence of which the doctrine cannot consistently admit. Yet descriptions of supposedly constitutive perceptual judgments always turn out to be descriptions of perceptual receptivity. For intellectualism, that is, "Perception is a judgment, but one that is unaware of its own foundations,[16] which amounts to saying that the perceived object is given as a totality and a unity before we have apprehended the intelligible law governing it" (PP 52/42/48). What Descartes describes as the innate inclinations of the mind, and what Malebranche calls "natural judgment," is just perception itself in its receptive aspect, in contrast to the spontaneity of the intellect. "The result," Merleau-Ponty concludes, "is that the intellectualist analysis ends by rendering incomprehensible the perceptual phenomena it is supposed to explain" (PP 43/34/39).

The perceptual foundations of judgment become clearer when we consider aspects or gestalts that shift even while the discrete parts of objects remain fixed. As Merleau-Ponty says, "perception is not an act of understanding. I have only to look at a landscape upside down to recognize nothing in it" (*PP* 57/46/54). Faces and handwriting undergo similar jarring transformations of character when viewed upside down or backward yet their objective structures remain the same from a purely intellectual point of view. Thus, Merleau-Ponty concludes that intellectualism, like empiricism, tacitly thrives on the constancy hypothesis: the sensory stimuli are in a certain sense objectively the same forward as backward, right side up as upside down; therefore, the qualitative difference in perceptual aspect can only be an artifact of a change of intellectual attitude. You cannot see what is not there, so when a perceptual effect fails to correspond to the supplied stimulus, you are not literally *seeing* what you seem to see, but merely *thinking* you see it. Arguments purporting to uncover massive illusions in normal visual experience take the constancy hypothesis for granted in just this way. You seem to see a regular pattern across a large expanse of wallpaper, more or less instantaneously, but your eyes cannot be saccading to all the discrete spots on the wall to piece together the pattern bit by bit; therefore, you must be *judging* rather than literally *seeing* its regularity. The illusion is not that you are seeing something that is not there, but that you think you are *seeing* what you are, in fact, merely *surmising*.[17]

But why should we accept the constancy hypothesis? Why not suppose instead that we often see things precisely by having them in our peripheral vision, especially in cases in which we are sensitized to notice just those salient features that make them relevant to what we are looking at, or looking for? Parafoveal vision is not just an impoverished form of foveal vision, otherwise phenomenologically equivalent. Peripheral vision has abilities and liabilities all its own, quite unlike those of direct visual scrutiny. By arbitrarily applying a single preconceived criterion of perceptual success across the board – namely, accurate registration of discrete stimuli – intellectualism systematically ignores the qualitative phenomenological differences that distinguish our diverse sensory capacities and therefore underestimates the complexity and sophistication of the perceptual mechanisms involved in opening the world up before our eyes.

For Merleau-Ponty, then, although perception is not grounded in sensations, the gestalts in which things are given perceptually constitute a primitive aspect of experience, irreducible to cognition: "there is a significance of the percept that has no equivalent in the universe of the understanding, a perceptual milieu that is not yet the objective world, a perceptual being that is not yet determinate being" (*PP* 58/46–7/54). Intellectualism ignores the indeterminacy of perception and helps itself uncritically to a view of the world as described by the physical sciences: "the real flaw of intellectualism lies precisely in its taking as given the determinate universe of science" (*PP* 58/47/54). Only by bracketing that fully objective description of the world, the description that aspires to a view from nowhere, as it were, and stepping back from the theoretical achievements of scientific theory to our ordinary situated perspective on our familiar environment can we recover the abiding naiveté that constitutes the positive organizing principle of our conscious lives. For the world as given in perception is not the world as described by science, nor even the world as described in prescientific cognition: "Perception is not a science of the world, it is not even an act, a deliberate taking up of a position; it is the background from which all acts stand out, and is presupposed by them" (*PP* v/x–xi/xi).

Perception understood as a background condition of intelligibility, the intelligibility both of judgments and of the misbegotten concept of sensation, is an inheritance we are already intimately familiar with as children, long before we are in a position to comprehend the world or ourselves from the depersonalized standpoint of science:

The child lives in a world he unhesitatingly believes to be accessible to all around him; he has no consciousness of himself or of others as private subjectivities, nor does he suspect that we are all, himself included, limited to a certain point of view on the world....Men are, for him, empty heads turned toward a single self-evident world. (*PP* 407/355/413)

That naive mentality of the child, Merleau-Ponty believes, harbors a wisdom of its own precisely in virtue of its prereflective, pretheoretical phenomenal integrity, which survives vestigially but unmistakably beneath the cognitive accretions of self-conscious maturity. Indeed, "it must be that children are right in some sense, as opposed to adults...and that the primitive thinking of our early years abides as an indispensable acquisition underlying those of adulthood, if there is to be for the adult a single intersubjective world" (*PP* 408/355/414). It is that underlying phenomenal inheritance or acquisition that an adequate phenomenology of perception must aspire to describe.

III. THE PHENOMENAL FIELD

Judgment is indeed grounded in perception, then, but perception is no mere cameralike confrontation with inert sensory particulars, à la the Myth of the Given. Yet if the concept of sensation is incoherent and the reduction of perception to judgment untenable, how are we then to characterize the perceptual field phenomenologically? Clearing a path between empiricism and intellectualism is one of the central aims of Merleau-Ponty's *Phenomenology*, one that requires a new conceptual framework and a new descriptive vocabulary with which to understand intentionality as the necessary interconnectedness of experience and the world. The notion of a primal interrelation, what Merleau-Ponty would later call the "intertwining" (*entrelacs*) or "chiasm" of body and world (*VI*, chapter 4), serves as an antidote to the abstractions of pure receptivity and pure spontaneity that have dominated traditional philosophy of mind. In *Phenomenology*, long before he began to describe the "flesh" common to percipients and their perceptible worlds (*VI* 169/127, et passim), Merleau-Ponty had already effectively reconceived perception itself as neither a mere passive registration of stimuli nor a radically free initiation of mental acts, but as the way in which the body belongs to its environment, the essential interconnectedness of sensitivity and motor response.

The point is not just that there is a close causal connection between perception and bodily movement, which nonetheless remain conceptually distinct. Even Descartes observes, "I am very closely joined and, as it were, intermingled with" my body, "so that I and the body form a unit."[18] If Merleau-Ponty's insistence on the overlap or dovetailing of perception and movement is more than mere rhetoric, it must constitute a fundamental challenge to the conceptual distinction between the mental and the material that generates the appearance of a mind-body problem to begin with, and that philosophers of mind today still take largely for granted. For Merleau-Ponty, that is, body and world are conceptually, not just causally, two sides of the same coin. The world and I are intelligible each only in light of the other. My body is perceptible to me only because I am already perceptually oriented in an external environment, just as the environment is available to me only through the perceptual medium of my body:

for if it is true that I am conscious of my body via the world, that it is the unperceived term in the center of the world toward which all objects turn their face, it is true for the same reason that my body is the pivot of the world: I know that objects have several faces because I could walk around them, and in that sense I am conscious of the world by means of my body. (PP 97/82/94–5)

What this essential interdependence of ourselves and the world entails is that our bodily orientation and skills constitute for us a normatively rich but noncognitive relation to the perceptual milieu. More precisely, what allows our perceptual attitudes to be right or wrong about the world in the most basic way is the sense of bodily equilibrium that determines which postures and orientations allow us to perceive things *properly*, and which, by contrast, constitute liabilities, incapacities, discomforts, distortions. We have, and feel ourselves to have, optimal bodily attitudes that afford us a "best grip" on things (PP 309/267/311), for example the best distance from which to observe or inspect an object, a preferred stance in which to listen or concentrate, to achieve poise and balance within the gravitational field. The intentionality of perception is thus anchored in what Merleau-Ponty calls the "motor intentionality" (PP 128/110/127) of our bodily skills. Indeed, even without our conscious or voluntary control, our bodies are constantly adjusting themselves to integrate and secure our experience and maintain our effective grip on things:

my body has a grip on the world when my perception offers me a spectacle as varied and as clearly articulated as possible, and when my motor intentions, as they unfold, receive from the world the responses they anticipate. This maximum distinctness in perception and action defines a perceptual *ground*, a basis of my life, a general milieu for the coexistence of my body and the world. (PP 289–90/250/292)

Our constant self-correcting bodily orientation in the environment constitutes the perceptual background against which discrete sensory particulars and explicit judgments can then emerge: "our body is not the object of an 'I think': it is an ensemble of lived meanings that moves to its equilibrium" (PP 179/153/177).

Perception is thus informed by what Merleau-Ponty calls a "body schema" (*schéma corporel*), which is neither a purely mental nor a merely physiological state. The body schema is not an image of the body,[19] and so not an object of our awareness, but rather the bodily skills and capacities that shape our awareness of objects. In the Schematism chapter of the first *Critique*, Kant conceived of schemas as organizing principles for the construction of images, principles he thought played an essential role in constituting the objectivity of experience. For Kant, however, a schema could play that structuring role only by being an explicit rule, a kind of cognitive content. So, although Merleau-Ponty's theory of intentionality is nonrepresentational and noncognitive, his concept of the body schema is analogous to Kant's insight that intentional content does not just magically crystalize in the mind but is so to speak sketched out in advance by the dispositions that allow things to appear to us as they do. Whereas Kant understood those dispositions as intellectual rules or procedures, Merleau-Ponty ascribes them to the bodily poise or readiness that gives us a felt sense rightness or equilibrium and so allows us to regard our own perceptions as either right or wrong, normal or skewed, true or false.

That bodily capacities and dispositions of various sorts *causally* underlie our perceptual orientation in the world is obvious; that those capacities and dispositions establish a *normative* domain, without which perception could not be intentional, is not. Indeed, what makes motor intentionality worthy of the name is precisely its normativity, that is, the felt rightness and wrongness of the different postures and positions we unthinkingly assume and adjust throughout our waking (and sleeping) lives. Felt differences between manifestly better and worse bodily attitudes thus constitute normative distinctions between right and wrong, true and false, perceptual appearances: the words on the chalkboard are a blur, so I squint and crane my neck to see them better; the voice is muffled, so I turn, lean forward, put my hand to my ear; the sweater looks brown until I hold it directly under the light and see that it is really green.[20]

It is easy to overlook the normativity of our bodily orientation in the world precisely because it is so basic and so familiar to us. Yet, Merleau-Ponty argues, that orientation constitutes a form of intentionality more primitive than judgment, more primitive even than the application of concepts. The rightness and wrongness of perceptual appearances is essentially interwoven with the rightness and wrongness of our bodily attitudes, and we have a feel for the kinds of balance and posture that afford us a correct and proper view

of the world. Perception is not just a mental or psychological effect in the mind, then, but the body's intelligent orientation in the
world. Abstracting perception from the body and from the world by
equating it with sensation or judgment means doing violence to the
concept of perception itself. More precisely, it means doing violence
to the experience that affords us an understanding of perception in
the first place, and surely the understanding of perception that is
actually informed and motivated by experience is the one worth
having.

NOTES

1. Intellectualism is roughly equivalent to what used to be called "rationalism" and what is nowadays called "cognitivism." Merleau-Ponty inher-
   its his terminology from fin-de-siècle psychology. In the first volume of
   The Principles of Psychology, for example, William James distinguishes
   between "Intellectualism" and "Sensationalism," and between "sensa-
   tionalist and intellectualist philosophies of mind" (vol. I: 244–5, 250).
   As we shall see, however, whereas James ascribes to intellectualists
   such as Helmholtz and Wundt the Kantian view that sensations exist,
   but *"are combined* by activity of the Thinking Principle" (vol. II: 27;
   cf. vol. II: 218–19), Merleau-Ponty identifies intellectualism as the more
   radical idea that perceptual content is itself constituted, not just organized or affected, by acts of judgment. Intellectualists of this latter sort,
   that is, for example Descartes and contemporary cognitivists like Daniel
   Dennett, intellectualize perception more thoroughly by construing it as
   cognitive or judgmental "all the way down."
2. John Searle makes much the same point, if more vividly, when he writes,
   "it is a category mistake to suppose that when I see a yellow station
   wagon the visual experience itself is also yellow and in the shape of a
   station wagon. Just as when I believe that it is raining I do not literally
   have a wet belief, so when I see something yellow I do not literally have
   a yellow visual experience. One might as well say that my visual experience is six cylindered or that it gets twenty-two miles to the gallon"
   (Searle, *Intentionality,* 43).
3. Wittgenstein, *Zettel,* §§418, 422.
4. Heidegger, *Being and Time,* 29.
5. Sellars, "Empiricism and the Philosophy of Mind," §§7, 29; *Science,
   Perception and Reality,* 132, 161.
6. See Köhler, "On Unnoticed Sensations and Errors of Judgment," in *The
   Selected Papers of Wolfgang Köhler.*

7. Michael White, "The Effect of the Nature of the Surround on the Perceived Lightness of Grey Bars within Square-Wave Test Gratings," Figure 1a.

8. "And so," Descartes writes in the Second Meditation, "something which I thought I was seeing with my eyes is in fact grasped solely by the faculty of judgment which is in my mind." *The Philosophical Writings of Descartes*, vol. II; AT VII 32. Similarly, Kant writes, "all synthesis, through which even perception itself becomes possible, stands under the categories, and since experience is cognition through connected perceptions, the categories are conditions of the possibility of experience" (Kant, *Critique of Pure Reason*, B161).

9. Descartes, *Philosophical Writings*, vol. II; AT VII 31, emphasis added.

10. Dennett, *Consciousness Explained*, 132.

11. In *Principles of Philosophy*, Descartes defines "thought" (*cogitationis*) as "everything which we are aware of as happening within us, in so far as we have awareness of it. Hence, *thinking* is to be identified here not merely with understanding, willing and imagining, but also with sensory awareness" (*Philosophical Writings*, vol. I, AT VIII 7; cf. *Meditations*, op. cit., vol. II; AT VII 34). The equation Descartes draws between sensory awareness and thought thus appears to fix the meaning of the latter term, rather than take the received sense for granted and assert something implausible. Dennett's theory is the implausible thesis itself.

12. Again, although "see" is usually understood as a success verb, the question is not whether something really is moving, but has to do instead with the content of our experience, what our experience purports. I therefore say "(apparent) movement" to indicate that the point here concerns the *experience* of seeing, not its veridicality. Alternatively, one could ask whether we *really seem to see* the movement.

13. Dennett describes experiments conducted by Paul Kolers in which subjects shown discontinuous changes in color and shape report seeing them occurring gradually and continuously, so that the perceptual effect could only have emerged in retrospect, which suggests that the subjects may be fabricating (false) beliefs after the fact regarding what they saw at an earlier moment. Dennett's conclusion, however, is that there is nothing to choose between the apparently conflicting claims that the experience was indeed a conscious perception and that it consisted simply in the formation of a retrospective belief. See Dennett, *Consciousness Explained*, 114–26.

14. *Consciousness Explained*, 366. By "phenomenology" Dennett doesn't mean the philosophical movement or method, but putative qualities of consciousness distinct from our judgments about them.

15. Dennett, "Real Consciousness." *Brainchildren*, 133–4.

16. Here Merleau-Ponty quotes the Sixth Meditation: "These and other judgments that I made concerning sensory objects, I was apparently taught to make by nature; for I had already made up my mind that this was how things were, before working out any arguments to prove it" (Descartes, *Philosophical Writings*, vol. II; AT VII 76).

17. Dennett, *Consciousness Explained*, 354–5. Cf. J. K. O'Regan, R. A. Rensink, and J. J. Clark, "Change-Blindness as a Result of 'Mudsplashes,'" 34; and S. J. Blackmore, G. Brelstaff, K. Nelson, and T. Troscianko, "Is the Richness of Our Visual World an Illusion? Transsaccadic Memory for Complex Scenes," 1075.

18. Descartes, *Philosophical Writings*, vol. II; AT VII 81.

19. Unfortunately, the standard English edition of *Phenomenology* mistranslates "*schéma corporel*" as "body image."

20. For a more detailed account of this kind of perceptual normativity, see Sean Kelly's essay in this volume.

3   Seeing Things in Merleau-Ponty

> *Just as the perceived world endures only through the re-*
> *flections, shadows, levels, and horizons between things . . .*
> *so the works and thought of a philosopher are also made*
> *of certain articulations between things said.*
>
>   Merleau-Ponty

This passage comes from the opening pages of "The Philosopher and His Shadow," Merleau-Ponty's essay on Edmund Husserl. It proposes a risky interpretive principle. The main feature of this principle is that the seminal aspects of a thinker's work are so close to him that he is incapable of articulating them himself. Nevertheless, these aspects pervade the work; give it its style, its sense, and its direction; and therefore belong to it essentially. As Martin Heidegger writes, in a passage quoted by Merleau-Ponty in the essay, "The greater the work of a thinker – which in no way coincides with the breadth and number of writings – the richer is what is unthought in this work, which means, that which emerges in and through this work as having not yet been thought."[1] The goal of Merleau-Ponty's essay, he says, is "to evoke this unthought-of element in Husserl's thought" (S 202/160).

The risk of such an interpretive strategy is evident. By identifying the essence of a thinker's work with ideas that he never explicitly endorsed, indeed, by allowing for the possibility that the ideas he did explicitly endorse are in contradiction with the essence of his thought, the interpreter runs the risk of recklessness. Yet there is something to the strategy.

In the first place, it seems clear that great works do have a style, a sense, a direction in which they point. This is true both for individual works of art and for the overall oeuvre of an artist. It is because

74

Titian's style runs throughout his work, for example, that we can often recognize a piece as a Titian without knowing which of his paintings it is. The Titian oeuvre has a style that is recognizable in all of its central works. Yet each individual work manifests the style in a different way. It is because a particular painting uniquely manifests an overall style that copying it can be such a difficult task. The style of a work is not something that one can copy as if mechanically tracing its lines. It is something that is manifest in the lines, but something that goes beyond them as well.

Moreover, the style of an oeuvre, like the style of an individual or an epoch, is so pervasive that it recedes into the background and is largely invisible to those who manifest it most. For this reason, Merleau-Ponty believes that *we* can recognize an artist's style better than the artist can himself. Merleau-Ponty writes, for example, in *The Prose of the World,*

To the extent that the painter has already painted and is in some measure master of himself, what is given to him with his style is not a certain number of ideas or tics that he can inventory but a manner of formulation that is just as recognizable for others and just as little visible to him as his silhouette or his everyday gestures. (*PM* 82/58)

Great works of philosophy, like great works of art, have this character as well. The style of a thinker's thought, its unthought element in other words, is more easily recognizable by others than it is by the thinker himself.

Finally, background phenomena like a style or a form of life are holistic and can therefore withstand local contradiction. We can say, for example, about a particular painting by Cézanne, not only that it is *in his style* but also that it is *not his style at its best*. This is an interpretive claim to be sure, but it need not be a reckless one. We need only admit that not everything produced *by* Cézanne is produced *in the style of* Cézanne, to make it possible for such a claim to be responsible.

Why are these comments apposite here? Although I do believe they provide a key to the interpretive strategy that Merleau-Ponty uses in his essay on Husserl, this chapter is not about interpretation. Rather, I begin with this discussion of background and style because I believe it both illustrates and licenses the interpretation of Merleau-Ponty's work that I give here. It illustrates my interpretation because, as I hope to argue, Merleau-Ponty's view of perception depends on the idea that the background of our perception of objects and their properties, like the background understanding of a thinker, must recede from view and yet functions everywhere to guide what is focally articulate. It licenses my interpretation because, as I will show, Merleau-Ponty didn't quite get his own view right.

I did not set out to write the essay this way. Indeed, when I realized that Merleau-Ponty does not say some of the things I thought he should, I wondered whether all along I had been seeing things in his work that simply are not there. I became convinced, however, that what he does say points unequivocally in the direction of an overall view that he seems not to have been able to articulate himself. I leave it to the reader to determine whether the interpretation I give is reckless or responsible. In any event, there is no doubt that it forms the type of history of philosophy that stands on the "middle-ground where the philosopher we are speaking about and the philosopher who is speaking are present together, although it is not possible even in principle to decide at any given moment just what belongs to each" (S 202/159). Merleau-Ponty, like Heidegger, thought that this way of engaging with a philosopher is the best way to be faithful to him. I hope he was right.

I. THE PROBLEM OF SEEING THINGS

Near the beginning of the *Phenomenology of Perception*, Merleau-Ponty makes an apparently astounding claim. It is part of my experience of the world, he says, that objects *see* one another:

To see is to enter a universe of beings which *display themselves*. . . . Thus every object is the mirror of all others. When I look at the lamp on my table, I attribute to it not only the qualities visible from where I am, but also those which the chimney, the walls, the table can "see"; the back of my lamp is nothing other than the face which it "shows" to the chimney. I can therefore see an object insofar as objects form a system or a world and insofar as each of them treats the others around it like spectators of its hidden aspects and a guarantee of their permanence. (*PP* 82–3/68/79, translation modified)[2]

The claim that I experience objects as *seeing* one another is central to Merleau-Ponty's understanding of the way in which I experience objects as *transcending*, or going beyond, my experience of them.

It is central, in other words, to Merleau-Ponty's understanding of what it is to see objects as full three-dimensional entities, despite only ever seeing them in perspectival presentations. Because of this, any attempt to understand Merleau-Ponty's account of object transcendence needs to grapple with this apparently astounding claim. Only in doing so will we be able to distinguish Merleau-Ponty's full-blooded phenomenology of perception from the more cognitivist accounts of perceptual experience found in such philosophers as Edmund Husserl and C. I. Lewis.

The problem of object transcendence poses itself most forcefully when we acknowledge the phenomenological distinction between experiencing something as a mere two-dimensional façade and experiencing it as a full three-dimensional entity. Indeed, until we have a good feel for this distinction, it can be difficult to understand the problem of object transcendence at all. In our everyday existence, however, this distinction is rarely made. The reason is that we almost always have experiences as of objects rather than as of mere façades. Despite only ever seeing my coffee mug from one perspective or another, for instance, I almost always experience it *as* a full three-dimensional entity. It is possible to experience something as a mere façade, however, whether it is one or not, and occasionally this happens.

Imagine visiting an old western movie set. When you first arrive, you might be amazed at how realistic everything looks. As you walk down the street, it really seems as though buildings rise up on either side. The bank really looks like it is a bank; the saloon really looks like it is a saloon; it really seems as though you've stepped into the Old West. Movie sets are constructed to fool you this way.

But they are movie sets after all, and a little bit of exploration reveals this fact. Walking through the saloon doors is nothing like walking into a saloon. The anticipation of a cool sarsaparilla, and even the anticipation of a room with chairs in it and a bar, is immediately frustrated in the movie set saloon. When you walk through the doors you see nothing but the supporting apparatus for the saloon façade and perhaps some stage materials hidden away. The same for what earlier looked to be a bank. It is revealed instead as a very convincing face supported by some two-by-fours and bags of sand. And so on for every structure on the street.

If you explore the set enough in this way, then an amazing thing can happen. Now as you walk down the street, it doesn't look realistic at all. Instead of buildings on either side, it looks as if there are mere façades. Instead of feeling as if you're in the Old West, it feels as if you're on an Old West movie set. This is not because you can see through the doors to their empty backsides, or, indeed, because you "see" anything different at all (at least in one very limited sense of "to see"). Let us stipulate, in fact, that every light ray cast onto your retina is exactly the same as it was when you first arrived on the set. Still, your experience of the set can change, a gestalt shift can occur, so that the whole thing looks like a set full of façades instead of like an Old West town. This is the phenomenon I have in mind.[3]

Husserl was the first to identify this phenomenon as a central problem for philosophical theories of perception. Given that the only information projected onto the retina is information in (roughly) two dimensions, the fact that there is a difference between experiencing something as *having* only two dimensions (a façade) and experiencing it as *having* three (an object) is a puzzle. To do justice to this phenomenological distinction, Husserl argued, we must admit that the features of perceptual experience are not limited to those of the sense data occasioned by the object's front.[4] Indeed, Husserl claimed, we need to give some account of the way in which the *hidden* aspects of an experienced object – the backside it is experienced to have, for instance – are present to me in my experience of it. Without such an account, we have no resources to distinguish between the case in which the thing looks to be a façade and the case in which it looks to be an object.

In Husserl's account of object transcendence, the principal move is to distinguish between the features of the object that are experienced by me as *determinate* (roughly, those features for which I have sense data) and the features of the object that are experienced by me as *indeterminate* (roughly, everything else). Following Husserl, Merleau-Ponty adopts this terminology as well. I argue here, however, that Merleau-Ponty's understanding of the category of the indeterminate is totally different from Husserl's. As a result, Merleau-Ponty's understanding of object transcendence is totally different, too. The puzzling passage about objects seeing one another, I claim, makes perfect sense once we have in mind Merleau-Ponty's complicated and interesting story about the experience of objects as three-dimensional.

I develop this interpretation in four stages. In section II, I discuss some textual evidence for the distinction between Husserl's account of the indeterminate and the account given by Merleau-Ponty. The distinction between absence and positive presence, I claim, is an important clue in teasing apart their positions. In section III, I begin to put some meat on Merleau-Ponty's notion of the indeterminate as a positive presence. In particular, I develop Merleau-Ponty's important idea that the visual background is indeterminate, in the sense that it is experienced normatively instead of descriptively. The test case for this story is that of color and its background lighting context. In section IV, I build on this idea to explain Merleau-Ponty's account of the transcendence of objects to our experience of them. In this section, I hope to make clear why Merleau-Ponty says that we experience objects as seeing one another. Finally, after a brief summary of the dialectic in section V, I offer some concluding thoughts in section VI. My main goal here is to contrast Merleau-Ponty's full phenomenological account of object perception with the more familiar, but less successful, kind of phenomenalist account found in the work of authors such as C. I. Lewis.[5]

II. MAKING THE INDETERMINATE A POSITIVE PHENOMENON

Merleau-Ponty gets from Husserl both the idea that we perceive objects as transcending what we determinately see of them and also the idea that one project of phenomenology is to describe the details of this experience. He moves beyond Husserl, however, in his characterization of the way in which we experience the indeterminate features of an object. The main difference between their views is that Husserl claims the indeterminate features of an object are *hypothesized but sensibly absent*, whereas Merleau-Ponty claims that they have a *positive presence* in our experience.

I have argued elsewhere that Husserl's account of object transcendence relies on a particular story about how the hidden features of an object are presented in experience.[6] The hidden features of an object include, for example, the color, shape, and size of the side of the object that is now hidden from view. Given that my perception of an object always takes place from one spatial point of view or another, I can only experience the object as a three-dimensional entity if I experience it as having a hidden side. Yet in what way, if at all, do I experience the various features of the hidden side, such as its color, shape, and size?

On Husserl's account, these features are completely absent from the sensuous aspects of my experience. Rather, I *know* or *believe* or *hypothesize* or *expect* that the object has certain hidden features, but I do not, properly speaking, *see* it as such. In an early set of lectures, in fact, Husserl says that the hidden features of the per- ceived object appear to the subject only in an "improper" mode; "im- properly appearing moments of the object," he says, "are in no way presented."[7]

On Husserl's account, therefore, the hidden features of an object are *indeterminate* in the sense that I have *not yet sensibly deter- mined* what they are. I may have a certain hypothesis or belief about the shape of the backside of the object, but until I go around to the back and look, I will not have *determined* it for sure. In particular, there is nothing in "the material of sensation"[8] to indicate that the backside is any shape at all. In this sense, therefore, Husserl believes that the hidden features of an object are absent in my perceptual experience of it.

According to Merleau-Ponty, however, "we must recognize the in- determinate as a positive phenomenon" (*PP* 12/6/7). The indetermi- nate features of the object are not merely features of which I have no current experience. As he says, "the perceived contains gaps which are not mere 'failures to perceive'" (*PP* 18/11/13). Rather, the inde- terminate features are those that I am experiencing, although *not as determinate* features of the object: "There occurs here an *indeter- minate vision, a vision of I do not know what (vision de je ne sais quoi)*," which nevertheless "is not without some element of visual presence" (*PP* 12/6/6). The project, for Merleau-Ponty, is to say what this positive but indeterminate experience is.

The distinction between the indeterminate as a perceptual ab- sence and the indeterminate as a positive presence is crucial to under- standing the relation between Husserl and Merleau-Ponty. I do not know of anywhere in the voluminous literature on these authors, however, where this distinction has previously been discussed. In part, it may have gone unnoticed because of an inadequacy in the standard English translation of Merleau-Ponty's text. Even once the text is clear, however, the distinction can be difficult to identify. Let me begin by stating why I believe the standard translation is inadequate.

Merleau-Ponty describes an "indeterminate vision," the kind of visual experience we have of the hidden side of an object, for example, as a *"vision de je ne sais quoi."* In the standard English translation of Merleau-Ponty's text, this is rendered as a "vision of something or other." This translation precisely covers up the difference between Husserl and Merleau-Ponty. According to Merleau-Ponty, I do not have a vision of some *thing* or another, a thing which is itself determinate but which I have not yet determined. Rather, on Merleau-Ponty's view, I have a positive presentation of something indeterminate, a presentation of *an I do not know what*. The correct translation of the phrase, therefore, is quite literal: my experience of the backside of an object is "a vision of I do not know what."

Even with the corrected translation, however, the distinction between the two views can be difficult to discern. Let me therefore state it as clearly as I can. The difference is properly understood as a distinction in the scope of the indeterminacy. Husserl thinks that it is indeterminate, from the point of view of the current visual experience, what the features of the backside of the object are. Merleau-Ponty, by contrast, thinks that my current visual experience contains something that is itself an indeterminate presentation of the back. For Husserl, it is not yet determined what I see; for Merleau-Ponty, what I see is indeterminate.

By analogy, consider the case of belief. There is a difference between not yet having made up your mind whether *A* or *B* on one hand, and positively affirming that *either A or B* on the other. In the first case, it is indeterminate (in the Husserlian sense of not yet determined) what you believe. In the second case, what you believe is indeterminate. This second case is not completely analogous to Merleau-Ponty's account of the indeterminacy of perception, however. The reason is that my perception of the hidden features of an object, according to Merleau-Ponty, is not indeterminate in the sense of being merely disjunctive. In what sense it is indeterminate, however, is a complicated question. This is the question I hope to answer in the following two sections.

III. THE INDETERMINACY OF THE VISUAL
BACKGROUND: A NORMATIVE ASPECT OF
VISUAL EXPERIENCE

The canonical kind of indeterminate visual presence, for Merleau-Ponty, is the visual presence of the background against which a figure appears. The background, insofar as it is experienced as a background, is visually present to a subject even though it makes no *determinate* contribution to his experience. To take a simple example, if I am looking at the lamp in front of me, then there is a sense in which the books, the wall, and the door behind it are all part of my visual experience. They are not determinate in my experience of them, however, the way the lamp might be thought to be. They are, in some sense yet to be clarified, present to me as indeterminate. In this section, I argue that, according to Merleau-Ponty, the indeterminacy of the visual background consists in its playing a normative rather than a descriptive role in visual experience.[9]

Perhaps the simplest example of visual background is the lighting context in which a color appears. Light itself can come in various colors, of course, and this can affect my experience of the color of an object in surprising and important ways. Yet even if we consider only the case of pure white light, the relative *brightness* of the light has an important effect on my experience of the color of the object to which I am attending. Within a certain range, the change in the brightness of the light will not affect the color I see the object *to be*. This is the so-called phenomenon of brightness constancy. Even if the color of the object seems to remain constant throughout changes in the lighting context, however, my experience of the color will change in some way or another whenever the surrounding light dims or brightens perceptibly. To do justice to the phenomenology of color experience, therefore, we must determine *in what way* changes in the lighting context affect my experience of the color of a thing. Merleau-Ponty will claim, against Husserl, that the experience of the lighting context is essentially normative; I see how the lighting *should* change in order for me to see the color better.

By contrast, consider first the view that Husserl holds. Husserl begins by emphasizing, with Merleau-Ponty, that changes in the context of perception produce changes in the experience of the color perceived.[10] He calls these changes "adumbrations"

(*Abschattungen*) of the perceived color. These are not changes in what color I experience the object *to be,* but changes in the *way that color looks.* Husserl highlights this distinction from early in his career. He writes the following in *Logical Investigations,* for example: "Here it is enough to point to the readily grasped difference between the red of this ball, objectively seen as uniform, and the indubitable, unavoidable *Abschattungen* among the subjective color-sensations in our percept."[11] The *Abschattungen* of the color, therefore, are the various ways it can look, given various changes in the context of perception. Yet how, according to Husserl, do changes in the lighting context in particular change the way a color can look?

Husserl must believe that the lighting context contributes sensuously to my experience of the color. I do not know of a place where he says this explicitly, but it would be extremely odd, and totally unmotivated by his view, if he treated the lighting context like the hidden features of the object. The lighting is precisely *not* hypothesized but sensuously absent. To claim that the lighting is sensuously absent would be to claim that it in no way affects the sensory image I get of the object; but this is clearly false. I can *see* the changes attributable to the lighting context, even if we understand *seeing* in the narrow sense of being presented with sense data. Changes in the lighting context affect what literally appears to me; I do not merely *hypothesize* these changes to have occurred.

If this is right, then Husserl's account of lighting must be very different from his account of the hidden features of an object. Insofar as the lighting is not *absent* from my experience, it cannot be indeterminate in the sense that Husserl uses the term.[12] Lacking Merleau-Ponty's notion of indeterminacy as a positive phenomenon, therefore, we must understand Husserl to believe that the lighting context is experienced as a *determinate* quantity. On such a view, the brightness of the surrounding light is registered in experience as some measurable amount – ten foot-candles, for instance. Because all sensible presence is determinate, according to Husserl, he has no other option available.[13] Indeed, this kind of Husserlian view has become the orthodoxy in perceptual psychology. The standard cognitivist theory of brightness constancy, for example, is predicated on the assumption that light is experienced in this measurable form.[14]

In contrast to the Husserlian approach, Merleau-Ponty claims that the lighting context is experienced as the background against which the color of the object appears. The background features of experience, according to Merleau-Ponty, make a positive contribution to the phenomenology of perception. They are not, however, determinate in experience in the way that foreground features might be thought to be. As Merleau-Ponty says,

> Lighting and reflection, then, play their part only if they remain in the background as discreet intermediaries, and *lead* our gaze instead of arresting it. . . . The shade does not become really a shade . . . until it has ceased to be in front of us as something to be seen, but surrounds us, becoming our environment in which we establish ourselves. (*PP* 357–8/310–11/361–2)

To say that the lighting *leads* our gaze, or that it *becomes our environment*, is to insist that it plays some positive role in our experience. This positive role appears to be very different, however, from the kind of determinate visual presence the lighting would have if I experienced it as a measurable quantity. What can we say about the kind of indeterminate visual presence that background lighting has in experience? Perhaps it is best to start with an example.

Suppose you are looking at an object that is uniformly colored but unevenly lit. Perhaps it is a tabletop with a natural pattern of shadows across its surface. If asked to determine the color of the table, your eyes move automatically to the part on its surface where the lighting is best. Which part of the surface this is depends at least in part on the color being lit. Darker colors are seen better in brighter light, whereas brighter colors are seen better in dimmer light. What you as a perceiver seem to know immediately is where to move your eyes to see the color best.[15]

Merleau-Ponty's suggestion is that this is how lighting typically figures in experience. The lighting context presents itself not as a determinate quantity but rather in terms of how well it enables me to see the thing I'm looking at. Because of the pattern of shadows covering its surface, not every part of the tabletop is an equally good place to look if you want to get the best view of its color. This is not because the shadows make the tabletop look like *it is* a variety of colors. We can assume that the variation in lighting falls within the range of the brightness constancy effect. Even if it looks as if the surface *is* the same color throughout, however, the pattern of shadows nevertheless affects the way that color *looks*. Merleau-Ponty's idea is that this effect is a normative one: *here* the color looks as if it is not presented in the optimum way; *there* it looks better. As Merleau-Ponty says about the related background phenomena of distance from and perspective on the object,

> For each object, as for each picture in an art gallery, there is an optimum distance from which it requires to be seen, a direction viewed from which it vouchsafes most of itself: at a shorter or greater distance we have merely a perception blurred through excess or deficiency. We therefore tend towards the maximum of visibility, and seek a better focus as with a microscope. (*PP* 348/302/352)

Like the distance from and perspective on the object, according to Merleau-Ponty, the lighting context figures in experience by leading my gaze to the optimum place where the lighting best presents the color.[16]

There is a cognitivist reconstruction of this view that is tempting and, therefore, important to avoid. On such an account, the lighting context "leads my gaze" by presenting me with a series of determinate observations about the quantity of light throughout the scene; along with this series of determinate observations, it also posits some knowledge on the subject's part about which determinate amount of light is optimal for his viewing needs. In the case of the tabletop, for example, such a view would first attribute to the subject knowledge of the determinate quantity of light that is optimal for viewing the color of the table. Perhaps the table is green and twelve foot-candles is optimal for viewing this color. Then, for each section of the table, it posits a determinate experience of the amount of light falling on it. With the knowledge of this light gradient, the subject can then search for the part of the table that has closest to twelve foot-candles of light falling on it. Thus, the lighting "leads the gaze."

This is not the view Merleau-Ponty has in mind. I never experience the light as a determinate amount, according to Merleau-Ponty. Instead, I see, in a direct bodily manner, *how the light would have to change* for me to see the color *better*. The current lighting context, in other words, is experienced as a deviation from an optimum. As Merleau-Ponty says, I do not experience the lighting as some determinate level "which increases or decreases, but [as] a tension which fluctuates round a norm" (*PP* 349/302/352).[17] To speak mathematically, I experience the light not as a determinate quantity but in terms of the direction, and perhaps even the slope, of the improvement

curve. If we think of the improvement curve as the curve that measures the quantity of light against the quality of the viewing conditions, then what my experience tells me at any given moment is
whether more or less light will improve my view, and also perhaps
how drastic the improvement will be. In this way, the lighting plays a
positive role in my experience but is never registered determinately.

My experience of the lighting context in this positive indeterminate sense is at the same time an experience of the color the object
is. Recall that the color or shade of color I see the thing to be co-
varies with the changes in lighting context that I see it to require.
Darker shades of green require brighter light to see them well; lighter
shades of green require dimmer light to see them well. Because different shades have different optimal lighting contexts, seeing the
optimum to be in *that* direction is at the same time seeing the color
to be one shade rather than another. Thus, Merleau-Ponty writes of a
unified structure that encompasses both the lighting and the color lit
(*PP* 354–6/307–8/357–9). This unified structure takes on its meaning for the perceiver through his direct bodily inclinations to act,
given certain perceptual needs, in the face of it. As Merleau-Ponty
writes, "Lighting and the constancy of the thing illuminated, which
is its correlative, are directly dependent on our bodily situation" (*PP*
358/310/362).

Because of their interdependence, insofar as the lighting context
is experienced in a direct, bodily manner as a deviation from a norm,
so, too, is the color correlative to it. This is a surprising result. Even
if the lighting is not experienced as a determinate quantity, you
might have thought that the color it illuminates could nevertheless
be experienced as a determinate shade. Because of the way figure
and ground are interrelated, however, this simple view cannot make
sense. Rather, each presentation of the color in a given lighting context necessarily makes an implicit reference to a more completely
presented *real* color, the color as it would be better revealed if the
lighting context were changed in the direction of the norm. This
real color, implicitly referred to in every experience, is the constant
color I see the object *to be*. Yet it is experienced not as a determinate
shade, but rather as the background to the particular experience I'm
having now. It is, in other words, like the normal context that reveals it, indeterminately present in every particular experience. As
Merleau-Ponty says, "The real color persists beneath appearances as

the background persists beneath the figure, that is, not as a seen or thought-of quality, but through a nonsensory [indeterminate] presence" (PP 352/305/356).

It is important to emphasize that the real color is *never* determinately seen. The reason for this is that the real color is defined as the color that is optimally illuminated by the lighting norm, and this lighting norm is never determinately experienced. Of course, the lighting norm may *be* determinate. It may be a fact of the matter, for example, that for a given subject on a given day a particular shade of green is seen optimally under twelve foot-candles of light. I have some doubts about whether this makes sense, but let us suppose it does.[18] Even when that subject on that day views that shade of green under twelve foot-candles of light, the real color is not presented to him determinately. The reason for this is that even when the lighting conditions are optimal, they are still experienced as a deviation from a norm, only in this case the current lighting is experienced as a "null" deviation from the norm. What I would have to do to get a better view of the shade is: nothing. I feel no inclination to look anyplace else at all to see the color better. Because this is still a normative feature of experience, the real shade it defines has features that the thing I see now does not: it remains constant, for example, as the lighting context deviates from the norm. The real color I see the object to be, therefore, is implicitly presented in every experience but always as the background to what I now see.[19]

Notice how unusual this notion of indeterminate visual presence is. Normally we think of perception as a kind of point for point descriptive representation of the visual features of the world. It is at root, on the traditional view, the projection of light rays onto the retina. To say that I see the lighting context as a deviation from a norm, however, is to say something radically different from this, namely, that it is a part of my visual experience that *my body is drawn to move,* or, at any rate, that *the context should change,* in a certain way. These are inherently normative, rather than descriptive, features of visual experience. They don't represent in some objective, determinate fashion the way the world *is*; they say something about how the world *ought to be* for me to see it better. In this way, Merleau-Ponty takes very seriously the idea that perception is a way of being involved with the world, not an objective, determinate way of recording it. As he writes, the system of experience is not arrayed before me as if I were God, it is lived by me from a certain point of view; I am not the spectator, I am involved, and it is my involvement in a point of view which makes possible both the finiteness of my perception and its opening out upon the complete world as a horizon of every perception. (*PP* 350/304/354)

IV. SEEING THINGS

When I introduced the notion of a visual background several pages ago, I gave perhaps the most obvious kind of example. I spoke there of the difference in my experience between the lamp I am looking at and the books, wall, and door that form the background to it. This is the kind of example Merleau-Ponty has in mind when he says that I experience objects as seeing one another. The way to get a handle on Merleau-Ponty's strange claim, therefore, is to try to figure out how the background objects are present to me in my experience of the figure on which I am focused. In this section, I extend the normative account of perception that we have already seen to the case of background objects and figural things.

1. Husserl on Spatial Figure and Ground

It is once again useful, by way of contrast, first to consider Husserl's view. Husserl addresses the issue of background objects explicitly in his later works under the name of the "outer horizon."[20] Even very early on, in the *Thing and Space* lectures of 1907, he is sensitive to the importance of the distinction between spatial figure and spatial ground. In the early works, Husserl sometimes calls the background objects "environing things" (*Dingumgebung*):

a perceived thing is never there alone by itself; instead, it stands before our eyes in the midst of determinate, intuited environing things. For instance, the lamp rests on the table, amid books, papers, and other things. The environing things are equally "perceived." As the words "amid" and "environment" signify, this is a spatial nexus, which unifies the especially perceived thing with the other coperceived things.[21]

According to this passage, the environing things are experienced as in some way distinct from the figure (thus the different names), even though the two are "equally 'perceived.'" Husserl is emphasizing, therefore, both *that there is a distinction* between experienced figure and experienced ground and *that both are essential* to experience. Yet what precisely is the distinction he has in mind? This passage does not tell us.

Husserl's answer to this question becomes clear a bit later in the text. The focal object, he claims, is the one to which we are *attending*; the background objects are the ones to which we are not now attending but to which we could, if we so desired, turn our attention: "What is perceived in the special sense is what we especially heed, what we attend to. The background things stand there, but we bestow on them no preferential attention."[22] On such a view, attention is a kind of mental searchlight that we can use to pick out certain objects instead of others. It is in terms of attention that Husserl hopes to explain the distinction between those objects that are experienced as figure and those that form the background against which the experienced figure stands out.

The main problem with this account is that it begs the question: attention seems to be a name for the distinction we are interested in rather than a characterization of it. Recall that Husserl is committed to the claim, as we saw in the previous passage, that both the focal object and the environing things are experienced as *determinate* entities. In this, therefore, our experience of each is on a par. The fact that we "attend" to one but not the others, that it is "perceived in the special sense" instead of merely "perceived," tells us only *that* figure and ground are experienced differently; it tells us nothing about *how* our experience of the figure is different from our experience of the ground.

Accordingly, Merleau-Ponty criticizes this notion of attention on the grounds that it destroys the phenomenological features of the figure–ground experience. In particular, he claims, it fails to allow for the possibility that the background objects could be presented indeterminately although positively, which is to say, *as background*.[23] If the environing objects are already determinate in my experience of the figure, there seems to be little sense to the claim that they form the background to it. Even though Husserl recognizes the *need* for a distinction between figure and ground, his account of the distinction obliterates it completely. Our task in developing Merleau-Ponty's account is to describe the way the environing objects are experienced *as background* to the focal thing.

2. Merleau-Ponty's Approach: The View from Everywhere as the Norm for Seeing Things[24]

Recall, as we learned in the case of lighting context, that background features of experience present themselves in terms of the effect they have on how the figure looks. In particular, they have a normative dimension: they tell me something about what should happen for me to get a better, fuller, or more complete experience of the focal thing. In the case of the lighting context, this just meant that the lighting was experienced in terms of how it would have to change for me to get a better view of the color. In the case of the background objects, although they do not actually shine light on it, they do stand in certain spatial relations to the focal thing. The way I understand these spatial relations, as we will see, can change my experience of the thing I am looking at.

To understand the background features of experience normatively, we defined the notion of a *normal* or *optimal* lighting context.[25] The normal lighting context, recall, is the one that allows me to get a maximum grip on the color I am looking at; it is the context that best reveals the color as it really is. Furthermore, the normal context is a *norm*: it is always that from which the current context is felt to be a deviation.[26] We can define a similar notion in the domain of spatial relations to the object. To do so, we must answer the following question: what is the perspective or point of view that would give me a maximum grip on something experienced as a three-dimensional object, that would most reveal the object as it really is? What is the *normal* spatial relation to it, in other words, from which all other perspectives are felt to deviate?

Here is where the analogy between lighting context and perspective begins to break down. Because objects are three-dimensional, there is no single point of view on the object that I could have that would reveal it maximally. There was such a lighting context (we were willing to suppose) – I could get lucky or even manipulate the situation in such a way as to make it the case that the lighting is just perfect for me to see the color. But there is no point of view that *I* could be in from which the full three-dimensional object would be fully revealed.

Nevertheless, the notion of an ideal point of view has a rich history. One traditional name for the ideal view on an object is the "view from nowhere." Merleau-Ponty attributes to Leibniz the notion that the view from nowhere is ideal, saying that Leibniz believes it is this "geometrized projection (*géométral*) of . . . all possible perspectives, that is, the perspectiveless position" that most reveals an object as it really is. From the start, however, we have said that seeing is in its nature perspectival, and so Merleau-Ponty naturally rails against such a view: "But what do these words mean? Is not to see always to see from somewhere? To say that the house itself is seen from nowhere is surely to say that it is invisible!" (*PP* 81/67/77). The idea of a *view* from *nowhere*, in other words, is a contradiction.

It is a contradiction that is motivated by a genuine insight, however, for it is true, of course, that no single point of view reveals the object fully. When we add that each point of view nevertheless reveals something about the object, then the proper notion of an ideal or normal perspective becomes clear. It is not the house seen from nowhere, but the house seen from everywhere all at once:

Our previous formula must therefore be modified; the house itself is not the house seen from nowhere, but the house seen from everywhere. The completed object is translucent, being shot through from all sides by an infinite number of present scrutinies which intersect in its depths leaving nothing hidden. (*PP* 83/69/79)

The view from *everywhere*, in other words, is the optimum perspective from which to view the object, the perspective from which one grips it maximally.[27]

It should be clear, as I have already emphasized, that the view from everywhere is not a view that *I* can have.[28] Although it is not itself achievable by me, the view from everywhere is nevertheless an ideal from which I can sense myself to be deviating. It is the *norm*, in other words, with respect to which all actual points of view are understood. In this way, the optimal view from everywhere plays the same kind of normative role that the other optimal phenomena do.

Understood in this fashion, it becomes clear why the background objects cannot be experienced as determinate things, for objects understood merely in terms of their determinate features cannot play the proper normative role. Merleau-Ponty's account, instead, is that the background objects are experienced as stand-ins for the point of view one gets on the focal thing from the position in which they sit. Although *I* can never stand everywhere at once, I can see all the objects surrounding my focal thing as together making up the view from everywhere. It is in this sense that I experience objects as seeing one another. Indeed, Merleau-Ponty suggests, to look at an object is just to see it as the spatial center of focus onto which all the objects surrounding it converge:

> To look at an object is to inhabit it, and from this habitation to grasp all things in terms of the aspect which they present to it. But in so far as I see those things too, they remain abodes open to my gaze, and, being potentially lodged in them, I already perceive from various angles the central object of my present vision. (PP 82/68/79)

In this way, although the view from everywhere is not a view I myself can have, it is a view I can now see as *being* had, a view from which my own perspective is felt to deviate. To get a proper feel for this claim, we need to see better how different felt deviations from the norm affect my experience of the focal thing.

3. The Normativity of Points of View

Every point of view on an object that I can actually have is a deviation from the norm. If I could *per impossibile* take up the view from everywhere, it would give me a better grip on the object than any single point of view could. This is not to say that every point of view deviates equally from the norm; some points of view are better than others. Thus, to see the background objects in terms of their point of view is already to understand the background normatively.

To see that some points of view are better than others, it will help to consider a simple example. If I experience the object to be a flat façade, I will experience the points of view that look sideways on to it as the least revealing ones. Insofar as I am trying to get the best sense of the façade as a whole, I will immediately feel solicited to move around to see it from the front.[29] In general, depending on the shape I see the object to be, different perspectives on it will seem to be better or worse deviations from the norm. Indeed, just as with the relation between lighting and color, sensing that *here* is a better perspective from which to view the object is already sensing the object to be one thing rather than another.

Whether I sense a perspective on an object to be better or worse does not necessarily depend on *how much* of the object it reveals.

Rather, the better perspectives are the ones that reveal more of the object's *revealing* features. Suppose I have a coffee mug with a handle on it. The perspective from which the handle is completely hidden may be a less revealing perspective on the object than the one from which it is fully seen. This might be true even if I see more of the surface area of the object from the perspective in which the handle is hidden than I do from the perspective in which it is seen. Because the handle is a particularly revealing feature of the object, points of view from which it is seen are by their nature experienced as more revealing. It is an interesting empirical fact that we seem immediately to see certain features of objects as more revealing than others and that we seem immediately to prefer correlative perspectives on it.[30]

Although I emphasized, in the last section, an important difference between the view from everywhere and the optimal lighting context, it should be clear from the description I have just given that there are important similarities as well. In the first place, my experience of other points of view is normative in the way that my experience of other lighting contexts is: *that* point of view looks to me *better* than the one I have now; *that other* point of view looks to me *worse* than mine. Better points of view immediately solicit me to take them up, and worse points of view are immediately avoided. To say that I see other objects as having points of view on the focal thing is just to say that I am immediately solicited either to see or not to see what is now revealed from where those objects are.[31]

Furthermore, as with the relation between lighting and color, which points of view I see to be better and worse already determines what I see the object to be. We have seen this already with the case of object and façade discussed earlier, but it is true for the other spatial features of an object as well. To see the backside of the mug as having a handle, for example, is already to experience the point of view on the backside as a particularly revealing one. The spatial identity of the object, in other words, is guaranteed by my experience of the value of the various points of view that are now had on it. As Merleau-Ponty says, background

objects recede into the periphery and become dormant, while, however, not ceasing to be there. Now with them I have at my disposal their horizons, in which there is implied, as a marginal view, the object on which my eyes at present fall. The horizon, then, is what guarantees the identity of the object throughout the exploration. (*PP* 82/68/78)

The relation between the spatial identity of an object and my experience of its spatial ground is the high point in Merleau-Ponty's account of seeing things. Unfortunately, it is at just this point that Merleau-Ponty falters. Let us see precisely how.

4. The Identity of the Real, Constant Thing

What exactly is the real, constant thing, and how is its identity bound up with the experience of the spatial ground? There is an easy way to misunderstand what Merleau-Ponty's view requires, and it is once again exemplified by Husserl's approach. Recall that for Husserl the hidden sides of an object are hypothesized but sensuously absent. This fact has repercussions for what Husserl understands the real object to be. In particular, it suggests that the real object is not the kind of thing that could be presented in *any* perspectival presentation. Because the real object actually has a hidden side, and because the hidden side of the object is never presented in experience, no experience of an object could possibly present it as it really is. Indeed, the problem is worse than that. There are literally an infinite number of possible presentations of the real object that are not now being given. For Husserl (as for phenomenalists such as C. I. Lewis), the real object is identified with the whole system of these perspectival presentations taken together – what Husserl sometimes calls the "nexus of appearances." Every "appearance refers, by virtue of its sense, to possibilities of fulfillment, to a continuous-unitary nexus of appearance, in which the sense would be accomplished in every respect, thus in which the determinations would come to 'complete' givenness."[32] Similarly, "[I]f we were to retain [a given] . . . appearance while cutting off the other multiplicities of appearances and the essential relations to them, none of the sense of the givenness of the physical thing would remain."[33] This system of perspectival presentations, which Husserl sometimes also calls the "circle of complete givenness,"[34] is the "real" object to which each perspectival presentation refers but which none by itself is able to present. It can be understood intellectually, although not presented perceptually, by

imagining yourself walking around the object or by imagining it rotating before you.[35]

This cannot be Merleau-Ponty's view. The real object should not
be defined as the sum of all the perspectives on it, for Merleau-Ponty,
any more than the real color is defined as the color seen in the optimal lighting context. The view from everywhere, which is the optimal spatial context, is the view that would give me the *maximum
grip* on the object (if I could have it). Even if I could have this view,
however, it would not present the real thing as a determinate particular, any more than the optimal lighting context presents the real
color determinately. Like the color, the real thing should be that
which stands as the background to every particular presentation of
it. It is the *norm* from which I experience the object as presented in
my current perspective to be deviating. We must say about the real
thing, in other words, what Merleau-Ponty has already said about the
real color, namely, that it "persists beneath appearances as the background persists beneath the figure, that is, not as a seen or thought-
of quality, but through a nonsensory [indeterminate] presence" (*PP*
352/305/356). In contrast with Husserl, therefore, Merleau-Ponty's
account should hold that the real thing is present in *every* perspectival presentation of it, although, of course, it is never presented
determinately in any one.

I believe that this is a crucial point. Indeed, it is the only way to
make sense of Merleau-Ponty's important and interesting idea that
the background is experienced normatively. It is the only way to
make sense, in other words, of his central claim that we experience
the perceptual context in terms of how it ought to change to see
the object better. Everything he says leads him to this view. Yet,
amazingly, I can find no place where he states it explicitly. He does
make the important claim, as we saw earlier, that the identity of the
object is guaranteed by the horizon of the points of view on it, but
he never seems to state further that this horizon is the *norm* from
which every perspective is felt to deviate. Indeed, there is no talk
of a "tension that deviates round a norm" anywhere in the vicinity
of this discussion. Worse yet, in some of his less formal work, he
carelessly posits just the Husserlian view that he opposes – the view
that the real thing is the *sum* of the points of view on it rather than
the *norm* defined by the sum.[36]

These lacunae in the text and lapses in the occasional pieces are troubling indeed. I cannot account for them except by the interpretive strategy with which we began. I have become convinced that what Merleau-Ponty does say – the overall sense and style of his view – points unequivocally in the direction of a position he was not able to articulate. In any case, I find this intended position extremely intriguing. After a brief summary of the dialectic so far, I conclude in the final section by distinguishing Merleau-Ponty's full phenomenological account of object perception from a more familiar position in its neighborhood.

V. SUMMARY BY WAY OF INTERLUDE

Let me summarize what I've said so far. We began with the phenomenological distinction between experiencing something as an object and experiencing it as a mere façade. The problem, addressed by Husserl, Merleau-Ponty, and others, is to account for this distinction. Everyone agrees what the first move is: we must admit that when we experience something as a full-fledged three-dimensional object, there is some sense in which we experience it as having sides that are now hidden from view. Here, however, opinions begin to diverge.

One natural, but mistaken, idea is that our experience of the hidden side of an object is not a properly perceptual one. This is the approach that Husserl prefers. It is motivated by the intuition that perception begins with the presentation of determinate sense data; any putative aspect of perception that is not attributable to such a presentation is not properly part of perception at all. To the extent that we experience the object as having a hidden side, on Husserl's view, it is because we *hypothesize* the side's existence, not because we *perceive* it. The hidden side of the object is *indeterminate* in experience in the sense that we have not yet determined perceptually what its determinate features are.

Merleau-Ponty, by contrast, says that we really do perceive the hidden side of the object. This is not because he believes we are presented with determinate sense data from it. Rather, it is because he believes that perceptual experience is not the presentation of sense data. The most basic unit of perceptual experience is the presentation of a figure against a ground. Sense data cannot make the figure–ground distinction. To account for this distinction, according to Merleau-Ponty, we need to admit that there is a positive but essentially indeterminate aspect of perception. The hidden side of the object is positively presented in experience, but it is presented indeterminately.

Merleau-Ponty's main challenge is to characterize the indeterminate aspect of perception. Perception is indeterminate, on his view, because it is essentially *normative*. Determinate sense data *describe* the world – they amount to a presentation of it feature by feature. When we perceive things, however, we are constantly sensitive not only to what we perceive but also, and essentially, to *how well* our experience measures up to our perceptual needs and desires. The norms involved in perception, therefore, are norms about how best to see the thing perceived.

The visual background is always experienced in terms of these norms: we do not see a determinate level of light, we see how the light needs to change to see the color better; we do not see a determinate object behind the figure, we see a point of view on the figure, a point of view that solicits us to take it up. Generally, our experience of the visual background is the experience of a tension around a norm. We can describe this mathematically as sensitivity to the direction and slope of the improvement curve.

The figure is also experienced normatively. This is because figure and ground are essentially intertwined. For every figure, there is an optimal context in which to see it: dark colors are best seen in brighter light, façades are best seen from the front, objects in general are always better seen from the perspective that best reveals their revealing features, and so on. Thus, the interplay between figure and ground is an essential feature in the identity of each. Which color I perceive to be in front of me is already anticipated by my immediate bodily inclination to look, say, at the more brightly lit areas of the surface to get a better view of it.

Finally, the real color or thing, the one that remains constant throughout various presentations, is itself experienced normatively. It persists beneath every particular presentation as a background persists beneath a figure. The real, constant color or thing, in other words, is experienced as that maximally articulate norm against which every particular presentation is felt to deviate. Merleau-Ponty is clear about this in the case of color but falters in his discussion of the real, constant thing.

This final kind of normativity gives us the answer to our initial problem. On Merleau-Ponty's view, I experience an object as now having sides that are hidden from me because I experience it as now seen from everywhere. This view from everywhere is the norm against which my particular presentation is felt to deviate. It is the background against which my perspectival presentation makes sense. In the concluding section, I contrast Merleau-Ponty's account with the phenomenalist account found in the work of authors such as C. I. Lewis. I hope to make it clear not only what Merleau-Ponty *means* when he says that objects see one another, but also why this account of perception is *better* than all its competitors.

VI. PHENOMENOLOGY VERSUS PHENOMENALISM

We have seen how the view from everywhere is the optimal view on an object; we have seen also that this optimal view presents itself as the background against which every particular presentation makes sense. It might still be natural to ask, however, why we must say that objects *see* one another.[37] A fairly natural theory of perception, which is defended by phenomenalists such as C. I. Lewis, seems to allow for a view from everywhere without ungainly mention of objects that see. In this concluding section, I show why Merleau-Ponty's account is superior to the phenomenalist approach.

The phenomenalist account of perception, of which I give no more than a caricature here, is sensitive to the problem that Husserl emphasized: it wants to explain how I can experience something as a three-dimensional object despite only ever having perspectival presentations of it. To solve this problem, as we have seen, one must have something to say about the hidden sides of the experienced object. The phenomenalist approach depends on a counterfactual analysis: the experienced object is seen *thus* from the perspective I am in now, would be seen *thus* if I were over there, and would be seen *thus* if I were in that other place. The experienced object therefore, as a full-fledged, three-dimensional entity, comprises the sum of all the possible perspectives that I could have on it.

We have already seen one weakness with a view like this: as with Husserl's account, the real object is *never* seen. I would like to focus on another aspect of the phenomenalist view, however: its penchant for defining the experienced object in terms of a series of experiences that *I* can have. The problem with this approach is that from the perspective that I am in *now*, I cannot have these other determinate experiences. Yet I nevertheless experience the object as a three-dimensional thing. The way I *now* experience the hidden side of the object is simply not the way I *would* experience it if I were on the other side. I do not now have the point of view from the other side, so my experience of that side of the object is not now what it would be if I were over there.

Merleau-Ponty's approach is tailor-made to avoid this difficulty. According to Merleau-Ponty, I now have a positive presentation of the hidden side of the object, but it is not the same as the presentation of that side that I would have if I were looking directly at it. To say that I see the object standing behind my focal thing *as having a point of view on it*, is simply to say that I see the hidden side as now presented, but not as now presented *to me*. Still, it would be nice to understand this metaphor more clearly. Let me try to explain.

The crucial passage is one that we have considered already. In discussing the way I experience background objects while focusing on the figure, Merleau-Ponty writes,

to look at an object is to inhabit it, and from this habitation to grasp all things in terms of the aspect which they present to it. But insofar as I see those things too, they remain abodes open to my gaze, and, being potentially lodged in them, I already perceive from various angles the central object of my present vision. (*PP* 82/68/79)

It is clear from this passage that the experience I now have of the hidden side of the object, according to Merleau-Ponty, is not the experience I would have if I were behind it. Rather, "I already perceive" the hidden side of the object because I am "potentially lodged in" the background object that now stands behind the figure. To understand the account fully, therefore, we must understand what it means *now* to be potentially lodged in another point of view.

The best way to understand this idea is by comparison with Merleau-Ponty's account of motor intentionality.[38] In skillful, un-reflective coping activities, such as grasping a coffee mug to drink from it, I have a direct bodily understanding of the shape, size, and weight of the mug. This direct bodily understanding is manifest in my body's unreflective tendency to form its grip with a certain shape and size and to prepare itself to lift an object of a certain weight. The tendency to perform these bodily preparations is more than merely a reflex because it is directed toward and responsive to the features of the mug. In this sense, we can call the activity intentional, but it is an essentially bodily understanding of those features and, indeed, can be had without any determinate visual experience of them at all.[39] For these reasons, Merleau-Ponty puts this kind of skillful coping activity into a new category that he calls "motor intentionality." Motor-intentional activity is reducible neither to any form of determinate cognitive intentionality nor to a series of merely reflexive movements. The motor-intentional understanding I have of the coffee mug in grasping it is a kind of bodily readiness for its relevant features.

This kind of full bodily readiness for something is what I believe Merleau-Ponty is pointing to when he says that I am now "potentially lodged in" the other points of view on the object. It is not a matter of now having a determinate experience of what is seen from those points of view, any more than the motor-intentional understanding of the mug is a matter of having a determinate visual experience of its features. Rather, it is a kind of bodily readiness to take up those points of view, a readiness that is reducible neither to a determinate cognitive understanding of what is seen in the view nor to a series of merely reflexive bodily movements. To see the coffee mug as now having a handle on its hidden side, for example, is to be prepared to pick it up from the back with a grip of a certain shape and size. To be potentially lodged in the point of view from behind the mug is now to be ready, in a direct bodily manner, to deal with the features of the mug that are now presented fully to the thing that is currently behind it.

This kind of bodily readiness for the features of an object, whether they are now hidden from view or not, is manifest throughout my interactions with the thing. So, for example, when directed to push her hand through an oriented slot, scientists have observed that a subject begins to rotate her hand in the appropriate direction as soon as it leaves the starting position.[40] For this reason Merleau-Ponty says about motor-intentional activities such as grasping that "from the outset the grasping movement is magically at its completion" (*PP* 120/103–4/119). It is in this sense that we should understand his further claim that, in being potentially lodged in other points of view, I "already perceive" what is seen from them. I already perceive the hidden side of the object in the sense that I am now ready, in a direct bodily manner, to deal with the features that are, I take it, now seen of it from behind. If I took the mug not to have a handle on the hidden side, then I would experience the point of view had by the object behind it differently. This difference would manifest itself in a different bodily readiness to deal with the hidden side of the mug.

The phenomenon of *now* experiencing the backside of the object a certain way is something the Lewisian phenomenalist cannot account for. Even so, it may still seem as though one could account for this phenomenon without any reference to seeing things. After all, in the version I have given so far, I have described the whole phenomenon in terms of bodily readiness. Even if this readiness is *motor* intentional, surely it is still *my* readiness, not one ascribed to other things.

This is a tricky point, but we have come across it already in section III.[41] Recall that we were trying to make sense of Merleau-Ponty's claim that lighting "leads" the gaze. I said that lighting leads the gaze in the sense that I have a direct bodily inclination to look where the lighting is best in order to see the color of a thing. This is a motor-intentional activity: my eyes move to a particular place on the object, but they do not identify that place in terms of its determinate features. Indeed, the inclination to move my eyes in a particular direction is so immediate and tied so directly to the lighting context that it may be misleading even to say that it is *my* inclination. As Merleau-Ponty says, "The lighting directs my gaze and causes me to see the object, so that in a sense it [the lighting] *knows* and *sees* the object" (*PP* 358/310/361).

We can say the same thing about the inclination to prepare my body in a particular way to deal with the hidden side of the coffee mug. In some sense it is *my* bodily readiness at stake. Yet how much credit can *I* take for this? Is it up to me alone that as soon as my hand leaves the starting position it begins to form an appropriate grip? I certainly did not know that my hand was doing that. Yet the activity is intentional from the start. It is directed toward and responsive to what my body takes to be the features of the hidden side of the mug.

As with the lighting, therefore, we must say that I experience my grip as *being led* to form itself in a certain way, led by something other than myself, something that knows more about the hidden features of the mug than I am capable of knowing from here. I have to say that objects see one another, in other words, to account for the motor intentionality of my activity, an intentionality that does not belong entirely to me.

The motivating idea here is that we experience our environment at least partly in terms of the activities it immediately leads us to perform. The environment solicits certain motor-intentional activities and suppresses others. As the ecological psychologist J. J. Gibson says, developing this view of Merleau-Ponty's, the perceived world is full of affordances to act, affordances that the involved perceiver responds to in an immediate and unreflective way.[42] When things are working well, these affordances in the environment lead us to act in ways that are consonant with it. I find myself forming a certain grip, through no determinate effort of my own, and lo and behold the grip forms perfectly to the hidden handle of the mug. Because the formation of the grip is so obviously intentional, and because it is equally obvious that I am not its principal cause, Merleau-Ponty puts the intentionality directly in the world.[43] Seeing things, in other words, requires seeing things.

VII. CONCLUSION

I said at the start that Merleau-Ponty's interpretive strategy both licenses and illustrates my account of his view. Now we should be able to understand why. Merleau-Ponty's account of object perception, like his account of the style of a thinker's thought, depends on the possibility that something can at once be closest to me and farthest away. In the case of object perception, motor-intentional solicitations are so hidden from me that I do not experience myself as their proximal cause. Indeed, a full account of the phenomenology of object perception requires me to say that I experience the world and its objects as intentional. Yet what could be closer to me than the way I hold my body in preparing to perform a task? So, too, the overall style of a thinker's thought guides and directs him as if from afar. Just as the subject's hand moves immediately and unreflectively to the coffee mug, so too the philosopher knows intuitively what must be said. His thought is guided by something outside himself to which he is responsible, something that knows his subject better than he. The style of a thinker's thought, in other words, illustrates the normative dimension of the figure–ground experience.

Yet Merleau-Ponty's approach licenses my interpretation as well, for I have argued that he misunderstands a crucial feature of his own view; this is precisely the kind of thing that Merleau-Ponty's interpretive strategy leads us to expect is possible. Because the style of a thinker's thought is hidden from him, "what is given to him with his style is not a certain number of ideas or tics that he can inventory but a manner of formulation that is just as recognizable for others and just as little visible to him as his silhouette or his everyday gestures" (*PM* 82/58). We have seen that it takes a scientist or a very subtle phenomenologist to observe certain crucial features of a subject's motor-intentional activity. That the subject's hand moves in the appropriate direction as soon as it leaves the starting position, for example, is often a surprise to the subject himself. So, too, with the details of an author's view. Although the style pushes him to say certain things and not others, the details that his position requires are often difficult for him to identify. In the résumé for a course he taught at the Collège de France in 1959 and 1960, Merleau-Ponty makes this point explicitly. In this passage, with which I will conclude, Merleau-Ponty is discussing the assumption that only an "objective" method of interpretation – one that says "just what was said or directly implied" by the thinker – would give us the proper account of his thought:

Such an assumption would only be plausible if [a philosopher's] thought . . . were simply a system of neatly defined concepts, of arguments responding to perennial problems, and of conclusions which permanently solve the problems. But what if the meditation changes the sense of the concepts it employs and even the sense of the problems; what if its conclusions are merely the results of a progression which was transformed into a "work" by the interruption – an interruption which is always premature – of a life's work? Then we could not define a philosopher's thought solely in terms of what he had achieved; we would have to take account of what until the very end his thought was trying to think. Naturally, words, which delimit and circumscribe it, must attest to this unthought. But then these words must be understood through their lateral implications as much as through their manifest or frontal meaning. (*HLP* 5)[44]

NOTES

1. Heidegger, *The Principle of Reason*, 71.

2. There is very little discussion in the secondary literature of this difficult but extremely important passage. There is no discussion that I know of that is at all helpful.

3. Three other points are subsidiary to the phenomenology but worth mentioning anyway. First, the thing I'm looking at need not *be* a façade for me to experience it as one. When I leave the set, for instance, and I'm walking down the street of a real town, I can experience its buildings as façades even if they're not. Again, with enough exploration – opening the door to the bank and seeing a real bank inside, for instance – I will come to see these buildings as the real thing. But whether they are real buildings is not conclusive in determining whether I will experience them to be so. Second, my *knowledge* that something is a façade or a real building is neither necessary nor sufficient for me to experience it as such. I knew the structures on the movie set were façades when I first walked in, but that didn't make me experience them as façades; only exploring them had that effect. So knowing that something is a façade is not sufficient for experiencing it as one; we can be fooled. Likewise, knowing that something is a façade is not necessary for experiencing it as one. Indeed, when I walk through the real town after visiting the movie set, I might know that the structures I'm looking at are *not* façades, even though I can't help experiencing them that way. Finally, and related to this, seeing something *as* a façade or seeing it *as* a full three-dimensional entity is not just *consciously* giving a particular interpretation to otherwise neutral sense data. We have already seen that nothing I *know* about the scene guarantees that I will experience it one way or another. More generally, however, it is important to point out that gestalt shifts between object and façade, like gestalt shifts generally, are not under the conscious control of the subject at all. The subject is *given* an already formulated take on the world; he does not *impose* it. It is this fact that Merleau-Ponty hopes to explain by claiming that I experience objects as seeing one another.

4. Husserl called these sense data the *hulê* – literally, the matter – of sensation. There is much dispute about what Husserl took the *hulê* to be. A rough approximation regards them as akin to sense data as Russell understood these in *The Problems of Philosophy*, although this is no doubt false in detail. In any event, for the purposes of this discussion it suffices to know that the perceiver has *hulê* for the front of a perceived object but not for its back.

5. I regard this essay, in part, as a development of positions I gestured at in §3 of "The Non-Conceptual Content of Perceptual Experience."

6. See my "Husserl and Phenomenology."
7. Husserl, *Thing and Space*, 57.
8. *Thing and Space*, 55.
9. It is worth commenting that the visual background is an absolutely pervasive aspect of experience. This is because, as the Gestalt psychologists clearly recognized, the most basic kind of experience is that of a figure against a ground. This Gestalt psychological principle was at the very foundation of Merleau-Ponty's approach to perception. See *PP* 10/4/4.
10. There are obviously a large number of contextual features that make some contribution to my experience of an object or its properties. These include, for example, the lighting context, the distance to the object, the orientation of the object, and so on. In Husserl's discussion of these issues, it is not always clear which contextual features he has in mind.
11. Edmund Husserl, *Logical Investigations*, esp. Investigation V, §2: 538. The importance of the notion of *Abschattungen* has been noticed in the Husserl literature, but I do not believe it has been given enough attention. One difficulty is that the various English translations of Husserl's texts render this term differently. In the passage quoted earlier, for instance, Findlay uses the phrase "projective differences," whereas the Kersten translation of *Ideas I* systematically employs the preferable term "adumbration." See Husserl, *Ideas I*, 70. Husserl himself sometimes uses other phrases for this phenomenon as well. In the text leading up to the passage quoted earlier, for example, he uses the phrase "the appearance of the object's coloring" to characterize the *Abschattungen*. See *Logical Investigations*, Investigation V, §2: 537. See my "Husserl and Phenomenology" for a more extended discussion of the role this concept plays in Husserl's work.
12. Recall that for Husserl a perceptual feature of an object or property is indeterminate if my experience has not yet determined what it is. In this case, the feature is hypothesized but sensously absent.
13. See Mulligan, "Perception," especially §6.1 for some discussion of Husserl on the phenomena of perceptual constancy.
14. See Rock, *Indirect Perception*.
15. It can be misleading to say that you "know" where to move your eyes. Whatever this "knowledge" consists in, it is certainly not articulated conceptual knowledge about the interplay of color and light. Rather, the knowledge is of a direct and bodily sort. When confronted with the task of determining the color of the table, you have a direct bodily inclination to move your eyes in one direction rather than another. This inclination is so immediate and tied so directly to the lighting context, that it may be misleading even to say that it is *your* inclination. As Merleau-Ponty says, "The lighting directs my gaze and causes me to see

the object, so that in a sense it [the lighting] *knows* and *sees* the object" (*PP* 358/310/361). In his later work, Merleau-Ponty suggests that it is not possible to say whether the subject or the environment is in command: "The look, we said, envelops, palpates, espouses the visible things. As though it were in a relation of preestablished harmony with them, as though it knew them before knowing them, it moves in its own way with its abrupt and imperious style, and yet the views taken are not desultory – I do not look at a chaos, but at things – so that finally one cannot say if it is the look or if it is the things that command" (*VI* 175/133). In any event, if it is *my* knowledge about where to move my eyes, this "knowledge" is of an extremely unusual kind. In *Phenomenology of Perception*, Merleau-Ponty gives the name "motor intentionality" to our direct bodily inclination to act in a situated, environmental context. See my "Logic of Motor Intentional Activity" for an account of some of the striking logical features of this kind of intentionality.

16. The treatment of distance and perspective is exactly analogous. I experience the distance to the object (when I am within the range of the size-constancy effect) in terms of how well it allows me to see the object's size. I do not experience the distance as a determinate, measurable amount. Indeed, many people are astoundingly bad at judging distances, but the distance to the object is always part of my experience of it nevertheless. The distance figures in my experience in a normative way: I *ought to get closer* to see the object *better,* or I *ought to move back* to take it in. Needless to say, these are not conscious judgments but immediately felt bodily inclinations to act. So, too, with perspective. I experience the perspective I have on the object in terms of how well it allows me to see the object's shape. Of course, there are many other contextual features as well.

17. Merleau-Ponty is describing the way I experience the distance to an object in this passage, but the same point holds for the way I experience the lighting context. I experience it not as a measurable quantity of brightness, but instead in terms of how well it allows me to see the thing I am drawn to see.

18. My doubts stem principally from the particular statement of the claim here. I suspect that what the lighting norm is in a given situation can depend on an indefinite array of situational features. Here I have listed only three – the subject, the day, and the shade in question – and so it seems likely that this statement of the claim is false. It seems to me likely, for example, that the lighting norm will change also depending on what the object is that manifests the color, how far away the subject is standing from the object, what direction the lighting comes from, what

the color of the light is, perhaps the subject's emotional state, and so on. I suspect it will be difficult ever to determine what all the relevant situational features are.

19. Unfortunately, Merleau-Ponty is not completely consistent about this crucial point. He says, for instance, mistakenly, "I run through appearances and reach the real color or the real shape when my experience is at its maximum of clarity" (PP 367/318/371). This amounts to the claim that the real color is the color presented focally when the lighting context is best. This claim contradicts the more interesting and important idea that the real color is seen as the *background* to every contextual presentation of it, even the presentation that is maximally clear.

20. See, for example, Husserl, *Cartesian Meditations*, esp. §19, and *Experience and Judgment*, esp. §8.

21. Husserl, *Thing and Space*, 80.

22. *Thing and Space*, 81.

23. See the chapter in *Phenomenology of Perception* titled "'Attention' and 'Judgment.'"

24. Notice that there will be different norms for different purposes. I am describing here only the norm for seeing something as a full three-dimensional entity.

25. It should be obvious by now that the "normal" context is not the one I am normally or usually in. Rather, it is the context that serves as the standard or norm by which all other relations are measured; it is the norm with respect to which all other views are felt to deviate.

26. Recall that this is a bit tricky. Although the current lighting context could in fact be the one that gives me the best view of the color (perhaps), it could not be the one that is the *norm*. The norm is that from which any given context is felt to be deviating – it is where the lighting *should* be and is therefore defined by its normative pull. Even if the actual lighting context is perfect, it still stands somewhere in relation to where it *should* be. (See section III of this chapter.)

27. There is an interesting question about the scope of "everywhere," as Mark Alfano has emphasized to me. If it is the *perceived* object that we're talking about, the real object *as it is perceived*, then the view from everywhere must really be the view from all the *normal perceptual* perspectives one can take on an object. This would not include, for example, the electron microscope view from within the bowels of the plumbing. Merleau-Ponty is not always very clear about this, even in the quote I included earlier. I believe that when he is emphasizing the infinity of possible views on the object, he is pushing in the direction of a constructivist ontology that is at odds with his actual view, but I will not pursue the point here.

28. If it were, then the object of perception would have a kind of cubist presentation in which every side of it is presented simultaneously *to me* in my single point of view. See "Husserl and Phenomenology," where I argue that Brentano's account of intentionality, when applied to perception, unintentionally yields this bizarre understanding of the object as perceived.

29. Naturally, what perspective I sense to be the best will depend on my perceptual needs and desires. If I am trying to figure out whether *it is* a façade, for example, the sideways on view may be the *most* revealing. If I already see it as a façade, however, I will sense that there is more to be gained from the front.

30. Recent empirical work has shown that there are preferential views even for objects never seen before. In one study, when subjects were allowed actively to explore new objects, they "spent most of their time studying only four views of the objects, all of which were rotations about the vertical axis. These four views corresponded to the front, back and two side views of the objects. Subjects tended to spend very little time studying particular intermediate views between these angles." It is interesting to discover that, as these authors argue, some views are seen immediately as better than others, even for objects I have never seen before. It is even more interesting, as they further suggest, that the better views cluster around what the subject immediately takes to be the vertical axis of the object. Not only are some perspectives on the object immediately experienced as more revealing, but, moreover, this is because one side of the object is immediately experienced as its base. As the authors write, subjects "treated the flat surface of the object as the 'bottom' and generally kept the objects oriented so that this surface was always face down." The normative aspect of object perception, in other words, seems to be part of our perceptual experience of objects even from our very first interactions with them. See Harman, Humphrey, and Goodale, "Active Manual Control of Object Views Facilitates Visual Recognition."

31. It is worth pointing out in this context, however, one possible dissimilarity with the lighting case that arises from our discussion in section IV.2. That is, which points of view seem to me more revealing of an object can change as I have further experience with it. This *can* happen in the case of lighting and color, but it is not normal. It can happen, for example, when my experience of the color shifts dramatically upon seeing that the lighting has been tricking me. In that case, which lighting contexts I experience as better and worse can change as well. This is not the normal case, however, once we are within the bounds of the constancy effect, familiarity with the color does not change my experience of it. (One possible exception to this is found in the case of master painters

like Cézanne and Van Gogh, who may come to have different bodily anticipations for colors as they perfect their art. Let us leave this case aside.) By contrast, I will certainly experience the hidden features of a new object differently as I become more familiar with them. As I explore the object, I will come to have fuller and fuller bodily anticipations about what I will see on the other side. This is an important fact about object perception. I relegate this fact to a footnote, however, because it is somewhat to the side of my purposes here. For no matter how familiar I am with an object, my bodily anticipations will never reveal to me explicitly its hidden features in the way they are now revealed to the point of view on it from behind. For that reason, I will always experience other points of view on the object in terms of how they solicit me to take them up. This similarity between the normativity of the lighting context and the normativity of the spatial background is what I wish to emphasize.

32. Husserl, *Thing and Space*, 124.

33. Husserl, *Ideas I*, 82.

34. *Thing and Space*, 129.

35. See *Thing and Space*, 127. For Merleau-Ponty's criticism of this view, which he calls Kantian and intellectualist, see *PP* 347–8/301–2/351.

36. In one discussion piece, for instance, he writes, "in perception [the thing] is 'real'; it is given as the infinite sum of an indefinite series of perspectival views" (*PrP* 48/15).

37. This is, of course, shorthand for the more careful statement of Merleau-Ponty's view. The claim is not that objects *do* see one another, but rather that *we experience* objects as seeing one another.

38. See my "Logic of Motor Intentional Activity" for a fuller account of this notion.

39. The recent work by Mel Goodale and David Milner with a patient known as D. F. shows this clearly. Because of a brain lesion, D. F. has a condition known as visual form agnosia – she cannot see the shapes of things. Nevertheless, she is capable of acting differentially with respect to those shapes, and indeed of doing things like grasping coffee mugs. See Milner and Goodale, *The Visual Brain in Action*.

40. See *The Visual Brain in Action*, 128.

41. See note 15.

42. See chapter 8 of Gibson, *The Ecological Approach to Visual Perception*.

43. At least he does so some of the time. In his later work, he comes more strongly to emphasize that the knowledge about how to act in motor intentional situations belongs neither completely in the subject nor completely in the thing (see note 15). For this reason, he creates a new ontological category – the flesh (*la chair*) – that is neither subject nor

object, neither perceiver nor perceived, but an essential intertwining of the two. It is interesting to note that even in *Phenomenology of Perception*, Merleau-Ponty sometimes flirts with a view like this. So, for instance, he writes, "The subject of sensation is neither a thinker who takes note of a quality, nor an inert setting that is changed by it; it is a power that is born into and simultaneously with a certain existential environment.... Just as the sacrament not only symbolizes ... an operation of Grace, but is also the real presence of God ... in the same way the sensible ... is nothing other than a certain way of being in the world suggested to us from some point in space, and seized and acted upon by our body ... so that sensation is literally a form of communion" (*PP* 245–6/211–12/245–6).

44. In developing these ideas I owe several important debts of gratitude. Thanks go in the first place to Hubert Dreyfus, who recommended the epigraph and with whom I had many fruitful discussions on the topic of the paper more generally. Thanks also to Taylor Carman for several helpful comments, and to Cheryl Kelly Chen for that and so much more.

4   Motives, Reasons, and Causes

A measure of the remarkable influence of Cartesian dualism is found in the fact that it often constrains even the ways in which it is rejected. Few accept, it is true, the basic picture of a dualism of mental and physical *substances*. A dualism still shapes the philosophy of mind, however – for instance, in that almost everyone sees as central the task of figuring out the relation between mind and body. It sometimes seems as if the only possible accounts of human beings consist in either giving a mental or a physical description, or explaining how the mental descriptions and the physical descriptions relate to one another.

Merleau-Ponty, by contrast, argues that no such variation, played out on the Cartesian register, will ever account for the human mode of being in the world. "There are two classical views," he notes;

one treats man as the result of the physical, physiological, and sociological influences which shape him from outside and make him one thing among many; the other consists of recognizing an acosmic freedom in him, insofar as he is spirit and represents to himself the very causes which supposedly act upon him.

For Merleau-Ponty, "neither view is satisfactory" (*SNS* 88–9/71–2); any adequate account of human existence will need recourse to a mode of explanation that is neither causal nor rational, and it will need to see the content of human states as neither physiological nor logical. Merleau-Ponty argues that the model for understanding human being can be neither that of the inferential and justificatory relations of explicit thought nor that of the blind and mechanistic workings of material causality. Instead, he proposes that the paradigm should be the "perception of our own body and the perception of external things," which, when properly understood, "provide an example ... of consciousness not in possession of fully determinate objects, that of a logic lived through which cannot account for itself, and that of an immanent meaning which is not clear to itself and becomes fully aware of itself only through experiencing certain natural signs" (PP 61/49/57). The dualist assumption of minds in an objective, material world, in other words, mistakes both the objects of experience and the consciousness of those objects – the former it treats as fully objective and determinate, the latter as self-evident and fully available for reflection. If we are to capture the true character of our experience of the world, Merleau-Ponty suggests, "a complete reform of understanding is called for" (PP 60/49/56).

The complete reform required consists in disrupting the dualism by introducing a "third term" that is irreducible to either of the other two – instead of mind and matter, the lived body; instead of causes and reasons, "motives." A full account of this disruption would require that one show how so-called motor intentional behavior, together with much of our experience of the world, is not reducible to a purely physical event, nor commensurable with mental predicates. Although I will say something in passing about this, I do not attempt such a demonstration here; I want instead to focus on the way in which relationships between experiential states and objects in the world are neither causal nor rational relationships. Nevertheless, an account of motives as a third term between reasons and causes is certainly relevant to justifying the claim that the lived body is outside of the Cartesian mind–body dualism. For if it turns out that the body as we live it in experience and motor-intentional action cannot be seen to stand in either rational or causal relations to thoughts and objects in the world, that will give some reason for refusing to treat it as itself essentially a mental or essentially a physical substance.

In what follows, then, I begin with a brief exposition of Merleau-Ponty's claim that the lived body resists treatment in the terms of the familiar and tired mind–body dualism and a review of his phenomenology of motivations. I then explain Merleau-Ponty's account of motivations – exploring what they are, how they work, and how they cannot be reduced to either logical or causal terms. I conclude by suggesting how such a view can explain the mind-to-world connection in a nondualistic fashion – that is, I explore how motives could ground our thoughts and experiences in the world.

I. THE PHENOMENOLOGY

Merleau-Ponty's case for the body as a third term in between mind and matter, and for motives as a nonrational and noncausal means of grounding us in the world, is based on a phenomenology of lived experience.

One half of overcoming the dualistic account of mind is to show that human experience is not (always) mental – that is, not conceptually articulated or constituted. Of course, one could hardly deny altogether that we entertain thoughts and hold beliefs; such acts and states have as their content propositions and stand in logical relationships to other propositions. Such states are not the only modes of human comportment, however – indeed, they are relatively rare in the overall course of human existence.

For example, Merleau-Ponty notes that "just as we do not see the eyes of a familiar face, but simply its look and its expression, so we perceive hardly any object." He explains, "in the natural attitude, I do not have *perceptions*, I do not posit this object as beside that one, along with their objective relationships, I have a flow of experiences which imply and explain each other both simultaneously and successively" (*PP* 325/281/327). Acts of explicit perception – perception in which we see determinate objects in determinate relationships to one another – only emerge from "ambiguous perceptions." By this, I take it, Merleau-Ponty means that a perceptual experience is articulated in a way that would lend itself to discovering rational relations only when a particular need arises, such as when the ambiguity of the situation resists any ready response and thereby prevents us from proceeding transparently in the "flow of experiences." As a consequence, such derived forms of perceptual experience should not be taken as paradigmatic: "They cannot be of any use in the analysis of the perceptual field, since they are extracted from it at the very outset, since they presuppose it and since we come by them by making use of precisely those set of groupings with which we have become familiar in dealing with the world" (*PP* 325–6/281/328). Thus, Merleau-Ponty's phenomenology leads him to the view that much of our experience of the world is articulated according to the "groupings" of our familiar, practical dealings with the world and that this articulation is incommensurate with conceptual articulations.

But if experience in the natural attitude is not conceptually articulated, Merleau-Ponty argues, neither is it causally constituted. Such experience, and the comportment in the world that accompanies it, "remains inaccessible to causal thought and is capable of being apprehended only by another kind of thought, that which grasps its object as it comes into being and as it appears to the person experiencing it, with the atmosphere of meaning then surrounding it" (*PP* 139–40/120/138). What a causal account cannot capture, Merleau-Ponty argues, is the way that we experience ourselves as always already inserted into a situation that is meaningfully articulated.

It is important to note, however, that for Merleau-Ponty (as for phenomenologists in general), it is not the case that all meaning needs to be understood in terms of linguistic meaning. Instead, linguistic meaning is a particular species of a more general class of experiences in which one thing arouses an expectation of another. Nonlinguistic entities, too, can have meaning in this sense – they lead us to anticipate something else – and the meaning they hold is not necessarily a conceptually articulated one. Merleau-Ponty notes, for example, that if part of my visual field contains something that looks like "a broad, flat stone on the ground," then "my whole perceptual and motor field endows the bright spot with the significance 'stone on the path.' And already I prepare to feel under my foot this smooth, firm surface" (*PP* 343/296–7/346). In this example, the significance of the object is a motor significance – that is, it arouses in me a bodily expectation.

In our normal experience of the world, then, we find the environment acting on our bodies, arousing expectations in our bodies. By the same token, our projects and intentions "polarize the world, bringing magically to view a host of signs which guide action" (*PP* 130/112/129). That is, the way we are ready for the world and acting in the world readies us to experience particular kinds of things: "my body centers itself on an object which is still only potential, and so disposes its sensitive surfaces as to make it a present reality" (*PP* 276/239/278). In anticipating the arrival of a friend, for instance, I find myself readied for an event – say, the noise of a passing car – that might otherwise go unnoticed.

What the phenomenology of lived experience teaches us, Merleau-Ponty believes, is that our primary way of being in the world is a bodily existence that, for its part, is experienced neither as a mental mode of comportment, with determinate conceptual contents, nor as a merely physical interaction with physical objects. In fact, the phenomenology of lived bodily experience shows that thoughts – "mental" states and events – and "physical" objects themselves actually bear on the body in ways that are meaningful but not rational. The phenomenon of motor significance makes this clear; there, we see that worldly objects speak to our body in myriad ways, drawing us into actions, while often remaining only tacitly present in our experience of things. The motivating object has "an ambiguous presence," Merleau-Ponty notes, "anterior to any express evocation. . . . It must exist for us even though we may not be thinking of it" (PP 418/ 364/424).

This has implications for the way we think about motivations. As a result of the fact that motor significations speak to our bodies, rather than through the mediation of thoughts, we cannot ever get completely clear about what moved us to act in a particular case. This is true even when we are moved to perform an intentional act like asserting. Merleau-Ponty observes that it is "not that we can ever array before ourselves in their entirety the reasons for any assertion – there are merely motives" (PP 452/395/459). He explains,

If it were possible to lay bare and unfold all the presuppositions in what I call my reason or my ideas at each moment, we should always find experiences which have not been made explicit, large-scale contributions from past and present, a whole 'sedimentary history' which is not only relevant to the *genesis* of my thought, but which determines its *significance*." (PP 452–3/395/459)

That is to say, if we reflect on the way our body is actually moved by the world, we arrive at the phenomenon of *motivation*, in which we see ourselves as moved by things of which, in many cases, we are only vaguely (if at all) aware. The objects and situations that we encounter in the world thus act on us through an ambiguous and indeterminate motor signficance. Our natural encounter with a thing is "packed with small perceptions that sustain it in existence. . . . Confronted by the real thing, our comportment feels itself motivated by 'stimuli' that fill out and vindicate its intention" (*PP* 391/339/395, translation modified).

II. THE RELATIONSHIP OF MOTIVATION

For this notion of motivation to do any work in explaining human existence, however, Merleau-Ponty needs to provide an account of how such motives, in working through our body, ground our thoughts and experiences in the world that we inhabit. To avoid backsliding into the problems associated with traditional dualisms, the account needs to show that the grounding is neither rational nor causal in nature. I will turn in a moment to explaining how experience in the natural attitude can ground propositional states and attitudes – that is, states and attitudes with which it is incommensurable in content – and how it can itself be grounded in the world. First I would like to examine a little more closely what precisely a motive is and how it differs from a reason or a cause.

It should be apparent by now that Merleau-Ponty's use of the term "motive" diverges from the ordinary use. In the usual sense of the term, a motive is the intentional state that prompts or moves one to act. For example, a desire to avoid public embarrassment might motivate (that is, move or impel) one to lie under oath. Merleau-Ponty's broader use of the term follows in the Husserlian tradition of phenomenology,[1] and he draws on the work of Edith Stein,[2] who defined a relationship of motivation as a connection between experiences and their antecedents in which there is "an *arising* of the one *from* the other, an effecting or being effected of one *on the basis* of the other, *for the sake of* the other."[3] Stein is quite self-conscious about broadening the usual meaning of the term "motive," and Merleau-Ponty follows her in adopting this broadened sense.

Merleau-Ponty, like Stein before him, sees intentional motives as instances of the more general type. The more general characterization, of course, in no way distorts the description of motives in the ordinary cases. If one's motive is the desire to avoid public embarrassment, then it is perfectly correct to say that the desire to avoid public embarrassment gives rise to the act of lying under oath for the sake of the desire to avoid public embarrassment. But the more general characterization of motivations allows Merleau-Ponty to extend the notion of motivation in important ways. For instance, motives need not be intentional states – that is, states characterizable with a proposition. Indeed, Merleau-Ponty also treats the objects, events, and states of affairs in the world as motives.[4] In addition, the more general characterization encompasses not just cases in which one is moved to *act*, but also cases where something simply gives rise to an experiential state, or event, or disposition.

Because motives thus characterized extend beyond intentional relationships, the relationship of motivation cannot be reduced to a rational relation. We can easily see that not all reasons are motives, because I can have a reason to do something without being moved to do it. Neither is it the case that all motives are reasons, however. To recognize this, we need simply to see that in many cases we are moved or impelled to act by something that does not and cannot function as a reason for the action – either because it is not available to thought or because it is not itself propositionally articulated as reasons must be (or both).

As we've already noted, Merleau-Ponty argues that our motivations include objects or states or events that are present only tacitly in our experience. To see how this undermines that idea that motives could be analyzed as reasons, let's look at one of Merleau-Ponty's examples of a nonthetic or not-explicitly-experienced motive. Merleau-Ponty notes that

Only after centuries of painting did artists perceive that reflection on the eye without which the eye remains dull and sightless as in the paintings of the early masters. The reflection is not seen as such, since it was in fact able to remain unnoticed for so long, and yet it has its function in perception, since its mere absence deprives objects and faces of all life and expression. The reflection is seen only incidentally. It is not presented to our perception as an objective, but as an auxiliary or mediating element. It is not seen itself, but makes us see the rest. (*PP* 357/309/360, translation modified)

My seeing a live person standing in front of me, it turns out, has its roots in a variety of features of the visual field of which I am usually only tacitly aware. One of these is the reflection of light in the eye of the person. Such tacit or "nonthetic" elements are a part of what I see, but not present in such a way that they are available for use as a *reason* for my seeing that there is a person there. The fact that the reflection remained unnoticed, even in the face of centuries of efforts to capture faithfully what it is that we *do* see, provides prima facie evidence that what we saw was not available to thought and, thus, could not ground an inference (from the fact that I see a reflection on the eye to the conclusion that I see a person, for instance), or could not serve to justify the belief that I see a person. The role the reflection plays, instead, is to dispose me to seeing a person there in front of me (rather than, say, a mannequin). A motive does not necessarily function as a reason, then, because we need not have an "*express* experience of it" (*PP* 299/258/301).

Generalizing on such examples, Merleau-Ponty argues that all our conceptually articulated perceptual experiences are motivated by the existential grasp we have on the world around us – that is, by a preceding familiarity with the world and how to act in it. Because this familiarity with the world is itself the condition of our ability to see that anything is the case and, hence, of our ability to reason, it is not itself generally available for use in inference and justification. To take another example, our ability to see objects in the world is motivated by our bodily familiarity with space. "The poplar on the road which is drawn smaller than a man," Merleau-Ponty notes, "succeeds in becoming really and truly a tree only by retreating toward the horizon" (*PP* 303/262/306). That we see it as a tree (and thus as conceptually describable) depends, in other words, on our ability to situate it spatially. Yet there is no *reason* for situating the tree spatially in the way that we do; we can appeal to no conceptually articulated feature of our experience of the drawing that justifies the spatial organization we find in it, if only because everything we see in the picture is equally a consequence of, and thus not a basis for, the spatiality into which it gets organized. If there is no reason for seeing the tree as receding toward the horizon, and hence as a tree, then what makes us see it in this way? As we shall see, it is motivated by the fact that seeing it in that way gives us the best practical grip on the scene. Our way of being in the world is one in which we are ready for objects to be situated at varying depths. This readiness, no doubt, is ingrained into our bodies by the fact that the world itself is arrayed about us in three dimensions. As a result, our mode of being in the world motivates us to see objects as arrayed three-dimensionally. Our mode of being, in other words, grounds our perception by motivating our seeing of the object at the appropriate depth.

We thus can see that, because motives *move* us rather than necessarily giving us a reason for what they motivate, they cannot be reduced to a species of reason. Indeed, we are often motivated to have experiences or to act in ways for which we not only lack reasons but have good reasons to reject, as when our bodily readiness impels us toward beliefs that we know are wrong.[5] As examples of such a phenomenon, Merleau-Ponty discusses perceptual illusions such as the way the moon looks bigger when low on the horizon than when directly overhead or Zöllner's illusion (Figure 3, page 64). Although we can demonstrate to ourselves that the moon is always the same size, still the "various parts of the field interact and *motivate* this enormous moon on the horizon" (*PP* 40/31/36). Likewise, we can easily convince ourselves that the lines in Zöllner's illusion are, in fact, parallel, but the overall configuration of lines "motivates the false judgement" by producing a bodily readiness that disposes us to the contrary beliefs (*PP* 45/35/41).

Of course, it is true that we can treat a motive as a reason, but in doing that, Merleau-Ponty notes, "I crystallize an indefinite collection of motives" (*PP* 342/295/345). In other words, because motives are functioning on a bodily level, in ways of which we are only barely, if at all, aware, any attempt to transform them into reasons ends up focusing on some narrow subset of a rich and complex set of motives. In the process, it may end up treating the selected motive as more determinate and prominent than it actually was in our experience of it. Sexual motivations are, for Merleau-Ponty, a clear example of this: "it is impossible to determine, in a given decision or action, the proportion of sexual to other motivations" (*PP* 197/169/196).

Yet if motives don't function as reasons, could they function as causes? Merleau-Ponty offers a number of arguments to show that they could not, most of which turn on the fact that motivated experiences or events occur "for the sake of" the motive. Merleau-Ponty calls this the "reciprocity" of motives – the fact that motive and motivated are each sensitive to the meaning or significance of the other. This gives motivational relationships a characteristic typical of intentional relationships – namely, a lack of extensionality. Causal relationships, by contrast, are extensional in the sense that the relationship holds between the relata regardless of the mode by which the relata are presented to us. A test for this is the fact that sentences describing causal relations preserve their truth value through substitutions in the sentence of a coreferring singular term. If the sentence "The stimulation of hair cells in my cochlea caused the firing of

neurons in my auditory cortex" is true, then substitution of coextensive predicates or singular terms should not change the truth value of
the sentence. This is because causal relations are relations between
events or states of affairs in the world. Although it may be that some
descriptions of the relata are better than others in illuminating a law
that governs the causal relation, no particular description is necessary for asserting that the causal relation holds.[6] Thus, if it turns
out that the stimulation of hair cells in my cochlea is identical to
the sounding of the trumpet, and the firing of neurons in my auditory cortex is identical to my hearing the trumpet, then we could
equally well state the causal relationship by noting that "The sounding of the trumpet *caused* my hearing the trumpet." It is a different
matter, however, when we are trying to capture a motivational relationship such as, "The death of Polyneices *motivated* Antigone to
defy Creon." Here, the relationship we are naming is not the relationship that holds between events in themselves, but the relationship in
terms of which an antecedent operates on an agent to dispose her to
a particular act or experience. This means that we cannot be indifferent to the way the relationship is described; instead, we only capture
the motivational relationship if we describe the relationship as it
exists for the agent. As Merleau-Ponty observes, a motive "is an antecedent which acts only through its significance" (*PP* 299/259/301).
Thus, even if Polyneices is the would-be tyrant of Thebes and Creon
is the rightful ruler of Thebes, it may well be the case that the death
of the would-be tyrant of Thebes in no way served as a motive for
Antigone to defy the rightful ruler of Thebes.[7]

This notion of reciprocity might seem to be in tension with the
fact we observed earlier – namely, that motives often operate tacitly.
Because we are in many instances unaware of them, just as we are
unaware of the causal processes that give rise to a conscious experience, it might seem that tacit motives are readily assimilable to
causes. There is, however, an important difference in the way that
we lack awareness of motives – namely, motives have a motor significance for us that we inhabit, and thus we *can* become (at least
imperfectly) aware of them, even though we often pay no express
attention to them. That is to say, as we are moved by motives, our
actions or experiences are shaped in such a way that we can only
understand ourselves as working out the significance the motives
have for us.

In making this point, Merleau-Ponty notes that "to experience a structure is not to receive it into oneself passively; it is to live it, to take it up, assume it and discover its immanent significance" (*PP* 299/258/301). Thus, one has not captured a motivational relationship if one has described it in a way that it cannot or does not bear on my mode of life. For example, a sound might motivate me because it operates in my experience as something toward which I can direct my attention, even if I am not aware of it in all its detail. In contrast, the vibration of hairs in my cochlea caused by sound waves cannot motivate me to do anything because that vibration is not something for the sake of which I can act, or the significance of which I can explore.

It might well be, of course, that the motive, redescribed in a suitable way, might be identical with the cause of a conscious experience. Likewise, it might be possible to describe a motive in such a way that it serves as a reason for an action – indeed, we often do precisely this. This doesn't reduce motivation to either a causal influence or a rational justification, however, because the relationship that holds between motive and motivated is different in kind from causal or rational connections. Nonphenomenological approaches to explaining the way conscious experience is grounded in the world fail, Merleau-Ponty argues, because they "can choose only between reason and cause." With the introduction of the "the phenomenological notion of *motivation*," however,

we get back to the phenomena. One phenomenon releases another, not by means of some objective efficient cause, like those which link together natural events, but by the meaning which it holds out – there is a raison d'être for a thing which guides the flow of phenomena without being explicitly laid down in any one of them, a sort of operative reason. (*PP* 61/49–50/57)

A motive, in other words, does not blindly and mechanistically produce the motivated because it only gives rise to it in virtue of its significance. The motive often only tacitly guides or gives rise to the motivated (and there is always some tacit motive at work), however, so that it functions as an "*operative* reason" – a prepredicative basis according to which phenomena are organized and made sense of – but not a justification. Thus, the motive also does not provide the sort of inferential or justificatory connection that a reason gives to a thought.

To summarize this account of the relationship of motivation, we can say that the fundamental workings of motivations are found in the way that our environment and body work together to dispose us to particular ways of acting and experiencing. The world works by drawing on our skillful bodily dispositions: "In perception we do not think the object and we do not think ourselves thinking it, we are given over to the object and we merge into this body which is better informed than we are about the world, and about the motives we have and the means at our disposal for synthesizing it" (*PP* 275–6/238/277). Thus, to return to the example of the stone in the path, the different parts of the visual field act directly on my body to draw out of it the proper responses for coping with the situation. The disposition of the visual field as a whole "suggest[s] to the subject a possible anchorage" (*PP* 325/280/327) – that is, it helps me know what to fix on in making the most sense of the situation. Each part of the visual field can be seen, in this way, to motivate a certain significance for the rest, in the same way that each line in a perspective drawing motivates the way we see each of the others: "the field itself … is moving toward the most perfect possible symmetry … The whole of the drawing strives toward its equilibrium" (*PP* 303/262/305–6). This equilibrium, I take it, consists in our having the proper disposition for fluidly responding to what the situation presents to us.

III. MOTIVES AS GROUNDS

We are now ready to discuss how the grounding function performed by motivational relationships differs from that performed by either reasons or causes. Let us first compare a motivational relationship to a relationship of rational grounding.

An experience is able to provide rational grounding to the extent that it is available for use in inference and justification. Thus, we can conclude that if the experience that gives rise to the thought is not available for use in inference and justification, then the thought is not rationally grounded. As we have seen, it is often the case that we are motivated by some features of our perceptual experience that are not available for use in thought but that nevertheless dispose us (rather than cause us) to have the thoughts that we do. Thus, motives stand to the thoughts they motivate not in a way that justifies or supports them, but rather in that they impel us toward having them.

If motives don't ground thoughts in the world by providing a rational connection between thoughts or experiences and what they are experiences of, neither do they establish a merely causal link between thoughts or experiences and what occasions them. This becomes clear when we consider that motives can connect propositional states to particular features of the world that give rise to them, and they can do this in a way that causes can't.

In the empiricist tradition, thoughts are grounded by discovering their causal connection to the world. In other words, the content of our thoughts is more or less directly "keyed," as Quine says, to causal stimulations of our sensory surfaces. "Two cardinal tenets of empiricism remain," according to Quine, "unassailable": "One is that whatever evidence there *is* for science *is* sensory evidence. The other ... is that all inculcation of meanings of words must rest ultimately on sensory evidence."[8] In Quine's case, the content of our observation sentences is tied to "the temporally ordered class of receptors triggered during the specious present."[9] But, as Quine made clear in the course of his attack on the "Two Dogmas of Empiricism," the causal triggering of a thought is insufficient to establish any tight connection between sentences or thoughts on one hand and particular causal interactions with the world on the other.

More recently, Davidson has developed this point by noting that any theory that attempts to ground our thoughts in causal intermediaries – things such as sensations, which are supposed to mediate the causes of our thoughts with our thoughts about them – must be able to explain "what, exactly, is the relation between sensation and belief that allows the first to justify the second?" The problem is that "the relation between a sensation and a belief cannot be logical, since sensations are not beliefs or other propositional attitudes."[10] If Davidson's argument is correct, we're left with two potentially incompatible assumptions about how perception grounds belief: first, that our perceptual encounter with the world is a causal transaction; second, that thoughts, being propositional in content, are rationally responsive only to other propositional entities. The assumptions are incompatible if we can see no way to move from a causal transaction to a propositional content.

One obvious way to avoid the incompatibility is to see the causal transaction as generating in us a propositional state – a belief about the world. This, in fact, is Davidson's view: "What then is the relation? The answer is, I think, obvious: the relation is causal. Sensations cause some beliefs and in this sense are the basis or ground of those beliefs."[11] Davidson calls this kind of interaction with the world "propositional perception." With language, he argues, comes the capacity for propositional thought. In virtue of this capacity, the world can cause us directly to have perceptual beliefs, but then there is no need to give perceptual experience itself a justificatory role in relation to those beliefs:

Of course, our sense-organs are part of the causal chain from world to perceptual belief. But not all causes are reasons: the activation of our retinas does not constitute evidence that we see a dog, nor do the vibrations of the little hairs in the inner ear provide reasons to think the dog is barking. "I saw it with my own eyes" is a legitimate reason for believing there was an elephant in the supermarket. But this reports no more than that something I saw caused me to believe there was an elephant in the supermarket.[12]

Thus, on Davidson's view, we are, as physical organisms, interacting causally with the world, and this interaction bears no information with a propositional content. It does, however, in virtue of our linguistic capacities, causally give rise to perceptual beliefs.

This is a coherent story to tell, but it does nothing to secure the connection between thoughts and particular occasions of those thoughts in the world. As long as the world acts only causally in the production of our beliefs and causes cannot serve as reasons for holding beliefs, it follows that we can be indifferent about which causes we correlate with which beliefs. The result is an indeterminacy of reference – that is, an inability to find any unique correlation between a particular object as causally constituted and a particular belief. The consequence of this indeterminacy is that we can put down no fixed linkages between our beliefs about the world and the particular features of the world. As Quine explained,

the total field [of beliefs] is so underdetermined by its boundary conditions, experience, that there is much latitude of choice as to what statements to reevaluate in the light of any single contrary experience. No particular experiences are linked with any particular statements in the interior of the field, except indirectly through considerations of equilibrium affecting the field as a whole.[13]

Yet without fixed linkages, John McDowell has argued, we undermine our confidence that our ideas are about the world at all:

we can make sense of the world-directedness of empirical thinking only by conceiving it as answerable to the empirical world for its correctness, and we can understand answerability to the empirical world only as mediated by answerability to the tribunal of experience, conceived in terms of the world's direct impacts on possessors of perceptual capacities.[14]

As McDowell explains,

if we do not let intuitions stand in rational relations to [thoughts], it is exactly their possession of content that is put in question. When Davidson argues that a body of beliefs is sure to be mostly true, he helps himself to the idea of a body of beliefs, a body of states that have content. And that means that, however successfully the argument might work on its own terms, it comes too late to neutralize the real problem.[15]

Thus, McDowell, in contrast to Davidson, argues that the idea of intentional content is only coherent if we can see our way to attributing to things in the world a more than causal role. McDowell proposes that we avoid the incompatibility between the causal structure of perceptual interactions with objects and the rational relations between perceptions and beliefs by supposing that, in causally interacting with us, the world draws on our conceptual capacities. Thus, the world is presented at the outset as being propositionally articulated. The difference is that, for McDowell, and not for Davidson, in our experience of the world itself, we can see the world as bearing the kind of content to which our thoughts can be responsive. In other words, McDowell's approach would redeem the idea of intentional content by explaining how our thoughts can be directly responsive to experience.

This disagreement illustrates the continuing influence of dualism. Despite their differences, McDowell and Davidson are both in agreement that if the content of perception is not conceptually articulated, then it can stand at best in a merely causal relationship to intentions. They differ only on whether the world presents itself to us in perceptual experience as conceptually articulated. Merleau-Ponty, in contrast, avoids the whole dilemma by holding that what ties thoughts to the world is neither a merely causal link nor a reason, but rather a bodily motivation. This motivation isn't a mere cause, because it has a meaningful structure. The motor significance of motivations means that the particular readiness for the world that we have in our prethematic involvement with the world is a direct response to specific features of the world.

Dualism is directly responsible for the puzzle over the way thoughts are grounded in the world because the heteronomy of reasons and mere causes means that we can be indifferent about the way we correlate particular thoughts with particular objects causally defined. "No appeal to causality can affect the determinacy of reference," Davidson notes, "if the only significant effects are responses to whole sentences."[16] This is because sentences can only be interpreted within the context of a whole pattern of beliefs that, in turn, is given content only by being mapped on to truth conditions. The current pattern of causal stimulations of the agent being interpreted are, of course, important features to take into consideration while carrying out the mapping, but they will be much too sparse as points of reference to fix the whole content of beliefs. As long as different mappings are equivalent in terms of preserving the overall truth and coherence of the beliefs being mapped, there is no basis for distinguishing between them.

The world as experienced in natural perception and the bodily readiness that motivate both natural and propositional perceptions are not indifferent to each other in the same way, however. A bodily readiness, although not necessarily responsive to conceptually delineated features of the world, nevertheless operates in a meaningfully ordered world and, as a consequence, will only respond to a meaningfully rather than causally delineated object. Because a particular kind of being ready is always a current involvement with particular things in a particular context, it can't be mapped arbitrarily onto whatever feature of the environing world we choose. A particular readiness will only be motivated by particular situations and will only uncover particular features of the world to us. Thus, it follows that motivational relationships are not merely causal influences on perception. Instead, they serve in an important sense as a ground of propositional thoughts because they connect our thoughts to particular objects or states of affairs. They succeed in doing this because we are motivated to have those thoughts by the meaning the object or state of affairs holds for our bodies – that is, its motor significance. Causes, on the other hand, can't ground our thoughts in particular objects or states of affairs. Therefore, we can conclude that motives are not causes.

The phenomenon of motivation, Merleau-Ponty believes, shows us how our mental life is directly grounded in a world that is not necessarily conceptually constituted – something not possible as long as it looked as if our thoughts could hook up to the world only rationally or causally. The phenomenology of motivation thus promises to move us beyond the Cartesian picture with all that it implies.

NOTES

1. See Husserl, *Ideas II*, §56.
2. Stein, "Beiträge zur philosophischen Begründung der Psychologie und der Geisteswissenschaften," cited in Merleau-Ponty, *PP* 39/31/36.
3. Stein, "Beiträge," 35ff.
4. See, for example, *PP* 38/29–30/34, where the object on which attention is focused is the motive for the act of attention, or *PP* 40/31/36, where "various parts of the visual field interact and *motivate* this enormous moon on the horizon." Stein also observes that it is the lightning, and not my perception of it, that is the "motive of the expectation of thunder." Likewise, "The motive of my joy is the arrival of the letter I have been longing for, not my cognizance of its arrival" (Stein, "Beiträge," 38).
5. I am indebted to Hubert Dreyfus for bringing this point home to me.
6. See Donald Davidson, "Laws and Cause."
7. Another way to see this reciprocity is in the fact that, in many motivational relationships, it is only possible to become aware of the motive through consideration of the event that it motivated. Such is undoubtedly true in cases such as those discussed earlier in the chapter in which the motive is not explicitly featured in our experience. It is only because we experienced the moon as big on the horizon that it can become clear on reflection how different parts of the perceptual field and our bodily disposition were cooperating to dispose us to certain experiences and judgments (like "the moon looks big").
8. Quine, "Epistemology Naturalized," 75.
9. Quine, *From Stimulus to Science*, 17.
10. Davidson, "A Coherence Theory of Truth and Knowledge," 141, 143.
11. "A Coherence Theory," 143.
12. Davidson, "Seeing through Language," 22.

13. Quine, "Two Dogmas of Empiricism," 42–3. See McDowell's discussion of this and the indeterminacy thesis at *Mind and World*, 129 ff.
14. *Mind and World*, xvii.
15. *Mind and World*, 68.
16. "Replies to Seventeen Essays," 55.

5   Merleau-Ponty and Recent Cognitive Science

In opposition to mainline cognitive science, which assumes that intelligent behavior must be based on representations in the mind or brain, Merleau-Ponty holds that the most basic sort of intelligent behavior, skillful coping, can and must be understood without recourse to any type of representation. He marshals convincing phenomenological evidence that higher primates and human beings learn to act skillfully without acquiring *mental* representations of the skill domain and of their goals. He also saw that no brain model available at the time he wrote could explain how this was possible. I argue that now, however, there *are* models of brain function that show how skills could be acquired and exercised without mind or brain representations.

I. THE FAILURE OF REPRESENTATIONALIST MODELS OF THE MIND

The cognitivist, Merleau-Ponty's intellectualist opponent, holds that, as the learner improves through practice, he abstracts and interiorizes more and more sophisticated rules.[1] There is no phenomenological or empirical evidence that convincingly supports this view, however, and, as Merleau-Ponty points out, the flexibility, transferability, and situational sensitivity of skills makes the intellectualist account implausible. Merleau-Ponty's most telling argument is that the intellectualist cannot explain how the organism could possibly use features of the current situation to determine which rule or concept should be applied. There are just too many features, so the selection of the relevant features requires that one has already subsumed the situation under the relevant concept.

129

In response to the difficulties of intellectualism, the empiricist claims that skills are acquired by the learner storing the memories of past situations as cases paired with successful responses. This approach is now known as case-based learning.[2] Case-based learning has not been successful, however, because as Merleau-Ponty saw, it faces the same problem that defeated the intellectualist. How can an organism classify cases so that the relevant case can be retrieved, even when, as is almost always the case, the organism finds itself in a situation that is not exactly like any of the stored cases? Cases would have to be classified by features, and, to be associated with a similar already stored case, a new situation would have to be recognized as having the appropriate defining features. As Merleau-Ponty again points out, however, there are too many ways in which situations are similar for the learner to consider all features in seeking those matching an already stored case. Thus, learners need to restrict themselves to the possibly relevant features, but which features these are can only be determined once the current situation has been understood as similar to an already stored case. As Merleau-Ponty puts it, "An impression can never by itself be associated with another impression. Nor has it the power to arouse others. It does so only provided that it is already *understood*" (*PP* 25/17/20).

Merleau-Ponty has turned out to be right. Neither computer programs abstracting more and more sophisticated rules nor those classifying and storing more and more cases have produced intelligent behavior. To understand how this problem of finding the relevant representations can be avoided, we need to lay out more fully than Merleau-Ponty did how one's relation to the world is transformed as one acquires a skill.[3]

II. A PHENOMENOLOGICAL ACCOUNT
OF SKILL ACQUISITION

Like a computer, beginners, who have no experience in a specific skill domain, must rely on *rules* and predetermined relevant *features*. For example, a beginning driver may be given the rule "shift at ten miles per hour." A more advanced beginner can be led to notice *prototypes* such as typical engine sounds and can then be given the *maxims* such as "shift down when the motor sounds like it's straining." Merleau-Ponty does not discuss these early stages of skill acquisition, except as they appear in pathological cases, such as that of Schneider, who cannot acquire new skills but must in each case reason out what to do like a rule-following computer.

Part of Schneider's problem may well be that he lacks the capacity for emotional involvement, for to progress to more flexible and context sensitive comportment, the learner must give up the detached rule-following or case-associating stance for a more involved relation to the skill domain. To learn to cope in any complex skill domain, the learner must adopt a perspective or goal so that features of the situation show up as more or less relevant and then act on this interpretation of the situation so as to find out which goals lead to success and which to failure. If the learner takes to heart his successes and failures, the resulting positive and negative emotional experiences seem to strengthen the neural connections that result in successful responses and inhibit those that produce unsuccessful ones, so that the learner's representations of rules and prototypical cases are gradually replaced by situational discriminations.[4] Then, in any given situation, rather than having to figure out which perspective to take or goal to pursue, the learner finds that *the situation directly shows up perspectivally*, but at this stage, which we might call mere proficiency, the learner still needs to *figure out* what to do.

If, however, the learner stays involved and dwells on her successes and failures, such involved experience will gradually turn the proficient performer into an expert. That is, starting with a variety of features, some of which are taken to be relevant to classifying a situation as requiring a specific response, with further experience the brain of the performer comes to recognize immediately the general situation, and the performer can then calculate consciously an appropriate response. Finally, with sufficient experience, the brain gradually decomposes each class of situations into subclasses, each of which elicits the type of response appropriate in that type of situation. No representation of rules, features, or cases is required.[5] An example of such a classification skill would be a radiologist's reading of X-ray pictures. To take a more extreme case, a chess grandmaster, when shown a position that could occur in an actual game, almost immediately experiences a compelling sense of the current issue and spontaneously makes the appropriate move. Experientially, as one becomes an expert, the world's solicitations to act take the place of representations as a way of storing and accessing what one has learned.

III. THE INTENTIONAL ARC AND SIMULATED NEURAL NETWORKS

The preceding sketch of a phenomenology of skillful coping makes clear that skills are acquired by dealing repeatedly with situations that then gradually come to show up as requiring more and more selective responses. This feedback loop between the learner and the perceptual world is what Merleau-Ponty calls the "intentional arc." He says, "the life of consciousness – cognitive life, the life of desire or perceptual life – is subtended by an 'intentional arc,' which projects round about us our past, our future, our human setting" (PP 158/136/157).[6] Merleau-Ponty refers to this feedback structure as a dialectical or circular relation of milieu and action: "the relations between the organism and its milieu are not relations of linear causality but of circular causality" (SC 13/15).

The notion of a dialectic of milieu and action is meant to capture the idea that, in learning, past experience is projected back into the perceptual world of the learner and shows up as affordances or solicitations to further action. As Merleau-Ponty puts it, a "person's projects polarize the world, bringing magically to view a host of signs which guide action, as notices in a museum guide the visitor" (PP 130/112/129).[7] On this account, the best "representation" of our practical understanding of the world turns out to be the world itself.

Merleau-Ponty argues persuasively that no representationalist model of mind or brain function can account for the way past learning is manifest in present experience so as to guide future action. Until recently, however, opponents of such a nonrepresentationalist view, such as Herbert Simon, could argue that intellectualist or associationist models must somehow explain skilled behavior because there was no way to understand how else it could be produced. Merleau-Ponty's response that the perception–action loop is "magical" did not help to win over his opponents.

Fortunately, however, there are now models of what might be going on in the brain of an active perceiver forming an intentional arc that do not introduce brain representations. Such models are called simulated neural networks. Simulated neurons are generally called nodes. Networks consist of a layer of input nodes, connected to a layer of output nodes by way of a number of intermediate nodes called hidden nodes. The simulated strengths of synaptic connection between neurons are called weights. The output of a neuron is called its activation. Running such a net means specifying the activations of the input neurons and then calculating the activation of the nodes connected to them using a formula involving the weights on these connections, and so on, until the activation of the output nodes is calculated.

Consider the case in which a net is to be trained, by a supervisor or by the environment, to respond appropriately to a number of different patterns. Each time the net associates an input pattern with an output response, the weights on the connections between the nodes are changed according to an algorithm that adjusts the weight on each connection in such a way as to cause the net to respond more appropriately the next time the same input occurs. The training is complete when each pattern used in the training evokes what the trainer has defined as the appropriate response.

In a network trained using such a sequence of input, output, adjustment of connection weights, and then new input, the current weights on the connections between the nodes correspond to what the net has already learned through prior training using a large number of inputs. The net with the current weighted connections is thus able to classify the current inputs and respond differentially to them. This corresponds to the discrimination ability that, according to Merleau-Ponty, the skilled organism brings to a situation, on the basis of which the situation solicits a specific response.

It is precisely the advantage of simulated neural networks that past experience with a large number of cases, rather than being stored as memories, modifies the weights between the simulated neurons, which in turn determine the response. New inputs thus produce outputs based on past experience without the net needing to represent its past experience as cases or rules for determining further actions. Simulated neural networks are thus able to avoid the problem posed by Merleau-Ponty concerning how to find the *relevant* rule to apply or how to associate the current input to the *relevant* past impression. For by changing neural connection weights and activation on the basis of past experience without remembering or in any way storing past cases, nets dispense with remembered cases altogether and so, too, with the problem of how to retrieve the appropriate one. The neural-net model thus suggests a nonrepresentational, and yet non-magical, brain basis of the intentional arc.

A fundamental problem of similarity recognition, however, reappears in any such disembodied model of neural-net learning. When a net is trained by being given inputs paired with appropriate responses, the net can only be said to have learned to respond appropriately when it responds appropriately to *new* inputs similar to, but different from, those used in training it. Otherwise, it could be regarded as merely having learned all the specific pairs used in the training. In one way, this is not a problem. Because of the way nets work, they always respond when given a new input by producing an output. If, however, the response is to be judged *appropriate* by human beings, the net must respond to the current input not merely in some arbitrary way. The net must respond to the *same similarities* to which human beings respond. But everything is similar to everything else and different from everything else in an indefinitely large number of ways. We just do not notice it. Thus, the insoluble problem of a disembodied mind responding to what is relevant in the input, which Merleau-Ponty notes concerning case retrieval and rule application, leads neural-network modelers to the basic problem of *generalization*.

Neural-network modelers agree that an intelligent network must be able to generalize. For a given classification task, given sufficient examples of inputs associated with one particular type of output, it should learn to associate further inputs of the same type with that same type of output. But what counts as the same type? The network's designer usually has in mind a specific type required for a reasonable generalization and counts it a success if the net generalizes to other instances of this type. When the net produces an unexpected association, however, can one say it has failed to generalize? One could equally well say that the net had all along been acting on a different definition of the type in question and that this difference has just been revealed. One might think of this unexpected response as showing an alien sort of intelligence, but if a neural net did not respond to the same types of situations as similar that human beings do, it would not be able to learn our skills, could not find its way about in our world, and would seem to us to be hopelessly stupid.

How, then, do human beings learn to generalize like other human beings so that they acquire the skills required to get along in the human world? Merleau-Ponty would no doubt hold that the fact that we all have similar bodies is essential to understanding how we generalize. There are at least two ways the human body constrains the space of possible generalizations. The first is due to the brain; the second is due to how our lived body copes with things.

First, the possible responses to a given input are constrained by brain architecture. This innate structure accounts for phenomena such as the perceptual constants and similarities the Gestalt psychologists investigated. These are given from the start by the perceptual system as if they had always already been learned. Merleau-Ponty calls them "a past that has never been a present" (*PP* 280/242/282).

This alone, however, would not be enough to constrain the generalization space so that, in a classification situation, all human beings would respond in the same way to the same set of inputs. It turns out, however, that in a net with a large number of connections with adjustable weights, not only the training cases but also the order and frequency of the cases determines the particular weights and, therefore, how a net will generalize. The training cases, as well as their order and frequency, are normally selected by the trainer. If, however, the net were to be set up to learn by itself, that is, if its connection strengths were arranged so as to adjust themselves on the basis of the input–output pairs that the net encountered in the world, then the order and frequency of the inputs would depend on the interaction of the structure of the embodied network and the structure of the world. For example, if the net controlled a robot with a body like a human body, things nearby that afforded reaching would be noticed early and often. Such body-dependent order and frequency would provide a second constraint on generalization.[8] Thus, while the generalization problem is inevitable for disembodied neural-net models, the problem might be solved for embodied organisms that share certain constraints on how they are able to cope.[9] As Merleau-Ponty says, "Although our body does not impose definite instincts upon us from birth, as it does upon animals, it does at least give to our life the form of generality" (*PP* 171/146/169).

Of course, the body-dependence of shared generalizations puts disembodied neural networks at a serious disadvantage when it comes to learning to cope in the human world. Nothing is more alien to our form of life than a network with no varying degrees of access, no up–down, front – back orientation, no preferred way of moving, such as moving forward more easily than backward, and no emotional response to its failures and successes. The odds are overwhelming against such a disembodied net generalizing the way we do, and so learning to classify situations and affordances as we do. It should therefore come as no surprise that such classification models have succeeded only in domains cut off from everyday embodied experience, such as discriminating between sonar signals reflected from a mine and those reflected from a rock.[10]

IV. MAXIMUM GRIP

The capacity of an embodied agent to feed back what it has learned into the way the world shows up – the intentional arc – is only the first half of Merleau-Ponty's story. His most important contribution is his description of a dynamic version of the dialectic of milieu and action. He gives an example from sports:

> For the player in action the football field is . . . pervaded with lines of force (the "yard lines"; those which demarcate the "penalty area") and articulated in sectors (for example, the "openings" between the adversaries) which call for a certain mode of action and which initiate and guide the action as if the player were unaware of it. The field itself is not given to him, but present as the immanent term of his practical intentions; the player becomes one with it and feels the direction of the "goal," for example, just as immediately as the vertical and the horizontal planes of his own body. . . . At this moment consciousness is nothing other than the dialectic of milieu and action. Each maneuver undertaken by the player modifies the character of the field and establishes in it new lines of force in which the action in turn unfolds and is accomplished, again altering the phenomenal field. (SC 182–3/168–9)

This kind of skillful response to a temporally unfolding situation is, of course, also exhibited by expert drivers and has been studied in chess players. Excellent chess players can play at the rate of 5 to 10 seconds a move and even faster without any serious degradation in performance. Simon has estimated that an expert chess player remembers roughly 50,000 types of position.[11] This is, of course, a case-based model that, as anyone who understands Merleau-Ponty would expect, has not produced expert chess play.[12] Rather, a careful description of the phenomenon suggests that, while beginners learn to distinguish specific patterns and follow rules for how to respond to them, the chess master, by playing thousands of games, has refined his dispositions to respond appropriately to each situation, and these changing dispositions to respond are correlated with changing lines of force on the board, which in turn solicit appropriate responses. So there is no need for the expert to *remember* or in any way store a repertoire of 50,000 typical positions. Still, the number of types of pattern on the chessboard the master has learned to respond to differentially must no doubt be as large as Simon estimates.[13]

In general, once an expert has learned to cope successfully, at each stage in a sequential, goal-directed activity, either he senses that he is doing as well as possible at that stage, or he senses a tension that tells him he is deviating from an optimal gestalt and feels drawn to make a next move that, thanks to his previous learning, is likely to be accompanied by less tension. As experts in getting around in the world, we are all constantly drawn to what Merleau-Ponty thinks of as a maximal grip on our situation. As Merleau-Ponty's puts it:

For each object, as for each picture in an art gallery, there is an optimum distance from which it requires to be seen, a direction viewed from which it vouchsafes most of itself: at a shorter or greater distance we have merely a perception blurred through excess or deficiency. We therefore tend towards the maximum of visibility, and seek a better focus as with a microscope. (PP 348/302/352)

Paintings are interesting special cases in which we are still learning, so that we have to experiment with each painting, making trial and error movements that oscillate around the optimum, in order to find the best grip, whereas, in everyday experience, once we have learned to cope with a certain type of object, we are normally drawn directly to the optimal coping point: "my body is geared onto the world when my perception presents me with a spectacle as varied and as clearly articulated as possible, and when my motor intentions, as they unfold, receive the responses they expect from the world" (PP 289–90/250/292). According to Merleau-Ponty, finite, involved, embodied coping beings are constantly "motivated" to move so as to achieve the best possible grip on the world.

Merleau-Ponty is clear that for this movement toward maximal grip to take place, one does not need a representation of a goal. Rather,

acting is experienced as a steady flow of skillful activity in response
to one's sense of the situation. Part of that experience is a sense of
whether or not coping is going well. When one senses a deviation
from the optimal body–environment gestalt, one's activity tends to
take one closer to an optimal body–environment relationship that
relieves the "tension." As Merleau-Ponty puts it, "our body is not
an object for an 'I think,' it is a grouping of lived-through meanings
that moves toward its equilibrium" (PP 179/153/177).

Skilled drivers or master-level chess players not only can sense at
each stage how well they are doing, they also sense whether their
actions are making their current situation better or worse. That is,
the learners' past involved experience of their successes and failures
results in a reliable sense that things are going well or that they are
deviating from a satisfactory gestalt – a gestalt that need not be represented in their brain or mind. Learners are simply drawn to respond
in a way that is likely to lower their sense of tension or disequilibrium. Thus, skillful coping does not require any representation of a
goal. It can be purposive without the agent entertaining a purpose.
As Merleau-Ponty puts it, "to move one's body is to aim at things
through it; it is to allow oneself to respond to their call, which is made
upon it independently of any representation" (PP 161/139/160–1).[14]

To distinguish this body-based intentionality from the representational intentionality presupposed by cognitivism, Merleau-Ponty
calls the body's response to the ongoing situation "motor intentionality" (PP 128/110/127). This term describes the way an organism is
sensitive to conditions of improvement without needing to represent
its goal, that is, the action's conditions of satisfaction.[15]

V. REINFORCEMENT LEARNING

So far, we have seen that artificial neural networks are normally
taught appropriate responses to situations by immediate feedback,
that is, the researcher (or the situation itself) determines what counts
as success and "rewards" the net when it makes a right association
and "corrects" it when it makes a wrong one. This is a useful model
of the formation of an intentional arc in the early stages of skill acquisition in which the beginner's brain is, for example, learning to
classify inputs such as motor sounds so as to make an appropriate
response. Most learning, however, is not of this static and passive

sort. Normally, the learner has to make a series of decisions that lead to a reward in the future. How is it possible to learn to make the right decision at an early stage without immediate feedback as to whether that decision increases or decreases the chance of a future reward many steps later? This would seem to be an even more magical capacity than that exhibited by the intentional arc.

We can find a clue in Merleau-Ponty's account of the tendency toward getting a maximal grip. As we have just seen, Merleau-Ponty's phenomenological account of the movement of the organism toward getting a maximal grip need not involve a representation of the goal, but only a sense of whether one's motor intentions, as they unfold, are affecting one's skillful performance as one expects. Researchers have recently developed a technique called *actor–critic reinforcement learning*, which makes use of an idea similar to Merleau-Ponty's, namely, that in learning a skill, a learner only needs to have a sense of how things are going at each stage of the action. Reinforcement learning techniques enable neural-net models to develop a reliable evaluation of how things are going from feedback based on the long-term successes or failures of their current actions.[16] Yet how, one may well ask, can the model evaluate how well it is doing without representing its goal and its current relation to it? How else could the far-off goal determine how the net evaluated its current action?

To understand the answer offered by the reinforcement learning model, we need first to recall that the frequency of electrical impulses produced by a neuron is called its "activation." Next we need to note that, unlike in the classification models discussed in section III, in reinforcement learning models, at each moment the *change in activation* of a particular node is a function of its *current activation*, together with its inputs from the other nodes connected directly to it, the activation of which in turn depends on the activation of still other nodes and the weights on their connections to that node.

Now, consider the case in which a net is to be trained to act appropriately at each step in a sequence of steps and to do so for a large number of such sequences. The input activation provided by the environment plus the current activation level of the nodes determined by all prior inputs and actions in a particular sequence is called a situation. (The current activation of a network at each moment during a sequence of actions can be said to correspond to the anticipation, or perspective, that, according to Merleau-Ponty, the skilled organism brings to the situation.) Each situation produces an activation of the output nodes. Given a situation during a training sequence, the simulated learner gradually learns to generate *two* outputs – one, of course, is the action that, in that situation, will produce the expectation of maximal reward, while at each moment the second output represents the prospect of future reward – all without needing to represent its goal.[17] This second output, according to the reinforcement learning model, is the key to learning a skill. It is also something skilled performers experience, as reflected in Merleau-Ponty's talk of the tension produced by actions that deviate from what in the past has led to an optimal grip. On the basis of how, in a sequence of actions, the current action affected the previously estimated prospect of reward, the network refines both its estimate of the prospect of reward and its choice of action.

There are more or less rewarding sequences, so the net's learning takes place, in each situation, by random explorations (small changes) in the action that its prior results have taught it, thereby finding out how this change would affect the prospect of reward. An action that improves the prospect of reward is then reinforced, and the value representing the prospect of reward is simultaneously increased. At each step, when the model makes a random variation that is less than optimal, the estimate of the prospect of reward goes down, and when the model improves its response, the estimated reward goes up. As the learning progresses, the actions represented in the model approach the optimal, and the anticipation of future reward becomes more accurate. Gradually the size of the random explorations necessary for learning is reduced to zero. A skill has been acquired when no experimental action improves the critic's estimate of future reward.

Thus, in *learning*, according to the model, the significance of the reward for the organism plays a crucial role. After the learning has established the most rewarding behavior, however, all the organism needs, according to the model, is the feedback at each stage, based on past experience, that the prospect of future reward is either increasing, decreasing, or remaining constant. At the end of the training, the organism represented in the model will act in such a way that the prospect of reward is optimal and stays constant.

The reward function has the interesting property that the behavior of the organism is, as the modelers say, "myopic."[18] The network simply reacts to the report of how it is doing in the current situation. It can be myopic and yet successful thanks to learning the prospect of reward. No representation of the goal is required in the model. The numerical value representing the prospect of future reward corresponds to the organism's sense of tension in getting further away from the optimal, or its sense that things are going as well as could be expected, which Merleau-Ponty describes as a sense of equilibrium. This tension, this sense of how things are going, is not just a sense of pleasure or pain, comfort or discomfort. It is a normative sensitivity to one's current situation as better or worse, relative to the optimal (ongoing) state. It is a sense of rightness and wrongness, success and failure, as ongoing processes, not as final goals. Thus, according to Merleau-Ponty, the organism's behavior is not simply *caused* by a feeling of how things are going, nor does the organism *infer* from the feeling what it should do next; rather, the feeling of how things are going *motivates* its behavior.[19]

The model really works. For example, a simulated neural net has learned to play backgammon at world-champion level after playing millions of games with itself, yet it does not "remember" any game or position, it has not abstracted any rules, nor does it represent its goal. It has acquired its skill simply by the weight changes made by the program, so that, when its current board position is the input, the output of the neural net, after a considerable number of games, approximates the maximal reward to the moving player. The program then chooses the move that yields the board position with the minimal reward for the opponent.[20]

We have just seen that, on this model, learning is controlled by trial-and-error variations that are tested on the basis of what, in the long run, is rewarding for the organism. Merleau-Ponty's description of learning a skill makes the same point. The organism, he tells us, "builds up aptitudes [skills], that is, the general power of responding to situations of a certain type by means of varied reactions which have nothing in common but the meaning. . . . Situation and reaction . . . are two moments of a circular process" (*SC* 140/130).[21]

Thus, the important insight of the reinforcement learning model is that, once learned, skilled behavior is sensitive to an end that is significant for the organism, and that this significance, encapsulated in the learned prospect of reward, directs every step of the organism's activity without being represented in the organism's mind or brain. Thus, Merleau-Ponty's claim that the representationalist account of our most basic and pervasive forms of learning and skillful action are mistaken and require a different account can be defended not only on phenomenological grounds, but on neuroscientific grounds as well.

VI. MERLEAU-PONTY'S RELATION TO NEUROSCIENCE

One important question remains. Granted that recent models of the role of the brain in learning and in skillful activity have features that are isomorphic with Merleau-Ponty's account of learning and coping without brain or mental representations, would Merleau-Ponty regard this development as support for his phenomenological account of perception and action?

Given his claim that the skilled organism is solicited by its environment to respond to its situation in a way that approaches an optimal gestalt, it might seem obvious that Merleau-Ponty would be happy with any brain model that attempted to generalize the Gestaltists' hypothesis that the structure of the perceptual field is isomorphic with field effects in the brain.[22]

Merleau-Ponty, however, rejects the Gestaltists' hypothesis for at least three related reasons. First, given that, according to him, the whole organism is geared into the whole world, even if one had an account of perceptual experiences in terms of local fields in the brain, one would find no isolable classes of events in the world correlated with isolable classes of events in the brain. For this reason, Merleau-Ponty rejected any causal account of the brain basis of phenomena when such an account claimed to explain the phenomena by psychophysical laws.[23]

Second, given his rejection of the possibility of psychophysical laws, Merleau-Ponty rejects any form of reductionism or eliminativism – the view he would call "naturalism." Presumably, he would even reject any form of mind–brain identity because he is sure that "perception is not an event of nature" (SC 157/145).

Third, contra the Gestaltists, Merleau-Ponty held that any account of the working of the brain in terms of *internal* forces and equilibria missed the most important feature of comportment, namely, that the organism does not respond to the stimuli impinging on its sense organs but determines and responds to the *significance* of the situation for the organism. Thus, the organism's sense of tending toward equilibrium is not just the result of gestalt fields *in* the brain tending toward a least energy configuration, like a soap bubble tending toward a spherical shape. Rather, the minimum whole reaching equilibrium must be the organism involved in the world. According to Merleau-Ponty,

The privileged state, the invariant, can no longer be defined as the result of reciprocal actions which actually unfold in the system.... [I]f one tried to hold with Köhler that preferred behavior is that involving the least expenditure of energy ... it is too clear that the organism is not a machine governed according to a principle of *absolute* economy. For the most part preferred behavior is the simplest and most economical *with respect to the task in which the organism finds itself engaged;* and its fundamental forms of activity and the character of its possible action are presupposed in the definition of the structures which will be the simplest *for it,* preferred *in* it.... This signifies that the organism itself measures the action of things upon it and itself delimits its milieu by a circular process that is without analogy in the physical world. (*SC* 158–61/146–8)

Merleau-Ponty's important point, then, is that any acceptable explanation of the brain activity underlying and giving rise to our comportment requires that the organism be actively involved in seeking a grip on the world and that it constantly receive feedback as to its successes and failures, which guide and refine its tendency to move toward a maximal grip on its environment. The brain basis of comportment, therefore, cannot be an equilibrium formed in the brain alone, but a tendency toward equilibrium of the active organism in the situation that reflects the meaning of that situation for the organism.

VII. CONCLUSION

It seems clear that the neural-net models discussed here meet all of Merleau-Ponty's requirements. They offer a circular model of brain function according to which the brain picks up what is significant to the organism in the world, while denying psychophysical laws – and so without reducing meaningful comportment and perception to brain functions. They could thus be the basis of the sort of organism-world relation Merleau-Ponty describes:

physical stimuli act upon the organism only by eliciting a global response which will vary qualitatively when the stimuli vary quantitatively; with respect to the organism they play the role of occasions rather than of cause; the reaction depends on their vital significance rather than on the material properties of the stimuli. Hence, between the variables upon which conduct actually depends and this conduct itself there appears a relation of meaning, an intrinsic relation. One cannot assign a moment in which the world acts on the organism, since the very effect of this "action" expresses the internal law of the organism. (SC 174/161)[24]

It would be satisfying to think that Merleau-Ponty would happily embrace some such model, but there are passages in *Phenomenology of Perception* in which Merleau-Ponty seems to foreclose the possibility of *any* account of brain function that could in any way be the basis of motor intentionality. He states categorically, "How significance and intentionality could come to dwell in molecular edifices or masses of cells is something which can never be made comprehensible, and here Cartesianism is right" (*PP* 403/351/409).

One would think that it is an empirical question whether and how brain activity underlies motor intentionality and that the conviction that a naturalized account *must be possible* (as Koffka[25] and John Searle, for example, maintain) or that it is inconceivable (as Merleau-Ponty contends in the preceding passage and as thinkers such as Thomas Nagel sometimes suggest) both go beyond what we have a right to claim. For the time being, one thing we can surely do is to follow Merleau-Ponty in rejecting the atomistic causal accounts offered by his contemporaries and by current mainstream neuroscience, while investigating with open minds the latest holistic and representationless brain models of learning and skillful coping that correct just what Merleau-Ponty found inadequate in the brain models that his contemporaries accepted.[26]

NOTES

1. As I use the term "cognitiv*ism*," it is synonymous with Merleau-Ponty's term "intellectualism." For the cognitivist, like the intellectualist, even

perception is a kind of thinking based on unconscious inferences and rule following. "Cognitive *science*," however, as I use the term, is the discipline that seeks to understand the mind or brain in whatever way turns out to work.

2. See for example, Schank, *What We Learn When We Learn by Doing.*

3. Although the French have a word for skill (*habilité*), Merleau-Ponty prefers to use the word "*habitude*" to stress the fact that we *have* our skills, that they are embodied (*PP* 203/174/202). The English edition correctly translates "*habitude*" as "habit," but the *Oxford English Dictionary* says "habit" refers primarily to "a settled disposition or tendency to act in a certain way, especially one acquired by frequent repetition of the same act until it becomes almost or quite involuntary." This rigid behavior is exactly what Merleau-Ponty is trying to distinguish from the flexible and situation-sensitive skills that make up *l'habitude* (see *PP* 166/142/164ff). So, wherever the translation says "habit," I substitute "skill." For a more detailed account of skill acquisition, see H. L. Dreyfus and S. E. Dreyfus, *Mind over Machine.*

4. If the learner resists involvement, he or she will remain merely competent. Patricia Benner has described this phenomenon in the training of nurses in *From Novice to Expert: Excellence and Power in Clinical Nursing Practice,* 164.

5. For the sake of simplicity, I am here describing the change from proficient to expert in the acquisition of skills that do not require continuous adaptation over time. I deal with sequential skills in section III.

6. Merleau-Ponty stresses that the intentional arc is tied up with the involved way in which the organism projects its activity into the future and, we should add, learns from the results. Thus, he concludes that Schneider's detached, robotic behavior comes from a weakening of the intentional arc, "which gives way in the patient, and which, in the normal subject, endows experience with its degree of vitality and fruitfulness" (*PP* 184/157/182).

7. It's important to note that Merleau-Ponty uses "magical" in two ways. Here "magically" means without needing to understand how we do it. But, in discussing how the mind can control movement, he says, "We still need to understand by what magical process the representation of a movement causes precisely that movement to be made by the body." He adds, "The problem can be solved provided that we cease to draw a distinction between the body as a mechanism in itself and consciousness as being for itself" (*PP* 163n/139n/160n). Here he is using the term "magical" pejoratively to mean that a causal claim is based on an ontology that makes it *impossible* to account for how that claim could be implemented.

8. For a worked-out account of human body structure and how it is correlative with the structure of the human world, see Samuel Todes, *Body and World*.

9. Giving robots bodies is a much more complicated problem than it first appeared to be. At the Massachusetts Institute of Technology (MIT) in the 1970s, researchers tried building a shoulder, arm, wrist, and hand, all guided by a television camera, which were collectively to be able to pick up blocks. Merleau-Ponty would have been pessimistic as to the success of the project. He had already pointed out in *Phenomenology of Perception* that the objective body is in objective space; therefore, to move such a body, one would have to calculate how to get its hand from one objective location to another, which in turn involved locating the shoulder, arm, wrist, hand, and fingers and moving them in a coordinated way, whereas our bodies are given to us directly in phenomenal space, in which we can directly move our limbs to a location relative to our body. He says, for example, "if I am ordered to touch my ear or my knee, I move my hand to my ear or my knee by the shortest route, without having to think of the initial position of my hand, or that of my ear, or the path between them" (*PP* 169/144/167).

As Merleau-Ponty would have expected, the MIT researchers found that the robot arm had so many degrees of freedom that they could not solve the problem of how to coordinate, in objective space, the movements of all the components. Now, however, neural nets promise a solution that does not use rules to determine how to move each joint in objective space. See the suggestion of how reaching and grasping could be solved as a problem of dealing with multiple simultaneous constraints in David Rumelhart and James McClelland, *Parallel Distributed Processing*, Vol. 1, 4–6.

For a more worked-out proposal using attractor theory to explain a kind of skillful coping, see H. C. Kwan et al., "Network Relaxation as Biological Computation." As Sean Kelly explains,

On the conceptualization of movement generation suggested by Borrett and Kwan, a movement is conceived as the behavioral correlate of the evolution or relaxation of a recurrent neural network toward a fixed point attractor. Thus, the initial conditions of the network represent the initial position of the limb, the relaxation of the network toward the attractor state represents the movement of the limb, and the final state of the network at the fixed point attractor represents the position of the limb at its desired endpoint.

The initial conditions of the model, like the initial intention to grasp, is sufficient to ensure, in normal circumstances, that the limb will reach the appropriate endpoint in the appropriate way. In this sense we can say that the neural-net model of limb movement reproduces the central phenomenological features of grasping behavior since, as with grasping, the model is from the outset "magically at its completion" (Sean Kelly, "Grasping at Straws: Motor Intentionality and the Cognitive Science of Skilled Behavior").

10. R. P. Gorman and T. J. Sejnowski, "Learned Classification of Sonar Targets Using a Massively-Parallel Network."

11. Simon, *Models of Thought*, 386–403.

12. Deep Blue might seem to be an exception to this claim, but actually it confirms it. This program, which defeated the world chess champion, is not an expert system operating with rules and cases. Rather, Deep Blue uses brute force to look at a billion moves a second and so can look at *all* moves approximately seven moves into the future. Except for a crude evaluation function that selects which beginning move ends in the best situation seven moves down the line, Deep Blue is no more intelligent than an adding machine.

13. That amateur and expert chess players use different parts of the brain has been confirmed by recent magnetic resonance imaging research. See Ognjen Amidzic et al., "Patterns of focal γ-bursts in chess players." These researchers report the following: "We use a new technique of magnetic imaging to compare focal bursts of γ-band activity in amateur and professional chess players during matches. We find that this activity is most evident in the medial temporal lobe in amateur players, which is consistent with the interpretation that their mental acuity is focused on analysing unusual new moves during the game. In contrast, highly skilled chess grandmasters have more γ-bursts in the frontal and parietal cortices, indicating that they are retrieving chunks from expert memory by recruiting circuits outside the medial temporal lobe." It should be noted that the claim that these MRI results support Simon's assumption that experts "are retrieving chunks [i.e., representations of typical chess positions] from memory" is in no way supported by this research. What the research does suggest is the researchers' weaker claim that "These marked differences in the distribution of focal brain activity during chess playing point to differences in the mechanisms of brain processing and functional brain organization between grandmasters and amateurs."

14. To help convince us that no representation of the final gestalt is needed for the skilled performer to move toward it, Merleau-Ponty uses the analogy of a soap bubble. The bubble starts as a deformed film. The bits of soap respond to local forces according to laws that happen to work so as to dispose the entire system to end up as a sphere, but the spherical result does not play a causal role in producing the bubble.

15. For a detailed account of the difference between propositional *conditions of satisfaction* and nonpropositional *conditions of improvement*,

see Hubert L. Dreyfus, "The Primacy of Phenomenology over Logical Analysis."

16. See Richard Sutton and Andrew Barto, *Reinforcement Learning*.

17. The numerical value representing the prospect of reward in the reinforcement learning model represents the organism's sense of how well it is doing. The organism itself, however, need not represent how it is doing. It simply feels the flow directly or feels drawn to modify its behavior.

18. In Merleau-Ponty's example of the soap bubble, the bits are myopic with respect to the sphere they end up producing.

19. Likewise, in the reinforcement learning model, the prospect-of-reward value represents a state of the brain that is not just a state of pleasure or pain, comfort or discomfort, but is a measure of the *significance* of the results of previous actions for the organism. This sensitivity to significance comes as near as any brain models we have to instatiating nonrepresentational intentionality.

20. G. J. Tesauro, "TD-Gammon, A Self-Teaching Backgammon Program, Achieves Master-Level Play." Unlike the way a net learns according to the reinforcement learning model, the backgammon program learns only the prospect of reward, not optimal actions, because the rule that restricts legal moves in backgammon enables the program to examine *all* legal moves in each position and choose the best one based on the prospect of reward. A full-fledged actor–critic account of skill learning can be found in Rajarshi Das and Sreerupa Das, "Catching a Baseball: A Reinforcement Learning Perspective Using a Neural Network."

21. In the reinforcement learning model, the reward is thought of as that which satisfies a need of the organism, whereas for Merleau-Ponty, it seems that, although the organism must of course have specific needs and satisfy them, ongoing coping is an end in itself. Thus, he says, "the preferred behavior is the one that permits the easiest and most adapted action: for example, the most exact spatial designations, the finest sensory discriminations. Thus each organism, in the presence of a given milieu, has its optimal conditions of activity and its proper manner of realizing equilibrium" (*SC* 160–1/148). It seems that what we are trying to do in our motor-intentional behavior, according to Merleau-Ponty, is not merely achieve some specific goal, but maintain the feedback we expect as we act. For example, we try to stay in the groove when playing jazz, and in the flow in sports. The tension between these two accounts of what human beings are ultimately aiming at, whether it is a goal or an ongoing activity, is reflected in Merleau-Ponty's example of the movement toward maximal grip as the tendency to achieve the goal

of getting the best view of a picture in an art gallery. As Todes puts it, we are constantly involved in making our indeterminate situation more determinate (see *Body and World*, chapter 4). Perhaps the best way to think about the relation between the goal-directed aspect of skilled comportment and what Merleau-Ponty refers to as the tendency toward a "maximum sharpness of perception and action" (*PP* 290/250/292) is to note that ongoing coping forms the background necessary for any specific goal-directed activity.

22. The Gestaltists sought to show, for example, that unstable figures such as the Necker cube flipped from one stable form to another when the correlated brain field became saturated and weakened and the brain switched to a fresh organization.

23. This is similar to the view Donald Davidson calls "anomalous monism"; see his "Actions, Reasons, and Causes."

24. Walter Freeman has worked out a different model of how the brain learns to classify experiences according to what they mean to the organism. His model uses chaotic attractors (see Walter J. Freeman, "The Physiology of Perception"). Such an approach could be adapted to show how the brain, operating as a dynamical system, could cause a series of movements that achieve a goal without the brain in any way representing that goal in advance of achieving it (see H. L. Dreyfus, "The Primacy of Phenomenology over Logical Analysis"). In addition, Freeman, like Merleau-Ponty, is opposed to linear transmission models of brain activity. He argues that they face what is called the binding problem, the problem about how activity in one part of the brain communicates its results to just those other parts where the results are relevant. He proposes that the attractors formed in acquiring a skill are like local storm patterns in that they communicate with other areas of the brain not by linear transmission, but by setting up overall field effects that are selectively picked up by the parts of the brain attuned to the relevant patterns. Merleau-Ponty seems to anticipate an attractor view like Freeman's when he says, "It is necessary only to accept the fact that the physicochemical actions of which the organism is in a certain manner composed, instead of unfolding in parallel and independent sequences (as the anatomical spirit would have it), instead of intermingling in a totality in which everything would depend on everything and in which no cleavage would be possible, are constituted, following Hegel's expression, in 'clusters' or in relatively stable 'vortices'" (*SC* 166/153).

25. Merleau-Ponty quotes Koffka as saying, "I admit that in our *ultimate* explanations, we can have but *one* universe of discourse and that it

must be the one about which physics has taught us so much" (Koffka, *Principles of Gestalt Psychology*, 48; Merleau-Ponty, *SC* 144/133).

26. I thank Stuart Dreyfus for the account of skill acquisition used in this paper. I'm also indebted to him for helping me understand how the reinforcement learning model of brain function supports Merleau-Ponty's phenomenology of representation-free coping.

6 The Silent, Limping Body of Philosophy

I

In the field of Western philosophy, Maurice Merleau-Ponty is something like the patron saint of the body. Although La Mettrie, Diderot, Nietzsche, and Foucault have also passionately championed the bodily dimension of human life, none can match the bulk of rigorous, systematic, and persistent argument that Merleau-Ponty provides to prove the body's primacy in human experience and meaning. With tireless eloquence that almost seems to conquer by its massive unrelenting flow, he insists that the body is not only the crucial source of all perception and action, but also the core of our expressive capability and thus the ground of all language and meaning.

Paradoxically, while celebrating the body's role in expression, Merleau-Ponty typically characterizes it in terms of silence. The body, he writes in *Phenomenology of Perception*, constitutes "the tacit *cogito*," "the silent *cogito*," the "unspoken *cogito*." As our "primary subjectivity," it is "the consciousness which conditions language," but itself remains a "silent consciousness" with an "inarticulate grasp of the world" (*PP* 461–3/402–4/468–70). Forming "the background of silence" (*S* 58/46) that is necessary for language to emerge, the body, as gesture, is also already "a tacit language" (*S* 59/47) and the ground of all expression: "every human use of the body is already *primordial expression*" (*S* 84/67).

There is a further paradox. Although surpassing other philosophers in emphasizing the body's expressive role, Merleau-Ponty hardly wants to listen to what the body seems to say about itself in terms of its conscious somatic sensations, such as explicit kinesthetic or proprioceptive feelings. The role of such feelings gets little attention in his texts (much less, for example, than in William James or even Wittgenstein), and they tend to be sharply criticized when they are discussed. They are targets in Merleau-Ponty's general critique of representations of bodily experience, along with other "thematized" somatic sensations.

This chapter explores the reasons for Merleau-Ponty's insistence on somatic silence and neglect of explicitly conscious body feelings by showing how these themes emerge from and illustrate his specific goals for a phenomenology of embodiment and a revaluation of our basic spontaneous perception that has been the target of philosophical denigration since ancient times. But his commitment to the silent body may also reflect a more general conception of philosophy that he strikingly advocates. Just as Merleau-Ponty paradoxically describes the body's expressiveness in terms of silence, so – in his paper "In Praise of Philosophy" (his project-defining, inaugural lecture at the Collège de France) – does he stunningly describe philosophy as "limping" (EP 59/58) and yet goes on to celebrate it precisely in terms of this crippling metaphor: "the limping of philosophy is its virtue" (EP 61/61).

Why should a brilliant body philosopher like Merleau-Ponty use such a metaphor of somatic disempowerment to characterize his philosophical project? My chapter explores this question too, while contrasting his philosophical vision with the more practical, reconstructive pragmatist approach to somatic philosophy that pays much more attention to explicit or reflective somatic consciousness in its attempt to effect not only a theoretical rehabilitation of the body as a central concept for philosophy, but also a more practical, therapeutic rehabilitation of the lived body as part of the philosophical life. This greater emphasis on the value of explicit somatic consciousness and on a more practical, meliorative dimension of body philosophy (which is inspired by the experiential-centered pragmatist tradition of William James and John Dewey and is elaborated in my theory of somaesthetics) could provide a useful complement to Merleau-Ponty's philosophy of embodiment.[1]

Merleau-Ponty's reasons for insisting on somatic silence are not always clearly articulated, perhaps because they are sometimes so closely tied to his basic philosophical vision that he simply presumed them. He may have not really seen them clearly by seeing through them, just as we see through our eyeglasses without seeing them clearly (and the more clearly we see through them, the less clearly they will be seen). Moreover, his neglect of the positive role of explicit somatic sensations can be interpreted in different ways. He could have neglected them simply because he thought they were irrelevant to his particular philosophical project of showing the body's indispensable role in directly perceiving the world without the further need of a mediating awareness of the body's own feelings to achieve such perception. Besides this weaker thesis of neglect through mere indifference or presumed irrelevance, however, a case can be made that Merleau-Ponty did not really want to affirm the value of consciously thematized bodily feelings because he presumed that such recognition could actually challenge his philosophical project of defending the adequacy of the body's tacit, unreflective mode of perception and because he thought that greater attention to explicit somatic feelings could hamper not only the understanding of our perception, speech, thought, and action, but even the efficiency of their performance.

This stronger thesis of resistance to somatic feelings finds support in Merleau-Ponty's sharp critique of their use as representations in intellectualist theories of perception and behavior, but also in his critique of Bergson's view that our basic lived attention to the world involves our "awareness . . . of 'nascent movements' in our bodies" (*PP* 93/78/91). Moreover, Merleau-Ponty sometimes suggests that explicit attention to the feelings *of* one's body disturbs one's more efficient direct perception and spontaneous action *through* one's body, because such attention to bodily feelings distracts us *to* the body itself rather than directing us effectively through the body to the things with which the body puts us in touch through its silent, nonexplicit, unreflective consciousness. Our body, he insists, wonderfully "guides us" but "only on condition that we stop analyzing it and make use of it" (*S* 97/78). "On the condition that I do not reflect expressly upon it, my consciousness of my body immediately signifies a certain landscape about me" (*S* 111/89). In short, body consciousness effectively guides us in perceiving and navigating the world only when it is a tacit, unthematized, and unreflective sense of bodily self in the world, but *not* when it is a focused, self-conscious awareness of what is being felt *in* rather than *with* our bodily self. Such focused attention to bodily feelings, which allows them not merely to be *had* in silence but also to be reflectively "heard," known, and utilized seems to have no real place in Merleau-Ponty's philosophical project. Whether we interpret this absence as mere neglect or as resistance, it can be properly understood only against the background of Merleau-Ponty's general strategy for rehabilitating the body in philosophy.

II

The key to Merleau-Ponty's strategy is to transform the recognition of the body's weakness into an analysis of its essential, indispensable strength. The pervasive experience of bodily weakness may be philosophy's deepest reason for rejecting the body, for refusing to accept it as defining human identity. Overwhelming in death, somatic impotence is also daily proven in illness, disability, injury, pain, fatigue, and the withering of strength that old age brings. For philosophy, bodily weakness also means cognitive deficiency. As the body's senses distort the truth, so its desires distract the mind from the pursuit of knowledge. The body, moreover, is not a clear object of knowledge. One cannot directly see one's outer bodily surface in its totality, and the body is especially mysterious because its inner workings are always in some way hidden from the subject's view. One cannot directly scan it in the way we often assume we can examine and know our minds through introspection. Regarding the body as at best a mere servant or instrument of the mind, philosophy often portrayed it as a torturous prison of deception, temptation, and pain.

One strategy for defending the body against these familiar attacks from the dominant Platonic–Christian–Cartesian tradition is to challenge them in the way Nietzsche did. Radically inverting the conventional valuations of mind and body, he argued that we can know our bodies better than our minds, that the body can be more powerful than the mind, and that toughening the body can make the mind stronger. Concluding this logic of reversal, Nietzsche insisted that the mind is essentially the instrument of the body, even though it is too often misused (especially by philosophers) as the body's deceptive, torturing prison.[2]

Although appealingly ingenious, this bold strategy leaves most of us unconvinced. The problem is not simply that its radical transvaluation of body over mind goes too much against the grain of philosophy's intellectualist tradition. Nor is it merely that the reversal seems to reinforce the old rigid dualism of mind and body. Somatic deficiency is, unfortunately, such a pervasive part of experience that Nietzsche's inversion of the mind–body hierarchy seems too much like wishful thinking (particularly when we recall his own pathetic bodily impotence). Of course, we should realize that our minds are often impotent to explain discursively what our bodies succeed in performing, and that our minds often fatigue and strike work while our bodies unconsciously continue to function. But despite such mental deficiencies, the range of what we can do or imagine with the power of our minds still seems far superior to what our bodies can actually perform.

In contrast to Nietzsche's hyperbolic somaticism, Merleau-Ponty's argument for the body's philosophical centrality and value is more shrewdly cautious. He embraces the body's essential weaknesses but then shows how these dimensions of ontological and epistemological limitation are a necessary part and parcel of our positive human capacities for having perspectives on objects and for having a world. These limits thus provide the essential focusing frame for all our perception, action, language, and understanding. The limitation the body has in inhabiting a particular place is precisely what gives us an angle of perception or perspective from which objects can be grasped, and the fact that we can change our bodily place allows us to perceive objects from different perspectives and thus constitute them as objective things. Similarly, although the body is deficient in not being able to observe itself wholly and directly (because the eyes' view is fixed forward in one's head, which it therefore can never directly see), this limitation is part and parcel of the body's permanent, privileged position as the defining pivot and ground orientation of observation. Moreover, the apparent limitation that bodily perceptions are vague, corrigible, or ambiguous is reinterpreted as usefully true to a world of experience that is itself ambiguous, vague, and in flux.

This logic of uncovering the strengths entailed in bodily weakness is also captured in Merleau-Ponty's later notion of "the flesh." If the body shares the corruptibility of material things and can be characterized as "flesh" (the traditional pejorative for bodily weakness in Saint Paul and Augustine), then this negative notion of flesh is transformed to praise and explain the body's special capacity to grasp and commune with the world of sensible things since its flesh is itself sensible as well as sensing.

Before I go further into how Merleau-Ponty's strategy of rehabilitating the body leads him to neglect or resist the role of explicitly
conscious somatic sensations, let me make some introductory remarks about such somatic sensations and their use. These are conscious, explicit, experiential perceptions of our body: they include
distinct feelings, observations, visualizations, and other mental representations of our body and its parts, surfaces, and interiors. Their
explicit or represented character distinguishes them clearly from the
kind of primary consciousness that Merleau-Ponty advocates. Although these explicit perceptions include the more sensual feelings
of hunger, pleasure, and pain, the term "sensation" is meant to be
broad enough to cover perceptions of bodily states that are more cognitive and do not have a very strong affective character. Intellectual
focusing or visualization of the feel, movement, orientation, or state
of tension of some part of our body would count as a conscious body
sensation even when it lacks a significant emotional quality or direct
input from the body's external sense organs. Conscious body sensations are therefore not at all opposed to thought but instead are understood as including conscious, experiential body-focused thoughts
and representations.

Among these explicitly conscious bodily sensations, we can distinguish between those that seem dominated by our external senses
(such as seeing, hearing, etc.) and those more governed by propri-
oception such as kinesthetic feelings. I can consciously sense the
position of my hand by looking at it and noting its orientation, but
I can also close my eyes and try to sense its position by kinesthet-
ically feeling (in terms of its felt sensorimotor input) its relation to
my other body parts, to the force of gravity, and to other objects in
my field of experience.

By instructing us about the condition of our bodies, both these
kinds of conscious somatic sensations can help us to perform better.
A slumping batter, by looking at his feet and hands, could discover
that his stance has become too wide or that he is choking up too far
on the bat. A dancer can glance at her feet to see that they are not
properly turned out. Besides these external perceptions, most people have developed enough internal somatic awareness to know (at
least roughly) where their limbs are located. And through systematic
practice of somatic awareness, this proprioceptive awareness can be
significantly improved to provide a sharper and fuller picture of our

body shape, volume, density, and alignment without using our external senses. These two varieties of explicitly conscious somatic sensations constitute only a relatively small portion of our bodily perceptions, which exhibit at least four levels of consciousness.

First, there are perceptions of which I am not really consciously aware at all but that Merleau-Ponty seems to recognize as belonging to our more basic "corporeal intentionality" (S 111/89). When Merleau-Ponty says "that my body is always perceived by me" (PP 107/91/104), he surely must realize that we are sometimes not consciously aware of our bodies. This is not simply when we are concentrating our consciousness on other things, but because we are sometimes simply unconscious *tout court* as in deep, dreamless sleep. Yet even in such sleep, can we not discern a primitive bodily perception of an unconscious variety that recalls Merleau-Ponty's notion of basic "motor intentionality" (PP 128/110/127) or "motility as basic intentionality" (PP 160/137/158–9)? Consider our breathing while we sleep. If an object such as a pillow comes to block our breathing, we will typically turn our heads or push the object away while continuing to sleep, thus unconsciously adjusting our behavior in terms of what is unconsciously grasped.[3]

A more conscious level of bodily perception could be characterized as conscious perception without explicit awareness. In such cases, I am conscious and perceive something, but I do not perceive it as a distinct object of awareness and do not posit, thematize, or predicate it as an object of consciousness. If my reflective attention is then explicitly directed to what is perceived, I could, in turn, perceive it with explicit awareness as a determinate, thematized, or represented object. The introduction of such reflection and explicit consciousness, however, would mean going beyond this level of consciousness, which Merleau-Ponty celebrates as "primary consciousness," describing it as "the life of unreflected consciousness" and "prepredicative life of consciousness" (PP x–xi/xv–xvi/xvii).

Consider two examples of this basic consciousness. Typically, in walking through an open door, I am not explicitly aware of the precise borders of its frame, although the fact that I perceive the borders is shown by the fact that I smoothly navigate the opening, even if it is a completely new doorway and the passage is not very wide. Similarly, I can perceive in some vague sense that I am breathing (in the sense of not feeling any suffocation or breathing impediment) without being explicitly aware of my breathing and its rhythm, style, or quality. In a state of excitement, I may experience shortness of breath without my being distinctly aware that it is shortness of breath I am experiencing. Such shortness of breath is here *not* represented to consciousness as an explicit object of awareness or what Merleau-Ponty sometimes calls a thematized object or representation.

But perception can also be raised to a third level in which we are consciously and explicitly aware of what we perceive. We observe the doorway as a distinct object of perception; we explicitly recognize that we are short of breath or that our fists are clenched. At this level, which Merleau-Ponty regards as the level of mental representations, we can already speak of what I call explicitly conscious somatic sensations. I would also add a fourth layer of still greater consciousness in perception, a level that is very important in many somatic disciplines. Here we are not only conscious of what we perceive as an explicit object of awareness, but we are also conscious of this consciousness, and we focus on our awareness of the object of our awareness through its representation in our minds. If the third level can be called conscious perception with explicit awareness, then the fourth and still more reflective level should be described as self-conscious (or self-reflective) perception with explicit awareness. On this level, we will be aware not simply that we are short of breath but also precisely how we are breathing (say, rapidly and shallowly from the throat or in stifled snorts through the nose, rather than deeply from the diaphragm). We will be focused on our awareness of how our fists are clenched in terms of both tightness and orientation of thumb and fingers in the clenching.

Merleau-Ponty's philosophy poses a challenge to the value of these two higher (or representational) levels of conscious somatic perception. It does so not merely by celebrating the primacy and sufficiency of nonreflective "primary consciousness" but also by specific arguments against body observation and the use of kinesthetic sensations and body representations. An adequate defense of somatic reflexivity must do justice to the details of this challenge.

III

One principal aim in Merleau-Ponty's phenomenology is to restore our robust contact with "the things themselves" (*PP* iii/ix/ix–x) and our "lived world" (*monde vécu*) as they "are first given to us" (*PP* 69/57/66). This means renewing our connection with perceptions and experience that precede knowledge and reflection, "to return to that world which precedes knowledge, of which knowledge always *speaks*" (*PP* iii/ix/x). Phenomenology is therefore "a philosophy for which the world is always 'already there' before reflection begins – as an inalienable presence; and all its efforts are concentrated upon reachieving a direct and primitive contact with the world, and endowing that contact with a philosophical status" (*PP* i/vii/vii).

Philosophy is perforce a reflective act, but phenomenology's "radical reflection amounts to a consciousness of its own dependence on an unreflective life which is its initial situation, unchanging, given once and for all" (*PP* ix/xiv/xvi). "It tries to give a direct description of our experience as it is" in our basic prereflective state (*PP* i/vii/vii), pursuing "the ambition to make reflection emulate the unreflective life of consciousness" (*PP* xi/xvi/xvii). Such philosophy "is not the reflection of a preexisting truth" (*PP* xv/xx/xxiii), but rather an effort "of describing our perception of the world as that upon which our idea of truth is forever based" (*PP* xi/xvi/xviii); it aims at "relearning to look at the world" with this direct, prereflective perception and to act in it accordingly (*PP* xvi/xx/xxiii). Such primary perception and prereflective consciousness are embodied in an operative intentionality that is characterized by immediacy and spontaneity (*S* 111–16/89–94). "Thus the proper function of a phenomenological philosophy" would be "to establish itself definitively in the order of instructive spontaneity" (*S* 121/97); and this basic, embodied "order of instructive spontaneity" constitutes a worldly wisdom and competence that all people share. Merleau-Ponty therefore concludes that the special knowledge of the philosopher

is only a way of putting into words what every man knows well.... These mysteries are in each of us as in him. What does he say of the relation between the soul and the body, except what is known by all men who make their souls and bodies, their good and their evil, go together in one piece? (*EP* 63/63)

Three crucial themes resound in such passages. First, Merleau-Ponty affirms the existence and restoration of a primordial perception or experience of the world that lies below the level of reflective or thematized consciousness and beneath all language and concepts but that is nevertheless perfectly efficacious for our fundamental needs and also provides the basic ground for higher reflection. This nondiscursive level of intentionality is hailed as the "silent consciousness" of "primary subjectivity" and "primordial expression." Second, he urges the recognition and recovery of *spontaneity* that is characteristic of such primordial perception and expression. Third is the assumption that philosophy should concentrate on conditions of human existence that are ontologically given as basic, universal, and permanent. Hence, the study of perception and the mind–body relationship should be in terms of what is "unchanging, given once and for all" and "known by all men" (and presumably all women) or at least all men and women deemed "normal."[4]

Even the first theme alone would discourage Merleau-Ponty from sympathetic attention to explicitly conscious bodily sensations. Not only do those sensations go beyond what he wishes to affirm as prereflective consciousness, they also are typically used by scientific and philosophical thought to usurp the explanatory role and deny the existence of the primary perception or consciousness that Merleau-Ponty so ardently advocates. This primordial consciousness has been forgotten, he argues, because reflective thought assumed such consciousness was inadequate to perform the everyday tasks of perception, action, and speech; so it instead explained our everyday behavior as relying on "representations," whether they be the neural representations of mechanistic physiology or the psychic representations of intellectualist philosophy and psychology. Merleau-Ponty's arguments are therefore devoted to showing that the representational explanations offered by science and philosophy are neither necessary nor accurate accounts of how we perceive, act, and express ourselves in normal everyday behavior (and also in more abnormal cases such as "abstract movement" and "phantom limb" experience).

His excellent criticisms of the various representational explanations are too many and detailed to rehearse here, but they share a core strategy of argument. Representational explanations are shown to misconstrue the basic experience or behavior they seek to explain by describing it from the start in terms of their own products of reflective analysis. Furthermore, such explanations are shown to be inadequate because they rely in some crucial way on some aspect of experience that they do not actually explain but that can be explained by primordial perception. For instance, to account for my successful passing through the threshold of an open door, a representational explanation would describe and explicate my experience in terms of my visual representations of the open space, the surrounding door frame, and of my conscious kinesthetic sensations of my body's width and orientation of movement. But normally I do not have any such conscious representations when passing through a door. These representations, Merleau-Ponty argues (much as William James and John Dewey did before him), are reflective, theoretical, explanatory notions that are falsely read back or imposed onto original experience.[5] Even if I did have these various visual and kinesthetic explanatory representations, they cannot themselves explain my experience because they cannot explain how they are properly sorted out from other, irrelevant representations and synthesized together in successful perception and action. Instead, claims Merleau-Ponty, it is our basic unreflective intentionality that silently and spontaneously organizes our world of perception without the need of distinct perceptual representations and without any explicitly conscious deliberation.

Although this basic level of intentionality is ubiquitous, its very pervasiveness and unobtrusive silence conceal its prevailing presence. In the same way, its elemental, common, and spontaneous character obscures its extraordinary effectiveness. To highlight the astounding powers of this unreflective level of perception, action, and speech, Merleau-Ponty describes it in terms of the marvelous, miraculous, and even the magical. The "body as spontaneous expression" is like the unknowing "marvel of style" in artistic genius.

As the artist makes his style radiate into the very fibers of the material he is working on, I move my body without even knowing which muscles and nerve paths should intervene, nor where I must look for the instruments of that action. I want to go over there, and here I am, without having entered into the inhuman secret of the bodily mechanism or having adjusted that mechanism to the givens of the problem. . . . I look at the goal, I am drawn by it, and the bodily apparatus does what must be done in order for me to be there. For me, everything happens in the human world of perception and gesture, but my "geographical" or "physical" body submits to the demands of this little drama which does not cease to arouse a thousand natural marvels in it. Just my glance toward the goal already has its own miracles. (S 83/66)

If representations of body parts and processes are negatively described as mechanistically inhuman, the unreflective use of the body not only is linked to the human and the artistic, but also suggests – through its miraculous marvels – the divine. In a section of *Phenomenology of Perception* in which Merleau-Ponty is criticizing the use of kinesthetic sensations, he likewise insists on the miraculous nature of bodily intentionality, describing its immediate, intuitive efficacy as "magical." There is no need to think of what I am doing or know where I am in space, I just move my body "directly" and spontaneously achieve the intended result without even consciously representing my intention. "The relations between my decision and my body are, in movement, magic ones" (*PP* 110/94/108).

Why should a secular philosopher hail our ordinary body intentionality in terms of miracle and magic? True, our mundane bodily competence can, from certain perspectives, provoke genuine wonder. But emphasizing the miraculous or magical also serves other functions in Merleau-Ponty's somatic agenda. To celebrate the primal *mystery* of spontaneous body proficiency is a strong antidote to the urge to explain our bodily perception and action through representational means, precisely the kind of explanation that has always obscured the basic somatic intentionality Merleau-Ponty rightly regards as primary. Moreover, celebration of the body's miraculous mystery deftly serves Merleau-Ponty's project of foregrounding the body's value while explaining it as silent, structuring, concealed background. "Bodily space... is the darkness needed in the theatre to show up the performance, the background of somnolence or reserve of vague power against which the gesture and its aim stand out." More generally, "one's own body is the third term, always tacitly understood, in the figure–ground structure, and every figure stands out against the double horizon of external and bodily space" (*PP* 117/100–1/115). The body is also mysterious as a locus of "impersonal" existence, beneath and hidden from normal selfhood. It is "the place where life hides away" from the world, where I retreat from my interest in observing or acting in the world, "lose myself in some pleasure or pain, and shut myself in this anonymous life which subtends my personal one. But precisely because my body can shut itself off from the world, it is also what opens me out upon the world and places me in a situation there" (*PP* 192/164–5/190–1).

Merleau-Ponty may also have a more personal reason for advocating the hidden mystery of the body: a deep respect of its need for some privacy to compensate for its function of giving us a world by exposing us to that world, by being not only sentient but part of the sensible flesh of the world. Some of his remarks express a strong sense of corporeal modesty. "Usually man does not show his body, and, when he does, it is either nervously or with an intention to fascinate" (*PP* 194/166/193). And when Merleau-Ponty wants to exemplify "those extreme situations" in which one becomes aware of one's basic bodily intentionality, when one grasps that "tacit *cogito*, the presence of oneself to oneself ... because it is under threat," the threatening situations that he gives are "the dread of death or of another's gaze upon me" (*PP* 462/404/470).

Merleau-Ponty's notion of bodily intentionality defies philosophical tradition by granting the body a kind of subjectivity instead of treating it as mere object or mechanism. But he is still more radical in extending the range of unreflective somatic subjectivity far beyond our basic bodily movements and sense perceptions to the higher operations of speech and thought that constitute philosophy's cherished realm of *logos*. Here again, the efficacy of spontaneous body intentionality replaces conscious representations as the explanation of our behavior:

thought, in the speaking subject, is not a representation.... The orator does not think before speaking, nor even while speaking; his speech is his thought.... What we have said earlier about "the representation of movement" must be repeated concerning the verbal image: I do not need to visualize external space and my own body in order to move one within the other. It is enough that they exist for me, and that they form a certain field of action spread around me. In the same way I do not need to visualize the word in order to know and pronounce it. It is enough that I possess its articulatory and acoustic style as one of the modulations, one of the possible uses of my body. I reach back for the word as my hand reaches toward the part of my body which is being pricked; the word has a certain location in my linguistic world, and is part of my equipment. (*PP* 209–10/180/209–10)

In short, just as "my corporeal intending of the object of my surroundings is implicit and presupposes no thematization or 'representation' of my body or milieu," so "Signification arouses speech as the world arouses my body – by a mute presence which awakens my intentions without deploying itself before them. . . . The reason why the thematization of the signified does not precede speech is that it is the result of it" (S 112–13/89–90).

Merleau-Ponty likewise highlights the marvelous mystery of this silent, yet spontaneously flowing somatic power of expression:

> like the functioning of the body, that of words or paintings remains obscure to me. The words, lines, and colors which express me . . . are torn from me by what I want to say as my gestures are by what I want to do . . . [with] a spontaneity which will not tolerate any commands, not even those which I would like to give to myself. (S 94/75)

The mysterious efficacy of our spontaneous intentionality is surely impressive, but it alone cannot explain all our ordinary powers of movement and perception, speech and thought. I can jump in the water and spontaneously move my arms and legs, but I will not reach my goal unless I first learned how to swim. I can hear a song in Japanese and spontaneously try to sing along, but I will fail unless I have first learned enough words of that language. Many things we now spontaneously do (or understand) were once beyond our repertoire of unreflective performance. They had to be learned, as Merleau-Ponty realizes. But how? One way to explain at least part of this learning would be by the use of various kinds of representations (images, symbols, propositions, etc.) that our consciousness could focus on and deploy. But Merleau-Ponty seems too critical of representations to accept this option.

Instead, he explains this learning entirely in terms of the automatic acquisition of body habits through unreflective motor conditioning or somatic sedimentation. "The acquisition of a habit [including our habits of speech and thought] is indeed the grasping of a significance, but it is the motor grasping of a motor significance"; "it is the body which 'understands' in the acquisition of habit." There is no need for explicitly conscious thought to "get used to a hat, a car or a stick," or to master a keyboard; we simply "incorporate them into the bulk of our own body" through unreflective processes of motor sedimentation and our own spontaneous corporeal sense of self (PP 167–9/143–4/165–7). The lived body, for Merleau-Ponty, thus has two layers: beneath the spontaneous body of the moment, there is "the habit-body" of sedimentation (PP 97/82/95, 150–1/129–30/149–50).

Affirming the prevalence, importance, and intelligence of unreflective habit in our action, speech, and thought, I also share Merleau-Ponty's recognition of habit's somatic base. Both themes are central to the pragmatist tradition of James and Dewey that inspires my work in somatic philosophy. But there are troubling limits to the efficacy of unreflective habits, even on the level of basic bodily actions. Unreflectively, we can acquire bad habits just as easily as good ones. (This seems especially likely if we accept the premise that the institutions and technologies governing our lives through regimes of biopower inculcate habits of body and mind that aim to keep us in submission.) Once bad habits are acquired, how do we correct them? We cannot simply rely on sedimented habit to correct them, since the sedimented habits are precisely what is wrong. Nor can we rely on the unreflective somatic spontaneity of the moment because that is already tainted with the trace of the unwanted sedimentations and thus most likely to continue to misdirect us.[6]

This is why various disciplines of body training typically invoke representations and self-conscious somatic focusing in order to correct our faulty self-perception and use of our embodied selves. From ancient Asian practices of meditation to modern systems such as the Alexander Technique and Feldenkrais Method, explicit awareness and conscious control are key, as is the use of representations or visualizations. These disciplines do not aim to erase the crucial level of unreflective behavior by the (impossible) effort of making us explicitly conscious of all our perception and action. They simply seek to improve unreflective behavior that hinders our experience and performance. In order to effect this improvement, however, the unreflective action or habit must be brought into conscious critical reflection (although only for a limited time) so that it can be grasped and worked on more precisely. Besides these therapeutic goals, disciplines of somatic reflection also enhance our experience with the added richness, discoveries, and pleasures that heightened awareness can bring.

In advocating the unreflective lived body in opposition to the abstract representations of scientific explanation, Merleau-Ponty creates a polarization of "lived experience" versus "representations" that neglects the fruitful option of "lived corporeal reflection," that is, concrete but representational and reflective body consciousness. This polarizing dichotomy is paralleled by another misleading binary contrast that pervades his account of behavior. On the one hand, he describes the performance of "normal" people whose somatic sense and functioning is totally smooth, spontaneous, and unproblematic. His contrasting category of discussion concerns the abnormally incapacitated: patients such as Schneider who exhibit pathological dysfunction and are usually suffering from serious neurological injury (such as brain lesions) or grave psychological trauma.

This simple polarity obscures the fact that most of us so-called normal, fully functional people suffer from various incapacities and malfunctions that are mild in nature but that still impair performance. Such deficiencies relate not only to perceptions or actions we cannot perform (though we are anatomically equipped to do so) but also to what we do succeed in performing but could perform more successfully or with greater ease and grace. Merleau-Ponty implies that if we are not pathologically impaired like Schneider and other neurologically diseased individuals, then our unreflective body sense is fully accurate and miraculously functional. For Merleau-Ponty, just as my spontaneous bodily movements seem "magical" in their precision and efficacy, so my immediate knowledge of my body and the orientation of its parts seems flawlessly complete. "I am in undivided possession of it and I know where each of my limbs is through a body image in which all are included" (PP 114/98/112–13).

While sharing Merleau-Ponty's deep appreciation of our "normal" spontaneous bodily sense, I think we should also recognize that this sense is often painfully inaccurate and dysfunctional.[7] I may think I am keeping my head down when swinging a golf club, but an observer will easily see I do not. I may believe I am sitting straight when my head and torso are instead tilted. If asked to bend at the ribs, many of us will really bend at the waist and think that we are complying with the instructions. In trying to stand tall, people usually think they are lengthening their spines when they are in fact contracting them. Disciplines of somatic education deploy exercises of representational awareness to treat such problems of misperception and misuse of our bodies in the spontaneous and habitual behavior that Merleau-Ponty identifies as primal and celebrates as miraculously flawless in normal performance.

Although he exaggerates our unreflective somatic proficiency, it is hard to condemn Merleau-Ponty for overestimating the body's powers. For he also stresses the body's distinctive weakness in other ways, including its grave cognitive limitations of self-observation. Indeed, his insistence on the miraculous efficacy of the spontaneous body (and on the consequent irrelevance of representational thought for enhancing our somatic performance) helps keep the body weaker than it could be by implying that there is no reason or way to improve its performance through the use of representations. Conversely, his compelling defense of bodily limitations as structurally essential to our human capacities could also discourage efforts to overcome entrenched somatic impediments, for fear that such efforts would ultimately weaken us by disturbing the fundamental structuring handicaps on which our powers in fact rely.

This suggests another reason why Merleau-Ponty might resist the contribution of reflective somatic consciousness and its bodily representations. Disciplines of explicit somatic awareness are aimed not simply at *knowing* our bodily condition and habits but at *changing* them. Even awareness alone can (to some extent) change our somatic experience and relation to our bodies. Merleau-Ponty acknowledges this when he argues that reflective thinking cannot really capture our primordial unreflective experience because the representations of such thinking inevitably change our basic experience by introducing categories and conceptual distinctions that were not originally given there. He especially condemns the posits of representational explanations of experience (whether mechanistic or rationalistic) for generating "the dualism of consciousness and body" (*PP* 162n/138n/160n), while blinding us to the unity of primordial perception.

However, the fact that representational explanations do not adequately explain our primordial perception does not imply they are not useful for other purposes, such as improving our habits. Change of habits can in turn change our spontaneous perceptions, whose unity and spontaneity will be restored once the new, improved habit becomes entrenched. In short, we can affirm the unity and unreflective quality of primary perceptual experience while endorsing self-reflective body consciousness that deploys representational thought for both the reconstruction of better primary experience and the intrinsic rewards of reflective somatic consciousness.[8]

In modifying one's relation to one's body, somatic disciplines of reflection (like other forms of body training) also highlight differences between people. Different individuals often have very different styles of body use (and misuse). Moreover, what one learns through sustained training in somatic awareness is not simply "what every man knows well" through the immediate grasp of primordial perception and unthinking habit. Many of us do not know (and may never learn) what it is like to feel the location of each vertebra and rib proprioceptively without touching them with our hands. Nor does everyone recognize, when he or she is reaching out for something, precisely which part of his or her body (fingers, arm, shoulder, pelvis, or head) initiates the movement.

If philosophy's goal is simply to clarify and renew the universal and permanent in our embodied human condition by restoring our recognition of primordial experience and its ontological givens, then the whole project of improving one's somatic perception and functioning through self-conscious reflection will be dismissed as a philosophical irrelevancy. Worse, it will be seen as a threatening change and distraction from the originary level of perception that is celebrated as philosophy's ultimate ground, focus, and goal. Indeed, to recognize differences and changes in the primary experience of different people might even seem to challenge the very idea of a fixed and universal primordial perception. Merleau-Ponty's commitment to a fixed, universal phenomenological ontology based on primordial perception thus provides further reason for dismissing the value of explicit somatic consciousness. Being more concerned with individual differences and contingencies, with future-looking change and reconstruction, with pluralities of practice that can be used by individuals and groups for improving on primary experience, pragmatism is more receptive to reflective somatic consciousness and its disciplinary uses for philosophy. If William James made somatic introspection central to his research in philosophy of mind, John Dewey affirmed the use of heightened, reflective body consciousness to improve our self-knowledge and performance.

IV

Given his philosophical agenda, Merleau-Ponty has adequate motives for neglecting or even resisting reflective body consciousness. But do they constitute compelling arguments, or should we instead conclude that Merleau-Ponty's project of body-centered phenomenology and fundamental ontology could be usefully supplemented by a greater recognition of the functions and value of reflective body consciousness? We can explore this question by re-casting our discussion of Merleau-Ponty's motives into the following seven lines of argument.

(1) If attention to reflective somatic consciousness and its bodily representations obscures our recognition of primary unreflective embodied perception and its primary importance, then reflective somatic consciousness should be resisted. This argument has a prob-lematic ambiguity in its initial premise. Our reflective somatic con-sciousness does distract us for a time from unreflective perception (attention to anything inevitably means a momentary obscuring of some other things). But such consciousness need not always or per-manently do this, especially because this consciousness is not (nor is meant to be) constantly sustained. The use of somatic reflection in body disciplines of awareness is not meant to permanently replace but to *improve* unreflective perception and habit by putting them into temporary focus so they can be retrained. If such body disciplines can affirm the primacy of unreflective behavior while also endors-ing the need for conscious representations to monitor and correct it, then so can somatic philosophy. Besides, if we adopt Merleau-Ponty's claim that experience always depends on the complementarity of figure–ground contrast, we could then argue that any real appreci-ation of unreflective perception depends on its distinctive contrast from reflective consciousness, just as the latter clearly relies on the background of the former.

(2) Merleau-Ponty rightly maintains that reflective consciousness and somatic representations are not only unnecessary but inaccu-rate for explaining our ordinary perception and behavior which are usually unreflective. From that premise, one might infer that rep-resentational somatic awareness is a misleading irrelevancy. But this conclusion does not follow; first, because there is more to explain in human experience than our unproblematic unreflective perceptions and acts. Representational somatic consciousness can help us with respect to cases in which spontaneous competencies break down and where unreflective habits are targeted for correc-tion. Moreover, explanatory power is not the only criterion of value. Reflective somatic consciousness and representations can be useful not for explaining ordinary experience, but for altering and supple-menting it.

(3) This prompts a further argument. If the changes that somatic reflection introduces into experience are essentially undesirable, then, on pragmatic grounds, it should be discouraged. Merleau-Ponty compellingly shows how reflection's representations form the core of both mechanistic and intellectualist accounts of behavior that promote body–mind dualism. Reflective somatic consciousness thus seems condemned for engendering a falsely fragmented view of experience, a view that eventually infects our experience itself and blinds us to the unreflective unity of primary perception.[9] But the misuse of representational somatic thinking in *some* explanatory contexts does not entail its global condemnation. Likewise, to affirm the value of representational somatic consciousness is not to deny the existence, value, or even primacy of the unreflective. Such reflection, I repeat, can serve alongside somatic spontaneity as a useful supplement and corrective.

(4) Merleau-Ponty prizes the body's mystery and limitations as essential to its productive functioning. He repeatedly touts the miraculous way we perform our actions without any conscious reflection at all. Could he, then, argue pragmatically that reflective somatic consciousness should be resisted because it endangers such mystery and "effective" weakness? This argument rests on a confusion. The claim that we can do something effectively *without* explicit or representational consciousness does not imply that we cannot also do it *with* such consciousness and that such consciousness cannot improve our performance. In any case, plenty of mystery and limitation will always remain. Somatic reflection could never claim to provide our bodies with total transparency or perfect power because our mortality, frailty, and perspectival situatedness preclude this. The fact that certain basic bodily limits can never be overcome is not, however, a compelling argument against trying to expand, to some extent, our somatic powers through reflection and explicit conscious direction.

(5) Here we face a further argument. Somatic reflection impairs our somatic performance by disrupting spontaneous action based on unreflective habit. Unreflective acts are quicker and easier than deliberatively executed behavior. Moreover, by not engaging explicit consciousness, such unreflective action enables better focusing of consciousness on the targets at which action is aimed. A well-trained batter can hit the ball better when he is not reflecting on the tension in his knees and wrists or imagining the pelvic movement in his

swing. Not having to think of such things, he can better concentrate on seeing and reacting to the sinking fastball he must hit. Somatic self-reflection would here prevent him from reacting in time. Deliberative thinking can often ruin the spontaneous flow and efficacy of action. If we try to visualize each word as we speak, our speech will be slow and halting; we may even forget what we wanted to say. In sexual behavior, if one thinks too much about what is happening in one's own body while visualizing to oneself what must happen for things to go right, there is much more chance that something will go wrong. Such cases show that explicit somatic consciousness can often be more of a problem than a solution. The conclusion, however, is not to reject such consciousness altogether, but rather to reflect more carefully on the ways it can be disciplined and deployed for the different contexts and ends in which it can be most helpful. That there can sometimes be too much of a good thing is also true for somatic awareness.

(6) Describing the body as '*la cachette de la vie*' ("the place where life hides away" in basic impersonal existence), Merleau-Ponty suggests yet another argument against somatic reflection. Explicit concentration on body feelings entails a withdrawal from the outer world of action, and this change of focus impairs the quality of our perception and action in that world: "when I become absorbed in my body, my eyes present me with no more than the perceptible outer covering of things and of other people, things themselves take on unreality, behavior degenerates into the absurd." To "become absorbed in the experience of my body and in the solitude of sensations" is thus a disturbing danger from which we are barely protected by the fact that our sense organs and habits are always working to engage us in the outer world of life. Absorbed somatic reflection thus risks losing the world, but also one's self, because the self is defined by our engagement with the world (*PP* 192–3/164–5/190–2).

Merleau-Ponty is right that an intense focus on somatic sensations can temporarily disorient our ordinary perspectives, disturbing our customary involvement with the world and our ordinary sense of self. Nevertheless, it is wrong to conclude that absorption in bodily feelings is essentially a primitive impersonal level of awareness, beneath the notions of both self and world, and thus confined to what he calls "the anonymous alertness of the senses" (*PP* 191/164/190). One can be *self-consciously* absorbed in one's bodily feelings;

somatic self-consciousness involves a reflective awareness that one's self is experiencing the sensations on which one's attention is focused. Of course, this "turning in" of bodily consciousness on itself involves to some extent withdrawing attention from the outside world, though that world always makes its presence somehow felt. A pure bodily feeling is an abstraction. One cannot feel oneself somatically without also feeling something of the external world. (If I lie down, close my eyes, and concentrate on scanning my body, I will feel the way it makes contact with the floor and sense the volumes between my limbs, just as I will recognize that it is I who is lying on the floor and focusing on my bodily feelings.) In any case, if somaesthetics' deflection of attention to our bodily consciousness involves a temporary retreat from the world of action, this retreat can greatly advance our self-knowledge and self-use so that we will return to the world as more skillful observers and agents. It is the somatic logic of *reculer pour mieux sauter*.

Consider an example. If one wants to look over one's shoulder to see something behind one's back, most people will spontaneously lower their shoulder while turning their head. This seems logical but is skeletally wrong; dropping the shoulder constrains the rib and chest area and thus greatly limits the spine's range of rotation, which is what really enables us to see behind ourselves. By withdrawing our attention momentarily from the world behind us and by instead focusing attentively on the alignment of our body parts in rotating the head and spine, we can learn how to turn better and see more, creating a new habit that eventually will be unreflectively performed.

(7) Merleau-Ponty's most radical argument against reflective somatic observation is that one simply cannot observe one's own body at all, because it is the permanent, invariant perspective through which we observe other things. Unlike ordinary objects, the body "defies exploration and is always presented to me from the same angle. . . . To say that it is always near me, always there for me, is to say that it is never really in front of me, that I cannot array it before my eyes, that it remains marginal to all my perceptions, that it is *with* me" (*PP* 106/90/104). I cannot change my perspective with respect to my body as I can with external objects. "I observe external objects with my body, I handle them, examine them, walk round them, but my body itself is a thing which I do not observe: in order to be able to do so, I should need the use of a second body" (*PP* 107/91/104). "I

am always on the same side of my body; it presents itself to me in one invariable perspective" (*VI* 194/148).

It is certainly true that we cannot observe our own lived bodies in exactly the same way we do external objects, since our bodies are precisely the tools through which we observe anything, and since one cannot entirely array one's body before one's eyes (because our eyes themselves are part of the body). It does not follow from these points, however, that we cannot observe our lived bodies in important ways. First, it is wrong to identify somatic observation narrowly with being "before my eyes." Although we cannot see our eyes without the use of a mirroring device, we can, with concentration, observe directly how they feel from the inside in terms of muscle tension, volume, and movement, even while we are using them to see. We can also observe our closed eyes by touching them from the outside with our hands. This shows, moreover, that our perspective with respect to our bodies is not entirely fixed and invariant. We can examine them in terms of different sense modalities; and even if we use a single modality, we can scan the body from different angles and with different perspectives of focus. Lying on the floor with my eyes closed and relying only on proprioceptive sensing, I can scan my body from head to foot or vice versa, in terms of my alignment of limbs or my sense of body volume, or from the perspective of the pressure of my different body parts on the floor or of their distance from the floor. Of course, if we eschew somatic reflection, then we are far more likely to have an invariant perspective on our bodies – that of primitive, unfocused experience and unreflective habit, precisely the kind of primordial unthematized perception that Merleau-Ponty champions.

Merleau-Ponty's notion of bodily subjectivity might provide a last-ditch argument against the possibility of observing one's own lived body. In his critique of "double sensations" (*PP* 109/93/106), he insists that if our body is the observing subject of experience, then it cannot at the same time be the object of observation. Hence, we cannot really observe our perceiving bodies, just as we cannot use our left hand to feel our right hand (as an object) while the right hand is feeling an object. Even in his later "The Intertwining – The Chiasm," in which Merleau-Ponty insists on the body's essential "reversibility"of being both sensing and sensed as crucial to our ability to grasp the world, he strongly cautions that this reversibility of being both observer and observed, although "always imminent," is "never realized in fact" through complete simultaneity or exact "coincidence." One cannot at the very same time feel one's hand as touching and touched, one's voice speaking and heard (*VI* 194/147–8). In short, one cannot simultaneously experience one's body as both subject and object. So if the lived body is always the observing subject, then it can never be observed as an object. Besides, as G. H. Mead claims, the observing "I" cannot directly grasp itself in immediate experience, because by the time it tries to catch itself, it has already become an objectified "me" for the grasping "I" of the next moment.

Such arguments can be met in a few ways. First, given the essential vagueness of the notion of subjective simultaneity, we could argue that, practically speaking, one *can* simultaneously have experiences of touching and being touched, of feeling our voices from inside while hearing them from without, even if the prime focus of our attention may sometimes vacillate rapidly between the two perspectives within the very short duration of time we phenomenologically identify as the present and which, as James long ago recognized, is always a "specious present," involving memory of an immediate past.[10] Part of what seems to disrupt the experience of simultaneous perception of our bodies as both sensing and being sensed is simply the fact that the polarity of perspectives is imposed on our experience by the binary framing of the thought-experiment, a case in which philosophy's reflection "prejudges what it will find" (*VI* 172/130). Moreover, even if it is a fact that most experimental subjects cannot feel their bodies feeling, this may simply be due to their undeveloped capacities of somatic reflection and attentiveness.

Indeed, even if one cannot simultaneously experience one's own body as feeling and as felt, this does not entail that one can never observe it, just as the putative fact that one cannot simultaneously experience one's own mind as pure active thinking (i.e., a transcendental subject) and as something thought (i.e., an empirical subject) does not entail that we cannot observe our mental life. To treat the lived body as a subject does not require treating it *only* as a purely transcendental subject that cannot also be observed as an empirical one. To do so would vitiate the essential reversibility of the perceiving sentience and the perceived sensible that enables Merleau-Ponty to portray the body as the "flesh" that grounds our connection to the world. The "grammatical" distinction between the body as subject of experience and as object of experience is useful in reminding us that we can never reach a full transparency of our bodily intentionality. There will always be some dimensions of our bodily feelings that will be actively structuring the focus of our efforts of reflective somatic awareness and thus will not be themselves the object of that awareness or the focus of consciousness. There also will always be the possibility of introspective error through failure of memory or misinterpretation. Nor should we desire simultaneous reflexive consciousness of all our bodily feelings. But the pragmatic distinction between the perceiving "I" and the perceived "me" should not be erected into an insurmountable epistemological obstacle to observing the lived body within the realm provided by the specious present and short-term memory of the immediate past.[11]

Ultimately, we can also challenge Merleau-Ponty's argument against bodily self-observation by simply reminding ourselves that such observation (even if it is merely noticing our discomforts, pains, and pleasures) forms part of our ordinary experience. Only the introduction of abstract philosophical reflection could ever lead us to deny its possibility. If we take our pretheoretic commonsense experience seriously, as Merleau-Ponty urges us to do, then we should reject the conclusion that we can never observe our own lived bodies, and we could therefore urge that his philosophical project be complemented by greater recognition of reflective somatic consciousness.

V

Given the insufficiency of these reconstructed arguments, Merleau-Ponty's neglect of or resistance to explicit somatic consciousness can be justified only in terms of his deeper philosophical aims and presumptions. Prominent here is his desire for philosophy to bring us back to a pure, primordial state of unified experience that has "not yet been 'worked over'" or splintered by "instruments [of] reflection" and thus can "offer us all at once, pell-mell, both 'subject' and 'object,' both existence and essence," both mind and body (*VI* 172/130). Such yearning for a return to prereflective unity suggests dissatisfaction with the fragmentation that reflective consciousness and representational thinking have introduced into our experience as embodied subjects. Philosophy can try to remedy this problem in two different ways. First, there is the therapy of mere theory.

Philosophical reflection can be used to affirm the unity and adequacy of unreflective body behavior, to urge that we concentrate on this unreflective unity, while rejecting somatic reflection and representational somatic consciousness as intrinsically unnecessary and misleading. Here, the very mystery of unreflective bodily actions is prized as an enabling cognitive weakness that proves superior to performances directed by representational reflection. A second way to remedy dissatisfaction with our experience as embodied subjects moves beyond mere abstract theory by also actively developing our powers of reflective somatic consciousness so that we can achieve a higher unity of experience on the reflective level and thus acquire better means to correct inadequacies of our unreflective bodily habits. Merleau-Ponty urges the first way; pragmatist somatic theory urges the second, while recognizing the primacy of unreflective somatic experience and habit.

The first way – the way of pure intellect – reflects Merleau-Ponty's basic vision of philosophy as drawing its theoretical strength from its weakness of action. "The limping of philosophy is its virtue," he writes, in contrasting the philosopher with the man of action by contrasting "that which understands and that which chooses." "The philosopher of action is perhaps the farthest removed from action, for to speak of action with depth and rigor is to say that one does not desire to act" (*EP* 59–61/59–61). Should the philosopher of the , then, be the farthest removed from her own lived body, because s overwhelmingly absorbed in struggling with all her mind to yze and champion the body's role?

This is an unfortunate conclusion, but it stubbornly asserts itself in the common complaint that most contemporary body philosophy seems to ignore or dissolve the actual active body within a labyrinth of metaphysical, social, and gender theories. Despite their valuable insights, such theories fall short of considering practical methods for individuals to improve their somatic consciousness and functioning. Merleau-Ponty's body philosophy exemplifies this problem by devoting intense theoretical reflection to the value of unreflective bodily subjectivity, but dismissing the use of somatic reflection to improve that subjectivity in perception and action. As opposed to men of action, the philosopher, says Merleau-Ponty, is never fully engaged in a practical "serious" way in what he affirms. Even in the causes to which he is faithful, we find that "in his assent something massive and carnal is lacking. He is not altogether a real being" (*EP* 60/60).

Lacking in Merleau-Ponty's superb advocacy of the body's philosophical importance is a robust sense of the real body as a site for practical disciplines of conscious reflection that aim at reconstructing somatic perception and performance to achieve more rewarding experience and action. Pragmatism offers a complementary philosophical perspective that is friendlier to full-bodied engagement in practical efforts of somatic awareness. It aims at generating better experience for the future rather than trying to recapture the lost perceptual unity of a primordial past, a "return to that world which precedes knowledge" (*PP* iii/ix/x).

If it seems possible to combine this pragmatist reconstructive dimension of somatic theory with Merleau-Ponty's basic philosophical insights about the lived body and the primacy of unreflective perception, this is partly because Merleau-Ponty's philosophy has its own pragmatic flavor. Insisting that consciousness is primarily an "I can" rather than an "I think" (*PP* 160/137/159), he also recognized that philosophy is more than impersonal theory but also a personal way of life. If he urged philosophy as the way to recover a lost primordial unity of unreflective experience, if he defined philosophy as "the Utopia of possession at a distance" (*EP* 58/58)* – perhaps the recapture of that unreflective past from the distance of present reflection, were there reasons in his life that helped determine this philosophical yearning? Was there also a personal yearning for a utopian past unity – primitive, spontaneous, and unreflective – and recoverable only by reflection from a distance, if at all?

We know very little of the private life of Merleau-Ponty, but there is certainly evidence that he had such a yearning for "this paradise lost." "One day in 1947, Merleau told me that he had never recovered from an incomparable childhood,"[12] writes his close friend Jean-Paul Sartre.

Everything had been too wonderful, too soon. The form of Nature which first enveloped him was the Mother Goddess, his own mother, whose eyes made him see what he saw.... By her and through her, he lived this

---

* The sentence containing this phrase appears in the 1953 edition of *Éloge de la philosophie*, but not in the 1960 edition, *Éloge de la philosophie et autres essais*, or thereafter. – Eds.

"intersubjectivity of immanence" which he has often described and which causes us to discover our "spontaneity" through another.[13]

With childhood gone, "one of his most constant characteristics was to seek everywhere for lost immanence."[14] His mother, Sartre explains, was essential to this utopic "hope of reconquering" this sense of childhood spontaneity and "immediate accord" with things. "Through her, it was preserved – out of reach, but alive." When she died in 1952, Sartre recounts, Merleau-Ponty was devastated and essentially "became a recluse."[15] There remained the consolation of philosophy: the ontology of the porous intertwining of the visible and the invisible, the immanent and the transcendent, presence and absence, the chiasm of what is and what is not, in the endless flow of continuous becoming.

NOTES

1. Introspective attention to bodily feelings is a central feature of William James's famous *Principles of Psychology*, and it plays a large role in his explanation of the self, the emotions, and the will. Such emphasis on bodily feelings forms the focus of Wittgenstein's critique of James's explanation of these concepts, although Wittgenstein allows other uses for bodily feelings. For a comparative discussion of James's and Wittgenstein's treatment of such bodily feelings, see my "Wittgenstein on Bodily Feelings: Explanation and Melioration in Philosophy of Mind, Art, and Politics." John Dewey was a fervent advocate and student of the Alexander Technique, a method of somatic education and therapy that is based on heightening reflective awareness of our bodily states and feelings. Alexander's emphasis on conscious constructive control of the self through reflective awareness of one's somatic feelings also plays a vital role in Dewey's theoretical writings in philosophy of mind. For more on the Dewey–Alexander relationship, see F. P. Jones, *Body Awareness in Action: A Study of the Alexander Technique* and my *Practicing Philosophy: Pragmatism and the Philosophical Life*. In the spirit of the James–Dewey tradition of experiential, embodied pragmatism, I have been advocating the role of explicit somatic consciousness as part of a disciplinary field I call somaesthetics. The basic aims and structure of this field are outlined in *Practicing Philosophy*, chapter 6, and *Performing Live*, chapters 7 and 8.
2. For a more detailed discussion of this Nietzschean strategy, see my *Performing Live*, chapter 7.

3. When Merleau-Ponty defines consciousness as simply "being towards-the-thing through the intermediary of the body" in a relationship not of "I think" but of "I can" (*PP* 160/137/159), it would seem that purposeful action in sleep should be construed as the actions of consciousness. One could then wonder to what extent we can ever speak of unconscious human life, let alone unconscious human acts or intentions. On the other hand, Merleau-Ponty sometimes speaks of consciousness as if it demanded a further "constituting" function: "To be conscious is to constitute, so that I cannot be conscious of another person, since that would involve constituting him as constituting" (*S* 117/93).

4. There have been feminist critiques that Merleau-Ponty's notion of a primordial, universal bodily experience that is ungendered in fact produces an account of embodied existence that is androcentric rather than neutral. See, for instance, Judith Butler, "Sexual Ideology and Phenomenological Description: A Feminist Critique of Merleau-Ponty's Phenomenology of Perception."

5. Dewey described this as "*the* philosophic fallacy," while James called it "the psychologist's fallacy." See Dewey, *Experience and Nature*, 34, and James, *The Principles of Psychology*, vol. I: 196, 278; vol. II: 281.

6. Nor, I should add, can we rely on mere trial and error and the formation of new habits because the sedimentation process would likely be too slow, and we would be most likely to repeat the bad habits unless those habits (and their attendant bodily feelings) were critically thematized and brought to explicit consciousness for correction. F. M. Alexander stresses these points in arguing for the use of the representations of reflective consciousness to correct faulty somatic habits. See Alexander, *Man's Supreme Inheritance; Constructive Conscious Control of the Individual; and The Use of the Self*.

7. As Alexander documents our "unreliable sensory appreciation" or "debauched kinaesthesia" with respect to how our bodies are oriented and used, so Feldenkrais argues that because the term "normal" should designate what should be the norm for healthy humans, then we should more accurately describe most people's somatic sense and use of themselves as "average" rather than normal. For a comparative account of the nature and philosophical import of Alexander Technique and Feldenkrais Method, see my *Performing Live*, chapter 8. The cited phrases are from Alexander's *Constructive Conscious Control*, 148–9.

8. Dewey recognizes this by advocating the reflective "conscious control" of Alexander Technique, while continuing to urge the importance of unreflective, immediate experience. For a discussion of the fruitful dialectic between reflective body consciousness and body spontaneity, see my *Practicing Philosophy*, chapter 6.

9. Merleau-Ponty complains that reflective thought "detaches subject and object from each other, and ... gives us only the thought about the body, or the body as an idea, and not the experience of the body" (*PP* 231/198–9/231). This cannot be true for disciplines of self-conscious somatic reflection that focus on the body as concretely experienced.

10. For James on the specious present, see *The Principles of Psychology*, vol I: 608–10. For the elusive vagueness of the notion of mental simultaneity and the intractable problems of determining "absolute timing" of consciousness, see Dennett, *Consciousness Explained*, 136, 162–6.

11. Mead himself wisely allows this. In making his famous "I–me" distinction, Mead did not conclude that the "I" was unobservable and absent from experience. Although "not directly given in experience" as an immediate datum, "it is in memory that the 'I' is constantly present in experience." The fact that "the 'I' really appears experientially as a part of a [subsequent] 'me'" does not, therefore, mean we cannot observe ourselves as subjective agents but only that we need to do so by observing ourselves over time through the use of memory. See Mead, *Mind, Self, and Society*, 174–6.

12. Sartre, "Merleau-Ponty," *Situations*, 157; "Merleau-Ponty *vivant*," in Stewart, *The Debate between Sartre and Merleau-Ponty*, 566.

13. *Situations*, 162; *Debate*, 570.

14. *Situations*, 167; *Debate*, 575.

15. *Situations*, 208; *Debate*, 610.

7 Merleau-Ponty and the Touch of Malebranche

The English-language reception of Merleau-Ponty's phenomenology of the body focuses mainly on two texts, *Phenomenology of Perception* and the posthumous *The Visible and the Invisible*. In the former, he interrogates the body as a site of mobility and spatiality, arguing that these fundamentally corporeal ways of relating to the world subtend and structure the intentionality of consciousness. In the latter work, the doctrine of intentionality is further displaced by a concept of the flesh, understood as a relation of tactility that precedes and informs intersubjective relations, necessarily disorienting a subject-centered account. The flesh is not something one has, but, rather, the web in which one lives; it is not simply what I touch of the other, or of myself, but the condition of possibility of touch, a tactility that exceeds any given touch, and that cannot be reducible to a unilateral action performed by a subject. The most extended and controversial discussion of touch takes place in the final chapter of *The Visible and the Invisible*, "The Intertwining," although that text, posthumously published and unfinished in many ways, can only suggest the radical challenge to a subject-centered conception of intentionality. Something is prior to the subject, but this "something" is not to be understood on the model of a substance. The grammar that would posit a being prior to the subject operates within the presumption that the subject is already formed, merely situated after the being at issue, and so fails to question the very temporality implied by its presentation. What Merleau-Ponty asks in this last work and, indeed, what he began to trace over a decade earlier, is the question, how is a subject formed from tactility or, perhaps put more precisely, how is a subject formed by a touch that belongs to no subject?

To speak of <u>a founding touch</u> is no doubt a romantic conceit and, as we shall see, it has its theological precedents. To speak in this way only makes sense if we understand that <u>the "touch" in question is not a single act of touching but the condition by virtue of which a corporeal existence is assumed</u>. Here it would be a mistake to imagine tactility as a subterranean sphere of existence, self-sufficient or continuous through time. The term "tactility" refers to the condition of possibility of touching and being touched, a condition that actively structures what it also makes possible. We cannot locate this condition independently, as if it existed somewhere prior to and apart from the exchange of touch that it makes possible. On the other hand, it is not reducible to the acts of touch that it conditions. How, then, are we to find it? What does it mean that it can be named but not found, that it eludes our touch, as it were, when we try to lay hold of it? What is it about touch that eludes our touch, that remains out of our reach?

In what follows, I return us to a consideration of Merleau-Ponty's engagement in 1947–8 with the work of Nicolas Malebranche (1638–1715), a set of lectures transcribed by Jean DePrun as *L'Union de l'ame et du corps chez Malebranche, Biran et Bergson*.[1] Malebranche was a speculative and theological philosopher whose work on metaphysics and ethics was published in the late seventeenth century. His work had an important effect on Bishop Berkeley and was considered in many ways a serious response to Descartes, one that sought to show the theological and intelligible underpinnings of any account of sentience and sensuousness. Whereas Malebranche embraced a Cartesian view of nature, he sought to rectify Descartes's understanding of mind, arguing that the order of ideal intelligibility is disclosed through sentient experience. Whereas one can have "clear and distinct" ideas of a priori truths, such as mathematical ones, it is not possible to have such clarity and distinctness with respect to one's own self, considered as a *sentiment intérieur*. Against Descartes's argument in the *Meditations* that introspection is the method by which truths of experience may be discerned, Malebranche argued for an experimental rather than intuitive approach to the idea of our own being. We acquire such a sense of ourselves through time, and always with some degree of unclarity and imperfection. This *sentiment intérieur* is occasioned by a divine order that, strictly speaking, cannot be felt; it is derived from an order that remains opaque and irrecoverable. Although Malebranche accepted Descartes's postulation that "I think, therefore I am," he did so for reasons that are at odds with those that Descartes supplies. For Malebranche, the proposition is not a direct inference, but a manifestation of the divine "word" as it makes itself present in experience itself. And although Malebranche separates the "pure" thought of God from its sensuous manifestations, there is no sensuous manifestation that is not derivable from God and does not, in some way, indicate divine presence and activity (only a full and final passivity would withdraw the demonstration of the divine).

Although in his *The Search after Truth*, Malebranche makes clear that to know what one feels is not the same as knowing what one is,[2] he also argues that sensation offers a demonstration for God, precisely because it cannot, by itself, be the cause of what one feels. That cause comes from elsewhere, and no separate or independent being is its own cause.[3] Although sense experience does not give us adequate knowledge of ourselves or of the order from which we are created (and can lead us astray), it nevertheless indicates that order by virtue of its own enigmatic and partial character. We are caused by God, but not fully determined by him: our actions become "occasions" by which the way we are acted on (by the divine) transforms (or fails to transform) into our own ethical action. The moral life is one that sustains a close relation (*rapport*) with the divine, attempting to establish a mode of human conduct that parallels the divine action by which our conduct is motivated.[4]

Although not a systematic philosopher, Malebranche offered a sustained speculative response to Cartesianism, adapting Augustine to his own purposes, and pursuing an empiricism paradoxically grounded in theological premises. The sentiments of the soul could not be dismissed as bodily contaminations but had to be reconsidered as created experiences that, through their very movement, give some indication – through the presumption of parallelism – of divine origination. Thus, Malebranche disputed the Cartesian distinction between body and soul, arguing that the very capacity to feel is not only inaugurated by an act of "grace," but that sentience itself maintains a referential connection to a spiritual order defined by the incessant activity of self-incarnation.

Merleau-Ponty's considerations in these lectures moved from Malebranche to Biran and Bergson, <u>reconsidering the relation of the</u>

<u>body to thought</u> in each instance and elaborating the contours of a prospective philosophical psychology that insists on <u>the centrality of the body to the act of knowing</u> and to the limits imposed on self-knowledge by the body itself. The notes of these lectures appeared in book form in France in 1978, although they only appeared in English in 2001. One reason, the editors of the English version conjecture, is that these are not precisely Merleau-Ponty's words, although many of them may well be verbatim citations.[5] In addition, Merleau-Ponty is providing an *explication de texte,* but is he offering his own interpretation of the importance of these thinkers to his own philosophy? My suggestion is that he is doing both, deriving resources from the tradition he explicates and, in so doing, disclosing his own relation to the tradition of sensuous theology. It may not at first seem easy to reconcile the focus on embodiment, often conceived as an antidote to forms of religious idealism that postulate a separable "soul," with theological works such as Malebranche's.

In his essay "Everywhere and Nowhere,"[6] Merleau-Ponty situates Malebranche as a precursor of French twentieth-century philosophy, noting that the influential Léon Brunschvig understood Malebranche, among others, to have established "the possibility of a philosophy which confirms the discordancy between existence and idea (and thus its own unsufficiency)." This Merleau-Ponty compares with the view of Maurice Blondel "for whom philosophy *was* thought realizing that it cannot 'close the gap,' locating and palpating inside and outside of us a reality whose source is not philosophical awareness" (S 177/140). Elaborating on the Christian philosophy bequeathed to contemporary philosophy, Merleau-Ponty makes free with the doctrine to show its promise for his own perspective:

Since it does not take "essences" as such for the measure of all things, since it does not believe so much in essences as in knots of signification (*nœuds de significations*), which will be unraveled and tied up again in a different way in a new network of knowledge and experience. (S 178–9/142)

Merleau-Ponty makes plain that Malebranche not only shows how the religious order, the order of intelligibility, or "the divine Word" intersects with lived experience, indeed, with the senses themselves, but also comes to understand the human subject as the site of this ethically consequential intersection.

If man is really grafted onto the two orders, their connection is also made in him, and he should know something about it.... In our view, this is the significance of Malebranche's philosophy. Man cannot be part "spiritual automaton," part religious subject who receives the supernatural light. The structures and discontinuities of religious life are met with again in his understanding.

He continues, "We are our soul, but we do not have the idea of it; we only have feeling's obscure contact with it" (*le contact obscur du sentiment*). It is in this sense, he writes, that "the slightest sense perception is thus a 'natural revelation'" (*S* 181/143–4). The divine does not appear as itself in the sensuous, and neither can the sensuous be said to "participate" in the divine according to a Platonic notion of mathesis. Rather, there is a certain division or discordance (*un clivage transversal*) that takes place within sense perception, so that its divine origin is obscurely felt, even as it cannot be apprehended.

It is this very discordancy that one would have to take as one's theme if one wanted to construct a Christian philosophy; it is in it that one would have to look for the articulation of faith and reason. In so doing one would have to draw away from (*s'éloignerait*) Malebranche, but one would also be inspired by him. For although he communicates something of reason's light to religion (and at the limit makes them identical in a single universe of thought), and although he extends the positivity of understanding to religion, he also foreshadows the invasion of our rational being by religious reversals, introducing into it the paradoxical thought of a madness which is wisdom, a scandal which is peace, a gift which is gain. (*S* 183/145)

If an initial skepticism toward the role of Malebranche in Merleau-Ponty's thinking restrains us from considering the usefulness of these lectures, doubt is ameliorated rather quickly, I would argue, when one understands the extent to which Malebranche sought to ground theology in a new conception of the body and, in particular, in the grounding and formative function of touch. Indeed, Malebranche offers Merleau-Ponty the opportunity to consider how the body in its impressionability presupposes a prior set of impressions that act on the body and form the basis for sentience, feeling, cognition, and the beginnings of agency itself. These impressions are, importantly, tactile, suggesting that it is only on the condition that a body is already exposed to something other than itself, something by which it can be affected, that it becomes possible for a sentient self to emerge.

I move too quickly in speaking of a "self" in this regard: a primary impressionability or receptivity forms the condition of experience itself for Malebranche, so that, strictly speaking, one does not experience a primary touch, but a primary touch inaugurates experience. This makes of "touch" a speculative notion, to be sure, unverifiable on empirical grounds, that is, on grounds of an "experience" already knowable. In another sense, however, touch reopens the domain of speculation as a necessary precondition for the theorization of embodiment and tactility. This point is made in a different way when we consider that the "tactility" from which touching and being touched both draw is not discernible as a discrete ontological substance of some kind. Another way of putting this is simply to say that touch draws on something it cannot fully know or master. That elusive condition of its own emergence continues to inform each and every touch as its constitutive ineffability. In fact, touch – understood neither simply as touching or being touched – not only is the animating condition of sentience, but continues as the actively animating principle of feeling and knowing. What is at least first modeled as a bodily impression turns out to be the condition for cognitive knowing, and in this way the body comes to animate the soul.

Let me offer a sentence from Malebranche that becomes crucial to Merleau-Ponty's own meditation on the unity of the soul and the body. Malebranche writes, "I can only feel that which touches me" (U 24/43).[7] Merleau-Ponty cites these words to show that the "I" who feels comes about only consequent to the touch, thus avowing a primacy of the undergoing of touch to the formation of the feeling self. Malebranche's claim is, despite its simplicity and, indeed, its beauty, a quite disarming and consequential claim. First, it postulates the origins of how I come to feel, of what I come to sense, and of sentience itself. Malebranche is claiming that the "I" that I am is one who feels. Although he does not claim here that there is no "I" prior to feeling or apart from feeling, it becomes clear from his argument in favor of the unity of the soul and body that feeling, precipitated by touch, initiates the "I" or, rather, institutes its self-representation. After all, what Merleau-Ponty cites from Malebranche is an autobiographical report, which then raises the question, under what conditions does the "I" become capable of reporting on what it feels? We are thus prompted to ask a more fundamental question: is feeling the condition under which self-reporting in language first takes place? In this citation, offered as a first-person report, feeling does not appear outside of the report on feeling, which suggests that feeling is given form through an autobiographical account. The "I" is not simply a self that comes into being prior to language but is designated primarily, in the citation at hand, as an act of self-reference within language, a self-reference not only prompted by affect, but animating affect in the act.

If "I" only feel on the condition of being touched, and if feeling is what inaugurates my capacity to report on myself, then it would seem to follow that feeling becomes mine as a distinctly linguistic possibility. But if feeling becomes mine on the condition of an autobiographical report in language, and if feeling follows from a touch that is not mine, then I am, as it were, grounded in, animated by, a touch that I can know only on the condition that I cover over that primary impression as I give an account of myself. "I can only feel what touches me" sets into grammatical form a grammatical impossibility insofar as the touch precedes the possibility of my self-reporting, provides its condition, and constitutes that for which I can give no full or adequate report.

If there can be no "I" without feeling, without sentience, and if the "I" who speaks its feeling is at once the I who feels, then feeling will be part of the intelligible "I," part of what the "I" can and does make intelligible about itself. Indeed, the citation offered us by Merleau-Ponty is an example of the "I" trying to make itself intelligible to itself, considering the prerequisites of its own possibility, and communicating those in language to an audience who, presumably, shares these prerequisites. Yet how would we know whether we do share these prerequisites? The "we" seems ruled out of the scene, and, in its place, we listen to another's self-presentation, and inhabit the "I" vicariously from a distance. On the one hand, the utterance is an address, delivering a challenge to Descartes and, indeed, to the notion that the "I," the one who speaks and knows, is one who is composed of a thinking substance that is, strictly speaking, distinct from any and all bodily extension – *res cogitans* rather than *res extensa*.

Yet Malebranche does *not* say, "I can only feel what touches me, and the same goes for you." He is constrained by an autobiographical form that is at once citational, that is, a citation of Descartes, meant to expose the impossibility of Descartes's own position. The markedly citational autobiography gives a partial lie to itself because it is the story of the one who speaks it, and it is, at once, someone else's story – with a twist. With Descartes, there is something of the threat of solipsism because we do not know if there is a "you" in the scene. "I think, therefore I am" is clearly not the same as "I can only feel what touches me." In neither instance, however, do we know to whom the statement is addressed or whether I can report on what another person feels, thinks, or is.

Can I speak of anything that is not mine, that does not become mine by virtue of being my feeling? So there is, we might say, at the beginning of this sentence, a certain scandal, a certain challenge, the one that conjoins the "I" with feeling, the one in which the "I" asserts itself as a feeling being. And it is not that the "I," on occasion, feels. No, it is rather the case that whatever the "I" will be, will be a feeling being. So the "I" is not reporting on this or that stray feeling, but asserting itself on the condition of feeling, which is to say that feeling conditions the "I," and there can be no "I" without feeling. Even though there is a touch that is not mine, it is unclear whether it comes from one who is otherwise like me. It seems not to. The touch is not provided by another self, for Malebranche, and so something in the touch leads us to wonder: where is the other? If it is the touch of God that animates me, am I then animated only in relation to an irrecoverable and ineffable origin?

If I can only feel what touches me, that means that there is a restriction on what I can feel. Many consequences follow from this claim: I cannot feel if nothing touches me, and the only thing I can feel is that which touches me. I must be touched to feel, and if I am not touched, then I will not feel. If I will not feel, then there is no way to report on what I feel, so there is self-reporting, given that feeling is what appears to animate my entry into linguistic self-representation. Although this last is not a claim that Malebranche explicitly makes, it is an act that he nevertheless performs for us, by (a) asserting the primacy of feeling to what I am and (b) performing the autobiographical account as a consequence of the primacy of feeling. If there is no "I" outside of feeling, and if the "I" makes this case through giving a report on its feeling, then *the narrative "I" becomes the transfer point through which the animated "I" launches an autobiographical construction.* For the "I" is the one who can and does feel, and if there is no touch, there is no "I" who feels, and that means that there is no "I," considered both as the animated effect of feeling and the subject of an autobiographical account. To be touched is, of course, to undergo something that comes from the outside, so I am, quite fundamentally, occasioned by that which is outside of me, which I undergo, and this undergoing designates a certain passivity, but not one that is understood as the opposite of "activity." To undergo this touch means that there must be a certain openness to the outside that postpones the plausibility of any claim to self-identity. The "I" is occasioned by alterity, and that occasion persists as its necessary and animating structure. Indeed, if there is to be self-representation, if I am to speak the "I" in language, then this autobiographical reference has been enabled from elsewhere, has undergone what is not itself. Through this undergoing, an "I" has emerged.

Note as well, however, that the sentence implies that I can only feel what touches me, which means that I cannot feel any other thing. No other thing can be felt by me than what touches me. My feeling is prompted, occasioned, inaugurated by its object, and the feeling will be, quite fundamentally, in relation to that object, structured by that object or, put in phenomenological terms, passively structured in an intentional relation to that object. I do not constitute that object through my feeling, but my capacity to feel and, indeed, therefore to announce myself as an "I" and, thus, to be capable of acting, will follow only on this more fundamental undergoing, this being touched by something, someone. It would appear to follow as well that if I cannot be touched, then there is no object, no elsewhere, no outside, and I have become unutterable with the absence of touch. And if I cannot be touched, then there is no feeling, and with no feeling, there is no "I," the "I" becomes unutterable, something unutterable to itself, unutterable to others. If touch inaugurates a feeling that animates self-representation, and if self-representation can never give a full or adequate account of what animates it, then there is always an opacity to any account of myself I might give. But if there is no touch, there is no account. This is perhaps the difference between a partial account, occasioned by touch, and a radical unaccountability, if not an aphasia, occasioned by a primary destitution.

So what can we conclude so far? That there is in the emergence of the "I," a certain passive constitution from the outside, and that the "I" is borne through feeling, through sentience, and that this sentience is referential: it refers, if only indirectly, to the outside by which it is induced. This would be a passivity prior to the emergence of the "I," a relation that is, strictly speaking, nonnarratable by the "I," who can begin to tell its story only after this inauguration has taken place. Yet can one understand this "passivity," or is this very phrase, and the very grammatical inflexion we use, "being touched," already a fiction retroactively imposed on a condition that is, as it were, before active and passive, that does not, and cannot, know this distinction?

When we consider that for Merleau-Ponty in his late writing "The Intertwining," there will come to be no disposition of being touched that is not at once touching, that the two will be implicated in each other, constituting the *entrelacs* of the flesh itself, how are we to understand this consideration, twelve years earlier, of the constituting condition of the "I"? If being touched precedes and conditions the emergence of the "I," then it will not be an "I" who is touched – no, it will be something before the "I," a state in which touched and touching are obscured by one another, but not reducible to one another, in which distinction becomes next to impossible, but where distinction still holds and where this obscurity, nonnarratable, constitutes the irrecoverable prehistory of the subject. If the touch not only acts on the "I" but animates that "I," providing the condition for its own sentience, and the beginnings of agency, then it follows that the "I" is neither exclusively passive nor fully active in relation to that touch. We see that acting on and acting are already intertwined in the very formation of the subject. Moreover, this condition in which passive and active are confounded, a condition, more accurately put, in which the two have not yet become disarticulated, is itself made possible by an animating exteriority. It is not a self-sufficient state of the subject but one induced by something prior and external. This means that this feeling that follows from being touched is implicitly referential, a situation that, in turn, becomes the basis for the claim that knowing is to be found as an incipient dimension of feeling.

For Merleau-Ponty reading Malebranche, sentience not only preconditions knowing, but gains its certainty of the outside at the very moment that it feels. This sentience is at the outset unknowing about itself; its origin in the passivity of the touch is not knowable. If I feel, there must be an outside and a before to my feeling.

My feeling is not a mere given; it is given from somewhere else. Spatial and temporal experience effectively follow from the touch, are induced from the touch retrospectively as its animating conditions. If I feel, then I have been touched, and I have been touched by something outside of myself. Therefore, if I feel, I reference an outside, but I do not know precisely that to which I refer. Malebranche contends, against Descartes, that "nothing is more certain than an internal sentiment [feeling] to establish knowledge that a thing exists" (U 18/38), but there is no way for sentiment itself to furnish the grounds for the existence of anything; it attests to an existence that is brought into being by an elsewhere, a constitutive alterity. What Malebranche calls "sentiment" is that which "alone reveals to us a dimension of the divine life; this profound life of God is only accessible through grace" (U 36/53). So we see that grace, understood as the moment of being touched by God and as the rupture that such a touch performs, reveals to us the divine life, where that life is understood, if "understanding" is the word, as an interruption of understanding, a sudden interruption of our time and perspective by that of another. If we stay within the terms of the temporal account that Malebranche offers, however, we would be compelled to say that the rupture, or the interruption, is inaugural; it does not intervene on a preconstituted field but establishes the field of experience through a traumatic inauguration, that is, in the form of a break, a discordance, or a cleavage of temporalities.

This disorientation within human perspective, however, is not merely occasional. It happens within all thinking. Merleau-Ponty paraphrases Malebranche this way: "No idea is intelligible on its own. It is 'representative of...' 'directed toward...'" (U 19/39). Thus, every idea is borne, as it were, in and through the sentient relation to an animating alterity. Malebranche, for Merleau-Ponty, therefore anticipates the Husserlian doctrine of intentionality, or so it would seem in light of the language Merleau-Ponty uses to explicate Malebranche's view. Whereas Husserl was always at odds with the *hulê*, the *matter* of the ego and of its objects, Malebranche seems at least occasionally clear that the body offers the formula for ideas, that the body is not discrete time and space, but exists in and as a "secret rapport" with consciousness, and so is clearly relational and referential. In this sense as well, the body carries within it what remains enigmatic to consciousness, and so exposes the insufficiency

of consciousness: consciousness is *not* a term to which the body corresponds, but the form the body takes when it becomes ideational.

As a result, we should not expect the *cogito* to be discrete and self-
knowing. There are, in fact, three parts to the *cogito* as Malebranche
understands it: the first is self-knowledge, which is, by definition,
obscure; the second is a knowledge of visible ideas of myself, which
involves an understanding of myself as a bodily being; and the third
is the knowledge of God. The knowledge of God exists in me when I
understand the illumination that God provides, an illumination that
subsequently informs my ideas, a "light" that is at once a "touch"
that God delivers (and, hence, a synaesthesia), which gives me my
sentience in general and, hence, my relation to an order of intelligibility. One might be tempted to understand that touch is itself
highly figural here, cast as light, emanating from a divinity that,
strictly speaking, has no body. It is unclear, as we will see, however,
whether the body is abstracted and rendered figural in this account or
whether theology is conceding its grounds in a bodily materialism. If
there will turn out to be a unity of body and soul in Malebranche, it
will not be a simple conjunction of discrete entities, but a dynamic in
which ideation follows from tactile impressionability; in this sense,
we are working with a theological empiricism of a rather singular
kind.

Although ideation follows from the body, bodily experience is not
primary. It is animated by that which is not fully recoverable through
reflective thought. When Malebranche remarks that "I am not the
light of myself" (*U* 18/38) and refers to a "created reason," he understands the "I" as necessarily derivative, deprived fundamentally
of the possibility of being its own ground. I think, but the referent
for my thought transcends the idea that I have because my idea is
never self-sufficient. My idea is derived from, and implicitly refers
to, what is given to me. To the extent that I have ideas, they come
to me not merely as gifts but as miracles, events for which I can give
no full account, certainly no causal one. Merleau-Ponty understands
Malebranche to be offering a theory of an obscure self-knowledge,
obscure but not for that reason illegitimate. It is obscure precisely
because I cannot capture the soul that I am through any idea I may
have of it. "I can construct a 'pseudo-idea' of the soul with the notion of extension" (*U* 21/40). Extension will not refer, transparently,
to the kind of being that I am. It is not a metaphysical concept that

corresponds to a reality, but a necessarily errant metaphor that seeks to capture in conceptual terms what must resist conceptualization itself. In Merleau-Ponty's language, "the soul will remain indeterminate, and the idea we have of it will rest on a half-thought" (*U* 21/40). The soul is not that to which I can have a transparent relation of knowledge: it is partially disclosed, or obscure, precisely because its origins lie elsewhere.

What is the relation between this errant metaphor, this half-thought, and the obscurity that accompanies the originary obscurity of the touch? For Merleau-Ponty, there is in Malebranche an effort to enter deliberately into a *philosophie l'irréfléchi*, a philosophy of the unreflected, of that for which no reflection is possible. Merleau-Ponty writes,

I am naturally oriented toward my world, ignoring myself. I only know that by experience I can think the past; my memory is not known to me by being seized directly as an operation. My reference to the past is not my work. I receive certain memories that are given to me. I am therefore not a spirit who dominates and deploys time, but a spirit at the disposition of some powers, the nature of which it does not know. I never know what I deserve (*vaux*), whether I am just or unjust. <u>There is a way that I am simply given to myself, and not a principle of myself</u>. (*U* 22/40–1)

If I am given to myself but am not a principle of myself, how am I to think this givenness, if I can? As we have already established, it will be a givenness that will never be captured by an idea or a principle, for it will be a nonnarratable and nonconceptualizable givenness (and in this sense *irreflechi*), what I will try to point to with the help of what Merleau-Ponty calls the "entrelacs" or "the intertwining" but where each word will be repelled, indifferently, by that which it seeks to name.

What is Merleau-Ponty doing here as he reads and rereads this speculative theology of the late seventeenth century? Merleau-Ponty's enormously provocative final work, *The Visible and the Invisible*, contains within it some of the most beautiful writing we have from him, a writing that not only is about vision and touch but that seeks, in its own rhythms and openness, to cast language in the mold of the relation he attempts to describe. I would wager that this chapter is the most important work for most feminists not only because it anticipates what Luce Irigaray will do when she imagines two lips touching (the *deux lèvres* were, in fact, first introduced explicitly in this very chapter by Merleau-Ponty, although tragically lost in the English translation), but because it attempts in a certain way to offer an alternative to the erotics of simple mastery. It makes thinking passionate, because it overcomes, in its language and in its argument, the distinction between a subject who sees and one who is seen, a subject who touches and one who is touched. It does not, however, overcome the distinction by collapsing it. It is not as if everyone is now engaged in the same act or that there is no dynamic, and no difference. No, and this is where the distinction between active and passive is confounded, we might say, without being negated in the name of sameness.

This final project of Merleau-Ponty's was dated 1959, two years before he died, and so we see what he was trying to understand more than ten years earlier when he gave his lectures on the speculative theology of Malebranche. Let me state what I think is at stake in this turn, so that my purpose here will not be misunderstood. It is one kind of philosophical contribution to claim that the Sartrian model of the touch or the gaze relies on an untenable subject–object relation and to offer an alternative that shows the way in which the acts of seeing and of being seen, of touching and of being touched, recoil upon one another, imply one another, become chiasmically related to one another. This is a brilliant contribution, one for which Merleau-Ponty is well known. It is another philosophical contribution, however, one attributed to Malebranche, to claim that all knowing is sentient and that sentience has its referential dignity, as it were, that it is a mode of knowing, that it relays the intelligible. By implication, it is a strong and important claim to make that sentience is the ground of all knowing. Yet we are still, in each of these contributions, concerned with a knowing subject, with an epistemological point of departure, with an "I" who is established and whose modes of knowing and feeling and touching and seeing are at issue. How can they be described and redescribed? How can they be accorded a greater philosophical dignity than they have previously enjoyed? Consider that what is happening in the lectures on Malebranche is a different and, I would say, more fundamental philosophical movement, for there the task is *not to provide an account of sentience as the ground of knowing* but to inquire into the point of departure for sentience itself, the obscurity and priority of its animating condition.

So the question is not how to conceive of sentience as the point of departure for knowing but *how to conceive, if we can, of the point of departure for sentience*. How to understand, if we can, the emergence of the subject on the condition of touch whose agency cannot fully be known, a touch that comes from elsewhere, nameless and unknowable.

On one hand, this is a theological investigation for Malebranche. It is not only that I cannot feel anything but what touches me, but that I cannot love without first being loved, cannot see without being seen, and that in some fundamental way, the act of seeing and loving are made possible by – and are coextensive with – being seen and being loved. Malebranche writes in *The Search after Truth*, "it might be said that if we do not to some extent see God, we see nothing, just as if we do not love God, i.e. if God were not continuously impressing upon us the love of good in general, we could love nothing."[8] So to love God is to have God continuously impress his love upon us, and so the very moment in which we act, in which we are positioned as subjects of action, is the same moment in which we are undergoing another love, and without this simultaneous and double movement, there can be no love. Love will be the confusion of grammatical position, confounding the very distinction between active and passive disposition. But Malebranche in the hands of Merleau-Ponty – Malebranche, as it were, transformed by the touch of Merleau-Ponty – becomes something different and something more. For here, Merleau-Ponty asks after the conditions by which the subject is animated into being, and although Merleau-Ponty writes of the touch in "The Intertwining," it is unclear whether there is a fundamental inquiry into the animating conditions of human ontology. Was that thought in the background of his writing? Does the confounding of active and passive verb form that follows from the theological inauguration of human sentience in Malebranche not prefigure the chiasm that becomes fundamental to Merleau-Ponty's return to the matter of touch in his posthumous writing? Reading Merleau-Ponty on Malebranche thus resituates the unfinished inquiry that constitutes "The Intertwining," his posthumously published essay, suggesting that this inquiry is not only a local ontology of the touch, but that it offers touch as the name for a more fundamental emergence, the emergence of the "I" on the basis of that chiasm.

To review briefly, then, what is that chiasm? In "The Intertwining," Merleau-Ponty writes,

the flesh is an ultimate notion...it is not the union or compound of two substances, but thinkable by itself, if there is a relation of the visible with itself that traverses me and constitutes me as a seer, this circle which I do not form, which forms me, this coiling over (*enroulement*) of the visible upon the visible, can traverse, animate other bodies as well as my own. (*VI* 185/140)

Later,

the flesh we are speaking of is not matter. It is the coiling over of the visible upon the seeing body, of the tangible upon the touching body, which is attested in particular when the body sees itself, touches itself seeing and touching the things, such that, simultaneously, *as* tangible it descends among them. (*VI* 191–2/146)

Already then we see that the body is a set of relations, described through a figure, the figure of a coiling or rolling back, and then again, within sentences, as a "fold," anticipating Deleuze. So touched and touching are not reciprocal relations; they do not mirror one another; they do not form a circle or a relation of reciprocity. I am not touched as I touch, and this noncoincidence is essential to me and to touch, but what does it mean? It means that I cannot always separate the being touched from the touching, but neither can they be collapsed into one another. There is no mirror image, and no reflexivity, but a coiling and folding, suggesting that there are moments of contact, of nonconceptualizable proximity, but that this proximity is not an identity, and it knows no closure. At another moment, he calls the flesh "a texture that returns to itself and conforms to itself." This same sentence that I was reading continues. It is a long sentence, and it coils back on itself, refusing to end, touching its own grammatical moments, refusing to let any of them pose as final. Merleau-Ponty thus attempts to end his sentence this way: "*as* touching [the body] dominates them all and draws this relationship and even this double relationship from itself, by dehiscence or fission of its own mass." The flesh is not my flesh or yours, but neither is it some third thing. It is the name for a relation of proximity and of breaking up. If the flesh dominates, it does not dominate like a subject dominates. The flesh is most certainly not a subject, and although our grammar puts

* Burst open, gape, cut or wound (of a pod)
o dividing smthing into 2 or more parts

it in a subject position, the flesh challenges the grammar by which it is made available to us in language. For whatever reason, the domination that the flesh enacts is achieved through the dehiscence or fission of its own mass. It dominates, in other words, by coming apart: the flesh is that which is always coming apart and then back upon itself, but that for which no coincidence with itself is possible. So when one touches a living and sentient being, one never touches a mass, for the moment of touch is the one in which something comes apart, mass splits, and the notion of substance does not – cannot – hold. This means that neither the subject who touches nor the one who is touched remains discrete and intact at such a moment: we are not speaking of masses, but of passages, divisions, and proximities. He writes,

my left hand is always on the verge of touching my right hand touching the things, but I never reach coincidence; the coincidence eclipses at the moment of realization, and one of two things always occurs: either my right hand really passes over to the rank of the touched, but then its hold on the world is interrupted; or it retains its hold on the world, but then I do not really touch *it* – my right hand touching, I palpate with my left hand only its outer covering. (*VI* 194/147–8)

Why would it be the case that my hold on the world is interrupted if the hand by which I seek to touch the world passes over into the rank of the touched? What does it mean to pass over into the rank of the touched? I gather that here Merleau-Ponty is telling us that a pure passivity, understood as an inertness, the inertness of a mass, cannot be the condition of a referential touch, a touch that gives us access to the order of the intelligible. This makes sense, I think, if we reconsider that for Malebranche, to be touched by God is thus to be already, at the moment of the touch, animated into the world, and so comported beyond the position of being merely or only touched, being matter, as it were, at the mercy of another, and instead, becoming sentient. I would add the following here, now that we understand the chiasmic relation in which the touch is to be figured: to be touched by God is thus to be made capable of touch, but it would be wrong to say that God's touch precedes the touch of which I become capable. To the extent that I continue to be capable of touching, I am being touched, I am, as it were, having impressed on me the touch of God, and that undergoing is coextensive with the act that I perform.

So, at the very moment of that ostensible passivity, what we can only call, inadequately, "passivity," what Levinas in a parallel, although not identical, move had to call the passivity before passivity, we are activated, but not in such a way that we overcome the passivity by which we are activated: we are acted on and acting at the same instant, and these two dimensions of touch are neither oppositional nor the same. Clearly, we do not, as it were, turn around and touch God in Malebranche's sense, for there is a strict asymmetry in this inaugurative relation, but the asymmetry does not lead to an absolute distinction between touching and being touched. It implies only that they are not the same. So we are, here, in proximity to a relation that is relayed by the middle voice or by a continuous action, but where the acting and the acted on can always and only be figured, but not rigorously conceptualized, where the turn of the one into the other defies conceptualization, makes us grasp for words, leads us into metaphor, error, half-thought, and makes us see and know that whatever words we use at this moment will be *in*adequate and fail to capture that to which they point. Thus, it is not on the basis of our being touched that we come to know the world. It is on the basis of being touched in such a way that touched and touching form a chiasmic and irreducible relation. It is on the basis of this irreducible and nonconceptualizable figure, we might say, that we apprehend the world.

This chiasm, this coiling back, this fold, is the name for the obscure basis of our self-understanding, and the obscure basis of our understanding of everything that is not ourselves. Indeed, there is thus no clarity for me that is not implicated in obscurity, and that obscurity is myself. "If my soul is known through an idea, it must appear to me as a second soul in order to have that idea. It is essential to a consciousness to be obscure to itself if it is to encounter a luminous idea" (*U* 22/41). Here we see that this originary obscurity is the very condition of luminosity. It is not what brings luminosity forth, for the luminous is divine, and precedes the emergence of all things human. When we ask after the human access to this light, however, it will be made possible through its own obscurity, a certain dimming against which brightness emerges. To account for this obscurity means accounting for what is given to me, for that by which I am touched, which is irreducibly outside and which, strictly speaking, occasions me. Thus, we arrive at the problem of passivity:

"We inherit powers which are not immediately our own. I register the results of an activity with which I am not confused" (*confond*) (*U* 22–3/41). Thus, my passivity indicates the presence and passion of that which is not me and which is situated at the core of who I am as a fundamental scission. We are not far from Levinas at this moment, from the division that not only is fundamental to the subject, but that indicates the operation of alterity in the midst of who I am.

For Merleau-Ponty, following Malebranche, no unity resolves the tension of this internal relation, and this relation is not supported by a common space or a common shelter, named the subject. Indeed, the relation finds itself in a disunity with no promise of reconciliation. This is an inevitable "scission" in a philosophy where there must be a detour for going from the self to itself, a passage through alterity which makes any and all contact of the soul with itself necessarily obscure. This obscurity is lived not only as passivity, but, more specifically, as feeling, a sentiment of the self. This interior sense of myself – obscure, passive, feeling – is the way that God is, as it were, manifest in the human soul. It is by virtue of this connection, which I cannot fully know, between sentience and God, that I understand myself to be a free being, one whose actions are not fully determined in advance, for whom action appears as a certain vacillating prospect. The interior sense of freedom is the power that a man has to follow or not follow the way that leads to God. In fact, the interior sense of myself is sufficient to reaffirm my freedom, but this same sense of myself is insufficient to know it (*U* 23/41).

Indeed, there is no inspection of myself that will furnish any clear access to intelligibility, for that inspection of myself will of necessity refer me elsewhere, outside. For there to be an illumination that is necessary for understanding, indeed, in Merleau-Ponty's reading, "for there to be light, there must be, facing me, a *representative being* . . . otherwise, my soul will be dispersed and at the mercy of its states" (*U* 31/50). So a subject who has only its own feeling to rely on, whose feeling is given no face, encountered by a representative of "being," is one that suffers its own dispersion, living at the mercy of its own random feeling. What holds those states and feelings together is not a unity to be found at the level of the subject, but one only conferred by the object, in its ideality. It is the one addressed by such feeling who confers intelligibility on one's own desire. This other, the one to whom feeling is addressed, the one who solicits feeling, does so precisely to the extent that the Other represents being. For that Other to represent being is not for it to be being itself, but to be its sign, its relay, its occasion, its deflection.

The human heart is empty and transient without this being. To say, then, that sentience is referential in this context is to say, with Malebranche, that "there must be a being...which refers to reality, because the human soul is not by itself this agility and this transparence which alone is capable of knowledge" (U 31/50). So whatever this referent is will not be the same as its representative, and this means, for Malebranche, that God is not the same as his objects. For Merleau-Ponty, this claim is cast in such a way that one can see its resonance with the phenomenological claim that there is an ideal point according to which variations in perspectives become possible and that the beings we come to know are the various perspectives of that ideal. In a sense, Malebranche prefigures in his description of God as the one who "sees" and endows all things with his perspective, the conception of the noematic nucleus for phenomenology. This gives Merleau-Ponty a way to distinguish the order of intelligibility from the order of its signification. The "intelligible extension" that characterizes various kinds of beings is, significantly, "not close to the subject (it is not a fact of knowledge), nor is it close to the object (it is not an in-itself). It is the ideal kernel according to which real extension [substance] is offered to knowledge" (U 31/50). Thus, what one feels, if it is a feeling, if it is a sense, if it is love, or even if it is a touch, for instance, is sustained by the ideality of its addressee, of the uncapturability of the referent, the irreducibility of the ideal to any of its perspectival adumbrations.

So when Merleau-Ponty writes of Malebranche that "he does not conceive of consciousness as closed, its meanings are not its own" (U 33/51), he means to show how this consciousness is given over from the start, prior to any decision to give itself over, prior to the emergence of a reflexive relation by which it might, of its own accord, give itself over. It is given over to an infinity that cannot be properly conceptualized and that marks the limits of conceptualization itself. "A property of infinity that I find incomprehensible," writes Malebranche, "is how the divine verb hides (renferme) the body of its intelligible mode" (U 34/52). The divine verb, the linguistic action that the divine takes, is not made known in a verb that might be understood. No, that verb is hidden, shut up, concealed, *renfermer*, offered in an enigmatic fashion, unreadable within the grammar that we know. In the terms of conventional language, the verb is unintelligible, but its unintelligibility, from the human perspective, is a sign of the divine intelligibility it encloses. The divine verb renders the body enigmatic precisely as a way to enter the body into the intelligible mode: *le Verbe divin renferme les corps d'une manière intelligible*. So the verb wraps that body up in an intelligible mode, but what of the body exceeds that wrapping? And the divine verb, which is it? We are given the verb for what the divine verb does, although this is not, we must suppose, the divine verb itself. The word we are given is *"renfermer"*: to shut or lock up; to enclose, to contain, to include. *"Renfermer"* stands for the divine verb, and we might even say that it is the verb *qui renferme le Verbe divin*, the one which has that divine verb enigmatically contained within it, where what is contained – and so not contained at all – is "an incomprehensible thought of infinity."

This enigmatic infinity, however, pertains to bodies and to how they are included within the realm of intelligibility. There is something enigmatic there, and something infinite, something whose beginning we cannot find, something that is resistant to narrativization. It is difficult to know how the divine is instantiated in bodies, but also how bodies come to participate in the divine. Through what enigmatic passage do bodies pass such that they attain a certain ideality, such that they become, as it were, a representative of an ideality which is inexhaustible, infinite, something about which I could not give an account, for which no account would finally suffice? ?

In the edition of the lectures from 1947–8 that I have cited here, an appendix is included called "Les Sens et l'inconscient" (The Senses and the Unconscious), a brief lecture that Merleau-Ponty delivered in this same academic year but that was not formally linked to the lectures collected in the book. One can see at a glance why it is included, why it should be.* Merleau-Ponty writes, "the unconscious . . . is nothing but a call to intelligence, to which intelligence does not respond, because intelligence is of another order. There is nothing to explain outside of intelligence, and there is nothing to

---

* This appendix is not included in the English translation. – Eds.

explain here, but only something that asserts itself, simply" (U 116). Here Merleau-Ponty makes clear the sense of the "unconscious" that he accepts, and it has to do with the way in which the unknown, and the unknowable, pervades the horizon of consciousness. In this sense, he is concerned, as was Malebranche, with how an order of intelligibility that is not fully recoverable by consciousness makes itself known, partially and enigmatically, at the level of corporeity and affect. In his view, it would be a mistake to claim, for instance, that when I fall in love, and am conscious of every phase of feeling I go through, I therefore understand something of the form and significance that each of these lucid images has for me, how they work together, what enigma of intelligibility they offer up. It is necessary, he writes, to distinguish between being in love and knowing that one is in love. "The fact that I am in love is a reason not to know that I am, because I dispose myself to live that love instead of placing it before my eyes" (U 117). Even if I attempt to see it, Merleau-Ponty insists, "My eyes, my vision, which appears to me as prepersonal ... my field of vision is limited, but in a manner that is imprecise and variable ... my vision is not an operation of which I am the master" (U 118). Something sees through me as I see. I see with a seeing that is not mine alone. I see, and as I see, the I that I am is put at risk, discovers its derivation from what is permanently enigmatic to itself.

That our origins are permanently enigmatic to us and that this enigma forms the condition of our self-understanding clearly resonate with the Malebranchian notion that self-understanding is grounded in a necessary obscurity. What follows is that we should not think that we will be able to grasp ourselves or, indeed, any object of knowledge, without a certain failure of understanding, one which makes the grasping hand, the figure for so much philosophical apprehension, a derivative deformation of originary touch. If we think we might return to an originary touch, however, and consult it as a model, we are doubtless radically mistaken. For what is original is precisely what is irrecoverable, and so one is left with a pervasive sense of humility when one seeks to apprehend this origin, a humility that gives the lie to the project of mastery that underlies the figure of the mind "grasping" its origins. "An analysis should be possible," Merleau-Ponty writes,

which defines thought not by the plenitude by which it seizes its object, but
by the sort of stopping of the activity of spirit which constitutes certitudes,
one which subjects these certitudes to revision, without reducing them to
nothing. It is necessary to introduce a principle of thought's lack of adequation to itself. (*U* 118)

It is not that thought is lacking something, but that we are lacking in
relation to the entire field of intelligibility within which we operate.
We cannot know it fully even as it gives us our capacity to know.

   The point here is not to reduce Merleau-Ponty's phenomenology
of touch to a psychoanalytic perspective, but perhaps to suggest that
Merleau-Ponty recasts psychoanalysis as a seventeenth-century theology, bringing both together in a tactile revision of phenomenology.
"It must be possible," he claims, "to "recognize the origin of a principle of passivity in freedom." The passivity to which he refers is a
kind of primary undergoing for which we have always and only an obscure and partial knowledge. To recognize the origin of a principle of
passivity in freedom is not to understand passivity as derived from
freedom, but to understand a certain passivity as the condition of
freedom, supplying a limit for the model of freedom as self-generated
activity.

   What follows is that whatever action we may be capable of is
an action that is, as it were, already underway, not only or fully our
action, but an action that is upon us already as we assume something
called action in our name and for ourselves. Something is already
underway by the time we act, and we cannot act without, in some
sense, being acted upon. This acting that is upon us constitutes a
realm of primary impressionability so that by the time we act, we
enter into the action, we resume it in our name, it is an action that has
its source only partially and belatedly in something called a subject.
This action that is not fully derived from a subject exceeds any claim
one might make to "own" it, or to give an account of oneself. Yet our
inability to ground ourselves is based on the fact that we are animated
by others into whose hands we are born and, hopefully, sustained.
We are thus always, in some way, done to as we are doing, that we
are undergoing as we act, that we are, as Merleau-Ponty insisted,
touched, invariably, in the act of touching. Of course, it is quite
possible to position oneself so that one might consider oneself only

touched, or only touching, and pursue positions of mastery or self-loss that try to do away with this intertwining, but such pursuits are always partially foiled or struggle constantly against being foiled. Similarly, it may well be that some humans are born into destitution and fail to become human by virtue of being physically deprived or physically injured, so there is no inevitability attached to becoming animated by a prior and external touch. The material needs of infancy are not quite the same as the scene that Malebranche outlines for us as the primary touch of the divine, but we can see that his theology gives us a way to consider not only the primary conditions for human emergence but the requirement for alterity, the satisfaction of which paves the way for the emergence of the human itself. This does not mean that we are all touched well, or that we know how to touch in return, but only that our very capacity to feel and our emergence as knowing and acting beings is at stake in the exchange.

NOTES

1. Maurice Merleau-Ponty, *L'Union de l'âme et du corps chez Malebranche, Biran et Bergson.* All citations from this text are my own translations, although an English version, without the appendix, now exists under the title *The Incarnate Subject: Malebranche, Biran, and Bergson on the Union of Body and Soul.*
2. Malebranche, *The Search after Truth,* "Elucidation Eleven," 633–8; see also books one and two, 76–90.
3. See Craig Walton's "Translator's Introduction" to the *Treatise on Ethics (1684)* for a discussion of Malebranche's opposition to neo-Aristotelian accounts of the causal power of beings. For Malebranche, all created things are caused by the divine order and exercise power only in a derivative sense. This is the meaning of his "occasionalism."
4. See Malebranche, *Treatise on Nature and Grace,* 51–5, 169–94.
5. Jean Deprun explains in his introduction that he consulted the student notebooks from the two versions of this course that Merleau-Ponty gave in the same year and chose between divergent accounts on the basis of which formulation seemed most clear and explicit. He describes his experience as an editor of this volume as *facile,* arguing that editorial decisions in no way altered the substantive views of Merleau-Ponty. Although Jacques Taminiaux in his preface to the English version remarks that these are obligatory courses and maintain a tangential relationship to Merleau-Ponty's own explicit philosophical views, I differ with this conclusion because the preoccupation with touch, with alterity, and

with an order of intelligibility disclosed through sentience seems crucial to Merleau-Ponty's developing account of bodily experience and its relation to knowledge.

6. Originally published as an introduction to *Les Philosophes célèbres*.

7. The sentence is quoted from Malebranche's *Méditations chrétiennes et métaphysiques* and originally reads, "Il est nécessaire que je ne me sente qu'en moi-même, lorsqu'on me touche."

8. Nicolas Malebranche, *The Search after Truth*, 233.

8   A Phenomenology of Life

I would like to begin with a passage from Derrida's *Speech and Phenomena*. It concerns the parallel Husserl establishes between phenomenological psychology and transcendental phenomenology. For Husserl, the domain of pure psychological experience has the same scope as the whole domain of transcendental experience. There is, however, an irreducible difference between these two fields inasmuch as the domain of phenomenological psychology refers to the subject as part of the world, that is, as existing empirically, whereas transcendental phenomenology concerns a consciousness that is not threatened by the destruction of the world and that is therefore the condition of the possibility of the world qua phenomenon.

This is why Derrida writes that this irreducible difference between transcendental and empirical consciousness is nonetheless "nothing." For in fact *nothing* – at any rate, nothing that can be defined in the natural or ontical sense – distinguishes transcendental from empirical consciousness. Yet they can in no way be conflated. So, the notion of a parallel, used by Husserl, is indeed apt because two parallel lines are identical; they are no different geometrically, yet they are not *the same* line. Like parallel lines, empirical and transcendental consciousness are at once very near and very far from one another. Concerning this parallel in Husserl, Derrida writes the following:

But the strange unity of these two parallels, that which refers the one to the other, does not allow itself to be sundered (*partager*) by them and, by dividing itself, finally joins the transcendental to its other; this unity is *life*. One finds quickly enough that the sole nucleus of the concept of *psuchê* is life as self-relationship, whether or not it takes place in the form of consciousness. "Living" is thus the name of that which precedes the reduction and finally escapes all the divisions which the latter gives rise to.[1]

Indeed, "life" refers to a living being, that is, a worldly existence; it presupposes the natural existence of the world. Life as the object of biology, then, ought to be reduced by the phenomenological *epochê*.

Yet Husserl characterizes transcendental activity as *life*, and his descriptions employ words and concepts that come from the domain of life (*Leben, Erlebnis, lebendige Gegenwart*). Life escapes the phenomenological reduction, then, because it appears again on the transcendental level. In this way, life eludes the distinction between transcendental and psychological or natural consciousness. We might say that at the transcendental level "life" is used in a *metaphorical* sense. This does not solve the problem, however, and does not make it possible to reduce "life" to a natural concept. For even if transcendental life is only metaphorically life, it remains to be seen how this metaphor is *possible*, that is to say, which dimension of transcendental activity allows us to establish a relation to biological life. In other words, to account for the possibility of the metaphor, we would have to uncover a living dimension at the transcendental level, that is, a sense of life more basic than the difference between transcendental and natural consciousness.

The fact that Husserl describes the transcendental level by using concepts borrowed from life in truth shows that life escapes the duality established by transcendental phenomenology. This means that "life" in the natural sense, as the basic characteristic of living beings, involves a dimension that exceeds the natural level, that overlaps the transcendental domain: it seems as if natural life were more than itself, part of a more primordial life, the other side of which would be the transcendental one. In short, this reflection on the neutrality of life makes it possible to discover a new sense of worldliness, namely, according to Derrida, "a *worldliness* capable of sustaining, or in some way nourishing, *transcendentality*, and of equaling the full scope of its domain, yet without being merged with it in some total adequation."[2] Life is thus nothing other than the "nothing" that at once joins and divides the transcendental and the psychological, or rather life is the condition of the possibility of the nothing as the peculiar unity of transcendental phenomenology and phenomenological psychology.

Now one could say that the starting point, and probably the whole of phenomenology, is the phenomenological *reduction,* so that the central question for phenomenology is the question of the possibility of the reduction, and so of the connection between the natural attitude and the transcendental attitude, between the natural world and its phenomenality. It follows that the question of life, the question concerning the status, the meaning of the being of life, as that which comprises both the natural and the transcendental, is the main question of phenomenology. In this sense, I believe, phenomenology is essentially *phenomenology of life:* the problem posed by Husserl in *The Crisis of European Sciences and Transcendental Phenomenology* (§53) concerning the dual status of the subject – its being both part of the world and the condition of the world – is *the same as the problem of the status of life.*

I would like to show, then, that Merleau-Ponty's phenomenology is really a *phenomenology of life,* which means Merleau-Ponty's thought completes the project of Husserl's phenomenology. Indeed, we can say that Merleau-Ponty's main purpose, from beginning to end, is to give sense to the Husserlian *lifeworld* as it is described in the *Crisis.* Thus, Merleau-Ponty's purpose is to develop a phenomenology that takes into account the irreducibility of the lifeworld. In a note in *Phenomenology of Perception,* he writes,

Husserl in his last period concedes that all reflection should in the first place return to the description of the lifeworld (*monde vécu*) (*Lebenswelt*). But he adds that, by means of a second "reduction," the structures of the lifeworld must be reinstated in the transcendental flow of a universal constitution in which all the world's obscurities are elucidated. It is clear, however, that we are faced with a dilemma: either the constitution makes the world transparent, in which case it is not obvious why reflection needs to pass through the lifeworld, or else it retains something of that world and never rids it of its opacity. (*PP* 419n/365n/425n)

Thus, according to Merleau-Ponty, recognizing the specificity of the lifeworld calls into question the role of transcendental subjectivity. Indeed, if the lifeworld refers to "a *Weltthesis* prior to all theses . . . a primordial faith and a fundamental and original opinion (*Urglaube, Urdoxa*) which are thus not even in principle translatable in terms of clear and distinct knowledge, and which – more ancient than any 'attitude' or 'point of view' – give us not a representation of the world but the world itself" (S 207/163), if the lifeworld involves an irreducible opacity, then the project of constituting this world in (or by) a transcendental subjectivity is incoherent. In other words, there is an incompatibility between the prior presence of the world and the representational acts of transcendental subjectivity, between the opacity of the world and the transparency of constitution.

It is not surprising, then, that in every text dealing with Husserl, particularly in "The Philosopher and His Shadow," Merleau-Ponty calls into question the strict opposition between the transcendantal attitude and the natural attitude. The world of our natural life, such as it was defined, that is, as primal belief, cannot, in fact, be overcome, unless we define the natural world by already projecting into it the attitudes and categories of science – in which case we change the natural attitude into a naturalistic attitude. If we respect the irreducibility of the "*Weltthesis* prior to all theses," then we cannot take for granted the idea of a transcendental attitude radically different from the natural attitude. Indeed, according to Merleau-Ponty,

The truth is that the relationships between the natural and the transcendental attitudes are not simple, are not side by side or sequential, like the false or the apparent and the true. There is a preparation for phenomenology in the natural attitude. It is the natural attitude which, by reiterating its own procedures, seesaws (*bascule*) in phenomenology. It is the natural attitude itself which goes beyond itself in phenomenology – and so it does not go beyond itself. (S207/164)

Because the concept of constitution must itself be called into question, because the transcendental subject, at least as described by Husserl in *Ideas I*, does not make sense, is not relevant for the description of the natural world, the subject of the natural world, the subject of the *Welthesis*, stands in need of clarification. I believe Merleau-Ponty's goal is to try to define more precisely the status of the subject as subject of the "*Weltthesis* prior to all theses," as subject of the lifeworld, which is, in principle, irreducible to an act or a representation. The subject of the lifeworld is precisely *life*. Accordingly, the question concerning the subject of the world amounts to a question concerning life.

We must take into account the word Husserl originally used to refer to this world, namely, "*Lebenswelt*," that is to say, the world of, or for, life. Husserl did not choose this word arbitrarily: he took advantage of the double meaning of *Leben* in German, which is ambiguous in French as well. The meaning of "to live" is originally intransitive: to live means to be alive; life is that which characterizes living beings. In German the verb *leben* becomes the verb *erleben*, which has a transitive meaning (as does *vivre* in French): it means to experience, to feel, to perceive, and thus refers to an object, either immanent (one can *vivre* or *erleben* an emotion, as in having a passionate love affair) or transcendent (*vivre, erleben* a situation). This duality corresponds exactly to the duality between life as the object of biology and life as a dimension of the transcendental flow, that is to say, as constituting the world. To ask about the subject of the *Lebenswelt* is to ask about life – life for which and by which there is a world, and this is to call into question the duality of the natural subject and the transcendental subject, to look for the unity of the subject beyond the distinction between the empirical and the transcendental levels.

Merleau-Ponty acknowledges this horizon of reflection at least once in *Phenomenology of Perception*. The context is a reflection on sexuality, more precisely, on Freudian psychoanalysis. After showing that sexuality expresses the whole existence of the subject, he poses an objection: even if sexuality has an existential significance, "there can be no question of allowing sexuality to become lost in existence, as if it were no more than an epiphenomenon." So it remains to show why, in the case of neurosis, for instance, "sexuality is not only a symptom, but a highly important one." The answer is that,

as we have indicated above, biological existence is synchronized with human existence and is never indifferent to its distinctive rhythm. Nevertheless, we shall now add, "living" (*leben*) is a primary process from which, as a starting point, it becomes possible to "live" (*erleben*) this or that world, and we must eat and breathe before perceiving and awakening to relational living, belonging to colors and lights through sight, to sounds through hearing, to the body of another through sexuality, before arriving at the life of human relations. (*PP* 186/159–60/185)

Here Merleau-Ponty recognizes that if corporeal life transcends itself in an existential significance that goes beyond natural needs, it is also true that this significance, whatever it may be, is rooted in corporeal life. In other words, it is life itself that transcends its natural or biological dimension and involves the whole realm of meaning: thus, just as we need a sexual body to develop meaningful relationships with others, so, too, we must be alive and have sense organs to experience anything and, finally, to perceive a world.

The heart of Merleau-Ponty's philosophical inquiry is therefore the movement by which a living being transcends its materiality and gives rise to meaningful existence and, conversely, the fact that every meaning, whatever its degree of abstraction, has its roots in corporeal life.[3] This amounts to saying that Merleau-Ponty looks for a sense of life that transcends the opposition between biological and "metaphorical" life, that is to say, existence in all its dimensions, even that of abstract thought. In other words, as Merleau-Ponty writes in the end of the introduction of *Phenomenology of Perception*, "Reflection will be sure of having precisely located the center of the phenomenon if it is equally capable of bringing to light its vital inherence and its rational intention" (*PP* 65/53/62).

To account for the specificity of Merleau-Ponty's ontology, then, I believe it is relevant to study the place and the role of life in its biological sense, which is the original one. That is, Merleau-Ponty's characterization of phenomenality not only goes through but is based on a precise phenomenological analysis of life. Indeed, as we shall see, life is present everywhere in Merleau-Ponty's thought, even if not with the same importance in every book. Without a doubt, life is the center of *The Structure of Behavior*, which forms the basis of the analysis in *Phenomenology of Perception*. I argue here that the investigation concerning life enables Merleau-Ponty to pose the problem of the phenomenon, inasmuch as a living being exists as such for a consciousness. Neither in the first book nor in the second, however, does he manage to resolve the problem in a satisfactory way. On the contrary, in the lectures on nature he devotes a large part of his argument to the question of the status of living beings, and I believe it was deepening this point, questioning the ontological status of life, that led him to give up the concepts of *Phenomenology of Perception* and turn to an ontological approach.

Merleau-Ponty's phenomenology can thus be said to be a phenomenology of life in a *twofold sense*. First, life is for him a privileged subject; indeed, he develops a phenomenological approach to life, taking advantage of the contributions of contemporary biology. This investigation concerning life greatly influenced his turn to ontology in his later work, to such an extent that several concepts in *The Visible and the Invisible* emerge from his inquiry into living beings in the lectures on nature. Merleau-Ponty's phenomenology is therefore a phenomenology of life in another, stronger sense, namely, that in its final form it is based on a reflection on life and is defined by that reflection. It is a phenomenology whose strength and originality come from its taking into account the specificity of life, of biological life, as the identity of reality and phenomenon.

At the beginning of *The Structure of Behavior* Merleau-Ponty defines his subject in the following way: "Our goal is to understand the relations of consciousness and nature: organic, psychological or even social. By nature we understand here a multiplicity of events external to each other and bound together by relations of causality" (*SC* 1/3). Merleau-Ponty's aim is thus to avoid the dilemma between realism and idealism. As he says of his first book at the end of *Phenomenology of Perception*, "the problem was to link the idealist perspective, according to which nothing exists except as an object for consciousness, and the realistic perspective, according to which consciousnesses are introduced into the stuff (*tissu*) of the objective world and of events in themselves" (*PP* 489–90/428/497). To link these two perspectives, however, it is necessary to disclose a sense of being that is neither that of a thing nor of a consciousness. It is therefore necessary to show that neither the mere thing (*blosse Sache*) qua closed totality of determinations, nor consciousness qua transparent presence to itself, or pure immanence, yields the proper sense of being and so makes it possible to account for the perceived world. Indeed, Merleau-Ponty shows that these two kinds of reality refer to the same attitude, and finally to the same meaning of being. For there is a theoretical complicity between objectivism, which reduces the world to physical nature, and subjectivism, which defines the world as that which is constituted by consciousness.

From the beginning, then, Merleau-Ponty shows that the concepts by which traditional philosophy accounts for reality fail to correspond to the true meaning of its being. This is why it is necessary to carve a path between idealism and realism. It is worth noting that this approach already indicates a place for life, for in criticizing realism and idealism Merleau-Ponty proposes a meaning of being that is neither that of a pure consciousness nor that of a mere object. To that end, then, Merleau-Ponty takes as his starting point the concept of behavior, "because, taken in itself, it is neutral with respect to the classical distinctions between the 'mental' and the 'physiological' and thus can give us the opportunity of defining them anew" (SC 2/4). By taking the concept of behavior as his starting point, Merleau-Ponty makes possible an investigation concerning life because behavior is a more neutral and comprehensive notion referring to what all living beings have in common.

We must note, however, that while the concept of behavior indicates the domain of life, it is not sufficient in itself to escape materialism or idealism. Indeed, there are philosophers (behaviorists) who reduce behavior to a causal relation, and others who believe that the source of behavior is consciousness. So although the concept of behavior is important in virtue of its neutrality, what really matters is the methodology Merleau-Ponty adopts. Instead of describing behavior from an internal point of view by observing what happens when we behave, as one might expect from a phenomenological approach, Merleau-Ponty bases his inquiry on the results of the sciences that study behavior, namely, psychology and physiology, and, more precisely, Gestalt psychology and Goldstein's physiology. These sciences work in a naïve ontological framework; they assume the realistic attitude, for which nature is "a multiplicity of events external to each other and bound together by relations of causality." These sciences are led by their own results to call into question that naïve ontology, however. As Merleau-Ponty explains, at the beginning of *Phenomenology of Perception*,

In order not to prejudge the issue, we shall take objective thought on its own terms and not ask it any questions which it does not ask itself. If we are led to rediscover experience behind it, this shift of ground will be attributable only to the difficulties which objective thought itself raises. (*PP* 86/71–72/83)

And this is exactly what happens: the results of physiological psychology cannot be reconciled with its ontological presuppositions; it therefore demands an ontological reform (an ontological shift), the characterization of which is the work of the philosopher.

Behavior cannot be explained, as in the case of a reflex, as a reaction to the physical and chemical properties of an object, that is to say, as an event situated in a world in itself and dependent on causal relations. The animal reacts to what makes sense for it, to what takes place in its vital environment (*Umwelt*). It acts, for instance, in relation to that which is attractive or dangerous to it, what is prey or predator, and of course it is impossible to reduce predation or danger to physical or chemical properties. Accordingly, behavior cannot be reduced to a mechanical reaction: it reveals something like an intention. The scientific analysis of behavior thus enables us to give up the realistic, naturalistic point of view: behavior does not exist in itself. A living gesture, for instance, is not reducible to the succession of its positions: it reveals a unity that is nothing other than the intention that gives it life. This unity is not a part of reality in itself, but a meaning irreducible to that reality. In this sense, there is an obvious convergence between Merleau-Ponty's methodology and the reflexive attitude: both stress the fact that existence-in-itself is a contradiction and that no reality can exist without an act of grasping, which requires a consciousness.

The fact of this convergence, however, does not mean that the two approaches are the same. If they were, "a moment of reflection would have provided us with a certitude in principle" (*SC* 138/127), and all that empirical research would have been unnecessary. Merleau-Ponty's methodology is, in fact, quite specific, and its importance must be stressed. To say that behavior is irreducible to a thing in itself bound to causal relations is not to say that it is the expression of a pure consciousness. This is incidentally why studying animals from an external, objective standpoint is so important, for the meaning that emerges in their behavior does not necessarily refer to our consciousness. If it is true that all behavior exhibits an intention, here is a case that does not depend on a consciousness. To begin with, animal behavior is not directed toward a mere thing. It does not seize the thing that makes sense for it in a disinterested way, that is, as an object endowed with general properties. Instead, it encounters it in terms of its vital meaning; indeed, the thing is nothing but the incarnation of a vital need. Accordingly, the animal's understanding of the thing is indistinguishable from the reaction the thing causes, that is to say, the animal's behavior. Proceeding by way of the behavioral sciences thus enables us to overcome the naturalistic attitude and its naïve ontology. This does not mean we are led to reinstate consciousness, as we would by the "shortcut" of reflection. The fact that behavior is not a thing does not imply that it is "the envelope of a pure consciousness."

On the basis of the findings discussed in the first two chapters, Merleau-Ponty emphasizes the specificity of living beings, that is, their irreducibility to their physical parts and properties. Even if the organism is nothing *more* than its parts, knowledge of the properties, the parts, and the laws governing them cannot provide the knowledge of the organism as a whole. Like everything in the world, the organism falls under physicochemical laws, but its specificity as a living being is dissolved in those laws. For example, we cannot account for the difference between normal and pathological at the physicochemical level, because every event, normal and pathological alike, obeys the laws of physics and chemistry. So if we imagine an infinitely intelligent God who could intuit the laws of nature immediately, bypassing the phenomenal world, which is a mere appearence from the standpoint of physical knowledge, that God would have no idea which is a normal and which is a pathological behavior, nor even, for that matter, which beings are living beings. The difference between a living being and a nonliving being cannot be accounted for if we confine our investigation strictly to the physicochemical level. As Merleau-Ponty says,

A total molecular analysis would dissolve the structure of the functions and of the organism into the undivided mass of banal physical and chemical reactions. Life is not therefore the sum of these reactions. In order to make a living organism reappear, starting from these reactions, one must trace lines of cleavage in them, choose points of view from which certain ensembles receive a common signification and appear, for example, as phenomena of "assimilation" or as components of a "function of reproduction"; one must choose points of view from which certain sequences of events, until then submerged in a continuous becoming, are distinguished for the observer as "phases" – growth, adulthood – of organic development. (*SC* 164–5/152)

There is no doubt, then, that the living being as such is irreducible to its parts. How can we account for this? One solution is to posit a vital force. This is the argument of vitalism. The living being defies physicochemical explanation qua *living* being, which is to say its irreducibility to physicochemical analysis is due to the presence of *life* in it. Yet this hypothesis in no way enables us to account for the concrete functions of living beings. Appealing to a vital force as a principle of explanation does not solve the problem but simply conceals our inability to overcome it: vitalism is essentially an expression of powerlessness.

There is no need to dwell on this point. It is important to notice, however, that the notion of compensating for the inadequacies of scientific analysis by positing a vital force rests on an *ontological presupposition:*

the critique of mechanism leads back to vitalism only if it is conducted, as often happens, on the plane of being. To reject the dogmatic thesis according to which the unity of the organism is a superstructure supported by a really continuous chain of physicochemical actions would then be to affirm the antithesis, also dogmatic, which interrupts this chain in order to make place for a vital force. (*SC* 171/158)

In other words, the inadequacies of scientific explanation lead to vitalism only if physicochemical analysis is considered adequate to reality in itself, a faithful representation of reality as it is. In that case, the irreducibility of the organism to a physicochemical analysis necessarily entails the presence of another reality, that is to say, a vital one. If we give up this presupposition, however, and regard the organism as a phenomenon, and the physicochemical analysis as a hypothesis based on a theoretical presupposition, we may be in a position to account for the irreducibility of living beings without appealing to a vital force.

Putting aside this false solution, then, the problem is this: "It is impossible for the intellect to compose images of the organism on the basis of partitive physical and chemical phenomena; and nevertheless life is not a special cause" (*SC* 165/152–3). In other words, the organism is nothing *more* than the sum of its parts; there is no vital force. It is something *other* than its parts, however, inasmuch as its life is not reducible to those parts. So the only solution lies, at least apparently, in assuming that the specifically vital dimension is not part of the real organism but refers to our way of perceiving the organism: the irreducibility of the organism would derive from the fact we project our thoughts onto physicochemical processes. As Merleau-Ponty asks, if one grants that the physicochemical analysis is, in principle, unlimited, this being the condition of a scientific research, do not the properly vital categories – the sexual object, the alimentary object, the nest – and the modes of conduct directed toward these objects cease to be intrinsic determinations of behavior and organism; do they not belong rather to our human way of perceiving them; and, in the *final analysis* ought not constructions of stimuli and reflexes be substituted for them in an objective study? (*SC* 166/153)

This solution, which apparently satisfies the conditions set by the problem, prompts *two kinds* of objections. The first is factual. If the specificity of life actually refers to our human way of perceiving, the fact remains that we cannot project our vital experience onto everything in the world. Indeed, the theory of projection is marked by a vicious circle: "Every theory of 'projection,' be it empiricist or intellectualist, presupposes what it tries to explain, since we could not project our feelings into the visible behavior of an animal if something in this behavior did not suggest the inference to us" (*SC* 169/156).

Which brings us to the second objection. Explaining the specificity of the organism in terms of a theory of projection presupposes a distinction between pure subjectivity and reality in itself, the same assumption that underlies vitalism. In fact, explaining the specificity of living beings as a human projection takes for granted that the only objective way to account for organic reality is in terms of physicochemistry. Inasmuch as the organism qua physicochemical construction is the organism in itself, anything falling outside that domain is necessarily subjective. Such is the implicit attitude of the theory of projection.

This attitude with regard to the reality of the organism involves another, more profound assumption about the meaning of subjectivity. The use of the word "projection" reveals that what is projected, that is to say, the subjective experience, has no universal validity and can correspond to no external reality. In other words, subjectivity is understood as empirical subjectivity, that is to say, a substantial reality, totally closed, situated in the world like anything else. What is lived by such a subjectivity can have no significance over and beyond its own particular empirical situation. This is why the theory of projection makes no sense: it cannot ascribe real significance to what we live, our lived experience, because it reduces the content of our subjectivity to our particular human experience. The real issue, then, is not the appeal to subjectivity to account for the specificity of the organism, but the conception of subjectivity as *empirical subjectivity*.

There is, in fact, something right about the theory of projection. For to explain the irreducibility of the organism to the physicochemical level without positing a vital force, it is necessary to admit that the organism as such is not something existing in itself and, accordingly, that it involves a meaning, that it is a phenomenon. The only way of overcoming the alternatives we have confronted is to give up the ontological presupposition according to which organic reality is a reality in itself. But it is a mistake to refer to the organism as no longer belonging to reality in itself, to an empirical subjectivity. In short, there is no alternative between the reality of the organism and the position of consciousness. One need only define the living dimension of the organism as a signification (not as a vital force), and the subject of the perception of the organism as a transcendental subject. In that case, the subjective character of the experience is compatible with its objective value.

We are now in a position to understand Merleau-Ponty's solution. The problem was this: How can we account for the irreducibility of the organism without positing a vital force? How can we define the organism, allowing for the fact that it is at once *different* from the sum of its parts and yet nothing *more* than its parts? The answer is implicit in the question. On the level of being, of reality in itself, we have seen that there is no solution. So we must describe the organism from another level; we must alter our ontological presuppositions. Signification is indeed something different from the physicochemical parts of the organism, but because it is something *ontologically* different, because it is not a thing, it cannot be something *more* than the sum of the parts. As Merleau-Ponty says, "the idea of *signification* permits conserving the category of life without the hypothesis of a vital force" (*SC* 168/155).

Indeed, in *The Structure of Behavior* the concept of signification is introduced through the concept of *form*, which comes from Gestalt psychology. Thanks to the contributions of Gestalt psychology, Merleau-Ponty understands that a reality can be irreducible to the sum of its parts, can be more than an additive whole, without therefore being a merely subjective reality: a gestalt remains objective even though it is not an object in the sense of a sum of material parts. If "forms" are "total processes whose properties are not the sum of those which the isolated parts would possess" (SC 49/47), then organisms, as irreducible to physicochemical laws, are themselves *forms*. The concept of signification thus defines the ontological status of forms, that is to say, original realities, not contents of consciousness. Merleau-Ponty writes,

the significance and value of vital processes which science, as we have seen, is obliged to take into account are assuredly attributes of the *perceived* organism, but they are not extrinsic denominations with respect to the true organism; for the true organism, the one which science considers, is the concrete totality of the perceived organism, that which supports all the correlations which analysis discovers in it but which is not decomposable into them. (SC 169/156)

Indeed, we arrive at the reality of the organism, or the organism as a real entity, when several events, in themselves devoid of meaning, appear as moments of a unity, manifestations of a vital behavior: we arrive at life when we manage to find points of view from which ensembles acquire a common signification. Even if it requires a consciousness, the signification is not a mere projection, but the very reality of the organism. A grasp of the signification is a disclosure of the biological reality. The totality is not an appearance, then, but a phenomenon.

Merleau-Ponty's great discovery here is that life is a phenomenal reality, in the sense that it is *real qua phenomenon*. His analysis entails a twofold conclusion. The first has to do with the status of life, the second with the status of phenomena. If real life, real organism, can be grasped at the level of phenomena, it follows that phenomena are real, that they are not mere manifestations of another, more basic reality. The step back from reality in itself to phenomena enables us to arrive at the reality of life, while life enables us to discover the reality of phenomena. If life is real as, but only as, phenomenon, we may infer the autonomy of phenomena, that is, that the meaning of the being of entities is precisely phenomenality.

Now the difficulty is to understand the autonomy of phenomenal reality, to give sense to the identity of reality and phenomenality, which is what phenomenology demands. What exactly is the status of the kind of signification in terms of which Merleau-Ponty defines living beings? Under what conditions can we understand the autonomy of phenomenality and identify the phenomenality of life with its reality? It must be said that Merleau-Ponty's position in *The Structure of Behavior* is not entirely clear. This is particularly evident in his shifting terminology, which mixes phenomenological and Kantian vocabulary (the organism is an "ideal unity," a "signification," an "idea," an "essence"). In fact, when he wrote *The Structure of Behavior*, his concept of *phenomenon* was more Kantian than phenomenological, that is to say, referring to transcendental consciousness in contrast to the thing in itself. Indeed, in the last chapter, the purpose of which is to evaluate the philosophical significance of the results of the three first chapters, he draws a Kantian conclusion.

Still, substituting transcendental consciousness for empirical consciousness is not sufficient for accounting for the unity of phenomenality and reality, that is to say, for the ontological status of life. The opposition between objective reality and subjectivity is not thereby overcome but merely displaced, so that it now takes the form of the Kantian distinction between things in themselves and phenomena. This is why the resort to transcendental subjectivity in the Kantian sense remains unsatisfactory. The resort to criticism (the "critical tradition") makes sense negatively, in opposition to a causal way of thinking, but it cannot be the solution. Merleau-Ponty writes at the end of the book,

> this first conclusion stands in a relation of simple homonymy with a philosophy in the critical tradition. What is profound in the notion of "Gestalt" from which we started is not the idea of signification but that of *structure*, the joining of an idea and an existence which are indiscernible, the contingent arrangement by which materials begin to have meaning in our presence, intelligibility in the nascent state. (*SC* 222–3/206–7)

Defining living beings as phenomena in a Kantian sense is not at all sufficient because such phenomena refer to empirically real entities and so cannot exhaust the reality of that of which they are appearances. In other words, to say the phenomenon is autonomous is to recognize not just that it is a manifestation of an entity, but that it is *really identical with that entity*. This is why Merleau-Ponty emphasizes that the important point about form is the conjunction – indeed, the identity – of an idea and an entity because the two are in fact "indiscernible." Understanding the phenomenon, as it has been brought to light in the case of life, requires understanding how an idea and an existence can be indiscernible.

The problem is this: the phenomenon is not an appearance, but rather what is given by being itself. Being exists only as phenomenon, which is to say, phenomenality is reality. On the other hand, the appearing, the relation of manifestation, clearly entails a distinction between *what* is manifest and *the manifestation itself*. Even if phenomenality is autonomous, in the sense that it does not depend on another reality, it cannot be, qua phenomenality, a new reality. It is the manifestation *of* something, a "coming to light," and this entails a distinction. The problem, then, is how to account for phenomenality, which entails a distinction between the appearing and that which appears, without referring to consciousness. How is it possible to reconcile the autonomy, which is to say, the unity, of phenomenality with that distinction? More precisely, how can we reconcile the unity of being and phenomenality, as demanded by the phenomenological reduction, with their difference, as implied by the notion of manifestation? Merleau-Ponty's ontological aim is to address this problem, that is, to characterize a sense of being that meets these requirements. I would like to show that that characterization is based on an analysis of the sense of being of living beings and that for this reason the lectures on nature play a crucial role in the elaboration of Merleau-Ponty's ontology. In these lectures, the analysis of living beings, in the light of scientific findings, reveals an original meaning of being that sheds new light on the being of nature itself.

The lectures on nature, delivered in three years (1956-7, 1957-8, and 1959-60), occupy an important place because they coincide with the period during which Merelau-Ponty changed philosophical direction toward an ontology, which was to be worked out in *The Visible and the Invisible*. Because they are contemporary with this ontological turn, the lectures must have played a role in it. Indeed, in numerous unpublished notes for *The Visible and the Invisible*, Merleau-Ponty again takes up conclusions that emerged in the lectures. This is confirmed by the justifications that he gives for the choice of this topic. We do not seek a

philosophy of Nature as referring to a separate power of being, in which we would envelop the rest, or that at least we would posit separately, against the philosophy of Spirit or of History or of consciousness. – The theme of Nature is not a numerically distinct theme....Nature as a leaf or layer of total Being – the ontology of Nature as a way toward ontology – the way that we prefer because the evolution of the concept of Nature is a more convincing propaedeutic, [since it] more clearly shows the necessity of the ontological mutation. (N 265/204)

Far from being approached as a positive, autonomous object or potency, then, nature is the means by which Merleau-Ponty will be able to critique objective ontology. The portion of the text dedicated to physical nature has a primarily critical significance: it is a question of showing how, in every classical conception of nature, there is a dimension that escapes objective ontology. Yet with the exception of the chapter on Whitehead, Merleau-Ponty derives no positive notion of nature from the study of concepts of physical nature. It is rather the study of living nature that provides new concepts for his ontological project.

As early as the introduction, however, the definition he gives of nature is striking. He wants to explain the meaning of the *word* "nature," which goes back to Greek philosophy:

In Greek, the word "nature" comes from the verb *phuô*, which alludes to the vegetative; the Latin word comes from *nascor*, "to be born," "to live"; it is drawn from the first, more fundamental meaning. There is nature wherever there is a life that has meaning, but where, however, there is not thought; hence the kinship with the vegetative. Nature is what has a meaning, without this meaning being posited by thought: it is the autoproduction of a meaning. (N 19/3)

This text seems to comprise two distinct parts. First, Merleau-Ponty reminds us of the original meaning of nature, which refers to a process of development, of growth; in this sense, nature has an original relation to life, or rather, in life the original meaning of nature appears in a privileged way. He then explains this original meaning on a philosophical level. Yet even if he is merely trying to clarify the philosophical significance of the Greek and Latin concepts of nature, I think he is, in fact, already assuming this meaning, which suggests that, for him, too, nature is "the self-production of a meaning." This means, first, that in nature there is no difference between meaning and reality, and second, for this reason, that nature originally refers to life, that is to say, there is a natural self-production, which accounts specifically for life, but in fact involves all natural beings. Thus, I believe nature, as defined in these lectures, offers a new meaning of being that makes it possible to surmount the dualities in Merleau-Ponty's first two books, and thus to solve our problem. I also believe, accordingly, that this meaning of being emerges from a study of living beings, to such an extent that nature originally means life, or in other words that there is an original sense of nature that accounts for the possibility of life.

We must rely on detailed and accurate analysis in biology. The example of the embryogenesis of the axolotl, an American salamander, is particularly helpful.[4] The development of the nervous system of the embryo involves a reference to the salamander's future behavior, to its swimming. In fact, it appears that that future behavior, of which the embryo is yet not capable, governs the nervous growth: the anatomy is subject to the way in which the animal will behave. Every local development thus refers to a global behavior, and so to the animal as a whole; the present involves a reference to the future. The embryo exists not just as a present reality; rather, "there are affinities between the spatial parts of the embryo and the temporal parts of its life" (N 203/152, translation modified). The entire gesture or behavior therefore cannot be explained by the composition of the nerves because that entirety governs the nervous functioning of the parts spatially and the growth of the nervous system and of its connections temporally.

Moreover, we must notice that the organism as a whole, that is, as a style of behavior, exists only as a perceived reality. Indeed, to say that the organism as a whole is not reducible to its material parts amounts to saying that the whole has no material existence, that is, as we have seen, that it exists as a phenomenal reality. This account reiterates that of *The Structure of Behavior*, but in greater depth, inasmuch as it shows the efficacy of the whole in the growth, which is to say the material constitution, of the organism. What is again at stake here is the status of the whole. As Merleau-Ponty writes at the end of his analysis of Coghill's results,

When we rise to the consideration of the whole of the organism, the totality is no longer describable in physiological terms; it appears as emergent. How are we to understand this relation of totality of parts as a result? What status must we give to totality? Such is the philosophical question that Coghill's experiments pose, a question which is at the center of this course on the idea of nature and maybe the whole of philosophy. (N 194/145)

The problem is that "we must avoid two errors: positing a positive principle (idea, essence, entelechy) behind the phenomena, and not seeing any regulatory principle at all" (*N* 207/155). In other words, it is impossible to explain the development of the embryo by the action of a positive principle, as if the future organism already existed as an essence or an entelechy that could govern its own growth. In this way, on one hand, Merleau-Ponty's position is not Aristotelian, for if there is a teleology, it cannot rest on a positive finality, that is to say, a substance. Indeed, the whole is nothing *more* than the sum of the parts. On the other hand, it is impossible to deny the existence of a regulatory principle, whatever it is, because the organism is not reducible to the sum of its parts and the growth of the whole is not reducible to the growth of the parts. It is obviously impossible to understand the efficacy of the whole as a mere appearence, that is, as a human projection on the growth of the organism as, say, a retrospective illusion. How, then, can we conceive of the status of the whole, allowing for the fact that it is nothing positive or distinct from the parts and yet is that which governs the growth and relations of the parts and is, in this sense, irreducible to them?

Merleau-Ponty's solution consists in changing the level at which the totality is defined, that is, by characterizing the whole as an original reality, as he does in *The Structure of Behavior*, but now in a far more radical way. On one hand, we must assume that the whole, or rather the behavior and the animal as a whole, is *real* because it is efficacious, because nothing in the growth of the organism and its functioning can be explained without a reference to the whole. As Merleau-Ponty writes in an unpublished note, "the whole is no less real than the parts." Yet if the whole is no less real than its parts, it is not real *in the way* its parts are. Accordingly, the being of the whole has an original meaning that is necessarily different from that of the parts. On the other hand, this whole exists for someone; it involves reference to a point of view. As Merleau-Ponty writes in another unpublished note, "life is only visible on a certain scale of observation, macroscopic" (he adds, "but on this scale, [it is] entirely true and original"). This may be explained by the following passage from *Nature:*

the organism is not a sum of instantaneous and punctual microscopic events; it is an enveloping phenomenon, with the macroscopic style of an ensemble in movement. *Between* the microscopic facts, global reality is delineated like a watermark, never graspable for objectivizing-atomistic thinking, never eliminable from or reducible to the microscopic. (*N* 268/207)

In other words, even if the whole is real, it is phenomenal in the sense that it is irreducible to microscopic (physicochemical) events; it presupposes a point of view.

How can the organism be real, then, in the sense of efficacious and irreducible, and yet exist only from a point of view? This question seems insoluble, even contradictory, if we assume a certain definition of reality, if we define the true meaning of being in terms of microscopic existence. *If we contest this presupposition, however, and understand that reality is not necessarily reached through an analytic approach, then the totality will be at once phenomenal and real.* This is precisely the step Merleau-Ponty takes, which makes possible his ontological turn. Consider this very important passage:

To seek the real in a closer view would be to work against the grain. Maybe we must take the opposite path. The real is perhaps not obtained by pressing appearances; it perhaps is appearance. Everything depends our ideal of knowledge, which makes a *bloße Sache* of being (Husserl). Grasped only as a whole, however, perhaps the totality is not missing from reality. The notion of the real is not necessarily linked to that of molecular being. Why would there not be molar being? The model of Being would be elsewhere than in the particle; it might be, for example, in a being of the order of Logos, and not of the "pure thing." (N 209/157)

This text is decisive inasmuch as it brings to light the assumption underlying our concept of reality, an assumption that is ultimately atomistic: the real is local and not global, molecular and not molar, so that what is divisible is necessarily an appearence. In the case of a living being, if we divide it, we miss its reality, at least there is a level beneath which we no longer find life. Merleau-Ponty's genius here lies in giving up this strong assumption about the meaning of reality and recognizing that if life qua reality is accessible from a global, or "molar," point of view, we must conclude that the very *phenomenality of the whole is reality,* that there is no distinction to be drawn between real being and "appearance." Here Merleau-Ponty reveals the absolute identity between being and phenomenality and is thus in a position to provide a foundation for the autonomy of phenomenality.

Moreover, thanks to this rigorous analysis of life, Merleau-Ponty discovers a new meaning of being, situated beyond the distinction between the in-itself and the for-itself, thus overcoming the opposition between consciousness and object, which Merleau-Ponty knows he must abandon. It is noteworthy that already in the lectures on nature he uses the word "flesh" (*chair*). Reality is nothing other than its appearance, but appearance is an original and specific reality; it exists "in itself" as appearance and so does not depend on consciousness. Reality, then, is not phenomenal because it refers to consciousness (this was still the position of *The Structure of Behavior* and *Phenomenology of Perception*); rather, it refers to consciousness because it is *in itself phenomenal:* consciousness is a *dimension* or *consequence* of phenomenality, not a *condition* for it. We could say, borrowing from expressions that Merleau-Ponty uses in the last texts, that the phenomenality means visibility or perceptuality in itself. It is not that the world becomes visible because there is vision; rather, vision becomes possible because of the intrinsic visibility of the world.

Of course, it remains for us to understand, as Merleau-Ponty says, "how this vision, this being *at* [something] becomes mind (*esprit*) – or awakens (*suscite*) a mind" (*N* 272/210). Be that as it may, by an account of the meaning of life and its irreducibility to a summation of parts, Merleau-Ponty discovers an original meaning of being, irreducible to the objective and correlative to the subjective sense. In this way, the analysis of life plays an essential role in his elaboration of an ontology at the end of his life. Indeed, he describes the "flesh" exactly as he defines the phenomenal being of life in the lectures on nature: "the flesh of the world is of the Being-seen, i.e. is a Being that is *eminently percipi*, and it is by it that we can understand the *percipere*" (*VI* 304/250). The phenomenon – that is, the flesh – is pregnant with all possible perceptions, hence, the being-seen makes it possible to understand the perceiving, the *percipere*.

It remains to define this meaning of being in greater depth. We can no longer refer it back to a consciousness, as in *Phenomenology of Perception*; on the contrary, the meaning of the being of consciousness depends on the meaning of being of phenomenality. It is clear that, qua phenomenal being, it cannot exist like a thing, fully positive, self-identical. More precisely, if it is true that the whole is *nothing* more than its parts without being the sum of them, we must acknowledge that nothingness *has a certain reality*. If that which is nothing more than its parts has an efficacy, we can no longer oppose nothingness to being, and we must admit that the phenomenal totality is a singular form of nothingness, a negativity that is not absolutely opposed to positivity. The organism as such is not some-thing in the same sense in which the parts of it are something, but neither is it therefore pure nothingness. Recall here the Heideggerian definition of being (*Sein*) as nothing, in the sense of the negation of entities (*Seiende*); being is nothing in the sense of *no thing*, which is to say the negation of any entity. Be that as it may, Merleau-Ponty writes,

We must posit in the organism a principle that is either *negative* or based on *absence*. We can say of the animal that each moment of its history is empty of what will follow, an emptiness which will be filled in later. . . . The guiding principle is neither before nor behind; it's a phantom, it is the axolotl, all the organs of which would be the trace; it's the hollowed-out design of a certain style of action, which would be that of maturation; the arising of a need that would be there before that which will fill it. (*N* 207/155–6)

The organism is thus like a musical theme that is never played as such and so only appears in its variations. On one hand, the theme determines each variation and is in this sense effective: there would be no variations if they did not refer to this theme. On the other hand, the theme is absent from the variations because each variation is not itself the theme, but precisely a modification of it. In this example, the theme is present as absent, as that of which the variations are manifestations. In the same way, the organism is that unity without which the parts and the events would have no meaning but that is never present as such: the organism is present as absent, that is, as hidden in the events it governs.

This is why Merleau-Ponty writes, quite accurately, that "the re-ality of organisms supposes a non-Parmenidean being, a form that escapes the duality of being and nonbeing. One can therefore speak of the presence of the [common] theme of these realizations, or say that the events are grouped around a certain absence" (*N* 240/183). It amounts to the same thing to say on one hand that the theme, the totality governing the realizations, is present, and on the other hand that the totality to which every event refers is absent. Indeed, living being qua phenomenon or totality escapes the distinction between presence and absence: it is present – that is, real and efficient – as absent: it is, to be precise, the presence of a certain absence.

It is impossible not to recognize here the relation between the visible and the invisible by means of which Merleau-Ponty will characterize perception in *The Visible and the Invisible*. The invisible, which is synonymous with meaning, or condition of possibility, is in principle not something (it is not some *thing*) that could become visible. It lies in a dimension of invisibility *constitutive* of visibility: it is *as visible* that the visible is invisible. In other words, vision of something in the world requires a relation with the world as whole, as inexhaustible depth. A thing can be seen only if it is seen as something that exists, which is to say something belonging to the world, standing out against the world. A relation to this whole is thus involved in every perception, and in this sense the whole is present. As an inexhaustible totality, however, it cannot be present in itself (otherwise, it would no longer be a totality, but a thing in the world): it is, to be precise, present as absent. That which manifests itself, that which comes to light in every concrete perception, at the same time withdraws out of this presence: it presents itself by remaining absent. In short, as Merleau-Ponty writes in an important note,

The sensible is precisely that medium in which there can be *being* without it having to be posited; the sensible appearance of the sensible, the silent persuasion of the sensible is Being's unique way of manifesting itself without becoming positivity, without ceasing to be ambiguous and transcendent. (*VI* 267/214)

There is no doubt, then, that the way Merleau-Ponty conceives of the perceived world is influenced, if not determined, by his analysis of life, which reveals an efficacious presence of the totality as absent. We could say there is a sense in which Merleau-Ponty makes use of the notion of totality discovered by Gestalt psychology and by Kurt Goldstein to conceive of the relation between world and perceptual presence, that is, between transcendence and appearance. The living totality reveals a transcendence that is not the transcendence of a transcendent, or a reducible distance, and conversely the transcendence of the world is understood as an inexhaustible whole.

We must take one more step, however. The characterization of living being as a kind of nothing that is not opposed to being, which blurs the Parmenidean distinction between being and nonbeing, is still abstract. We must therefore deepen the characterization of the specificity of living beings. For if the whole is nothing more than the parts, that is to say, a totality immanent in the parts, it follows that the parts no longer exist as spatiotemporal parts, that they communicate with their own future and their own past. If the theme of the animal melody is nothing other than its realization, then the whole is nothing more than the parts themselves as transcending their own spatial and temporal locations. To say that every event of an organism manifests the presence of a whole as absent amounts to saying that every event is more than itself and, in this sense, includes a dimension of possibility and so transcends its own position as to encroach on other events. The whole is nothing but the transversal communication among the events. Indeed, a vital process, for example, cellular regeneration, refers to a form that is not yet present, of which the process is a realization.

There are two ways to understand this situation, which is typical of vital phenomena. If we maintain the classical idea of space and time as frameworks for successive or contemporaneous events, so that any event is situated in one single point of this framework, then the process of regeneration can be explained only by the active presence of a positive form, for example, an entelechy. In this case, we try to explain vital processes within the classical distinction between existence, which is spatiotemporally situated, and essence, which is not in space and time. We can also explain the process of regeneration by admiting "in the very fabric of physical elements a transtemporal and transspatial element we do not take account of by supposing an essence outside of time" (N 231/176). In this case, we take seriously the specificity of the process and draw the necessary ontological conclusion, namely, that the distinction between existence and essence is an *abstraction*. We must posit an essence if we first assume a spatiotemporal framework. If the fabric of reality reveals a transversal communication, however, a dimension that exceeds every local and temporal position, then we can explain the communication and the kinship among events without appealing to the concept of essence. The whole, which escapes the distinction between being and nonbeing, must therefore be defined as that transversal dimension that links all spatiotemporal events, as the axis along which the events are equivalent, like a melody, which is nothing more than the notes, but precisely as they communicate with one another other.

This dimension refers to the vital whole, the mode of existence of which does not respect the dualities of being and nonbeing, of existence and essence. As Merleau-Ponty writes, "In a sense, there is only the multiple, and this totality that surges from it is not a totality in potential, but the establishment of a certain dimension" (*N* 208/156). We know that the aim of the chapter in *The Visible and the Invisible* titled "Interrogation and Intuition" is precisely to surmount this opposition and to disclose a deeper aspect, which he calls "wild essence," "dimension," and "hinge." I believe, then, that this notion of dimension, understood as a system of equivalences, which is Merleau-Ponty's concept of being, also derives from his analysis of life. Vital processes reveal a unity of style par excellence, that is, a kinship that is not based on any positive principle, such as an essence. Rather, vital processes reveal a communication among events beyond the spatiotemporal framework. The central concept of Merleau-Ponty's ontology derives from the phenomenology of life.

NOTES

1. Derrida, *Speech and Phenomena*, 14–15.
2. *Speech and Phenomena*, 13.
3. This movement is called "transcendance" or "existence" in *Phenomenology of Perception*, and the double meaning of life is called "ambiguity." In the ontological period of Merleau-Ponty's later work, however, the concept of "flesh" (*chair*) comprises all these dimensions.
4. See G. E. Coghill, *Anatomy and the Problem of Behavior*.

9   The Embryology of the (In)visible

With the 1995 publication of the notes to Merleau-Ponty's three lecture courses on the subject of nature, scholars of the philosopher have
been given a treasure trove of material with which to make sense of
the "ontological turn" in his late thinking and to reconstruct the possible trajectory and potentially radical implications of what, by the
necessity of accident, became his final work. These notes, assembled
under the collective title *Nature,* bring together materials from the
lecture courses of 1956–7, 1957–8, and 1959–60, respectively titled
"The Concept of Nature," "The Concept of Nature: Animality, the
Human Body, Passage to Culture," and "The Concept of Nature: The
Human Body."[1]

The importance of these lecture notes goes well beyond their contribution of a wealth of material relevant to Merleau-Ponty's final
project, fragments of which are presented in *The Visible and the
Invisible.* Indeed, the broad claim I want to make in this chapter
is that Merleau-Ponty's confrontation with the biological sciences
of his day, not unlike his earlier engagement with Gestalt theory,
psychology, and physiology (in both *The Structure of Behavior* and
Phenomenology of Perception), furnished him with the means necessary to make a crucial philosophical breakthrough: just as his early
turn to science allowed him, through a kind of immanent analysis,
to *discover* the incarnate experience of the body as the necessary implication of its scientific objectification, so, too, did his later engagement lead immanently to the discovery of a properly philosophical
concept of embodied life necessarily situated beneath the division
between consciousness and body, thought and extension, memory
and matter. In both cases, science can be said to have played an enabling role for philosophy: in the former, by furnishing a necessary

distance from the philosophical determination of the body as necessarily either an object of consciousness or simply identical with consciousness itself; in the latter, by introducing the "object" of a new ontology and a new natural history no longer beholden to the long-dominant conception of nature as pure positivity.

Taken too far or too literally, however, my parallel between these two engagements with science would quickly prove misleading because Merleau-Ponty's later turn to the biological sciences marks his attempt to overcome that very impasse at which his earlier engagement with science had left him: the impasse of a philosophy that takes as its starting point the distinction between consciousness and object. To be sure, Merleau-Ponty saw his task from the very beginning to be that of undermining this distinction, along with others tributary to it (spontaneity and receptivity, activity and passivity, *pour-soi* and *en-soi*), and his first turn to Gestalt psychology and physiology was made precisely in the name of such a task. Yet, as he gradually came to realize, this early recourse to science and the concept of the body it allowed him to introduce could not rise to the task because it proceeded by introducing the body as the solution to what remained a more fundamental dualism of consciousness and object. What was necessary – and what his second turn to science afforded – was the introduction of a concept of organism or living body as a unitary phenomenon constituted by the identity of behavior and development, a unitary phenomenon of which phenomenality and consciousness would simply be dependent aspects.

On this point, Merleau-Ponty's own evaluation of his accomplishment and future task is unequivocal, as is his emphasis on the role of natural science within his final work. In one of the working notes published in *The Visible and the Invisible,* he admits that the "problems posed in *Ph.P.* [*Phenomenology of Perception*] are insoluble because I start from the 'consciousness' – 'object' distinction" (*VI* 253/200). In another, he situates his future work accordingly, making explicit reference to the three parts of the *Nature* lectures: "I must show that what one might consider to be 'psychology' (*Phenomenology of Perception*) is in fact ontology," and "that the being of science can neither be nor be thought as *selbstständig*. Whence the chapters on: Physics and Nature – animality – the human body as *nexus rationum* or *vinculum substantiale*" (*VI* 230/176). Merleau-Ponty's second turn to nature, then, would appear to be motivated by the very failure of his earlier effort to deploy psychology and physiology as a means of situating the body "outside" or "beneath" the framework of a philosophy of reflection, and its purpose to be nothing less than the passage to ontology so provocatively and perplexingly presented in the notion of the "flesh" most systematically developed in the fourth chapter of *The Visible and the Invisible*.

For this reason, Merleau-Ponty's engagement with various quasi-autonomous domains of biological research merits concrete examination in and of itself. Still, because this engagement aims at the articulation of a new ontology – the ontology of the flesh – such an examination can hardly avoid issues of profound philosophical import and, for that reason, should let itself be guided by the philosophical leitmotifs orienting Merleau-Ponty's lectures on nature. Of these, there are (at least) four, and all can, not surprisingly, be stated as claims about the singularity of modern biological science: (1) the biological sciences form the basis for opposing the Cartesian ontology of nature, (2) they serve as a source of constraint concerning what philosophy can say about being, (3) they furnish ontic evidence for a philosophical conception of life rooted in a concept of negativity *within* being, and (4) they give the foundation for a conception of the body as a double being or "natural symbolism."

In this chapter, I want to evaluate Merleau-Ponty's second "turn to science" by examining several of his concrete engagements with the biological sciences of his time in the light of these philosophical leitmotifs. My first goal, accordingly, is simply expository: to give an introduction to a more or less obscure body of work available, until recently, only to a French-speaking public. Beyond that, I shall attempt to defend a claim that Merleau-Ponty's philosophical analysis of the biological sciences solves the impasse in his thinking in *Phenomenology of Perception* – the dead end of a philosophy that takes the duality of consciousness and object as its starting point – precisely by opening a new trajectory of thinking, a trajectory oriented by and toward a philosophical concept of life.

Schematically put, my claim is that the fundamental correlation of behavior and morphogenesis Merleau-Ponty discovers in his exploration of the biological sciences *grounds* the correlation of phenomenology and ontology in his late work, and that it does so precisely because it overcomes the dichotomy between mind and body on one side and world and environment on the other, a dichotomy Merleau-Ponty simply took for granted in *Phenomenology of Perception* and, indeed, up until his confrontation with Jacob von Uexküll's ethology. By rendering mind–body somehow already the stuff of the world, a part of the flesh, and by making the world integral to the operation and development of the mind–body, Merleau-Ponty's philosophical concept of life transforms his phenomenology into a philosophy of immanence – a philosophical account of the human body as a part of nature, of human experience as the phenomenalizing of the world itself.

My chapter develops this argument through three sections. In the first of these, I explore Merleau-Ponty's turn to the topic of nature by focusing on several of his important engagements with the biological sciences of his time. Concentrating on his analysis of embryology, phylogenesis, and neo-Darwinian evolution in particular, I attempt to gauge the stakes of Merleau-Ponty's critique of the Cartesian conception of nature and his effort to specify the human as a particular manner of being a body. These two valences of Merleau-Ponty's engagement with nature will culminate in his philosophical concept of life as negativity within being, the very concept that will allow him to overcome the impasse of *Phenomenology of Perception*.

In the second section, I analyze precisely how this philosophical concept of life informs the "ontological turn" in his late work. It is the living body qua living, I suggest, that allows Merleau-Ponty to dedifferentiate the two complementary processes of the flesh – the becoming-world of the flesh and the becoming-flesh of the world – and thereby to arrive at a properly systemic view of the coupling of mind–body and environment–world.

Finally, in the very brief third section, I defend the contemporary relevance of Merleau-Ponty's philosophy of nature by contrasting it with the work of an influential philosopher, Daniel Dennett, and an important biological scientist, Francisco Varela, both of whom explore the cusp of philosophy and science in interesting and productive ways. By offering a middle path between Dennett's antimetaphysical instrumentalism and Varela's cellular or molecular realism, Merleau-Ponty allows us to treat life in a philosophically significant manner: as the very basis of our embodied perceptual experience and as the basis of phenomenology itself.

I. LIFE

Perhaps the easiest way to circumscribe Merleau-Ponty's exploration of nature is the most literal one: by analyzing its points of orientation and culmination. If, for example, we consider the opening pages of the *Résumé de Cours* for the first set of lectures, we find Merleau-Ponty justifying his attention to nature, which he admits might seem "an untimely theme," precisely because of its neglect within the postidealist philosophical tradition. Reading it as a symptom rather than a valid judgment, Merleau-Ponty correlates this neglect with a blindness to the profound ontological implications of nature:

nature is not only the object, the partner of consciousness in a face-to-face [confrontation] with knowledge. It is an object out of which we have emerged (*surgi*), one in which our preliminaries have been set out little by little until the moment of joining together in an existence, and one which continues to sustain that existence and to furnish it with materials. Whether what is at stake is the individual fact of birth or the birth of institutions and societies, the originary relation of man and being is not that of a for-itself to an in-itself. Rather it continues in each human being who perceives. (*N* 356; *RC* 94/132–3)

From this passage alone, we can discern two of the most important factors that give the topic of nature its philosophical significance. On one hand, nature lies beneath the division of consciousness and extension, thinking and incarnation, which means that it provides a basis for an account of the human body as both emergent and prior to this division. On the other hand, nature names the very stuff of the human, such that the human body is itself both an element and expression of it.

When we turn to the motivating source of Merleau-Ponty's examination – the Cartesian conception of nature – we find the first of these factors both amplified and specified. In the *Résumé*, as in the course itself, Merleau-Ponty claims that Descartes's thematization of nature as pure positivity has dominated – and, hence, profoundly compromised – modern philosophy's understanding of nature. According to Merleau-Ponty, the Cartesian conception "compels all being, if it is not to be nothing, to be fully, without deficiencies (*lacune*), without hidden possibilities" (*N* 358–9; *RC* 98–9/137). This Cartesian obligation, as it were, stems historically and philosophically from a broader ontology that opposes being to nothingness and has the effect of confining being to actuality: a being is what it is because it cannot be anything else.

Now it is precisely to furnish an alternative to this all-or-nothing ontology that Merleau-Ponty embarks on his study of nature. As he recounts in the *Résumé* to the course on animality, this study should be understood as "an introduction to the definition of being": "it is a question of knowing if 'there is being' (*l'être est*) is a simple or self-sufficient proposition (*identique*), if one can say without further ado that 'there is being' and that 'there is not nothing' (*le néant n'est pas*)." Posed in relation to the "certain sector of being" that is nature, these properly philosophical questions will yield a different ontology, one that is not split between the vicious opposition of being and nothingness, between the irresolvable alternative of a "positivist" and a "negativist" thinking, but that can – precisely by containing all of the contradictions that arise between these – properly claim to underlie and to ground them both. It is by following the modern development of the concept of nature that Merleau-Ponty proposes to approach this new ontology: although, in the end, philosophy must intervene to expand the perspectives of science and unveil their "teleology," we must not forget that such intervention is possible only because the "so thoroughly un-Cartesian developments (*developpements si peu cartésians*)" of modern science reveal the very prospect of another ontology (*N* 359; *RC* 99/137).

At the other, far pole of Merleau-Ponty's engagement with nature, we find a concrete claim for the specificity of the human as a particular manner of being a body. This is, properly speaking, the fruit of the third lecture course devoted to the human body, and it stems from the necessary correlation of the ontology of life (developed in the second course) with the symbolic dimension Merleau-Ponty attributes to all embodiment: "the ontology of life," concludes Merleau-Ponty in the *Résumé* to the second course, "will emerge from confusion only by appealing . . . to brute being such as it is unveiled to us by our perceptual contact with the world" (*N* 376; *RC* 137/166). Two fundamental claims orient Merleau-Ponty's philosophical treatment of scientific research on embryology, phylogenesis, and neo-Darwinian evolution: first, the human is not simply the conjunction of animality and reason, which means that we must "grasp humanity above all as another manner of being a body" (*N* 269/208); second, the human is not built on the animal (as the evolutionary notion of descent alleges); rather "animality and human being are given only together, in the interior of a totality of being" (*N* 339/271).

Taken together, these two fundamental claims introduce a properly philosophical concept of emergence. This concept postulates that the human, as a manner of being a body, emerges out of the animal, or rather out of an *Ineinander* (intertwining) with animality (and, in the bigger picture, with being): it marks the introduction of a new dimensionality (a "vertical" dimension) that does not negate that from which it emerges and is indeed contained potentially in it:

Emergence of the flesh in life like that of life in the physicochemical: this "singular point" of life ... where the *Umwelt* [environment] is no longer dissimulated to itself – just as life is not in the physicochemical, but between the elements, as another dimension, so too *Empfindbarkeit* [sensibility] is not in the objective body or even in the physiological one. (*N* 280/217)

There is, accordingly, no "descent of a soul into a body, but rather the emergence of a life in its cradle, an instigated (*suscitée*) vision. This is because there is an interiority of the body, an 'other side,' for us invisible, of this visible" (*N* 280/218). Similarly, the "lateral union" of humanity and animality calls for a "bottom-up" conception of perception as emergent from our life as natural history:

Animal life refers to our sensible and our carnal life. This is not the idealist path, because our carnal, sensible life is not our human present or atemporal spirit. In the order of *Einfühlung* [sensitivity], of the "vertical" where our corporeity is given to us, there is precisely an opening to a visible, the being of which is not defined by the *percipi*, but where on the contrary the *percipere* is defined by the participation of an active *esse*. (*N* 338/271)

These claims mean that the elucidation of the human body as a perceiving body must recuperate and intensify the entire development, in the first two courses devoted to physical nature and life, respectively, by which Merleau-Ponty demonstrated that "there is finally no other way to think Nature than by perceived Nature." In the end, what such an elucidation will yield is a specification not simply of the immanence of human (qua manner of being a body) within being, but more significantly still, of the active participation of the human in the opening of the world: "it is only by recurring to nature as visible that we can understand...the emergence of an invisible perception in its relation to what it sees, as a gap (*écart*) in relation to the visible" (*N* 278/215).

This concept of emergence distinguishes Merleau-Ponty's second turn to science from his earlier engagement with Gestalt psychology and physiology. In particular, it furnishes a far richer explanation for the paradox of totality or unity: the paradox resulting from the fact that the organism (and here specifically the human body) is not reducible to the sum of its parts, and yet is nothing over and above these parts. Whereas *The Structure of Behavior* and *Phenomenology of Perception* approach this paradox via the Gestalt conception of form, and thus to some extent abstractly, in the *Nature* lectures, Merleau-Ponty concentrates his attention on the concretely irreducible macroscopic dimension of life:

the organism is not a   sum of instantaneous and punctual microscopic events; it is an enveloping phenomenon, with an allure of the whole, macroscopic. Global reality is sketched *between* the microscopic facts like a watermark (*en filigrane*), never graspable to objectifying-atomistic thinking, never eliminable or reducible to the microscopic: we had only a bit of protoplasmic jelly, and then we have an embryo, through a transformation that, always before or after, we are never witness to in our investment in a biological field. (*N* 268/207)

From where he stands in 1959–60, what is crucial for understanding this macroscopic dimension of being – and what allows it to resolve the paradox of totality – is the natural historical aspect of behavior understood as the active investment of biological space. Behavior, as Merleau-Ponty's analysis of morphogenesis shows, is precisely what fills the gap between function and structure. Whereas function can be explained in microscopic terms and within the space of the physicochemical, the production of structures is not governed exclusively by microscopic causality: accordingly, although everything that "takes place in embryonic regulation is physicochemistry, it is not physicochemistry that requires there to be an organism of typical form when the whole design is reconstituted from one of the parts" (*N* 268/207). The physicochemical, in short, cannot explain the development of macroscopic form, of the organism.

For Merleau-Ponty, the key to explaining the mystery of emergent totality lies in behavior. This is because behavior draws out a potential that is simply not there in the physicochemical, that emerges with and from the very movement it carries out. Behavior draws on the "dynamic anatomy," the "potentiality for growth," "intrinsic" to the organism: behavior is what transforms such intrinsic potentiality into history while simultaneously preserving it as a "source" for future growth.

Merleau-Ponty discovers the biological basis for this function of behavior in G. E. Coghill's study of the embryogenesis of the axolotl, a larval salamander native to Mexico and the western United States.[2] From Merleau-Ponty's perspective, Coghill's study demonstrates that behavior cannot be explained through microscopic analysis alone and, consequently, that behavior and emergent totality are of one piece. Thus the organization of the initial behavior of the axolotl is due not to neural function, but to the "growth of the whole organism": "The preneural system of integration 'steps beyond' (*enjambe*) nervous functioning and does not stop with its appearance." Furthermore, the capacity for *learning* characteristic of higher vertebrates – the very capacity strikingly manifest in the axolotl – stems from the "matrix of embryonic tissues" that surround nervous tissues: "This matrix must be the depositary of a potential for growth and, even once it has begun to function, the neuron must continue to grow, in a purely embryonic way" (*N* 192/143).

On the basis of these demonstrations, Coghill's work furnishes three fundamental principles for a philosophical understanding of the paradox of totality. First, Coghill rejects the notion of adaptation in favor of a conception of growth as a "solution" to a problem posed to the organism as a whole. Thus, the axolotl can be said to "transfer" the solution to the problem of living in water to the problem of living on land, thereby generating a new solution. Second, Coghill understands the development of the organism as the realization of a certain power – a "what it can do" – that forms a "possibility internal to the organism" and that is, strictly speaking, beyond its actual physiological function. This is why Coghill can claim that the embryo already contains a reference to its future. Third, and most consequentially, Coghill demonstrates that the maturation of the organism and the emergence of behavior are, effectively, of one piece. For the axolotl, existing from head to tail and swimming are two faces of a single process, or more exactly, a "double phenomenon": on one hand, a gradual expansion of total conduct across the body; on the other, the acquisition by the parts of the organism of an existence proper to them. In sum, behavior appears as a "principle immanent to the organism itself" and one that "emerges from the start as a totality" (N 194/145). It can hardly come as a surprise, then, that behavior lies right at the heart of the "philosophical question" orienting Merleau-Ponty's analysis of the idea of nature, which may well turn out to be the question of philosophy itself, namely, how should we understand the relation of the whole to the parts, what status must we give to the whole?

Merleau-Ponty's examination of behavior is further elaborated via Arnold Gesell's principles of "dynamic morphology." Like Coghill, Gesell identifies the organization of the body and behavior: for him the body is defined as the "site of behavior," a "grip (prise) on the external world" (N 196/146). Yet Gesell's work – perhaps because it addresses behavior at the human level – articulates several notions that will prove fundamental to Merleau-Ponty's philosophical definition of life. First, there is the asymmetry of behavior. Despite its bilateral construction, the organism confronts the world not frontally, but at an angle. As Merleau-Ponty puts it, the behavioral center of gravity tends to be placed in an eccentric position in relation to the organism's geometrical center. Although Gesell offers no explanation for this phenomenon of asymmetry, Merleau-Ponty is quick to extract its profound philosophical significance: "It is only in virtue of this asymmetry that there occur what Proust calls 'sides' (côtés). Objects must seem to me to diverge (en écart) from the symmetrical position which is the first position in the embryo, that is to say, the position of rest" (N 195/146). In what amounts to an "embryology of the (in)visible," Merleau-Ponty here rejoins the characteristic behavioral modality of higher-order organisms (i.e., movement) with the emergence of a dynamically constituted, perceptual, or phenomenological totality. (I return to this fundamental juncture in Section II.)

This notion of divergence reappears in two other crucial claims Gesell advances concerning behavior of higher-order organisms. On one hand, dynamic morphology is governed by "autoregulatory fluctuation," whereby a living being, insofar as it can be understood as a phenomenon in growth, is simultaneously in a state of relative equilibrium and in a state of disequilibrium (N 199/149); on the other hand, behavior has an "endogenous character" (N 201/151) or as Merleau-Ponty puts it, "the organism is the seat of an endogenous animation" (*N* 200/150), meaning of course that behavior does not descend from on high but emerges from below.

Together with the fundamental asymmetry of the living, these two principles form the basis of Merleau-Ponty's philosophical analysis of life as negativity within being. As he presents it initially in the course on animality, this analysis must toe the line between the two, closely correlated tendencies that haunt the paradox of totality by threatening to collapse it. On one hand, the analysis of life must avoid the error of placing a positive principle behind phenomena – whether it be idea, essence, or entelechy – that would (re)institute a transcendental cause. On the other hand, it must avoid the error of failing to introduce a regulatory principle, that is, a principle or "system of order"[3] which, by correlating the instability in one part of an organism with instabilities in other parts, would guarantee the endogenous origin of the organism's animation, its status as a "field," indeed "a true electric field," encompassing "a relation between parts and the whole" (*N* 200/150). Merleau-Ponty's philosophical concept of life emerges out of an effort to avoid these twin "errors."

Because of its fundamental significance for the philosophical payoff of Merleau-Ponty's second engagement with science, let me cite his analysis of life at some length:

It is necessary to introduce within the organism a principle that would be *negative* or *absence*. We can say of the animal that each moment of its history is a void of what will follow, a void to be filled later. Each present moment is not so much swollen with the future as propped up against it. If one considers the organism at a given moment, one will claim that there is the future in its present, because its present is in a state of disequilibrium.... The rupture of equilibrium appears as an operational nonbeing which prevents the organism from remaining in the previous phase.... Beyond this factor of disorder, of rupture of equilibrium, the present already traces the future in a more precise manner: from the moment of rupture, it is understood that the reequilibration will be not just any reequilibration, in the sense of an economic equilibrium ... as the return to zero.... And this disequilibrium is not defined in relation to certain pregiven external conditions that play the same role as weights in the balance; rather it takes account of the conditions instigated in the interior of the organism itself. The rough outlines (*ébauches*) of the organism in the embryo constitute a factor of disequilibrium.... These rough outlines must be considered as foreign bodies with respect to the present situation, and as a prioris for future development.... It is not a positive being but an interrogative being that defines life. (*N* 207/155–6)

Here we encounter the two fundamental facets of Merleau-Ponty's philosophical conceptualization of life: on one hand, the essential incompleteness or "disequilibrium" that opens the organism to the future; on the other, the embryonic equipotentiality from which such incompleteness stems. In a word, if the living being reaches beyond itself, exists in excess of itself, as originary desire (desire in the absence of any object), this is because, internally, it experiences itself as out of phase with itself, as haunted by "foreign bodies," by what *within itself* is nonactual, potential, to come. These poles are thus strictly complementary, and indeed, their very complementarity attests to the manner in which life is able to solve the paradox of totality (the nontranscendental nonidentity of the parts and the whole) and with it, the very problematic of the phenomenology of the flesh, namely, how the flesh can be both my flesh and the flesh of the world without the former being the vehicle of the latter.

On one hand, life as natural negativity is characterized by an "adhesion" (and not a "unity") among "elements of the multiple" or plurality of phenomena, meaning that its "reality" is, in a certain sense, nothing other than its appearance, that it cannot be located at the microscopic or molecular level, but has a "molar being" (*N* 209/157). On the other hand, life as natural negativity forms an interior within the living organism that is strictly correlative with its behavioral-cum-phenomenal field: "From the moment when the animal swims, there is a life, a theater, provided that nothing interrupts this adhesion of the multiple. It is a dimension that gives meaning to its surroundings" (*N* 208/156).

With this complementarity, we grasp nothing less than the identity of behavior and phenomenon, of movement and perception, that lies at the heart of Merleau-Ponty's phenomenology of life: without behavior to activate the negativity of life as a problem, there would simply be no phenomenal dimension at all; and without the natural negativity as a virtual interiority, there would be no possibility for such activation to occur in the first place. This is, finally, why Merleau-Ponty can claim a certain privilege for the human that does not abjure its immanence within nature. It is only in reference to the human body that we can truly *understand* the natural negativity and the interiority of the living, that we can grasp precisely why life does not comprise a positive power or spiritual force: "we install ourselves in perceived being/brute being, in the sensible, in the flesh where there is no longer a distinction between the in-itself and the for-itself, where perceived being is emphatically within being" (*N* 272/210).

II. SELF-MOVEMENT AND EXCESS: THE HUMAN BODY

Earlier I suggested that Merleau-Ponty's second engagement with science holds the key to making sense of his final project and thus to overcoming the impasse to which *Phenomenology of Perception* led him: the dead end of a philosophy that starts from an opposition of body–mind and object–world. How, we now need to ask, does his properly philosophical conceptualization of life inform the "ontological turn" in his late work? Why would a biological understanding of the body as both externally and internally, behaviorally and developmentally, *in excess of itself* succeed in accounting for the belonging-together of body and world while more properly philosophical paths of thought, such as the analysis of vision and touch, arguably do not? What is it about the living body *qua living* that allows it to dedifferentiate the two, strictly complementary, processes of the flesh: the becoming-world of the flesh and the becoming-flesh of the world? What, finally, are its consequences for our understanding of the trajectory of Merleau-Ponty's final work?

As we shall see, the answer to these questions has everything to do with the body's capacity, as a "natural negativity," to form a hinge between being and perception: by installing itself as negativity within being, the body phenomenalizes being from a position immanent within it. As Merleau-Ponty explains in the course on animality, what distinguishes the negativity specific to the living body from other, more abstract accounts of negation (Spinozist irreality, Hegelian determinate negation) is the principle of "divergence" (*écart*): both externally and internally, the living body operates by divergence, that is, through self-movement. Moving oneself means being "out of phase" with oneself, being in excess of one's actuality, both in the sense of originary desire (striving to fill a void that cannot be filled) and embryonic virtuality (the presence of the future within the present). As one working note puts it, "Absolute primacy of movement, not as *Ortsveränderung*, but as instability instituted by the organism (cf. F. Meyer), as *fluctuation organized by it*" (*VI* 284/230).

We might say, then, that if the living body solves the problem of the belonging-together of *esse* and *percipere*, it is precisely because – as essentially self-moving – it opens a divergence between itself and what it sees, a divergence that is filled by the flesh.[4] This is why Merleau-Ponty can assert that there is a correspondence "of my inside and [the world's] outside," just as there is a "correspondence of its inside and my outside" (*VI* 179n/136n). To say that the modality of the body's installation in being is self-movement is thus to move beyond the alternative *esse–percipere:* just as the world acquires an "inside" (the capacity to manifest itself through its own withdrawal) only because the body is constituted as an "outside" proper to it, so, too, does it possess an "outside" only because the body has an "inside" (the capacity to be out of phase with itself, to be in internal instability). The body's perception simply is the world's manifestation and vice versa. Accordingly, if the biological conception of the living solves the problem of the belonging-together of body and world, the reason must be that it can account for the identity of movement and perception.

To understand why this is so, let us now trace the evolution of the function of movement, and its correlation with the body, from *Phenomenology of Perception* to the final work.[5] Quite schematically, we can differentiate three "stages" in this evolution: (1) bodily movement as what constitutes the object and the world, (2) bodily movement as what opens the invisible, and (3) bodily movement as what constitutes the incarnation of the living. With the passage through these stages, Merleau-Ponty's analysis renders the body more primordial as it is shown to be more deeply biological. If in the end the body can be said to underlie (and to condition) the incarnation-consciousness dualism, it is precisely because it belongs to the world *as an essential modality of the living.*

PP Merleau-Ponty's description of the lived body (*corps propre*, one's own body) in *Phenomenology of Perception* aimed to uncover an originary intentionality anchored in the perceptual life of the body, and not in the reflective activity of thinking. Otherwise put, Merleau-Ponty attempted to show that intentionality is rooted in being-in-the-world and that the correlation between an act of think-ing (*noesis*) and a content of thought (*noema*) comprises nothing more than an abstraction from this primary modality of being re-alized by the body.[6] Accordingly, consciousness must be understood not as an "I think," but as an "I can," such that motility becomes strictly synonymous with intentionality: "Consciousness is being-toward-the-thing through the intermediary of the body. A movement is learned when the body has understood it, that is, when it has incor-porated it into its 'world,' and to move one's body is to aim at things through it" (*PP* 161/138–9/159–61). For this reason, the body forms something like a general medium between consciousness and the world: "Our bodily experience of movement is not a particular case of knowledge; it provides us with a way of access to the world and the object, with a 'praktognosia,' which has to be recognized as original and perhaps as primary" (*PP* 164/140/162). Insofar as consciousness is founded on this original and primary bodily motility, it must be understood to be exterior to itself, to transcend itself by going out into the world. Furthermore, movement itself must be viewed as synonymous with perception in the sense that this transcendence toward the world opens a gap that perception can in a certain sense be said to fill.

Strangely enough, the very strength of Merleau-Ponty's interven-tion – his revision of intentionality into a corporeal intentionality or "I can" – proves to be its own downfall, for the structure of transcen-dence toward the world ultimately leaves intact the consciousness-world dualism.[7] In becoming the "mediator of the world," the body continues to be defined by its correlation with consciousness: as the originary basis of consciousness, the body introduces an opac-ity into intentionality. We can thus conclude that the recourse to movement in the *Phenomenology of Perception,* and specifically in the chapter on "The Spatiality of One's Own Body and Motility," aimed to establish the necessary opacity in the intentional relation of consciousness and the world. What was important at this point in Merleau-Ponty's development was precisely the intentional char-acter of movement: if motility is fundamental, it is because it ac-complishes the transcendence of consciousness toward the world in a manner that is anchored in incarnation, not in thought.

As we have already seen, Merleau-Ponty understood this persis-tence of the consciousness–world dualism to be the fundamental limitation of his first two books. This is what I have been calling

[margin note:] Husserl: Ideas (chp. 9)

the "impasse" of his early thought. Even if he managed to displace the subject–object opposition by making both derivative of a more fundamental bodily intentionality, he was unable to think the body in its specificity because he could only identify it with consciousness, or better, because he could only conceive it as a more primordial account of consciousness. In *The Visible and the Invisible,* accordingly, Merleau-Ponty devotes himself to the task of grasping the body as a negation of consciousness, which is to say, as a part of the world itself. Once again, movement proves to be fundamental for Merleau-Ponty's trajectory, although for precisely the opposite reason, or better, with precisely the opposite effect: rather than opening a transcendence of the body outside of itself, movement is now understood as the very modality of the body's belonging to the world. In its ontological dimension, that is, movement operates the mixing together of the phenomenal and the transcendent, such that the body's movement beyond itself just *is* its belonging to the world.

This identification finds a perfect illustration in Merleau-Ponty's understanding of vision as both *of* the world and *in* the world. Vision is the movement from the body to the object perceived. Accordingly, vision belongs to the world just as much as the world belongs to vision. As Merleau-Ponty puts it in "The Intertwining – The Chiasm,"

since vision is a palpation with the look, it must be inscribed in the order of being that it discloses to us; he who looks must not himself be foreign to the world that he looks at. As soon as I see, it is necessary that the vision (as is so well indicated by the double meaning of the word) be doubled with a complementary vision or with another vision: myself seen from without, such as another would see me, *installed in the midst of the visible.* (VI 177/134, emphasis added)

To understand what "this prepossession of the visible" is, Merleau-Ponty suggests that we turn to the domain of "tactile palpation" where, he says, the questioner and the questioned are more closely linked. Following Merleau-Ponty's hints in "The Philosopher and His Shadow" and in some working notes to *The Visible and the Invisible,* we can see that this suggestion makes a crucial reference to Husserl's account of touch in *Ideas II.* There, Husserl demonstrates that the constitution of the lived body takes place through tactility and that a subject endowed only with the capacity for vision would have no body at all. In effect, Husserl argues that the lived body is

Husserl:
Ideas II
"Touch"

constituted through tactile contact with objects, which is to say, as
the field of localization of the resulting tactile sensations. This primacy of touch in the constitution of the lived body becomes acute
when the body touches itself, for in this case we do not have a series
of objective tactile sensations on one hand and a localization of those
sensations in the lived body on the other, but rather a mixing up of
the two.

M-P:
self-
"touch"

While Husserl remains unable to capitalize on this analysis because he can only conceive of the body as a physical thing that *possesses* the sensations it localizes, Merleau-Ponty takes it as the very
basis for his conceptualization of the flesh. For him, the experience
of self-touching, and the implicit reversibility it betokens, represents
the passage beyond the nature–spirit dualism of Husserl's account:
"I touch myself touching; my body accomplishes a 'sort of reflection.'...the touched hand becomes the touching hand, and I am
obliged to say that the sense of touch here is diffused into the body –
that the body is a 'perceiving thing,' a 'subject–object'" (*S* 210/166).
What the analysis of self-touching shows, then, is that the sensible is
more fundamental than the division of subject and object, spirit and
nature, and consequently that the body cannot be located within the
conceptual space opened by these oppositions. Rather, the body is the
sensible itself – the sensible incarnated *as sensible*, that is, beyond
the distinction between sensing and sensed. In sum, Merleau-Ponty
tempers the privilege accorded touch by Husserl and exposes a deeper
intersensory reversibility beneath it.

Consequently, we will be able to discern the primacy of movement
within Merleau-Ponty's conception of the sensible incarnate *only* by
exploring the correlation *between* vision and touch. Movement is
precisely that fundamental modality of the body's belonging to the
world that allows for the correlation of vision and touch:

as, conversely, every experience of the visible has always been given to me
within the context of the movements of the look, the visible spectacle belongs to the touch neither more nor less than do the "tactile qualities." We
must habituate ourselves to think that every visible is cut out in the tangible, every tactile being in some manner promised to visibility, and that
there is encroachment, infringement, not only between the touched and the
touching, but also between the tangible and the visible.... It is a marvel too
little noticed that every movement of my eyes – even more, every displacement of my body – has its place in the same visible universe that I itemize

and explore with them, as, conversely, every vision takes place somewhere in the tactile space. There is a double and crossed situating of the visible in the tangible and of the tangible in the visible; the two maps are complete, and yet they do not merge into one. The two parts are total parts and yet are not superposable. (*VI* 176–7/134)

Here we can discern the profound stakes of Merleau-Ponty's appropriation of the Husserlian analysis of touch. Rather than forming the modality proper to the constitution of the lived body, touch, along with vision and all other sensory modalities, participates in a larger nexus of the sensible, the connecting thread of which is bodily movement. The lived body understood as a (static) site for the localization of sensation – the body of Husserl's analysis – is thus displaced in favor of bodily movement.

If Merleau-Ponty thereby earns the right to generalize the reversibility exemplified in touch into a reversibility of the sensible itself (the reversibility of body and world), it is precisely because the essential motility of the body installs it *in between* the senses, as a divergence constitutive of the incarnate sensible. It is not because touch (or vision) produces itself in a body that this latter belongs to the world; rather, it is because sensation belongs to the world that there are (can be) such things as bodies. For Merleau-Ponty, the body is not that which constitutes the sensory world (as it is for Husserl); rather, the body is a sensible manifestation of the world's "sensation." The body simply *is* the divergence of the sensible. This is why Merleau-Ponty can claim that the body belongs to the world in a manner more radical than that of the object: if the body is "a thing among things," he says, "it is so in a stronger and deeper sense than they: ... it detaches itself upon them and, accordingly, detaches itself from them" (*VI* 181/137). It is also why Merleau-Ponty can claim that the body belongs to the world in a manner more radical than that of the subject: "Since the total visible is always behind, or after, or between the aspects we see of it, there is access to it only through an experience which, like it, is wholly outside of itself. It is thus, and not as the bearer of a knowing subject, that our body commands the visible for us." As a belonging to the world more fundamental than objectivity and subjectivity, the body does not explain or clarify the visible; rather, in what is properly a "paradox of Being, not a paradox of man," the body "only concentrates the mystery of [the visible's] scattered visibility" (*VI* 180/136).

Yet far from resolving the problem of the body's belonging to the world, this analysis of <u>movement as divergence</u> simply poses it at a more fundamental level: if the <u>body is not outside the world like a pure subject</u>, and if it is <u>not in the world like an object</u>, <u>how exactly does it belong to the world?</u> The answer toward which Merleau-Ponty was working just before his death – as demonstrated by several of the working notes and the *Nature* lectures – involves <u>a deepening of the correlation of the body</u> with movement and of <u>movement with perception</u>. Put bluntly, <u>the body is that being that is capable of *moving itself*</u>, and <u>perception</u>, profoundly considered, is nothing other than the correlate of such self-movement.

Merleau-Ponty came upon this solution as early as September 1959 when (in a working note) he considered the analysis of a cube; <u>in the perception of the cube</u>, he notes, there <u>occurs "an openness upon the cube itself</u> by means of a view of the cube which is a distancing, <u>a transcendence</u> – to say that I have a view of it is to say that, <u>in perceiving it</u>, I go from myself onto it, <u>I go out of myself into it"</u> (*VI* 256/202). In this <u>perceptual experience</u>, we encounter <u>a transcendence beyond the self</u> that, unlike the otherwise similar experience in *Phenomenology of Perception*, <u>does not polarize the body</u> and the world, but uncovers their more profound correlation. Because <u>perceptual transcendence is doubled by the self-movement of the body</u>, it constitutes an opening onto the object (and the world) and not a consciousness of that object (and world). <u>Perceptual transcendence</u>, that is, <u>does not happen as a modality of consciousness</u>, but rather <u>*in and as* the experience of the self-moving body</u>. Moreover, if the body transcends itself toward the world through its movement, the fact that this movement is self-movement means that the body rediscovers itself in this very transcendence.

The identification of perception and self-movement that is implied in this analysis of the cube becomes entirely explicit in the working notes from May and June 1960. Merleau-Ponty there speaks of a de jure invisible beyond the de facto invisible according to which my eyes are invisible for me:

I cannot see myself in movement, witness my own movement. But this de jure invisible signifies in reality that *Wahrnehmen* and *Sich bewegen* are synonymous: it is for this reason that the *Wahrnehmen* never rejoins the *Sich bewegen* it wishes to apprehend: it is another of the same. But, this failure, this invisible, precisely attests that *Wahrnehmen* is *Sich bewegen*, there is here a success in the failure. *Wahrnehmen* fails to apprehend *Sich bewegen* (and I am for myself a zero of movement even during movement, I *do not move away from myself*) precisely because they are homogeneous, and this failure is the proof of this homogeneity: *Wahrnehmen* and *Sich bewegen* emerge from one another. A sort of reflection by ec-stasis (*Ek-stase*), they are of the same tuft. (*VI* 308/254–5)

Wahrnehmen and *Sich bewegen* are synonymous in the profound sense that they name the poles of the body's fundamental divergence from itself. It is in the very act of moving itself, that is moving along with itself, remaining a "zero of movement," that the body moves out of itself, into the world – that, in short, it perceives the world. Accordingly, self-movement must be distinguished from movement within an objective exteriority, from the displacement of an object in space, just as perception must be understood as motor intentionality, as a phenomenalization of the world through the self-emanation of movement from the body. This is why Merleau-Ponty asks, "in what sense are these multiple chiasms but one?" and answers, "not in the sense of synthesis, of the originally synthetic unity, but always in the sense of *Übertragung*, encroachment, radiation of being" (*VI* 314–15/261). The divergence or chiasm between sense modalities (vision–touch), like that within them (seen–seeing, touched–touching), finds its source in the divergence constitutive of the body's belonging to the world: the divergence between *Wahrnehmung* and *Sich bewegen*.

How, then, does this fundamental divergence allow us to understand the body's mode of spatiality, which is, as we have observed, neither that of a subject (outside the world) nor an object (in extended space)? The various hints Merleau-Ponty lays down in the working notes return us to the *Nature* lectures and the definition of life with which we began. Thus, for example, Merleau-Ponty admits that the "vision–touch divergence" is in one sense simply a "fact of our organization," but he goes on to insist that this has absolutely "no *explicative power*"; simply put, "there is no physical explanation for the constitution of the 'singular points' which are our bodies" (*VI* 309/256). Elsewhere he speaks of "locality by investment," noting that the mind (*esprit*) is "no objective site, and yet it is invested in a site which it rejoins by its environs" (*VI* 275/222). As self-movement, the body is attached to the world without being located in objective space: it is "neither here, nor here, nor here" but is rather what Husserl calls "the ultimate central here": a here "which has no other here outside of itself, in relation to which it would be a 'there.'"[8] The body is a fundamental opening onto the world and thus not simply one among other things in the world; it is a "universal measurant," a "dimensional this" that is "dimensional of *itself*" (*VI* 313/260).

Notwithstanding its philosophical roots,[9] this "transspatial" modality of the body derives directly from Merleau-Ponty's study of the biological sciences and can only be understood through this study. Consider, for example, just how much richer Merleau-Ponty's description of the dimensionality of the flesh is in *Nature* than in the working note just cited. To explain how the flesh appears in life, Merleau-Ponty draws the following analogy: like life in relation to the physicochemical, the flesh as *Empfindbarkeit* is a

singular point where another dimensionality appears. *Empfindbarkeit* is, if not localized, at least not independent of locality: it is not in my head or in my body, but *even less* is it somewhere else.... [I]t emerges through investment in life – by opening of a depth, ... as a being-other, relative non-being...natural negativity. (*N* 286/224)

As this description suggests, Merleau-Ponty's philosophical redemption of biology is intended to furnish nothing less than the foundation for his final ontological phenomenology. Specifically, his conception of life as a transspatial emergence from the physicochemical introduces a fundamental correlation of behavior and morphogenesis that itself *grounds* the correlation of phenomenality and ontology.

This correlation – and the philosophical work it performs – is nowhere more manifest than in Merleau-Ponty's appropriation of Uexküll's ethology in both the second and third set of lectures. Not insignificantly, ethology enters the lectures devoted to the human body via its imbrication with self-movement:

the *Umwelt* (i.e., the world + my body) is not concealed from me. I am witness to my *Umwelt*. Likewise, my body is not concealed from me.... To know the *Umwelt* = more or less large divergence in relation to a zero body, to know the body = divergence in relation to the "there" of the *Umwelt*. This divergence is the inverse of the identification that I achieve through movement: *Wahrnehmen* and *Sich bewegen*. (*N* 278–9/216)

In this striking, indeed truly startling, philosophical elucidation of the "structural coupling" of the embodied human being with its environment,[10] we encounter nothing less than a model of the kind of unity or interiority the body must possess to be determinable as self-movement, as always in excess of itself. Rather than a substantial interiority produced through the inscription of "tactile sensations," this unity or "interiority" must be conceived as systemic – that is, constituted through the body's coupling with its environment. The *Umwelt* is therefore not outside the body, and the body is not other than the *Umwelt*; rather, as the passage specifies, the two terms must be understood as divergences with respect to one another: the *Umwelt* (i.e., that part of the environment selected by the body) is what makes the body self-dimensionalizing, a universal measurant, and the body is what makes the *Umwelt* transspatial, not an empirical "there," but an absolute "here." The coupling with an *Umwelt* is, then, precisely what clarifies the profound correlation of the body and the world, the belonging of one to the other that Merleau-Ponty calls the flesh.

Yet what exactly can Merleau-Ponty mean when he says that the *Umwelt*–body divergence is the *inverse* of the identification *Wahrnehmen – Sich bewegen*? Precisely this: like *Wahrnehmen* and *Sich bewegen*, the *Umwelt* and the body are synonymous *on account of their mutual divergence*; and yet, whereas the divergence of *Wahrnehmen* and *Sich bewegen* constitutes the body's mode of being in excess over itself, the divergence of *Umwelt* and body comprises what we might, taking all necessary caution, call the "internal" excess of the body, the embryonic equipotentiality that characterizes it as a particular form of the living. Since, however, the divergence of *Umwelt* and body reconnects "the activity that creates organs and the activity of behavior" (N 228/173) – that is, morphogenesis and self-movement – it serves in fact to *ground* the most fundamental chiasm of all: the chiasm between the internal excess (equipotentiality) and the external excess (disequilibrium) of the body.

This chiasm is the philosophical payoff of Merleau-Ponty's interpretation of Uexküll's work. What is truly new in Uexküll, Merleau-Ponty concludes, is the very notion of the *Umwelt* itself. Not insignificantly, this notion furnishes a view of the world that can be reduced neither to "a sum of external events" nor to "an interior which is not caught up in the world" (N 232/177). With the living – which is to say, with the production of an *Umwelt* – there appears "an event-milieu that opens a spatial and temporal field." Importantly, this appearance of a privileged milieu must not be understood as the manifestation of a new force, but precisely as an *emergence:*

The living operates only with physicochemical elements, but these subordinate forces knit among themselves wholly new relations. We can, from this moment on, speak of an animal.... The animal is like a gentle force.... The animal regulates, makes detours. There is an inertia of the animal. (*N* 233/177)

The *Umwelt,* in other words, is what allows us to see that the organism has an interiority that is not a goal or a substance, but something like a melody or a "theme that haunts consciousness" (*N* 233/178). When there is an *Umwelt,* there is a "living plan" (*N* 231/176), i.e., a structure with which the organism can regulate its own potentiality, can draw on the "transtemporal and transspatial element" that lies "in the very fabric of physical elements" (*N* 231/176). The way the organism does this is precisely through behavior, which, by regulating its interiority, turns this potentiality into natural history.

Only the analysis of the human body in its specificity will allow us to ground the phenomenality–transcendence divergence in the fundamental chiasm of the living, the chiasm between internal equipotentiality and external disequilibrium. As a "metamorphosis of life," our body emerges as a "body *of* the mind" (following the felicitous expression of Paul Valéry) (*N* 380; *RC* 177/196); it is what places our life as natural history (as the confluence of morphogenesis and self-movement) "before us" and what makes it "enveloping in relation to our 'thought.'" In this sense, the body holds a certain priority in the operation of phenomenalization–transcendence constitutive of the flesh. Specifically, it is that in virtue of which there is an other, hidden side of things, of the body, of the visible – what Merleau-Ponty so aptly describes as a "being for the living," a being that exists insofar as the living "has an *Umwelt.*" Precisely because it is a being for the living, the invisible is "not constituted by our thought, but lived as a variant of our corporeity, i.e., as an appearance of behaviors within the field of our behavior" (*N* 338/271). Such being-lived as a variant of our corporeity is precisely what defines the opening to the visible – that is, phenomenality itself – not as the being of a perceived (*percipi*) but as the activity of perceiving (*percipere*) defined through its participation in the activity of being as living (active *esse*).

Because phenomenality thus remains dependent on the activity of the living (human) body, Merleau-Ponty's final work articulates a philosophy of immanence in which the body's self-transcendence simply *is* its mode of belonging to the world. The body maintains a privilege because it constitutes the negativity within being that allows for the manifestation of being in the very act of its withdrawal. Most important, this privilege reflects the double excess of the body, its identity with the chiasm of the living identified earlier: on one hand, there is an excess of the body's potential in relation to its actuality (excess of the body over itself) and, on the other, an excess of the body in relation to being as cosmology (excess of being over the body). The former defines the field of development; the latter, the field of behavior. Significantly, *both* excesses involve a correlation of phenomenalization and transcendence, and they are imbricated within one another: the body manifests its potential (phenomenalizes itself) in the very act of preserving it as potential, and it only does so through its behavior, that is, by moving out from itself toward the world; and correlatively, the world manifests itself only in limiting itself, that is, in reserving itself, and it does so above all through actualization in the living body.

We can now fully grasp the primacy of the living (human) body within the philosophy of the "something" called for by Merleau-Ponty in the third set of lectures. The living (human) body is that negativity within being which, through its own determinate history of negations, brings the world to perception. It is thus not sufficient to say that Merleau-Ponty's final philosophy is a phenomenology of life, or that the body must be derived from life.[11] Rather, it is a phenomenology of the living *in the form of the human body*: a phenomenology inseparable from that concrete "pattern of negations" that has led to and continues to inform the "evolution" of the human as an emergence from animality, as a new mode of *being a* body.

This is precisely the philosophical lesson Merleau-Ponty extracts from embryology and phylogenesis. What embryology demonstrates, precisely by refusing Hans Driesch's opposition of preformation and epigenesis, is the probabilistic status of the living: neither simply actual, nor purely random, life is the "establishment of a level around which divergences distribute themselves." What this means is that the equipotentiality of the living is not limitless or purely formal but is, in fact, constrained by the concrete history, the determinate "pattern of negations" or "system of oppositions" that delimit the living, that "make it the case that what is not this is that" (*N* 302/238). Put another way, the opening onto the world constitutive of the living is not an "opening onto everything" but rather a "specified opening" (*N* 303/238), and this constraint or specification is precisely what accords concrete agency to the biological being rooted in negativity.

Something similar can be said about phylogenesis and neo-Darwinism, which, considered philosophically, furnish a picture of organisms as what Merleau-Ponty calls "phenomena-envelopes": emergent properties of evolution, not residues of selection; active expressions of an internal animation, not effects of an external mechanism. The organism (and the human body in particular) is the result neither of "pure chance" (Darwinism's random mutation and selection) nor of idealism (idealist morphology), but of "something in between": the "suture organism–milieu, organism–organism" (*N* 317/251). In phylogenesis no less than embryology, then, the organism has what Merleau-Ponty characterizes as a statistical being. Accordingly, the being of life must be defined "on the basis of phenomena," that is, of the organisms that emerge, "without any rupture with chemical, thermodynamic, and cybernetic causality, as 'fluctuation traps,' 'patterned mixedupness,' variants of a sort of 'phenomenal topology'" (*N* 379; *RC* 175–6/195–6). As he goes on to note, when the organism in question is the human body, the being of life that is phenomenalized is being itself, being expressed in the living (human) body opened to a specified world.

We can now say precisely in what way Merleau-Ponty's final philosophy comprises a phenomenology of the living or, alternatively, a philosophy of immanence according to which the living body's self-transcendence simply *is* its belonging to the world. As that concrete form of the living in which morphogenesis and behavior can be perceived in their complementarity, the human body both is itself *and* perceives itself as the expression of being. It is no less true that being happens in and through the human body than that the body phenomenalizes being, for in bringing together and revealing the interdependency between the self-unfolding of life and the self-movement toward the world, the living human body folds together phenomenology and cosmology – the being of life as phenomenon and the being of the cosmos itself.

III. PHENOMENOLOGY BETWEEN PHILOSOPHY
AND SCIENCE

Can a philosophy of nature rooted in the biological sciences of the first half of the twentieth century still speak to us today? Given the revolutionary impact of complexity and self-organizing systems over the past several decades, can Merleau-Ponty's philosophical concept of life as negativity within being still find a place in contemporary biological thinking? Is it possible that we can still learn from Merleau-Ponty's example, from his careful and considered reflection on the phenomenological significance of biological facts? Can we update his philosophical perspective in a way that brings it to bear, consequentially, on contemporary issues in the biological sciences?

To assess the continued relevance of Merleau-Ponty's final work, let us briefly contrast his approach with that of Daniel Dennett, whose *Darwin's Dangerous Idea* has done much to promote a properly philosophical perspective on evolution, and that of Francisco Varela, whose *The Embodied Mind* (with Thompson and Rosch) comprises a valiant and inspiring, if not entirely successful, effort to combine insights from cognitive science with a phenomenological approach.[12] I single out Dennett and Varela because their projects engage them in an effort to account for the transitions from seemingly blind mechanical processes to the higher-order processes that characterize mental life without introducing any transcendent cause. This is an aim very much at the heart of Merleau-Ponty's concern, as we have just seen. Yet, contrasted with these two alternative engagements with philosophy and science, Merleau-Ponty's approach proves unique in articulating a middle path between instrumentalism and biological realism – the middle path of phenomenology. Unlike Dennett, Merleau-Ponty takes seriously the metaphysical consequences of an evolutionary approach to the living while nonetheless accounting for the singularity of human intentionality. Unlike Varela, Merleau-Ponty privileges embodied human experience in his philosophical account of the biological paradox of totality while nonetheless insisting on its continuity with lower-order organisms.

In *Kinds of Minds*, his attempt to explain consciousness in the wake of *Darwin's Dangerous Idea*, Dennett begins by insisting that an "evolutionary perspective" is needed if we are to understand the "complex fabrics" that our minds are: such a perspective, he claims, "can help us to see how and why these elements of minds," some as old as life itself, others as new as today's technology, "came to take on the shapes they have," even if "no single straight run through time, 'from microbes to man,' will reveal the moment of arrival of each new thread."[13] Having made this promising claim in his preface, why then does Dennett proceed in the remainder of the book to vitiate the evolutionary perspective of any but the most trivial significance for our understanding of what minds are? The reason, in brief, is Dennett's commitment to what he calls the "intentional stance." *Kinds of Minds* is his attempt to mobilize the intentional stance as a general procedure for understanding other systems, including the "macromolecular machines" of which, he insists, we are made. For Dennett, the intentional stance is, quite simply, "the key to unraveling the mysteries of the mind ... all kinds of minds."[14]

Put bluntly, the problem with this deployment of the intentional stance is that it forbids us in principle from drawing ontological conclusions from the attribution of intentionality to the other candidates for mind as well as to those evolutionary processes responsible for forming us (humans) as minds gifted with second-order intentionality (Dennett's criterion for personhood[15]). In its broad deployment in *Kinds of Minds*, intentionality does not name properties of the system under exploration, but rather a means *for us* to understand that system. This, according to Dennett, is precisely its major advantage: "the intentional stance *works* (when it does) whether or not the attributed goals are genuine or natural or 'really appreciated' by the so-called agent."[16] Indeed, such a stance is necessary given the limitations of our perspective because we cannot know, for example, whether the macromolecule *really* wants to replicate itself or even what such a question could mean: "tolerance is crucial to understanding how genuine goal-seeking could be established in the first place." For Dennett, the bottom line is simply that the "intentional stance explains what is going on, regardless of how we answer that question."[17]

Dennett's ontological indifference (or "tolerance") would not be a problem if we were not dealing here with human experience as a phenomenon emergent from a more primitive biological heritage (the living). Because we are, however, Dennett's position would seem to involve a basic contradiction: he adopts an evolutionary perspective on intentionality to avoid recourse to a transcendent cause for the uniqueness of human intentionality (see, for example, his account of "The Tower of Generate-and-Test" in chapter 4); yet, when push comes to shove, he simply abandons the metaphysics to which he has helped himself, retreating to the agnosticism of the (in this case, unequivocally nonevolutionary) intentional stance.

This contradiction comes into focus in a particularly salient way around Dennett's (defensive) discussion of the anthropomorphism of the intentional stance. Following his already-mentioned disclaimer regarding the ontological commitment entailed by the intentional stance, he asks whether the intentional stance involves "a misapplication of our own perspective, the perspective we *mind-havers* share?" "Not necessarily," he answers, and his rationale is telling:

From the vantage point of evolutionary history, this is what has happened: Over billions of years, organisms gradually evolved, accumulating ever more versatile machinery designed to further their ever more complex and articulated goods. Eventually, with the evolution in our species of language and the varieties of reflectiveness that language permits . . . we emerged with the ability to wonder . . . about the minds of other entities.[18]

If the intentional stance does not involve a misapplication of our perspective, it is precisely because it has emerged out of the evolutionary process that has transformed primitive macromolecular machines into complex human beings. The ontology of emergence ensures a continuity of nature, and, specifically, of the evolving (that is, complexifying) function of intentionality as, precisely, a strategy of the living. Here, in short, Dennett leans heavily on the metaphysics of evolutionary emergence – and on the continuity of being it assumes – regardless of what his rhetoric might suggest. At best, he is guilty of conflating two distinct concepts of intentionality: on one hand, as a property of the living; on the other, as a descriptive device for understanding the living (which also happens to be a property of *certain* kinds of living beings).

Yet, far from invalidating Dennett's effort to embrace an evolutionary perspective, this contradiction merely serves to foreground the need for an ontologically serious account of evolutionary emergence. Such an account is precisely what Varela would seem to offer. In his paper, "Organism: A Meshwork of Selfless Selves," Varela presents a picture of the organism that appears remarkably congruous with Dennett's: in both cases, the organism is a modular entity

comprising functionally and evolutionarily quite distinct levels or
(in Varela's parlance) "selves."

Closer inspection, however, reveals a significant philosophical difference: for Varela, the question of the self as a network of selves is
emphatically an ontological one. Thus, he suggests, to address

the issue of the organism as a minimal living system by characterizing its
basic mode of identity . . . is, properly speaking, to address the issue at an
ontological level: the accent is on the manner in which the living system
becomes a distinguishable entity, and not on its specific molecular composition and contingent historical configurations.[19]

This focus on the "autopoietic organization" of the living allows
Varela to develop a criterion of minimal selfhood that forms an invariant across vastly divergent levels of selfhood: no matter what
concrete material basis is concerned, the pattern of ongoing self-
organization closed to the environment serves to distinguish the
minimal identity of any living system. In contrast to Dennett, then,
Varela deploys the concept of evolutionary continuity on ontological grounds: having established a minimal criterion for the living,
he can treat "other candidates for mind" (Dennett), no matter how
primitive, as cognitive systems in their own right, without needing
to take recourse to the intentional stance. This is why, for him, "the
more traditional level of cognitive properties, involving the brains of
multicellular animals, is in some important sense the *continuation*
of the very same basic process" that generated identity in a minimal
organism.[20]

One significant consequence of this approach is its vastly different
account of intentionality: for Varela, intentionality is a feature of the
basic cognitive level of selfhood and not something reserved for the
human mind or some other higher-level emergence.[21] On this understanding, intentionality emerges out of the coupling of the organism
with an environment, and specifically from the active selection by
the organism of a "world," a part of the environment that is specifically relevant for it. The coupling of organism and environment

is possible only if the encounters are embraced *from the perspective* of the
system itself. This amounts, quite specifically, to elaborating a *surplus signification* relative to this perspective. Whatever is encountered must be
valued one way or another . . . and acted on some way or another. . . . This
basic assessment is inseparable from the way in which the coupling event

encounters a functioning perceptuo-motor unit, and it gives rise to an *intention* (I am tempted to say "desire"), that unique quality of living cognition.[22]

For our purposes, this account is important less as a concrete corrective to Dennett's position than for the correlation it introduces between behavior and meaning. For Varela, the passage to a form of cognition at the level of a behavioral entity (as against that of a more simple, spatially bounded entity such as the minimal cellular organism) *coincides* with the creation of *surplus signification,* a world endowed with the potentiality crucial to the organism's continued life. This basic level of the "cognitive self" introduces a "double dialectic" between organism and environment[23] that is not so different from Merleau-Ponty's coupling of self-movement and transcendence. For Varela as for Merleau-Ponty, it is the self-movement of the organism that transforms its internal incompleteness (its status as originary desire[24] or equipotentiality) into the motor of its self-perpetuation, and it is also self-movement that opens the organism to the excess of the environment where it discovers nothing less than the potentiality on which its continuance depends.

When he chooses to privilege this basic level of the "cognitive self," however, Varela diverges markedly from Merleau-Ponty. Whereas the latter sought to discern the philosophical significance of the biological sciences (and specifically Uexküll's ethology) by deriving the chiasm of phenomenology and ontology from the correlation of behavior and morphology, the former concentrates on the organism as a strictly biological phenomenon derived from the double dialectic of identity and coupling and thus remains squarely within the empirical domain of science. For all of his efforts to supplement this basic level of biological selfhood in order to do justice to the singularity of human being,[25] Varela remains hampered by an overemphasis on the *biological* continuity across levels. For Merleau-Ponty, in contrast, the biologically emergent human body is the dynamic "site" where being and phenomenality come together: it is only in the *human* organism that body as a part of being comes together with the phenomenological experience of the body as part of being. To recall the conclusion to the preceding section: only the human body both is itself *and* perceives itself to be the experience of being. What this means is that the belonging-together of being and phenomenality in human embodiment marks a leap akin to that from the physicochemical to the living.[26] Even though it is not something over and above the biological, this belonging-together simply cannot be accounted for exclusively at the level of biological or evolutionary emergence.[27]

This is why, in the end, Varela's approach can only afford a third-person (observational) account of the necessarily first-person (operational) perspective of the living being, even when the being in question is the human being – that form of being equipped, biologically, with the means (language) to autonomize itself in relation to its basic cognitive self. His approach develops an *epistemology* of the living: an account of the identity and coupling necessary for a given organism to maintain itself as living. We arrive at a *phenomenology* of the living only when, with Merleau-Ponty, we recognize the philosophical implications of this epistemology – the way that, for a quintessentially first-person being like the human, the coupling of body–mind and world–environment necessarily implicates phenomenology in being and being in phenomenology.[28]

NOTES

1. As the editors suggest, these notes make up what we might call a hybrid text, and for two different, although closely related reasons: on one hand, they are themselves internally uneven (the first two being transcripts of dactylographic student notes, hitherto buried away in the library of the École Normal Superieur of Saint-Cloud; the last, a reproduction of Merleau-Ponty's own, often elliptical and fragmentary, course notes); on the other hand, they constitute neither a work composed but left unpublished by the philosopher during his lifetime (like *The Prose of the World*) nor a work reconstructed from notes and posthumously published (like *The Visible and the Invisible*), but written traces of a line of thinking that *had been* publicly presented by the philosopher. As such, they furnish us a kind of working view from within of the scope and aims of Merleau-Ponty's final thinking.

2. The axolotl ordinarily lives and breeds in the larval condition but is capable, when the pond it inhabits dries up, of losing its gills and fins and developing into a normal adult salamander.

3. Merleau-Ponty borrows this term from Conrad Waddington, as he is cited by Gesell. For Waddington, the regulatory principle is "a system

262 MARK B. N. HANSEN

of order such that the position taken by unstable entities in one part of the system would have a definite relation with the position taken by unstable entities in other parts" (N 200/150).

4. "[T]he fabric of possibilities that closes the exterior visible in upon the seeing body maintains between them a certain *divergence* (*écart*). But this divergence is not a *void*, it is filled precisely by the flesh as the place of emergence of a vision, a passivity that bears an activity – and so also the divergence between the exterior visible and the body which forms the upholstering (*capitonnage*) of the world" (VI 326/272).

5. My reconstruction owes much to the extremely insightful commentaries on Merleau-Ponty in Renaud Barbaras, *Le Tournant de l'experience*.

6. The *noesis–noema* correlation is introduced by Husserl in *Ideas* to describe the structure of intentional experience. See *Ideas*, chapter 9.

7. In this sense, Merleau-Ponty's concept of the "I can" repeats the error that plagued its philosophical source, Husserl's concept of the "I can": just as Husserl's "I can" fails to overcome the dualism of consciousness and body it was meant to remedy, so, too, Merleau-Ponty's "I can" fails to overcome the dualism of body and world it was introduced to dissolve. For Husserl's account of the "I can," see *Ideas II*, §38, and *Cartesian Meditations*, §44.

8. Husserl, *Ideas II*, §41: 158.

9. Beyond Husserl's conception of the "absolute here," his analysis of the Earth forms a by now well-recognized source for Merleau-Ponty's final conception of the flesh.

10. The notion of "structural coupling" comes from the autopoietic theory of Humberto Maturana and Francisco Varela, where it names the strict and ongoing correlation of an organism with a world or milieu it selects, via its sensory and perceptual capacities, from the environment as such. See their *Autopoiesis and Cognition*.

11. See the essay by Renaud Barbaras in this volume.

12. Dennett, *Darwin's Dangerous Idea*; Varela, Thompson, and Rosch, *The Embodied Mind*. For a critical account of Varela's effort to combine cognitive science and phenomenology, see Hubert Dreyfus's review of *The Embodied Mind*.

13. Dennett, *Kinds of Minds*, viii.

14. *Kinds of Minds*, 24, 27. The "intentional stance" is the strategy of interpreting the behavior of an entity *as if* it were a rational agent capable of making decisions more or less like we (humans) do.

15. See Dennett, "Conditions of Personhood."

16. *Kinds of Minds*, 31–2.

17. *Kinds of Minds*, 32.

18. *Kinds of Minds*, 33.
19. Varela, "Organism: A Meshwork of Selfless Selves," 84.
20. "Organism," 88.
21. I should point out here that he, too, thinks it important to extend intentionality beyond the human species. See, for example, his contempt for
    John Searle's distinction between "original" and "derived" intentionality. *Kinds of Minds*, 50 ff. In the end, however, Dennett cannot escape
    the constraints of an account of intentionality that was formulated prior
    to his evolutionary turn, and thus he ends up affirming the human as
    that being capable of being cognizant of its deployment of intentionality.
    At the very least, this means that there would be two kinds of intentionality: the minimal intentionality of goal-seeking systems (which may
    or may not correspond to real stuff) and the full intentionality of self-
    observing systems like ourselves (where self-observation attests to the
    real existence of intentionality).
22. Varela, "Organism," 96–7.
23. "[T]he organismic dialectic of self is a two-tiered affair: we have on the
    one hand the dialectics of identity of self; on the other the dialectics
    through which this identity, once established, brings forth a world from
    an environment. Identity and knowledge stand in relation to each other
    as two sides of a single process that forms the core of the dialectics of
    all selves" ("Organism," 102).
24. Here it is worth pointing out how closely Varela's conception of desire
    and the living correlates with Merleau-Ponty's philosophical concept of
    life as negativity within being: "the uniqueness of the cognitive self is
    this constitutive *lack* of signification which must be supplied faced with
    the permanent perturbations and breakdowns of the ongoing perceptuo-
    motor life. Cognition is action about what is *missing*, filling the fault
    from the perspective of a cognitive self" ("Organism," 99).
25. Most interesting here is his account of language as the capacity to bring
    the basic coupling of the biological self into play as a factor in the future
    behavior of the cognitive system. See Maturana and Varela, *The Tree of
    Knowledge*.
26. Justifying such a claim, we will recall, is precisely the burden of the
    third section of *Nature* and the rationale behind Merleau-Ponty's turn
    to the human body.
27. Varela's account of the self as a "network of selfless selves" can be
    understood as a take on the paradox of totality that Merleau-Ponty discovered in the biological sciences; see, for example, his introduction to
    "Organism" (79) and his discussion of emergence and self-organization
    (84). Unlike Merleau Ponty's conception of totality, however, Varela's
    remains biological: "it is very important to see how [the same motif of

identity and coupling] is shared from our most intimate and immediate everyday experience right down to the very basic levels of life and body. Only then can we avoid splitting the selves in an organism into disjointed categories and thus avoid splitting what is a totality ranging from cells to social minds into separate pulverized realms" (102).

28. I want to thank Taylor Carman for his generous comments on this chapter.

10 Merleau-Ponty's Existential Conception of Science

Maurice Merleau-Ponty is best known as a philosopher of science for his detailed investigations of psychology. Perhaps because of this, the significance of his work for a broader philosophical reflection on science has been overlooked, but Merleau-Ponty intended his work as a general investigation of the epistemological and onto-logical status of meaning and structure. The structures discovered through research in solid-state physics or molecular biology must be included within the scope of his inquiry as much as the more primary perceptual structures of color or visual depth. It is true he often insisted that science cannot account for or understand a par-ticular phenomenon and went on to contrast his phenomenological discoveries with the inadequate analyses produced by science. When Merleau-Ponty spoke of "science" in this way, however, he used the term interchangeably with "objective thought." The task remains to show that scientific investigation can also be freed from the tra-ditional prejudices of objective thought and exhibited as a mode of human existence. Merleau-Ponty was admittedly ambivalent about this possibility, and he rarely thematized scientific research in the course of his investigations. The aim of this chapter, however, is to develop an existential conception of science within the context of Merleau-Ponty's work. It seems clear to me that his project cannot be completed unless it incorporates science, and not just the body and the perceived world, poetry and history, painting and love.

Already in *The Structure of Behavior*, Merleau-Ponty insisted that the concept of "structure" or "form" employed by the Gestalt psy-chologists must be extended to the physical sciences as well: "But, in reality, what Köhler shows with a few examples ought to be extended to all physical laws: they express a structure and have meaning only within this structure" (SC 148–9/138). Merleau-Ponty's argument for this claim will be familiar to philosophers of science. The concepts and laws developed in science cannot be attached to the world one by one but only as a structural whole, because any attempt to match physical law or theory with the world brings into play a host of other theories and theoretically informed descriptions of initial conditions.

> The physical experiment is never the revelation of an isolated causal series: one verifies that the observed effect indeed obeys the presumed law by taking into account a series of conditions, such as temperature, atmospheric pressure, altitude, in brief, a certain number of laws which are independent of those which constitute the proper object of the experiment. (SC 150/139)

Merleau-Ponty was most concerned to investigate the philosophical significance of this sense of "structure." In *The Structure of Behavior*, his principal target of attack was realism. A structure (or a "system of complementary laws" in science) cannot be regarded as an object existing in itself but must be disclosed to a perceiving consciousness.

> Thus form is not a physical reality, but an object of perception; without it physical science would have no meaning, moreover, since it is constructed with respect to it and in order to coordinate it.... [F]orm cannot be defined in terms of reality but in terms of knowledge, not as a thing of the physical world but as a perceived whole. (SC 155/143)

Yet it is insufficient to say that structure always is essentially related to consciousness without clarifying what that relation is. Merleau-Ponty was equally insistent that structure cannot be constituted by a consciousness completely in possession of itself. His aim in *Phenomenology of Perception* was to investigate and undermine the shared assumptions that allowed realism and idealism to appear as opposed and exhaustive philosophical alternatives.[1] Only after thus clearing the ground can we develop a more adequate philosophical interpretation of the relation between consciousness, the structures of scientific laws, and the perceived world.

Realist interpretations of scientific theories have been widely discussed in recent philosophy of science. Many of the arguments for scientific realism acquire their force from critiques of idealism.[2] Merleau-Ponty's arguments against realism, and his attempt to articulate a nonidealist alternative to it, should thus be of more than just historical interest.

I

Merleau-Ponty's attack on the antinomy of realism and idealism in ontology (and of empiricism and rationalism in epistemology) proceeded in two stages. He first argued that neither the body nor the perceived world can be understood on the basis of this antinomy. Only then did he extend the argument to encompass all forms of cultural expression, science included. This strategy is particularly important in the case of science because Merleau-Ponty argued that the meaning of scientific concepts and laws is dependent on the world as disclosed through perception.

The whole universe of science is built upon the world as directly experienced, and if we want to subject science itself to rigorous scrutiny and arrive at a precise assessment of its meaning and scope, we must begin by reawakening the basic experience of the world of which science is a second-order expression. (*PP* ii–iii/viii/ix)

We shall have to return to this claim and clarify the relation between this "basic experience of the world" and the "second-order expression" of it in science. In order to do this, we must give some account of Merleau-Ponty's descriptions of sensation, the body, and the perceived world, which he regarded as the foundation of other meaningful structures.

Traditional analyses of perception begin with sensations, which are taken to be the given content of perceptual experience. Empiricists (as Merleau-Ponty used this label) take sensations to be the result of a causal interaction between the body and other objects in the world. Meaning arises through the habitual association of sequences of sensations. Rationalists (also Merleau-Ponty's descriptive label) regard the sensation as the given content on which consciousness reflects and imposes meaning. Merleau-Ponty believed that both positions share an error.

We started off from a world in itself which acted upon our eyes so as to cause us to see it, and we now have consciousness of or thought about the world, but the nature of this world remains unchanged: it is still defined by the absolute mutual exteriority of its parts, and is merely duplicated throughout its extent by a thought which sustains it. (PP 49/39/45)

Both accounts overlook the meaningful structure of the perceptual field itself. A perceived figure always stands out against a background. The ground is not a given content. Its content is indefinite, receding from awareness as the figure stands out. It is not given because it continues behind the figure (and is perceived as such) and is not confined by the physical limits of the visual field. The ground fades out and continues beyond what we explicitly see; it is there as a potential field to be explored, to be transformed into figure, and it is there perceptually. We do not have to imagine the continuity of the visual field, we see it (even though we do not see what it continues as) (PP 321/277/323).

There is more to the perceived figure, too, than is actually given. It has a back side whose "virtual figure" (its implicit presentation to a possible observer elsewhere) contributes to its perceived sense. If our sense of how the figure continues is violated by further exploration, its look is transformed upon return to our original view. The house which on further exploration turns out to be only a façade later looks like a façade. The figure stands out from the ground, but its sense is rooted in the ground, in what is perceptually present but not explicitly seen. As Merleau-Ponty pointed out, it is only through this horizonal structure that the perceived object retains its identity throughout our exploration of it (PP 82/68/78). When Merleau-Ponty said that "Perception ... is not even an act, a deliberate taking up of a position; it is the background from which all acts stand out, and is presupposed by them" (PP v/x–xi/xi), he was using the word "act" in two senses. Perceiving is not a pure activity of consciousness or an explicit synthesis or taking of a position; the perceived object in turn is not pure actuality but is laden with potentiality which can never be made fully determinate. We are situated in a perceptual field, which we cannot make fully explicit because we inhabit it. The body that we are is not an object in the world either. The body is unified not through an explicit synthesis of its parts but through a tacit grasp of its possibilities. The body is of space, not in it (PP 173/148/171). Thus, Merleau-Ponty insisted that

what counts for the orientation of the spectacle is not my body as it in fact is, as a thing in objective space, but as a system of possible actions, a virtual body with its phenomenal "place" defined by its task and situation. My body is wherever there is something to be done. (*PP* 289/249–50/291)

This grasp of possibilities, this "I can" that is embodiment, cannot be a purely intellectual synthesis either. The body is directed toward a situation and is not explicitly deployed but rather responds to that situation as a field of potentialities. The body touches and sees but is also seen and touched. It is subject to disease, to deformity, to clumsiness – in short, to incapacities that it cannot fully comprehend:

rationalism ... was itself unable to account for the variety of experience, for the element of senselessness in it, for the contingency of contents. Bodily experience forces us to acknowledge an imposition of meaning which is not the work of a universal constituting consciousness, a meaning which clings to certain content. My body is that meaningful core which behaves like a general function, and which nevertheless exists, and is susceptible to disease. (*PP* 172/147/170)

Merleau-Ponty argued that there is a mutual implication between the body as I live it and the perceived world. The ambiguity and potentiality with which I inhabit my body extend to the world as well. For Merleau-Ponty, the world cannot be taken for granted as something existing independently of us. He insisted that "we must not, therefore, wonder whether we really perceive a world, we must instead say: the world is what we perceive" (*PP* xi/xvi/xviii). The body is intentionally directed toward the world; we are a "motor project." Through its explorations, it acquires the capabilities which constitute it, and the world is disclosed to us. The structure and style of the world are correlates of our bodily style of investigation:[3]

we have found underneath the objective and detached knowledge of the body that other knowledge which we have of it in virtue of its always being with us and of the fact that we are our body. In the same way we shall need to reawaken our experience of the world as it appears to us in so far as we perceive the world with our body. (*PP* 239/206/239)

The body is its intentional relatedness to the world, and the world is likewise constituted through that relation.

Merleau-Ponty supported this claim by examining some of the important structures of the world as perceived. He extended his earlier arguments against reducing sensations to given contents by arguing that they are modulations of the world as inhabited by my body.

When we say that red increases the compass of our reactions, we are not to be understood as having in mind two distinct facts, a sensation of redness and motor reactions – we must be understood as meaning that red, by its texture as followed and adhered to by our gaze, is already the amplification of our motor being. (*PP* 245/211/245)

Just as the body is not a collection of discrete organs but a unified intentional project, so sensations have intersensory significance. Merleau-Ponty reported that we see and hear hardness and brittleness, that weight and elasticity are visible (*PP* 265–6/229–30/266–7), and that (citing Cézanne with approval) we should be able to paint even odors (*SNS* 28/15). He concluded,

the sensible has not only a motor and vital significance, but is nothing other than a certain way of being in the world suggested to us from some point in space, and seized and acted upon by our body, provided that it is capable of doing so, so that sensation is literally a form of communion. (*PP* 245–6/212/246)

The spatiality of the perceived world is likewise the intentional correlate of the spatiality and motility of the body. Space is oriented into vertical and horizontal fields, the senses of which are not interchangeable. Depth is not an interchangeable dimension either (it is not breadth turned endways). Indeed, it can never be understood objectively because, as Merleau-Ponty observed, "it quite clearly belongs to the perspective and not to things" (*PP* 296/256/298). Space is laid out along the course of our potential projects within it; it always already has a significance. "The vertical and the horizontal, the near and the far, are abstract designations for one single form of being in a situation, and they presuppose the same setting face to face of subject and world" (*PP* 309/267/311). Perceived movement is rooted in the bodily grasp we have upon the world as a situation into which we project ourselves. Only because our gaze is "lodged and anchored" in a setting and yet is "attracted" and "drags at its anchors" do we see movement (*PP* 322/278/324). Movement is a solicitation to our body to track the moving thing against a field in which we are already established. Thus, space as described in geometry cannot encompass orientation, movement, or significance. Only a space that is centered on and directed from the body can characterize the world perceived. Even the thing in space is a correlate of our embodiment. Its unity through a manifold of appearances reflects the felt unity of the body that explores it and that can track the exploration so as to record its present manifestation as the outcome of past exploration and a solicitation to encounter more of it.[4] "Thus the thing is correlative to my body and, in more general terms, to my existence, of which my body is merely the stabilized structure. It is constituted in the hold which my body takes upon it" (*PP* 369/320/373).

Merleau-Ponty had been arguing against the conception of the perceived world as a universe of objects in geometrical space. This argument attacks not just the realist sense of the world but also that of the idealist or social constructivist for whom the world (or its sense) is constituted by consciousness (or a community united by language, interest, or shared beliefs and norms). They share the same misconception: in neither case is subjectivity found within the world. Thus, Merleau-Ponty concluded, "We must conceive the perspectives and the point of view as our insertion into the world-as-an-individual, and perception, no longer as a constitution of the true object, but as our inherence in things" (*PP* 403/350–1/408). The relation between body and world cannot be understood abstractly because it depends on the real presence of body to world. Just as a motor skill cannot be accurately simulated in the absence of the object to which it skillfully responds, so the object cannot be adequately grasped without understanding its significance for the human capabilities it extends. Body and world become what they are through the motivated exploratory activities of embodied subjects.

I have the world as an incomplete individual, through the agency of my body as the potentiality of this world, and I have the positing of objects through that of my body, or conversely the positing of my body through that of objects, not in any kind of logical implication, as we determine an unknown size through its objective relations to given sizes, but in a real implication, and because my body is a movement toward the world, and the world my body's point of support. (*PP* 402/350/408)

This correlation between body and world does not imply some sort of relativism because the world is never possessed or determined by the body, and because the body is not a thing but an open system of possibilities. The world always exceeds what I make of it, and often resists it. I encounter the world as having irreducibly opaque and alien aspects, which cannot be accounted for by some other projection of the world that is the true one and thus explains the world's resistance to my projects:

any attempt to define the thing either as a pole of my bodily life, or as a permanent possibility of sensations, or as a synthesis of appearances, puts in place of the thing itself in its primordial being an imperfect reconstruction of the thing with the aid of bits and pieces of subjective provenance. . . . What is given is . . . something transcendent standing in the wake of one's subjectivity. (PP 375–6/325/379)

The body-subject does not remain unaffected by its encounter with transcendent things either. It does not impose a project and a perspective upon the world but rather discovers the world through its project, which it adjusts in response to what is discovered. Merleau-Ponty repeatedly described body and world as being in communication, each becoming what it is in response to the other.

II

We are now prepared to ask how the world conceived in scientific theory stands in relation to the perceived world. I have already cited Merleau-Ponty's claim that science is a "second-order expression" of the world that is disclosed prereflectively to the embodied perceiving subject. We can now see why this claim has no affinity to that empiricist approach to understanding science, which attempts to reduce the sense of its results to the contents of sensation. Merleau-Ponty thought perception is misunderstood if regarded merely as the presence of a certain sensory content. Perception is not something given but rather an openness to further determination. Perception gives us not sensations but a hold on the world. The perceiving subject is open to new forms of expression, including science, which reflect back on and even transform its original sense of the world. Merleau-Ponty's concern was not to show that science (or any other cultural form of expression) adds nothing original to the world as perceived but to show how its contribution is rooted in our prior familiarity with that world. Science presupposes perceptual consciousness without being reducible to it. Merleau-Ponty called this relation between science and the perceived world a

two-way relationship that phenomenology has called *Fundierung:* the founding term, or originator – time, the unreflective, the fact, language, perception – is primary in the sense that the originated is presented as a determinate or explicit form of the originator, which prevents the latter from reabsorbing the former, and yet the originator is not primary in the empiricist sense and the originated is not simply derived from it, since it is through the originated that the originator is made manifest. (*PP* 451/394/458)

At several points (*SC* 227/210; *PP* 152/130/149), Merleau-Ponty indicated that the model for his account of the relation of *Fundierung* is the relation between already acquired concepts and meanings and original speech that creates new meaning. Acquired meanings and originating speech always have a reciprocal relationship. All original speech rests on a background of already understood speech. Even the small child who does not yet speak encounters language as something already achieved, as a meaningful "world" already enveloping him or her, to which he or she must gradually catch on. When I speak, and do not merely repeat a thought previously articulated, I nevertheless build on a background of prior acquisitions.

Speech is, therefore, that paradoxical operation through which, by using words of a given sense, and already available meanings, we try to follow up an intention which necessarily outstrips, modifies, and itself, in the last analysis, stabilizes the meanings of the words which translate it. (*PP* 455–6/389/452)

This last phrase illustrates the other side of the reciprocal relation between constituted and originating speech. For if all speech rests on an already-acquired conceptual background, that background itself was acquired through earlier originating acts of speech. Merleau-Ponty took originating speech as that on which constituted speech is founded. Constituted language is made manifest only through the ways it is taken up and used, and yet it alone opens up the expressive possibilities that originating speech actualizes.

The decisive question for Merleau-Ponty was how original expression can be achieved. How, given a stock of words already at our command, can new meanings arise and be understood? He prepared his answer to this question by considering how we come to understand gestures. Gestures are not natural signs, which are simply seen as one might see an object. If they were, the specificity of our understanding of gestures would be inexplicable. If the meaning of a gesture

were given to me as a thing, it is not clear why my understanding of gestures should for the most part be confined to human ones. I do not "understand" the sexual pantomime of the dog, still less of the cockchafer or the praying mantis. I do not even understand the expression of the emotions in primitive peoples or in circles too unlike the ones in which I move. (*PP* 215/184/214)

The reason for this inability is that gestures are not signs that I interpret in a cognitive operation, but bodily possibilities that I comprehend by taking them up as an expressive potential of my own. It is not that I act out the gesture of the other, but rather that I recognize my own possibilities for expression in hers.

The communication or comprehension of gestures comes about through the reciprocity of my intentions and the gestures of others, of my gestures and intentions discernible in the conduct of other people. It is as if the other person's intention inhabited my body and mine his. (*PP* 215/185/215)

The meaning of a gesture is not self-contained but is inseparable from its insertion in a world that it points toward and further articulates as a space of possible expression. Gestures cannot simply be described as conventional because without some prior grasp of the expressive possibility of the gesture, it is unclear how the convention could ever be proposed and agreed on.

What is true of gestures is true of "linguistic gestures" (*PP* 217/186/216) as well. Merleau-Ponty claimed that "the spoken word is a genuine gesture, and it contains its meaning in the same way as the gesture contains its" (*PP* 214/183/213). There is, to be sure, a difference in that the gesture is mute and can indicate only relations with the surrounding world, whereas the spoken sentence "aims at a mental setting which is not given to everybody" (*PP* 217/186/216). Merleau-Ponty insisted, however, that the cultural background we share with others provides a surrogate "world" within which linguistic gestures may function. "Available meanings, in other words former acts of expression, establish between speaking subjects a common world, to which the words being uttered in their novelty refer as does the gesture to the perceptible world" (*PP* 217/186/216–17). Learning language, or learning a new meaning for a word within a language, is not a matter of grasping a meaning privately and cognitively, then assigning to it a conventional sign. I take up a possible use of a word and make it part of my repertoire of expressive skills. Constituted language is not a transparent acquisition but an expressive power bound to the situations to which it can respond.

The word has never been inspected, analyzed, known and constituted, but caught and taken up by a power of speech and, in the last analysis, by a motor power given to me along with the first experience I have of my body and its perceptual and practical fields. As for the meaning of a word, I learn it as I learn to use a tool, by seeing it used in the context of a certain situation. (*PP* 462/403/469)

Why is it, then, that words often seem straightforwardly comprehensible, independent of the particular vocal modulations or inscriptions in which they are embodied, and without reference to the situations within which I first learned them? Merleau-Ponty claimed that the familiarity of speech, and of the already-constituted meanings within which most of our speaking is confined, conceals from us the obscurity and ambiguity which lies behind those familiar expressions. We overlook that what is now habitual and obvious was once only an obscurely grasped possibility; the obscurity has been forgotten rather than removed.

We think that language is more transparent than music because most of the time we remain within the bounds of constituted language, we provide ourselves with available meanings, and in our definitions we are content, like the dictionary, to explain meanings in terms of each other. The meaning of a sentence appears intelligible throughout, detachable from the sentence and finitely self-subsistent in our intelligible world, because we presuppose as given all those exchanges, owed to the history of the language, which contribute to determining its sense. (*PP* 219/188/218–19)

I "inhabit" these acquired meanings analogously to the way I inhabit a familiar space, not through a familiarity born only of habit and repetition but through appropriating them into my capabilities. The meanings I acquire are not a fixed "conceptual scheme" that can be taken as a self-enclosed structure. They point beyond themselves toward the expressive possibilities that arise out of them, just as my body outruns itself toward the world:

my acquired thoughts are not a final gain, they continually draw their sustenance from my present thought, they offer me a meaning, but I give it back to them.... Thus what is acquired is truly acquired only if it is taken up again in a fresh momentum of thought, and a thought is assigned to its place only if it takes up its place itself. (*PP* 151/130/150)

It is thus not coincidental that Merleau-Ponty's phenomenology of perceptual consciousness ended in discussions of temporality and freedom. We have seen that originating speech (and the same could be said of other forms of expression) arises obscurely out of its history and projects itself indefinitely into the future. What is already achieved can only be understood through how it lends itself to that indefinite and ambiguously delineated future, which in turn is rooted in those prior achievements without being determined by them: "the meaning of a sentence is its import or intention, which once more presupposes a departure and arrival point, an aim and a point of view" (*PP* 491/430/499). We can infer that the relation of *Fundierung* that Merleau-Ponty claimed to hold between the theoretical constructions of science and the perceived world, which was modeled on the relation between originating and constituted speech, is essentially a temporal relation.

How might this affect the philosophy of science? Presumably Merleau-Ponty would have insisted, with Kuhn and Lakatos, that the philosophically significant unit of science must be the research program rather than the theory. The sense of a theory cannot be confined to its explicit content any more than could the sense of ordinary utterances. Theories have temporal horizons, which are integral to what they say about the world. They cannot be adequately understood except as the outcome of other theories proposed and investigated and as the progenitor of further research as yet only partially anticipated. Such research brings out dimensions of meaning only latent in the theories on which that research was based. The sense of current theories thus has yet to be fully disclosed; they are laden with potential. Only when those theories cease to play a role in ongoing research, that is, when they cease to be scientifically significant, will they escape this open-ended incompleteness.

This is why Merleau-Ponty rejected any formalized interpretation of scientific theories. Only a completed theory (or a theory taken as if completed, shorn of its temporal horizons) could be formalized, he would have argued. As a result, then, formal philosophies of science must overlook the elements of invention and discovery that comprise scientific research. Science formalized is science dead. Although attempts at formalization may be conceived,

it is in any case quite certain that they lay no claim to provide a logic of invention and, that no logical definition of a triangle could equal in fecundity the vision of the figure, or enable us to reach, through a series of formal operations, conclusions not already established by the aid of intuition.... [T]he fact that formalization is always retrospective proves that it is never otherwise than apparently complete, and that formal thought feeds on intuitive thought. (PP 441/385/448)

This emphasis might suggest that Merleau-Ponty's principal contribution to the philosophy of science, in Anglo-American terms, was to assign priority to the context of discovery over the context of justification. To read him this way is to overlook important subtleties in his position, however. Merleau-Ponty's work demands that we look at the relation between discovery and justification in a new way, and this can lead us to a new understanding of the philosophical issues surrounding justification.

There was never a question of justifying the atemporal validity of an utterance for Merleau-Ponty. Taken out of its historical context, the utterance has no validity. Whatever sense it makes rests on the obscurity of past utterances that now function as familiar and unquestioned acquisitions. It may be argued against this claim that the truth of an utterance does not depend on its history. No matter what led me to make a particular claim, its truth or falsity will depend only on how the world is. Yet Merleau-Ponty could offer at least three responses to this objection. The first is that there is more to justification than truth. Any utterance, he remarked, has a whole "sedimentary history" that not only is relevant to the *genesis* of my thought, but determines its *significance* (*sens*) (PP 453/395/459). Thus both the sense of what is being said about the world and the significance it has for science depend on this sedimentary history. There are, after all, innumerable truths with no scientific import and well-justified, significant scientific claims that are false. Scientific claims are evaluated for what they contribute to scientific understanding as a whole. Scientific understanding is not an accumulating stock of truths but involves ever-shifting capacities that are not simply the sum of their parts. It is constantly being renewed and reorganized. Thus, it is no accident that science continually outruns its textbooks because new discovery affects the significance of past achievements, if only by redirecting the project of research in terms of which that significance is assessed.

Merleau-Ponty's epistemological holism, which I cited earlier, is the basis for his second response. Scientific claims form a structure, from which the contribution of a particular claim cannot be disentangled. Confirming or challenging a scientific claim confirms or challenges a whole scientific approach to the world. Accepting or rejecting a particular claim never leaves unaffected the rest of the discipline to which it belongs. If one claim stands out as inviolable, or conversely as the likely source of error, this can only be on the basis of its place within an ongoing program of research. This consideration then leads to the third and final point. We have already seen that a scientific theory expresses more than its explicit content. Like the perceptual figure whose sense cannot be confined to what is given but must be understood as a solicitation to explore further, as a not fully definite anticipation of what is to come, the scientific claim points beyond itself. Its sense (and its truth) includes its anticipation of possibilities for further research.

The actual possession of the true idea does not, therefore, entitle us to predicate an intelligible abode of adequate thought and absolute productivity, it establishes merely a "teleology" of consciousness which, from this first instrument, will forge more perfect ones, and these in turn more perfect ones, and so on endlessly. (PP 453/395–6/460)

Scientific claims are justified not by their final correctness but by their contribution to further research. Thus, even false claims are justified through the eventual disclosure of their error and the significance this discovery has for subsequent research.

For there is not one of my actions, not one of even my fallacious thoughts, once it is adhered to, which has not been directed toward a value or a truth, and which, in consequence, does not retain its permanent relevance in the subsequent course of my life, not only as an indelible fact, but also as a necessary stage on the road to the more complete truths or values which I have since recognized. (PP 451/393/458)

Merleau-Ponty illustrated this claim that scientific statements must be understood with reference to their solicitation of further investigation with an extended discussion of geometrical proof. It may seem odd to take an example from mathematics without asking whether it could be straightforwardly extended to the empirical sciences. Merleau-Ponty, however, wrote in the context of Husserl's argument that what was essential to the development of a science of nature was the indirect application of geometry and geometrical thinking to the natural world.[5] To examine geometry in this philosophical context would *be* to examine the foundations of physical science. Merleau-Ponty began by pointing out that even the simplest geometrical proofs require constructions. Why is a line through the apex of the triangle and parallel to its opposite side significant when other equally constructable lines are not? How is there a direction (*sens*) to the proof? How, that is, is the movement possible from a given figure to the demonstration that its angles are equal to two right angles?

> It is because my perception of the triangle was not, so to speak, fixed and dead, for the drawing of the triangle on the paper was merely its outer covering; it was traversed by lines of force, and everywhere in it new directions not traced out yet possible came to light. Insofar as the triangle was implicated in my hold (*prise*) on the world, it was bursting with indefinite possibilities of which the construction actually drawn was merely one. The construction possesses a demonstrative value because I cause it to emerge from the *dynamic formula* of the triangle. (*PP* 443/386/449, emphasis added)

The point can clearly be extended to the theoretical constructions of empirical science, which are "not a collection of objective 'characteristics,' but the formula of an attitude, a certain modality of my hold on the world, a structure, in short" (*PP* 442/386/449).

Scientific theories are thus neither purely self-contained structures nor are they reducible to actual observations which embody them, as empiricists have tried to claim. In this respect, they are like the "virtual figures" we experience in perception (the figures anticipated as the outcomes of possible exploration). Thus, for example, physicists' concept of force is not reducible to any actual experience of forces in the world, but it cannot be understood without some appreciation of how it transforms how physicists see the world and cope with it (this, I believe, exemplifies what Merleau-Ponty meant by "a modality of my hold on the world"). His point here is comparable to one made by Kuhn in introducing the concept of a paradigm.[6] Kuhn suggested that the content of scientific theory was embedded in a range of concrete applications. Newton's Laws, he argued, cannot be appropriately understood apart from an ability to pick out the relevant forces, masses, and accelerations in an open-ended variety of actual problem situations. Merleau-Ponty's interpretation would have been that a paradigm in this sense is not reducible to a given content, but is grasped as a skill, which is flexibly applicable to new situations. Such further applications are neither totally unforeseen, nor fully worked out. In examining a new problem, the scientist sees it "traversed by lines of force," and "bursting with indefinite possibilities." These possibilities, as "virtual figures," are the intentional correlates of scientific skills, the ability to follow out those lines of force and develop explicitly the possibilities latent within one's present grasp of the situation. Just as in learning a physical skill like hammering a nail, I learn not a repetitive series of movements, but a flexible skill responsive to new demands (one can fairly easily hammer upside down or backhanded without having to relearn the skill completely); so in learning a scientific theory as a scientist does, one acquires a repertoire of skills for seeing, imagining, and manipulating the world in new ways.

III

We are now prepared to assess Merleau-Ponty's criticism of realist interpretations of science. It is a nuanced criticism rather than a total rejection of realism. "As philosophy, realism is an error because it transposes into dogmatic thesis an experience which it deforms or renders impossible by that very fact. But it is a motivated error; it rests on an authentic phenomenon which philosophy has the function of making explicit" (SC 233/216). What is this authentic phenomenon that realism supposedly misunderstands? It has two aspects, one linguistic, the other experiential. First, realism takes at face value the apparent transparency of language. Words seem to efface themselves and take us directly to things, but only because we take for granted their history. As we have already seen, Merleau-Ponty argued that the apparent clarity of familiar speech rests on our ability to appropriate a way of speaking as we might take up a gesture and make it our own, without clearly understanding it. "The act of speech is clear only for the person who is actually speaking or listening; it becomes obscure as soon as we try to bring explicitly to light those reasons which have led us to understand thus and not otherwise" (PP 448/391/455). To be sure, in speaking and hearing we direct ourselves toward the world, but not by discovering and articulating the way the world already is. There is always some opacity in reference, because words have a history. Realism proposes that there are truths that are independent of their history, the truth of which resides in the relation between words and things. Yet only through the history of their acquiring significance do words have a relation to things, Merleau-Ponty argued, or a "content" that could be true or false. Realism acquires its plausibility from our ability to overlook that history, but we can do that only because we have appropriated it into our capabilities.

To give expression is not to substitute, for new thoughts, a system of stable signs to which unchangeable thoughts are linked, it is to ensure, by the use of words already used, that the new intention carries on the heritage of the past, it is at a stroke to incorporate the past into the present, and weld that present to a future, to open a whole temporal cycle in which the "acquired" thought will remain present as a dimension, without our needing henceforth to summon it up or reproduce it. (*PP* 449–50/392/456)

Realism also reflects our experience of the achievement of perceptual permanence. Merleau-Ponty described this phenomenon most clearly in the case of visual perception.

I run through appearances and reach the real color or the real shape when my experience is at its maximum of clarity ... [D]ifferent appearances are for me appearances of a certain true spectacle, that in which the perceived configuration, for a sufficient degree of clarity, reaches its maximum richness. (*PP* 367/318/371)

The figure stabilizes and achieves a kind of practical certainty that makes it immune to doubt. Having seen the thing from the optimal point of view, "I commit (*j'engage*) a whole perceptual future" (*PP* 415/361/421). The certainty one thus acquires through perception is not a guarantee one receives but a commitment one makes to the world. As Samuel Todes and Hubert Dreyfus have pointed out, "The presumption that these permanent figures will never prove to be illusory is based merely on a perceptual faith – we would be astonished on disillusionment – but our experience is organized as if we had a perceptual guarantee to support this faith."[7] The past activity and future commitment of a perceiving subject underwrite this achievement of perceptual clarity and permanence, as a secure practical orientation rather than as epistemically indubitable.

Now the same phenomenon of stabilization and practical certainty, after an initial welter of appearances that were suggestive but inconclusive, occurs in scientific research. The correlate to the perceptual figure at *maximum prise* is the fact[8] that has been secured against the possibility of dissolving into artifact. At that point, scientific discourse seems to mirror a world of real objects independent of that discourse. "Previously, scientists were dealing with statements. At the point of stabilization, however, there appears to be both objects *and* statements about those objects. Before long, more and more reality is attributed to the object and less and less to the statement *about* the object."[9] Two points must be made about this phenomenon. The first is that here also (perhaps here especially), the possibility remains that this stabilization will turn out to be merely apparent. The stabilization (or "convergence") of scientific knowledge is not inconsistent with fallibilism. The achievement of scientific fact always rests in part on scientists' commitment to further research that takes those facts for granted. The second is that this stabilization is the product of scientific research and not its cause.[10] *Maximum prise* is the product of an embodied subject whose explorations lead her or him to an optimal *stance, from which* the thing shows itself as it is. The scientific fact is the significant outcome of a course of research through which it was achieved, and to which it owes its sense. Merleau-Ponty himself asked,

For what precisely is meant by saying that the world existed before any human consciousness? An example of what is meant is that the earth originally issued from a primitive nebula from which the combination of conditions necessary to life was absent. But... [n]othing will ever bring home to my comprehension what a nebula that no one sees could possibly be. Laplace's nebula is not behind us, at our remote beginnings, but in front of us in the cultural world (*PP* 494/432/502).

It is true that both scientific facts and perceived things can be partially freed from the contexts in which they were first disclosed. In the case of facts, however, this partial autonomy arises only because they are established in a standardized and often simplified form that allows those who take account of them to overlook the complexities that lay behind their original disclosure.[11] When they are to be used in ways unanticipated in their standard formulations, their origins must be recovered and their original production to some degree reenacted or reperformed. The reference to standardized facts is a specifically scientific example of the apparent clarity of speech that stems from unquestioning acceptance of familiar concepts and expressions but rests on the obscurity of its origins. This is not objectionable scientific practice, for it is what makes original research possible.[12] It is objectionable, however, when given a philosophical interpretation as scientific realism. The realist interpretation of the stabilization of scientific facts reflects what Merleau-Ponty would call the misinterpretation of the acquired as the eternal (PP 450/392/456–7). As he pointed out in the passage quoted at the beginning of this section, realism as a philosophical thesis makes the phenomenon it describes impossible because it leaves out of account the investigations that do not simply discover facts already there but bring them into being as culturally meaningful objects.

The rejection of realism compels us to ask anew about the relation between the world perceived and the world conceptualized in scientific research. To say that scientific theories are cultural objects is not to make them mere fictions or instruments. The realist is correct in asserting that the objects of scientific theory exist and that they are not ontologically dependent on the *objects* of the everyday world. What science does presuppose according to Merleau-Ponty is a prior and ongoing acquaintance with the world through perception, which he refers to as "preobjective" (PP xiii/xvii/xx). Without this prior familiarity, science would have nothing to refer to, and its theories would be empty formalisms.

To return to things themselves is to return to that world which precedes knowledge, of which knowledge always *speaks,* and in relation to which every scientific schematization is an abstract and derivative sign-language, as is geography in relation to the countryside in which we have learned beforehand what a forest, a prairie or a river is. (PP iii/ix/ix–x)

This analogy to geography (henceforth, to maps) can be usefully explored to reveal Merleau-Ponty's ontology of science. Consider the relations between a map, the terrain it represents, and its intended users. Maps do not simply reproduce the user's original sense of the terrain but instead select certain features to be represented, leaving others out. Reading a map presupposes a general acquaintance with terrain (e.g., knowing what a river is) but not with the particular terrain being mapped, nor even necessarily with all of the features to which the map refers. A map may indicate features of the terrain that are not directly perceivable or immediately apparent, but without some familiar features and some identifiable reference to the world, the map has no significance, except perhaps in play. Maps can be studied as self-contained objects, and their features analyzed internally, but their significance as maps depends on their possible reference to an actual place. Our original familiarity with the world is not left unchanged by our acquaintance with maps, for they often transform our subsequent perceptual awareness. An acquaintance with the schematic structure of a map can enable us to see new things in the world and to inhabit it in new ways. We see proximities or features that had not been apparent to us before mapping. Indeed, they are often then so obvious that we have difficulty understanding our previous failure to see them and cannot clearly recall or reproduce our original experience. Because maps are always selective, the possibility of alternative mappings always remains open. The notion of the ultimate or complete map, even of an exhaustive set of maps, is senseless because a map is always more or less suited to some purpose. Often our explorations with a map allow us to discover new concerns that would require new mapping if they are to be satisfied. Only if the range of possible human concerns could be somehow limited in advance would the "ideal" of a complete map make sense. Yet this does not mean that the features on the map are merely instrumental constructs; they represent real aspects of the world that we encounter as significant and intelligible through our concerns.

All of these aspects of the relations between maps and places mapped have analogues in the relations between scientific theories and the perceived world. Science does not simply reproduce the everyday world; some features of the latter have scientific significance, and others do not. Practicing science presupposes general familiarity with the world but not necessarily with the particular aspects of it which are under investigation (Rheinberger[13] offers detailed accounts of how such investigations of novel phenomena proceed with reference to prior familiarity in the cases of ultracentrifugation of cell components and electron microscopy of tissue-cultured cells). Scientific theories often refer to objects or aspects of objects that are not directly perceivable or not immediately apparent, but they must have some identifiable connection with ordinarily perceivable events, however tenuous that connection may be. Scientific theories can be, and often are, studied as self-contained objects and analyzed internally, but without some possible reference to phenomena in the world, they would not have scientific significance. Science certainly does not leave our everyday experience unchanged; it has taught us to see new things, while preventing some old things from ever looking the same again. Scientific theories can never be complete because which features of the world require scientific description or explanation depends on our cognitive and practical concerns. As our concerns change, our theories must also change (consider what the growing concern to understand weight relations did for and to chemical theory in the eighteenth century). There cannot be an ideal scientific theory any more than there can be an ideal map. There must always be, Merleau-Ponty claimed, a "surplus of the signified over the signifying" (*PP* 447/390/453).

On this view, scientific theories can be true or false just as maps can be accurate or inaccurate, but this truth and falsity is always contextual. Just as the perceptual figure achieved at *maximum prise* requires a compromise between clarity and richness, so scientific theories require choices between competing concerns (simplicity, comprehensiveness, detail, practical applicability, coherence with other theories, and so on). A theory is false when it directs us toward the world with expectations that cannot be satisfied. This outcome has a great deal to do with how things are in the world, but it also depends on which expectations the theory generates, and this cannot be fully understood except with reference to theory users' cognitive and practical concerns, their prior knowledge, and the history of research that brought them to that theory with certain expectations about how it attaches to the world. Theories thus occupy an ambiguous place between us and the world. They seem to be objects with properties independent of us (we discover rather than invent their implications, for example). Yet we also use them to explore the world and, in doing so, incorporate them into our own capacities, much as a blind man incorporates his cane. "Once the stick has become a familiar instrument, the world of feelable things recedes and now begins, not at the outer skin of the hand, but at the end of the stick" (*PP* 177/152/175–6). We do not *interpret* our perceptions in terms of our concepts and theories. The world begins for us at the "far end" of our theories, so that interpretation is not necessary.

That is Merleau-Ponty's version of the supposed theory-ladenness of observation. Scientific concepts and theories are incorporated into our bodily synthesis, that sense of our capabilities and skills through which we explore and disclose the world. Science thereby continually reshapes the world we inhabit.

The important question for Merleau-Ponty was which, if any, limits there are to such reshaping. It is clear on his account that science cannot totally alter or undermine our ordinary sense of the world.

If I try to imagine Martians, or angels, or some divine thought outside the realm of my logic, this Martian, angelic or divine thought must figure in my universe without completely disrupting it. My thought, my self-evident truth is not one fact among others, but a value-fact which envelops and conditions every other possible one. (PP 456/398/463)

What serves as a limit here is not the particular objects or forms of experience of my everyday life; it is the horizon of the world as perceived. In Sellars's terms, Merleau-Ponty does not assign priority to the manifest image over the scientific image of the world.[14] The priority belongs to the world itself, the actual presence of which to me as an embodied subject cannot be challenged. The world is the open context within which all my activities take place and against which both scientific and everyday concepts are measured. Further investigation may require that any particular element of our present understanding of the world be replaced, but the replacement takes place against the background of a world. "There is the absolute certainty of the world in general, but not of any one thing in particular" (PP 344/297/347). Yet there do seem to be some aspects of my everyday experience that Merleau-Ponty took to be irreplaceable. The experience of the body as lived cannot be replaced by a physiological description of it. The spatiality of everyday life cannot be replaced by or subordinated to a geometrical one, as we have seen. Perhaps the difference is that some structures of preobjective experience are essential and thus unchallengeable, whereas the elements of everyday experience are not.[15] This distinction might be difficult for Merleau-Ponty to sustain, however, because it is not clear how to distinguish essential structures of experience from contingent limitations of imagination. Moreover, some particular components of everyday experience seem to resist the encroachment of science as well. Merleau-Ponty would have no trouble saying that physicists see subatomic particles in cloud or bubble chambers, but neither they nor anyone else can see a table as a configuration of such particles (this example is, of course, highly artificial because physicists cannot even describe a table this way, but less problematic cases could be constructed). "Reflection can never make me stop seeing the sun two hundred yards away on a misty day, or seeing it 'rise' and 'set,' or thinking with the cultural apparatus with which my education, my previous efforts, my personal history, have provided me" (*PP* 74–5/61/71). Thus the extent of Merleau-Ponty's pragmatism is not fully clear. The phenomenal field (i.e., the preobjective world) is, he claimed, a transcendental field (*PP* 77/63/74); its structures are immune to empirical revision because they are presupposed by it. Yet there is no principled way (apart from the contingencies of imaginative variation) to distinguish such "structures" from what they structure. What aspects of our everyday, culturally informed *Lebenswelt* must always resist such revision is thus undetermined. At best, such phenomenologically described "structures" could have only a practical certainty comparable to that of the figure at *maximum prise*, and not any kind of transcendental necessity.

It should be clear that Merleau-Ponty's response to realism as I have outlined it also contains a response to skepticism. Any particular claim that we assert is fallible, but this fallibility presupposes an ability to distinguish truth and falsity. "We know that there are errors only because we possess truth, in the name of which we correct errors and recognize them as errors" (*PP* 341/295/344). We possess not particular truths, but truth, the openness to the world which we are by virtue of being a body. What Merleau-Ponty believed that both skeptics and those who would refute skepticism fail to see is that we are perceivers, to whom a world is present not as a spectacle to be described or misdescribed but as a situation to be explored and responded to. "Rationalism and skepticism draw their sustenance from an actual life of consciousness which they both hypocritically take for granted, without which they can be neither conceived nor even experienced" (*PP* 342/296/345). "We are in the realm of truth and it is the 'experience of truth' which is self-evident. To seek the essence of perception is to declare that perception is, not presumed true, but defined as access to truth" (*PP* xi/xvi/xviii). Realists may well respond that this fact (or "value-fact" as Merleau-Ponty described it in the passage quoted earlier), that a world is present to us as a field of truth and error, demands explanation. Why is it that some of our exploratory stances and conceptions lead to illusion, and others do not? What accounts for the difference between truth and error? Only a realist account of the world, it is said, can explain this without invoking miracles.[16] Merleau-Ponty responded that such a demand mistakenly places rationality outside of the world, outside of the experiences in which it is manifest.

> To say that there exists rationality is to say that perspectives blend, perceptions confirm each other, a meaning emerges. But it should not be set in a realm apart, transposed into Absolute Spirit or into a world in the realist sense. ... [T]he only preexistent Logos is the world itself ... and no explanatory hypothesis is clearer than the act whereby we take up this unfinished world in an effort to complete and conceive it. (PP xv/xix–xx/xxii–xxiii)

Rationality is not a problem to be solved. Science can never be made secure, if security must be found in the certainty of a given content. The rationality of science, like all rationality, is contingent. It is to be continually achieved, rather than secured once and for all. The "unmotivated upsurge of the world" (PP viii/xiv/xv) is the point at which both scientific and philosophical reflection begin and which neither can transcend or explain.*

NOTES

1. In *Representing and Intervening,* Ian Hacking has persuasively argued that recent Anglophone debates over realism are better construed as debates over classification (with realism and nominalism as the opposing positions) rather than over existence (realism versus idealism). For Merleau-Ponty, however, the dispute between realism and idealism concerned the constitution of meaning rather than existence. Moreover, because he understood conceptual content in terms of structures and inferential relations rather than classification, his challenges to realist and idealist accounts of meaning incorporate the issues between realist and nominalist accounts of classification.
2. Transcendental idealism is rarely taken seriously by Anglo-American philosophers of science. When they speak of "idealism," the word is usually interchangeable with "instrumentalism" or "empiricism," but

---

* An earlier version of this essay appeared in *Synthese* 66 (1986): 249–72. –Eds.

more commonly in philosophy of science nowadays, the debates are between realists and *social* constructivists rather than realists and empiricists. For a good recent survey of the debates, see Kukla, *Social Constructivism and the Philosophy of Science*. Because Merleau-Ponty's arguments against "idealism" attack the possibility of any autonomous source for the constitution of meaning, they readily extend to arguments against any of these forms of antirealism (empiricist, transcendental idealist, or social constructivist).

3. The interplay between intersubjective and personal aspects of bodily structure and style is an important topic that I am unable to discuss here.

4. For a detailed exposition of this claim, see Todes, *Body and World*, 262–5.

5. Husserl, *The Crisis of European Sciences and Transcendental Phenomenology*, 23–37, 353–78.

6. Kuhn, *The Structure of Scientific Revolutions*, 187–91.

7. Dreyfus and Todes, "The Three Worlds of Merleau-Ponty," 561–2.

8. Following Ravetz, I am not confining the denotation of "fact" to singular true statements: "'Invariance,' along with significance for further work and stability under repetition and application, is a necessary condition for a component of a solved problem to be accepted as a fact; and all three together are sufficient." Ravetz, *Scientific Knowledge and Its Social Problems*, 190.

9. Latour and Woolgar, *Laboratory Life: The Construction of Scientific Facts*, 176–7.

10. "Scientific research" must be understood not simply as the activity of scientists but as also incorporating the phenomena that are the focus of the research. Latour and Woolgar's claim about the splitting of statements is often read (misread, in my view, but I am not primarily concerned with how to interpret their work) as expressing a social constructivist, linguistic idealism. That reading is tenable only if "statements" are entities that function without dependence on their circumstances. I think Latour and Woolgar's claim only makes sense if one takes "statements" to be utterances-in-context (where the context includes their material setting), in which case no idealist or constructivist conclusions follow from it.

11. See Ravetz, *Scientific Knowledge and Its Social Problems*, 199–292; Fleck, *Genesis and Development of Scientific Fact*, 79, 84–7; and Latour and Woolgar, *Laboratory Life*, 176–83.

12. See, for example, Kuhn's discussion of the efficacy of normal science for producing new discoveries in *The Structure of Scientific Revolutions*, 52, 64–5.

13. See H.-J. Rheinberger, "From Microsomes to Ribosomes."
14. Sellars, *Science, Perception and Reality*, chapter 1.
15. For a fuller account of this distinction, see Dreyfus and Todes, "The Three Worlds of Merleau-Ponty," 560–5.
16. Putnam, *Meaning and the Moral Sciences*, 18–19; Boyd, "The Current Status of Scientific Realism."

11 Between Philosophy and Art

"Every theory of painting is a metaphysics," declares Merleau-Ponty in "Eye and Mind," his last major philosophical essay on the visual arts (Œ 42/171/132). The immediate target of his remark is Descartes, in whose brief comments on engravings Merleau-Ponty finds a denigration of art as but a handmaiden to perception, capable of disclosing only those features of the mind-independent world already available to ordinary vision. However, his claim is meant to apply much more broadly. By addressing the nature of representation, its content, means, and ends, and the relation of the artist to the world, a theory of painting entails a metaphysics: a conception of how the self, body, mind, and world interrelate. In his major essays on visual art – "Cézanne's Doubt" (1945), "Indirect Language and the Voices of Silence" (1952), and "Eye and Mind" (1961) – Merleau-Ponty draws on this internal relation between theories of painting and metaphysics to challenge prevailing philosophical and scientific accounts of perception, meaning, imagination, and human subjectivity.

Yet if every theory of painting implies a metaphysical theory, not every metaphysical theory offers a theory of painting. Art plays a central role in Merleau-Ponty's efforts to elaborate his phenomenology; however, even in the intense, searching reflection of "Cézanne's Doubt" on the painter's life and work, it is not clear that from such phenomenological inquiry there emerges a philosophy of art. Does the essay offer an analysis of Cézanne, of Cézanne's painting, of painters and paintings, or of artists and art in general of which Cézanne and his work are – in relevant ways – representative? If philosophy requires general applicability, does this mean that as Merleau-Ponty's discussion is more particularly focused, it is less philosophical? If a philosophy of art must be careful not to lose what may be distinctive about art in assimilating it to a more general account of human behavior, expression, and perception, does this mean that the more generally conceived Merleau-Ponty's theory is, the less it functions as a philosophy of art? In what follows, I want to suggest that these questions shaped Merleau-Ponty's essays on art, pulling in opposite directions, from the example to the general type, from a narrow focus to a broad one. I argue, more specifically, that this tension in Merleau-Ponty's essays between the attempt, on one hand, to offer a general philosophical theory and, on the other, to furnish particular explanations and interpretations of art, is ultimately left unresolved. That is, his deep commentaries on the arts illustrate and extend his general philosophical views but generate no philosophy of art in themselves.[1]

I. ART AND VISION

"Cézanne's Doubt" begins with a catalogue of some of the painter's mundane epistemic doubts (only later will his existential and metaphysical doubts be explored): he works alone, without the confirmation of students or the encouragement of critics; he wonders whether he has enough talent; he suspects that his unusual style may be owing to a defect in his vision. Merleau-Ponty dismisses the latter physiological explanation but flirts with ascribing some explanatory value to the various temperamental, physical, and psychological ills from which the painter suffered – his "morbid constitution," possible "schizophrenia," "alienation from humanity," "nervous weaknesses," and so on – only to dismiss the idea that the meaning of the artist's work could be determined from such features of his life. If this is ambiguous in implying alternatively that one could discover the meaning of the work through understanding the life or that the meaning of the work is produced by the kind of life its creator had, Merleau-Ponty appears to reject both accounts. Not only, he says, do Zola and Émile Bernard emphasize too much of their personal knowledge of Cézanne's life in understanding his art, but even Cézanne's "own judgment of his work" will not make that meaning clearer. Furthermore, although it is possible that part of the origin of Cézanne's art may reside in his mental illness, in its reception it is "valid for everyone" (*SNS* 15/11; *AR* 61).

Here, Merleau-Ponty argues not against the biographical or intentionalist explanations of art *as such* so much as the one-sidedness of such approaches. As we will see, Merleau-Ponty will reject the dichotomy between the self and its external attributes, actions, and experiences. In the domain of art, this means that Merleau-Ponty will eschew the dichotomy between internalist explanations of art, which find art's meaning in the artist's intentions or life, and externalist explanations, which look to social or other contextual sources of meaning. For Merleau-Ponty, art, artist, and artist's life are interdependent; each explains the other and the others explain each in turn. To anticipate, Merleau-Ponty will introduce a way of conceiving of art as reflecting its creator's life, but not transparently. That is, Merleau-Ponty will argue that there is an internal relation between work and life, but that this relation reflects contingencies in how the work and the life unfold.

But first Merleau-Ponty describes the particular working methods of Cézanne, in particular, his advances over the impressionism through which he initially developed his style. Although much of what Merleau-Ponty presents here might appear as a kind of art-historical précis of impressionist and postimpressionist aesthetics, it is around this account of Cézanne's pictorial aims – and what greater, extravisual significance those aims had for the artist – that the larger phenomenological themes of the essay are organized. For in his pictorial practice, Cézanne instantiates the kind of perception that phenomenology ascribes to all ordinary perception. Yet Cézanne makes thematic the content of that phenomenological description of what he sees, raising it to a level of perspicuity such that his painting is both the product of vision and *about* vision, both exemplifies the way in which we perceive our environment and pictorially describes or reflects on the way in which we perceive. At the same time, Cézanne faces the problem of such phenomenological description: the phenomenologist describes the prereflective and prejudgmental bases for our experience in the world, but in describing that experience freezes it, or corrupts it, turning it into what the partial (and thus falsely totalizing) account of perceptual experience offered by science would say it is. In this way, Cézanne's painting is both an object for Merleau-Ponty's phenomenological analysis and, like self-psychoanalysis, the source of a phenomenological analysis in itself.

In his interpretation of Cézanne, Merleau-Ponty generally follows those art historians and critics who sought to distinguish the painter from his impressionist and postimpressionist or symbolist contemporaries.[2] Postimpressionist painters such as Gaugin and Van Gogh charged that when impressionism disposed of academic conventions of composition and traditional narrative, moral, and allegorical content for the rendering of nature in its immediacy, it too readily dispensed with judgment and expression as well. That is, while impressionists thought that the rendering of nature in its visual totality – including the effects of water, wind, mist, smoke, and changing conditions of light – was the defining imperative of art, symbolists accused such work of being intellectually empty. Gaugin wrote, "the Impressionists study color exclusively [for its] decorative effect, but without freedom, retaining the shackles of verisimilitude . . . [It is a] purely superficial art, full of affectations and purely material. There is no thought there."[3] The symbolist response to the impressionist rendering of the appearance of the natural world was to turn away from it, subordinating the realist impulse to imagery that drew on fantasy, dreams, and individual expression and employing stylistic techniques drawn from nonnaturalistic traditions in painting such as that of Japanese screens.

Cézanne's mature work, however, followed neither the impressionists nor the symbolists. He did not turn away from the rendering of appearance but devoted himself more fully to it, to showing not the brute – what Merleau-Ponty called "inhuman" – appearance of the world, but the appearance of the world as it comes into being as a configured space of individuated forms for an observer. That is, instead of showing just the sensations that the impressionists treated – like contemporary positivists – as belonging to the given in experience, to be transparently recorded, Cézanne tried to render the process by which such sensations feed into the generation of the landscape or other objects of experience. In the process, Merleau-Ponty says, Cézanne would return the solidity to objects, their presence as objects, which evaporated in the impressionist rendering of mere appearance. For Merleau-Ponty, the painter offered not a picture of the world "as it is," but a picture of the world coming into being in the percipient's view of it, not before or after but *as* the attributes associated with use, significance, and value are applied. This is not the impressionists' quasi-scientific rendering of the appearance of the world, but a view of the world that makes salient the contribution of one's particular consciousness.

However, Merleau-Ponty also contests positivist theories of perception according to which the world appears to us as sense data that are then interpreted and given configuration in the mind. For he argues that the particular perspective of someone's consciousness is not to be understood as merely a screen of subjectivity that, were it removed, would allow access to the object itself. For the object of experience as understood by phenomenology is in part constituted by the perspective of consciousness. Against transcendental philosophies like neo-Kantianism that worried such a perspectival account of perception would sanction a kind of relativism about objects in the world, Merleau-Ponty followed Husserl in seeing a guarantee of the existence of independent objects in the very fact there are such multiple perspectives on a thing: "Perspective does not appear to me to be a subjective deformation of things but, on the contrary, to be one of their properties, perhaps their essential property. It is precisely because of it that the perceived possesses in itself a hidden and inexhaustible richness, that is a 'thing'" (*SC* 201/186).

Thus, Merleau-Ponty takes what was a long-standing artistic battle – between those who construed the *verité* of painting in terms of naturalism and those who found it in the expression of an inspired creative mind – and raises it to the level of competing metaphysical systems.[4] Neither system, nor the dichotomy they constitute together, will suffice as an account of the human grasp of the world. Furthermore, just as phenomenology rejected the dichotomy between realism and idealism, so Cézanne is described by Merleau-Ponty as refusing to be fixed between the poles of impressionism and symbolism, between a notion of art as rendering only appearances and a notion of art as grounded in an artist's personal, perhaps idiosyncratic response to the world.

II. VISION AND TECHNIQUE

Merleau-Ponty does not claim that Cézanne had some special capacity for vision that allowed him to render what others could not see. Indeed, if Merleau-Ponty is right that Cézanne shows us something about how we come to see the world, this would in principle be true of the impressionists' vision of the world as well. Rather, Cézanne shows us via pictorial means what Merleau-Ponty would otherwise describe by philosophical means: that our relationship to the world is as embodied beings, with a perspectival or incomplete grasp of the world in which the meaning of what we experience arises neither from some determinate and unchanging landscape of objects that our perception passively follows nor from our mind imposing preexisting categories on the world. Rather, the meaning of our experience comes from our bodily and perceptual confrontation with the world, from within it. Such meaning is given to the world prior to any meaning or significance that might come from our intellectual judgment of what we find around us. Objects are meaningful first because of our sensorimotor relation to them – such as the fact that the front of an object implies, for beings who can move through space, the object's back as well. Phenomenological description expresses the meaning objects have as a consequence of belonging to the orbit of such embodied beings: "the experience of a real thing cannot be explained by the action of that thing on my mind: the only way for a thing to act on a mind is to offer it a meaning, to manifest itself to it, to constitute itself vis-à-vis the mind in its intelligible articulations" (SC 215/199). This is so even if the organizing or meaning-giving activity of our embodied perception hides itself in its operation, leaving us to see things in the world habitually as if determinate and existing independently of us.

Merleau-Ponty interprets Cézanne, however, as refusing to surrender to this habitual way of seeing. In Cézanne's painting, we do not see the revelation of some feature of the world to which earlier vision had been blind, such as, say, the color that the impressionists showed to inhere in shadows. Rather, we see the conditions under which our vision of the world is achieved. Indeed, Merleau-Ponty points out a number of pictorial techniques by which this generation of our experience is represented, but where those pictorial techniques or features occupy no place in the real world. So, for example, Cézanne paints a multiplicity of outlines around a figure to undermine the usual impression that the edges of things exist prior to our sense-making perception of them: "Rebounding among these, one's glance captures a shape that emerges from them all, just as it does in perception" (SNS 20/15; AR 65).

Yet paintings, in representing things in the world, are things in the world themselves, and Merleau-Ponty does not explain how the image of the world Cézanne presents will escape being seen by us in the same way the rest of the world is. That is, if objects in the world take on form as we perceive them in the same way objects in a painting take on form as we perceive them, then what can the painting show us that looking at the real world doesn't already reveal (or fail to reveal)?[5] One response, suggested but not explicitly argued for by Merleau-Ponty, is that Cézanne's techniques constitute discoveries by which he is able to make salient or perspicuous something that is part of visual experience, but not *recreate* that visual experience. Thus, Merleau-Ponty distinguishes between a landscape painting by Cézanne in which he shows "nature pure" and a photograph of the same scene that would invariably suggest "man's works, conveniences, and imminent presence" (*SNS* 18/14; *AR* 64). If the mechanical reproduction displays such an already categorized and inhabited world, this would not be because the photographer intends it to be so but because the photographer in Merleau-Ponty's comparison lacks the technical means to show the world in any way except as we habitually see it. If Cézanne's painting prevents that experience of seeing an image just as one sees the world, it is not because his depiction of the landscape leaves features out that the photograph leaves in. It is because the painter, unlike the photographer, employs a technique that calls attention to – and does not just participate in – the ways in which objects are given individuation, meaning and form. So, in Merleau-Ponty's reference to what Émile Bernard described as "Cézanne's suicide – aiming for reality while denying himself the means to attain it," it is not just any painterly techniques that are denied, but those, such as mathematical perspective, by which a preformed, familiar, and naturalizing order is imposed on the flux of experience (*SNS* 17/12; *AR* 63).

Earlier artists had recognized the ways in which, despite the verisimilitude mathematical perspective offered, it was largely a conventional way of depicting the world that, when applied too rigorously, could result in distortions. Leonardo, for one, made a distinction between "natural perspective" which corresponds to how we view the world, and "artificial perspective, which is a feature only of art," after noticing such problems as inconsistencies in the scale of represented objects caused by foreshortened sides of very wide images and the way spheres must be always be rendered circular in an image to look natural, even if the application of perspective would transform them into elliptical shapes. What Cézanne does, however, in Merleau-Ponty's view, is thematize this use of perspective. That is, Cézanne makes the artificiality of perspective salient in his work, disclosing it in a way that allows it to be reflected on as a convention.

Cézanne's abrogation of perspective is also important for the way in which it demonstrates the painter giving up a kind of control, "abandoning himself to the chaos of sensations" (*SNS* 17/13; *AR* 63). Here, Merleau-Ponty refers to more than just exclusively *visual* sensations. For he argues that sensations are not experienced as arriving individually, one after the other, but holistically, each conditioning the others as they are all revealed. Sartre writes in this connection of how a

> lemon is extended throughout its qualities, and each of its qualities is extended throughout each of the others. It is the sourness of the lemon which is yellow, it is the yellow of the lemon which is sour... if I poke my finger into a jar of jam, the sticky coldness of that jam is a revelation to my fingers of its sugary taste.[6]

In the same vein, Merleau-Ponty refers to Cézanne's remark that "one should be able to paint even odors," such is the unity of the sensible properties of things in experience before they are submitted to the distinctions of the mind.[7] Such holistic sensations imply the role of the body in constituting the objects of experience. This is not the experience of someone affected by synesthesia, but an account of the grounds of experience – one's "lived perspective" – before it is submitted to the individuating and categorizing judgments of the intellect.

Merleau-Ponty describes this "lived perspective" in a passage on the work-table in Cézanne's portrait of Gustave Geoffrey (*SNS* 19/14; *AR* 64). Although a perspectival construction would dictate that the table be painted as a plane with receding sides, Cézanne paints it as if it were leaning over into the lower part of the picture because that is how one sees a table when standing before it, as a plane that slopes toward oneself as one looks over its surface. This does not mean Cézanne paints mere sensations instead of employing his preformed judgment about what he sees. Rather, Cézanne rejects the dichotomy between giving oneself over passively to sensation and applying one's judgment to organize sensation. Neither alternative, Merleau-Ponty stresses – neither the painter who sees nor the painter who thinks – captures the experience of seeing as a being in the world.

In his discussion of Cézanne's technique, Merleau-Ponty suggests that those artists who continue a tradition tend to be committed to such dichotomies as between sensation and understanding, whereas those who initiate traditions foreswear such dichotomies. So Cézanne does not choose between representing things as they are and the way they appear. Rather, he will "depict matter as it takes on form, the birth of order through spontaneous organization" (*SNS* 18/13; *AR* 63–4). This means that Cézanne draws contours of objects in a still life without employing a continuous line, for that would be to make "an object of the shape" (*SNS* 20/14; *AR* 65). Instead, he treats the outline as the ideal limit toward which the sides of the apple recede. Those visible sides thus refer – as presences to absences – to the sides of the apple that we do not see, but to which our sensori-motor presence in the world is oriented. Here, and again later in the essay, Merleau-Ponty refers to "philosophers and painters" as such initiators of a tradition, suggesting that the philosopher and painter are engaged in the same sort of project, despite differences in method and material. The important difference, then, between Cézanne's and Merleau-Ponty's investigations is not the result, but that the painter may not be aware, or at least not be able to articulate his awareness, of the truth of experience he has revealed, whereas the philosopher might be able to articulate the truth of experience he has uncovered.

Yet, unlike the painter's success in bringing features of that experience into perspicuity, the philosopher's articulation of the experience must contend with the risk of distorting it. The articulation of the experience risks introducing distortions because it casts the experience in just those explicit and objective representations that scientific description employs, but which phenomenology has stressed is alien to the experience as it occurs to an embodied consciousness. In his late, unfinished work, *The Visible and the Invisible*, Merleau-Ponty appears to seek to dissolve this contrast between experience and its linguistic articulation, suggesting that the structures of the two are interdependent. Here, at least, his treatment serves as a counterinstance to the charge that a philosophy of art invariably subordinates art to philosophy or deforms the art in making it amenable to philosophical analysis. Indeed, Merleau-Ponty acknowledges in a way that the artist can engage in a kind of philosophical analysis of experience that is not entirely open to the philosopher.

The distinction between philosopher and painter is posed once again in "Eye and Mind" where Merleau-Ponty describes the scientific point of view that treats objects and beings in the world as essentially susceptible to manipulation and control. Merleau-Ponty says, by contrast, that the domain of inquiry that belongs to the arts is precisely this human world that "operationalism" – a way of casting the world in instrumental terms – ignores. However, whereas literature (as well as philosophy) must appraise what it treats, must have a judgmental relation to its subject, the painter is "entitled to look at everything without being obliged to appraise what he sees." Merleau-Ponty says that the painter alone can stand outside the sphere of action and judgment, "as if in the painter's calling there were some urgency above all other claims on him." Merleau-Ponty asks what this calling is, "What, then, is the secret science which he has or which he seeks?" (Œ14–15/161/123). Although here he appears to invoke a modernist notion of artistic autonomy, in which art is in its essence held to be immune to the demands of the practical, moral, and political spheres, Merleau-Ponty understands artistic autonomy not as a rejection of the world's claims on the artist, but the pursuit of a claim that is greater. This claim, which Merleau-Ponty develops in "Eye and Mind" (in a way that represents a change from his predominant concern with vision in the earlier essays), addresses the artist's role in expressing a way of existing in the world that is not just his own but is that of the collective group, society, or milieu to which he belongs. Yet it is precisely in absenting himself, in a form of autonomous existence, from the demands of action and judgment that define membership in such a society that the artist is able to achieve such general, nonindividualistic expression.

III. EXPRESSION

In explaining his notion of a social or collective form of expression, Merleau-Ponty cites a phrase from Valéry: the painter "takes his body with him." By this, he refers first to the phenomenological understanding of what may be called "embodied vision," meant not in the sense of vision existing only when causally dependent on a physical being, but in the less easily characterized sense of one's vision being shaped by or expressive of the fact that it is a capacity of an embodied organism: one encounters the world as a physical being, not an abstract "point of view" for which the world is a picture or representation in the mind. He also uses Valéry's remark to stress the fact that as one sees, one inhabits a body – a body that is seen by others. One's body is simultaneously seeing and seen, and when it sees itself, it sees itself seeing, just as it can touch itself touching. This capacity of the body to be both its own subject and object leads Merleau-Ponty to describe the self as constituted nontransparently and nonautonomously, as both object and subject. Thus, against the notion of a unified subject that serves as the transcendental guarantee of the unity of the world, Merleau-Ponty introduces ways of speaking of a decentered self: one that is not immediately present to itself. There is, he writes, "another subject beneath me, for whom a world exists before I am here, and who marks out my place in it. This captive or natural spirit is my body" (*PP* 294/254/296).[8]

Instead of beginning with a notion of the autonomous self and then asking how one's knowledge of other minds is possible, Merleau-Ponty starts with the premise that as an embodied individual one is related – as both subject and object – to other embodied beings. Judgments about others can be made, including judgments about how those others relate to oneself, but the important point for Merleau-Ponty is that one's fundamental connectedness with others is prior to and the ground (not the result) of one's intellectual judgments about them. He stresses that such unity of sensing and sensed is part of being human, but such humanity is not a matter of "contingencies," such as the way our eyes are implanted in us: "The body's animation is not the assemblage or juxtaposition of its parts." Rather, it emerges from what Merleau-Ponty describes as "a kind of crossover" between the body as subject and the body as object: "between the seer and the visible, between touching and touched" (*Œ* 21/163/125). How to understand the relationships among these incarnations is a central question of Merleau-Ponty's late philosophy.

Merleau-Ponty contrasts the ordinary understanding of an image as showing the appearance of things with the notion that an image registers an attitude, a not exclusively visual point of view, toward the world. In looking at a cave painting on the walls of Lascaux, he says, "rather than seeing it, I see according to, or with it" (*Œ* 23/164/126). An artist's imagery presents a way of seeing that reflects the artist's embeddedness in the world, but in so doing it furnishes neither a visual likeness of the world nor an external presentation of some internal mental imagery. Now a given painting may both realistically represent something in the world and express, perhaps necessarily, an attitude or point of view toward its subject. Yet for Merleau-Ponty, the representative capacity of the image is derived from its registering an attitude and orientation toward the world. That attitude and orientation belong to our sensorimotor, prereflective, prejudgmental grasp of the world. So, Merleau-Ponty writes, "painting is an analogue or likeness only according to the body," meaning that it is not a visual identity that determines likeness between image and world but a fit between the understanding of the world the painter's image offers and our prereflective, prejudgmental sense-making experience of what we perceive (Œ 24/165/126). In this way, Merleau-Ponty reverses the familiar claim that through departures from a default form of realistic representation a painting expresses a particular attitude toward its subject. Instead, for Merleau-Ponty, the particular attitude a painting registers toward what it represents determines whether the painting appears realistic: it does if it coheres with our sensorimotor orientation toward its subject.

Yet however much we speak of realism in painting, there is for Merleau-Ponty, in principle, no possibility of an image "copying" or being a perfectly realistic rendering of the appearance of the visible world. For he recognizes no notion of a determinate and independent "visible world" that could serve as the end and measure of a painting of such a putatively exacting realism. This is not because human vision is always partial, say, because we cannot see all sides of a three-dimensional object at once. Rather, it is because the "visible world" is in part constituted in relation to its perceivers, but at a level more fundamental than the sense-making judgments of the mind. Thus, when referring to the visual density of Cézanne's brushstroke, Merleau-Ponty says that "expressing what *exists* is an endless task" (*SNS* 21/15; *AR* 66), he means it not so much honorifically as literally: "It is no more possible to make a restrictive inventory of the visible than it is to catalog the possible expressions of a language. . . . The eye is an instrument that moves itself, a means which invents its own ends." Here, the eye is defined not as an anatomical organ but, derivatively, as an attribute of one's experiences in the world. In the artist's case, the eye is "*that which* has been moved by some impact of the world, which it then restores to the visible through the traces of a hand" (Œ 26/165/127). What the artist restores to the visible is thus much greater for Merleau-Ponty than the "visible in the narrow and prosaic sense" (Œ 27/166/127). It includes those features of our existence in the world that attend to our bodily experience of it, such as our experience in looking at something that it exists in three dimensions, with an anterior side that is present to us in more than just an intellectual sense: "I see depth and yet it is not visible, since it is reckoned from our bodies to things" (Œ 45/172–3/133).

The same restoring of the visible is true of the experience of time, which accounts, Merleau-Ponty says later in the essay, for why a galloping horse in a photograph taken at the instant when all its legs are off the ground does not look like it is running, whereas Géricault's horses do appear to run, although they are painted in a posture foreign to those of real horses at a gallop. It is because the painter's horses bring us "to see the body's grip (*prise*) upon the ground and that, according to a logic of body and world I know well, these grips upon space are also ways of taking hold of duration.... Painting searches not for the outside of movement but for its secret ciphers" (Œ 80–1/185–6/145). Although Cézanne shows the world in a way that suspends our habitual tendency to consider things only in their relation to our ends or needs, Merleau-Ponty stresses that this is not, in any ordinary understanding of the term, a kind of naturalism. For once Merleau-Ponty has dispensed with the naive notion of naturalistic painting and introduced the ways in which paintings such as Cézanne's show us what motivates the appearance of things to us, not the appearance simpliciter, he wants to forestall any attempt to deal with these reservations through a modified theory of naturalism – one that, say, acknowledges the partiality and generative facts of human vision. This is because for Merleau-Ponty, at least in his later essays, art is fundamentally "a process of expressing" (*SNS* 23/17; *AR* 67–8).

Art expresses, but not just in the limited sense of articulating something that exists in one's mind prior to being made public. Rather, art expresses in the sense of bringing into being something that is only inchoately, if at all, conceived before it is given form. The English term "realization" has the dual meaning that expression does in this view: one can realize something in the sense of discovering some truth that was, in principle, available prior to its realization; however, one can also realize something in the sense of bringing it into being – in a sense, creating it. It is in this latter, Hegelian sense that Merleau-Ponty speaks of expression: "'Conception' cannot precede 'execution'" (*SNS* 24/19; *AR* 69).[9] Rules of art or design serve only as the means through which that expression, of which the painter is not the exclusive source, occurs. Thus, Merleau-Ponty refers to André Marchand's comment, after Paul Klee, "In a forest, I have felt many times over that it was not I who looked at the forest. Some days I felt that the trees were looking at me.... I think that the painter must be penetrated by the universe and not want to penetrate it" (Œ 31/167/129).

But Merleau-Ponty does not advocate a theory of art as idiosyncratically expressive. He says that an artist such as Cézanne "speaks as the first man spoke and paints as if no one had ever painted before," so that the risk is whether what is expressed can succeed in being extracted from the flow of experience and take on a meaning for the artist and for others (SNS 24/19; AR 69). Expression thus implies a kind of social context in which meaning can be shared, and consequently expression admits the possibility of failure of meaning as well. This, then, is the deeper, existential and metaphysical meaning of Cézanne's doubt, a doubt about whether his work can achieve meaningfulness at all. It is a doubt that springs from the contingency of meaning when the creation of art enjoins no preestablished language of forms but offers, in both content and form, a new order of expression. As in the quote referring to Klee, Merleau-Ponty conceives of such meaning as generated not exclusively by the artist, but by the world in which the artist is situated. In *The Visible and the Invisible*, he describes how in performance the musician "feels himself, and others feel him to be at the service of the sonata; the sonata sings through him" (VI 199/151). It is as if the artist – like the rhapsode in Plato's *Ion* – serves only as a vehicle for the expression of the artwork, rather than the reverse.

Merleau-Ponty employs this transitive conception of art in arguing against Sartre's relegation of visual art to a lower cognitive level than literature. Sartre allows that an image might serve as an imaginative projection of the artist, perhaps creating an affective relation with the viewer, but he withholds the possibility that visual art could enlighten audiences about the world in a way comparable to the capacity of literary works. Against this view – and, in concert with André Malraux's comment that works of art affect us not through what they represent but "through their styles" – Merleau-Ponty adopts a position akin to that of Heidegger in his essay, "The Origin of the Work of Art," construing visual art as a means of "disclosure" of the world – not in terms of resemblance, but in terms of showing through the artist's way of rendering the world what in experience resists articulation.[10] He writes, "The painter's vision is not a view upon the *outside,* a merely 'physical–optical' relation with the world. The world no longer stands before him through representation; rather, it is the painter to whom the things of the world give birth by a sort of concentration or coming-to-itself of the visible" (Œ 69/181/141). Thus, while Merleau-Ponty shares with romantic theories a stress on art's capacity to express truths about the world unavailable to ordinary cognition, he charges such expression with creating new, shared forms of meaning: "The painter can do no more than construct an image; he must wait for this image to come to life for other people. When it does, the work of art will have united these separate lives; it will no longer exist in only of them like a stubborn dream.... It will dwell undivided in several minds" (SNS 26/20; AR 70).

IV. STYLE

In "Indirect Language and the Voices of Silence," Merleau-Ponty suggests that the shared or intersubjective nature of artistic meaning can best be understood with reference to the concept of style. There he rejects two contrary theories of style, both of which he finds in Malraux's *Voices of Silence:* that style is an expression of some suprastylistic force, for example, a "spirit of the age," and that style describes the imposition on the world of a given artist's idiosyncratic imagination. Against such views, Merleau-Ponty contends that style should be understood as the expression of an individual's bodily perception of the world: style encodes what our embodied existence in the world makes salient about it, that is, how we, prior to any intellectual judgment, give meaning and configuration to the world. Yet just as our experience is perspectival, so, too, a style instantiates a particular point of view, one that serves to assemble and integrate features of the world into coherent objects, even as it shows the impossibility of perceptual closure. So all persons have a stylistic relation to the world; the artist, however, is the one who reveals that relation in material forms such as sculpture and painting.

Endorsing Malraux's suggestion that perception already stylizes, Merleau-Ponty describes how the painter does not simply represent a subject such as "a woman" or "an unhappy woman," but shows "a way of inhabiting the world, of treating it, and of interpreting it by her face, by clothing, the agility of the gesture and the inertia of the body," emblems of a certain way of being in the world. Such ways of inhabiting the world do not, Merleau-Ponty comments, already belong to "the woman seen"; rather they are "called for by her" (S 68/54; AR 91). This suggests a way in which the artist's style participates in a kind of exchange or debate with the world that already exhibits a style, a way or manner of existing: "the perceived world . . . is not a pure object of thought . . . it is, rather, like a universal style shared in by all perceptual beings."[11] This exchange occurs even though the painter may think of his project in unidirectional or monologic terms. Citing Malraux's anecdote of the garage keeper at Cassis who sees Renoir inexplicably painting a stream while standing before the open sea ("he didn't seem to be looking at anything in particular, and he was only tinkering with one little corner of the picture"), Merleau-Ponty says,

Renoir can paint women bathing and a freshwater brook while he is by the sea at Cassis because he only asks the sea . . . for its way of interpreting the liquid element, of exhibiting it, and of making it interact with itself. The painter can paint while he is looking at the world because . . . he thinks he is spelling out nature at the moment he is recreating it. (S 70/56; AR 93)[12]

The concept of style also enters into Merleau-Ponty's account of how to understand the relationship between the preconditions attending a person's life, the givens of context and character associated with that life, and the projects that give that life meaning. In this discussion, he makes what first seems to be an epistemological observation: that if we think we find in a life such as Cézanne's the "seeds" of his work, it is because we first come to know the work and then see the circumstances of his life, filtered, as it were, through the work, through those qualities in the work that we wish to understand or explain. Yet this observation, he shows, is underwritten by a deeper explanatory relation: the conditions of Cézanne's life could genuinely figure in his projects only by signifying for him *what* he had to live, not *how*. How he would live would be a matter of how he interpreted those givens. In other words, if one has no control over certain conditions of the life one leads, one does have a kind of freedom in the manner in which one leads it and the ends one chooses to recognize as one's own. This way of leading a life, by which one gives meaning to the given features or preconditions attending one's existence, can be called one's *style* of being in the world. Because, for Merleau-Ponty, such meanings are given to these conditions at a level of preconscious, sensorimotor experience, one's style is not in the first instance constituted by a conscious choice, and thus one's style may not be apparent to oneself or to others. This is analogous to the way in which, in Sartre's view, a person's fundamental project, although freely chosen and definitive of who one is, may not be recognized by the person until late in life, if at all.

Unlike Sartre, Merleau-Ponty does not speak of an absolute form of freedom, of an ability to stand "outside" the conditions of one's life and choose what to make of it with those contours and constraints in place. Rather, the freedom is of an internal sort; it is a freedom to act within an already constituted life, specifically to project forward into that life an intention or desire to realize a certain goal. It is in reference to this projected future that the present state of the life acquires a determinate meaning. So Cézanne's life did not determine his work as cause to effect, but the two were nonetheless internally related: the projection of the future work gave an interpretation to the present life from which that projection was made. Merleau-Ponty describes this as an "equilibrium" in Cézanne's life. This is why it feels natural to find "hints" of his later work in his earlier life – natural because what is significant and "essential" in the life is drawn out, or made perspicuous, through his relation to his projected future. The important point here is that this relation between life and work is not discovered extrinsically; rather, it describes the individual's *own* interpretation of his life from within: "We can only see what we are by looking ahead of ourselves, through the lens of our aims" (*SNS* 27/21; *AR* 71). The style of an artist's life and the style of the artist's work may be intertwined, then, not because one explains the other, but because a projection of what the work will be offers the artist an interpretation of the way in which his life emerged against the background of its preconditions. Yet style is not, for Merleau-Ponty, a choice as much as an achievement: describing the formation of a style he says, "the painter does not put his immediate self – the very nuance of feeling – into his painting. He puts his *style* there, and he has to win it as much from his own attempts as from the painting of others or from the world." Referring to an analogous comment by Malraux on a writer's style, he comments on "how long it takes the painter ... to recognize in his first paintings the features of what will be his completed work, provided that he is not mistaken about himself" (S 65/52; AR 89).

V. FREEDOM AND SELF-EMERGENCE

Merleau-Ponty asks whether defining a life in terms of the way in which one pursues one's goals might suggest an incompatibility with freedom. For if "we are from the start our way of aiming at a particular future," then how is this original feature of oneself to be distinguished from the other givens that attend one's life? In this picture, one might say one's life is free from external constraints, but only because what would count as limits on such a life serve among its defining features – a radically nonautonomous view of the self that Merleau-Ponty, borrowing from Kierkegaard, summarizes in the striking phrase, "if we experience no external constraints, it is because we are our whole exterior." Merleau-Ponty further suggests, "if there is true freedom, it can only come about in the course of our life by our going beyond our original situation and yet not ceasing to be the same" (SNS 27–8/21; AR 71–2).

It might be objected that to go beyond one's original situation or to change one's fundamental project is, within the confines of the theory Merleau-Ponty sketches, precisely to change one's self, to be a different person and thus realize freedom not within one's own life, but within the life of "another." Merleau-Ponty believes, however, that freedom within a given, original life is possible, for he insists that we never entirely change: "looking back on what we were, we can always find hints of what we have become" (SNS 28/21; AR 72). From an external standpoint, this reply would be unsatisfactory, for there is no guarantee that those features that survive a change in the self are *essential* features, rather than just accidental features that one can find in both the person's earlier and later incarnations. In Merleau-Ponty's theory, however, this retrospective understanding in which a life reflects a unity or sustained identity through time belongs first to the internal perspective of the person whose life it is. Thus, what matters for the sake of unity is whether the individual from his or her own perspective can see the ability or desire to go beyond the original situation as *anticipated* in that original situation. For Merleau-Ponty, an individual at any given time in his or her life is not just determined by the events of the past. Rather, he proposes, not only is the future determined by the past, but the past, through imaginative projection, is determined by the future. This is obviously not an understanding of determination in solely causal terms; it is a notion of *determination as interpretation*, which seeks a stable equilibrium between the events of one's life and one's interpretation of them. One's actions are seen in relation to a past and projected future, each of which shapes what in the other is taken to be significant or brought into relief. This is why Merleau-Ponty can assert that psychoanalysis – as a hermeneutic method – allows us to see our being free as amounting to the "creative repetition of ourselves, always, in retrospect, faithful to ourselves" (*SNS* 32/25; *AR* 75).

In his discussion of Leonardo, Merleau-Ponty illustrates this connection between the original conditions attending one's life and the nature of the life as it unfolds. He recounts Valéry's paean to the artist as a man for whom no dream, fantasy, or illusion colors his self-knowledge or mediates between what he wills and what he does. For Merleau-Ponty, Leonardo thus exemplifies a putatively free man whose actions are determined only by current concerns in his life and whose decisions are unaffected by any internal psychic factors of which he is unaware. Drawing on Freud's analysis of the artist, however, Merleau-Ponty suggests that even in the autonomous Leonardo we can see features of his childhood that entered unreflectively into the work of his mature self: he left his work unfinished, just as his father had abandoned him; his apparent lack of attachment to any woman is connected to his exclusive attachment to his mother, from whom he was taken when he was four; his mature scientific experiments display the same wonder as that of a child, and so on. Even if such psychoanalytic explanations in this particular case seem arbitrary or ad hoc, Merleau-Ponty suggests that what psychoanalysis in general confirms is the relationship between one moment of life and another.[13] Of course, this connection does not yet satisfy Merleau-Ponty's criteria for freedom because, even if there is such a connection between later and earlier stages of an individual's life, this does not entail that the individual will interpret them as thus connected. Yet Merleau-Ponty might want to insist that the connection is there nonetheless.

In Merleau-Ponty's (as well as the analyst's) view, the relationship between earlier and later events is not a linear cause to effect. Rather, "in every life, one's birth and one's past define categories or basic dimensions that do not impose any particular act but which can be found in all" (*SNS* 31–2/24–5; *AR* 75). Merleau-Ponty appears to operate with two positions here. One is that a person's life can be understood as more and more conditioned by actions and events as it is lived, such that at any one time the cumulative history of one's life shapes its subsequent history, even if it does not exhaustively determine it. The other position is that one's life is best conceived not as a chain of causes and effects but as exhibiting a kind of organic development, such that the nature of the person is not the result of the actions and events attending one's life, but rather emerges through them. This emergence gives a unity to the life not just from the outside, as the entity that happens to serve as the locus of those events, but from the self-interpreting inside as well. The nature of this self may not be visible in any greater degree to the individual herself than to external observers. Thus, Merleau-Ponty speaks of Cézanne as "never at the center of himself," needing to look to others for self-recognition (*SNS* 32/25; *AR* 75). Again, the analogy with an artist's style presents itself: an artist's style, once formed, may emerge into perspicuity only in the course of the artist's work, becoming visible to the artist and to others only late in his oeuvre. In "Indirect Language and the Voices of Silence," Merleau-Ponty speaks of an artist's style as "just as recognizable for others and just as little visible to him as his silhouette" (*S* 67/53; *AR* 90).

VI. ART HISTORY

The passage on Leonardo at the end of "Cézanne's Doubt" is quite brief in comparison with the attention devoted to Cézanne. Although the case of Leonardo offers Merleau-Ponty an opportunity to distinguish his own understanding of the implicit unity of a life from that of psychoanalysis, it leaves a sense of incompleteness in the essay, as if Merleau-Ponty might have aborted an attempt to offer an analysis of the Renaissance painter on a par with that he accorded Cézanne.

Perhaps the abrupt ending also suggests a sense of essential incompleteness in Merleau-Ponty's theory, as if the phenomenological investigation that was so fruitful in the case of Cézanne could only with difficulty be extended to others such as Leonardo. For considered as a theory of art, Merleau-Ponty's analysis is both too specific and too general. Too specific because although Merleau-Ponty found a nearly perfect visual expression of a phenomenological theory of perception in the work of Cézanne, he has not offered a theory of art that can easily be generalized and applied to other cases. This is because, ultimately, Cézanne functions in Merleau-Ponty's essay only as an illustration of a theory of experience and perception that, although it applies to the experience and perception of art, does so in the same way it applies to everything else in human experience and perception. Thus, the essay may appear too general because it does not isolate anything peculiar to art, artists, or artistic experience, nor anything essential to representation as art. To be sure, he makes compelling use of Cézanne's work in laying out his phenomenological theory – but this is because, in Merleau-Ponty's interpretation of the painter's work, it is a theory they, philosopher and artist, both share. But such a theory is not a theory of art, even if it is a theory of vision's relation to the world to which artists at certain times (as in early modernism) subscribed. Merleau-Ponty offers a model of painterly practice that has the same ahistorical, universal structure as does sensorimotor experience in his phenomenology. Yet although a phenomenological account of human existence in the world may be offered in ahistorical terms (even as it recognizes the role of historical change in shaping the content of that experience), a theory of visual art must recognize its historically changing dimensions.

Merleau-Ponty does suggest in "Eye and Mind" that modern art exhibits a "system of equivalences, a Logos of lines, of lighting, of colors, of reliefs, of masses – a nonconceptual presentation of universal Being," such that when artists attempt to invent new means of expression, or modify those already at hand, their effort is essentially an attempt to find new systems of equivalences for the transhistorical features of human existence they disclose. This would imply that whatever the differences are among various movements, periods, and styles of art, they share a common purpose: penetrating the "envelope of things" (Œ 71–2/182/142). Yet Merleau-Ponty's examples are largely drawn from the large, but by no means exhaustive, class of artists, such as Cézanne, Matisse, and Klee, for whom the organizing principle of art is the visual interrogation of the world. This interrogation is not, of course, to be understood on the model of naturalistic or mimetic fidelity: Cézanne wants to reveal what generates the appearance of things, and Klee, in Merleau-Ponty's interpretation, frees line from its putative subordination to how things appear

and lets it take on a generating power itself. But such a phenomenologically inflected principle of art could hardly be extended over the
whole of art history. Indeed, it might be said that such a model of
art – art as a competitor and an antidote to the scientific view of
the world – applies mainly to those artists (Leonardo, Monet in his
series paintings, Cézanne, Seurat) who looked to science, in part,
for their own self-definition and who sought to arrive, through their
own means and methods of art, at truths about a world otherwise
understood in scientific terms. (Recall that while Merleau-Ponty attributes to Cézanne the endeavor to depict form as it comes into
being, he acknowledges Cézanne's own understanding of his project
as committed to the representation of things as they are.)

Even if one finds no general theory of art in Merleau-Ponty's phenomenology, however, one can find a general theory of experience, a
theory that artists may indeed make central to their art. For example,
minimalist artists of the 1960s, such as Donald Judd and Robert Mor-
ris, found in *Phenomenology of Perception* a way of understanding
how the notion of "preobjective experience" underlying all perception could guarantee the meaningfulness of their work, even in its
complete visual abstraction and its eschewal of an animating conceptual core. A bit later, Richard Serra would draw on such a minimalist interpretation of phenomenology to create pieces such as *Shift*
of 1970–2, a site-specific work composed of six sections of concrete
(815 feet in total) laid down on a hilly field in King City, Ontario.
There the art's meaning is generated not through its appearance, nor
through its "concept," but through the way it structures the experience of individuals – as moving, seeing bodies – who start at opposite
ends of the work and try to keep each other in view as they traverse
the terrain in which "abstract geometries were constantly submitted
to the redefinition of a sited vision."[14]

Where Merleau-Ponty does allow history to enter into his analysis of painting is in his account of the nature and genesis of the
means of expression. He says that the various and changing interpretations that we give to great works of art over time issue, in fact,
from the works themselves: "It is the work itself that has opened
the perspective from which it appears in another light. It transforms
itself and *becomes* what follows; the interminable interpretations
to which it is *legitimately* susceptible change it only into itself"
(Œ 62/179/139). Here, the meaning and expression of a work of art

are not fixed features of the work, but they are also not simply projected onto the work by interpreters without constraints (drawn from
the work itself) over which interpretations are true. Rather, Merleau-
Ponty suggests that changes over time in the interpretation of a work
of art may reflect the self-generated transformations of the particular
work itself. Merleau-Ponty does not say what determines the validity of a given interpretation in that conception of art but does stress
how the interpretation of art, like the sense given to the objects of
one's experience, must be understood as an essentially situational
phenomenon, emerging in the confrontation of an individual with a
work.

Merleau-Ponty suggests that before art represents in its manifest
content something in experience, its imagery is "autofigurative," it
forms itself. That is, representational art shows not the painter's depiction of a determinate and independent world, even if the painter
sees his art in those terms, but the world shaping itself through the
painter: "The world no longer stands before him through representation; rather, it is the painter to whom the things of the world give
birth by a sort of concentration or coming-to-itself of the visible" (Œ
69/181/141). The history of painting likewise exhibits an evolution
(but not progress) that occurs, like Hegel's "cunning of reason," as
if behind the painter's back. Merleau-Ponty describes how even as
artists try to achieve their immediate goals in painting, as if it were
a stable practice with internal standards of success, they bring about
its transformation: "At the very moment when, their eyes fixed upon
the world, they thought they were asking it for the secret of a sufficient representation, they were unknowingly bringing about that
metamorphosis of which painting later became aware" (S 60/48; AR
85).

For Merleau-Ponty, this transformation is best understood as a
process in which artists respond to their immediate situation, including the tradition of art they find themselves in, but create art
that is pregnant enough in meaning that it "prefigures" art made by
individuals finding themselves in very different circumstances. "No
doubt one reason why our painting finds something to recapture in
types of art which are linked to an experience very different from
our own is that it transfigures them. But it also does so because they
prefigure it" (S 75/60; AR 97). The relation of art of the past to that of
the present is not one of causal influence but a kind of "continuous

exchange" in which today's art "activates" or makes salient forgotten or ignored features of past art, while past art serves to inaugurate a tradition. In this tradition, Merleau-Ponty writes, "The classical and the modern pertain to the universe of painting conceived as a single task" (S 75/60; AR 96–7), each artist "advancing the line of the already opened furrow" (S 73/58; AR 95).[15] This "task" is not the exposure of an independent and determinate world, but the disclosure of a point of view on that world. Here, it would be fair to describe such a historical task as akin to a general style: a way of representing the world that is generated in the art of a number of painters because of their shared tradition, context, or goals, even as each tries to realize the aims of his or her art alone.

Merleau-Ponty appears to believe, however, that such a general style is grounded in, and expresses, an even more fundamental phenomenon: a common human style of perceptual comportment. In this way, he offers a model of art history that is analogous to, but more radical than, theories of the internal evolution of art developed by such philosophically minded historians of art as Alois Riegl, Erwin Panofsky, and Henri Focillon. Riegl sought to uncover the unity within the various manifestations of art by appeal to universal "laws" of artistic development and a Hegelian concept of the *Kunstwollen*, a kind of aesthetic will or intention that operates through the artist. Panofsky tried to register the unity of historical periods in the idea of a symbolic form, a neo-Kantian notion of period-specific, a priori categories that structure thought and experience. And Focillon theorized that the unity of art through its changes was explained by the way those transformations were internally generated: "form liberates other forms according to its *own* laws."[16]

Merleau-Ponty, however, proposes a kind of unity much more fundamental than that offered by these theorists, one derived from the basic orientation of the human body in the world. If those art historians sought a general explanatory model of why art changes, Merleau-Ponty sought a way of understanding how, through its changes, art is in its essential features the same. Such a view of art history as inhering in and generated out of a universal style may offer an answer to the charge that Merleau-Ponty offers less a general theory of art than a thesis about a particular historical moment or form of art. For if all art is, in its fundamental motivation, the same, then to speak of one art is to speak of them all. In any case, if Merleau-Ponty's writings on art illuminate the experience of art, and the relations between artist, spectator, and world, without propounding a theory of art that would admit of universal application, that may be one of the sources of its depth. The artworks and artists he treats serve less as examples than as exemplary instances, chosen precisely because of the ways in which they serve as models of what art strives to be. Merleau-Ponty does not theorize about artistic practice in a way that detaches it from ordinary human experience but shows instead ways in which the two are continuous in their interrogation of the world.

NOTES

1. For a comprehensive commentary on the genesis and contents of Merleau-Ponty's writings on the visual arts, see the essays by Galen Johnson, forming the first part of Johnson and Smith's *Merleau-Ponty Aesthetics Reader: Philosophy and Painting.*

2. In addition to relying on the letters and conversations between Cézanne and Émile Bernard that the latter published as *Souvenirs de Paul Cézanne* (1912), Merleau-Ponty relies on generally antiformalist histories of the artist such as Joachim Gasquet's *Cézanne* (1921), a biography of the artist, and Fritz Novotny's pioneering series of articles on Cézanne's rejection of mathematical perspective. See Novotny's "Cézanne and the End of Perspective."

3. From "Diverses Choses, 1896–1897," an unpublished manuscript, part of which appears in Rotonchamp, *Paul Gauguin, 1848–1903*, 210, 216, 211; reproduced in Chipp, *Theories of Modern Art: A Source Book by Artists and Critics*, 65.

4. Baudelaire comments in his "Salon of 1859" on the distinction between artists who are faithful to the optical effects of nature and artists who are faithful to their own temperaments or singular understandings of their milieu: "The immense class of artists . . . can be divided into two quite distinct camps: one type, who calls himself *'réaliste'* . . . says, 'I want to represent things as they are, or as they will be, supposing that I do not exist. . . . And the other type, *'l'imaginatif,'* says: I want to illuminate things with my intellect and project their reflection upon other minds" (Baudelaire, "Salon de 1859," in Florenne, *Écrits sur l'art*, vol. 2, 36–7).

5. What can be called the "El Greco fallacy" is a version of this problem: it will not explain the elongated, tortured figures of El Greco's painting to posit that the painter had a form of astigmatism or other visual abnormality, for if El Greco saw the world as appearing this way, he would also see normally formed images of the world on his canvas this way, and

thus there would be no added impetus, were he to paint what he saw, to depict his figures in that elongated fashion. Merleau-Ponty rejects the physiological explanation of El Greco's work; see *SC* 219/203.

6. Sartre, *Being and Nothingness*, 227/257/209.

7. "An Unpublished Text by Maurice Merleau-Ponty: A Prospectus of His Work," *The Primacy of Perception*, 6.

8. Similarly, "If I wanted to render precisely the perceptual experience, I ought to say that *one* perceives in me, and not that I perceive" (*PP* 249/215/250).

9. Merleau-Ponty describes the incident in which a film recorded Matisse as he was drawing, which, when played in slow motion, showed the hesitations, false starts, and other gestures that were invisible to Matisse and others in real time. Merleau-Ponty comments that while Matisse would surely be wrong to treat the film as revealing the truth about his process of drawing, the slow-motion representation does demonstrate that Matisse's action was the result of a series of decisions made not at the level of conscious deliberation, but at that of habitual motor-reflexive "know-how." Nonetheless, they were choices of a sort, ones that reflected "a score of conditions that were unformulated and even unformulable for anyone but Matisse because they were only defined and imposed by the intention of executing *that particular painting which did not yet exist*" (*S* 58/46; *AR* 83).

10. Malraux, *The Voices of Silence: Man and His Art*, 320.

11. "An Unpublished Text by Maurice Merleau-Ponty: A Prospectus of His Work," *The Primacy of Perception*, 6.

12. Malraux, *Voices of Silence*, 280.

13. In a lecture given in 1951, Merleau-Ponty rejected the notion of the unconscious. What psychoanalysts call the unconscious, he said, corresponds only an "unrecognized, unformulated knowledge, that we do not wish to assume" (*S* 291/229).

14. Rosalind Krauss, *Richard Serra/Sculpture*, 31. For an account of the role of phenomenological themes in minimalist and earthwork sculpture generally see Krauss's *Passages in Modern Sculpture*, 266–88. Whereas Krauss has used phenomenology in describing the historical context and theoretical sources of art such as Serra's, the art historian and critic Michael Fried has used Merleau-Ponty's notion of embodiment as the core concept in his methodology of interpretation. See, for example, his *Courbet's Realism* and the essays collected in *Art and Objecthood*. Stephen Melville provides an overview of these and other uses of phenomenology in art history in his "Phenomenology and the Limits of Hermeneutics," 143–54.

15. For a similar theory of the retroactive transformation an artwork may have on one earlier in a history they both share, see Arthur Danto's account of the "style-matrix." Danto suggests that the discovery of new forms of art can enlarge the set of predicates in terms of which earlier forms of art are interpreted (e.g., the emergence of expressionist art, or nonrepresentational art, allows earlier art to be predicated with the opposite terms, "nonexpressionistic" or "representational"). Danto, however, sees this change as occurring a lot in the artwork put in its description. See Danto, "The Artworld."

16. Riegl, *Late Roman Art Industry*; Panofsky, *Perspective as Symbolic Form*; Focillon, *The Life of Forms in Art*, 97.

12 Understanding the Engaged Philosopher: On Politics, Philosophy, and Art

> *It is true, as Marx says, that history does not walk on its*
> *head, but it is also true that it does not think with its feet.*
>
> Merleau-Ponty[1]

I. CHALLENGING COMPANIONS

In *The Cambridge Companion to Sartre*, Rhiannon Goldthorpe entitles her essay on aesthetics and politics "Understanding the Committed Writer."[2] Similarly can we entitle this essay in *The Cambridge Companion to Merleau-Ponty*, although there is a difference. Whereas Sartre strives to be a *committed writer* as philosopher, playwright, and political "man of action," Merleau-Ponty strives to be an *engaged philosopher*.[3] Whereas, from Merleau-Ponty's perspective, Sartre thinks about commitment as neutral between roles, Merleau-Ponty regards engagement as role-dependent. Whereas Sartre thinks about commitment as one's taking sides in politics, Merleau-Ponty argues for the philosopher's engagement with truth. Characteristically, Merleau-Ponty writes, "One must be able to withdraw and gain distance in order to become truly engaged, which is, also, always an engagement with the truth" (*EP* 60–1/60).

This essay is about Merleau-Ponty's lifelong intellectual companionship with Sartre. It is also about the challenging companionship between the politician, the philosopher, the playwright, and the painter. Most specifically, it is about how Merleau-Ponty allowed his engagement as philosopher to determine and reflect his engagement with politics and the arts. It tracks, therefore, the sometimes surprisingly analogous arguments Merleau-Ponty develops in these different domains of discourse. The essay asks throughout whether in placing the philosopher's engagement between the apolitical engagement of the artist (more the painter than the playwright) and the political commitment of the politician (more the "man of action" than the policymaker), Merleau-Ponty gives the middle position enough content. This question is asked in recognition of its classical motivation in Socrates' trial, but also in recognition of the post-Hegelian possibility that, in the crisis of modern times, it may no longer be possible to do philosophy.

Goldthorpe succeeds in covering Sartre's view of commitment without even mentioning Merleau-Ponty. But then he is mentioned only seven times in the entire Sartre *Companion*, even though, in the opening line of another recent book, the editors state that Merleau-Ponty was "perhaps the most important French philosopher of the twentieth century."[4] The hesitation of the "perhaps" is appropriate because their statement is exaggerated. Still, they are right to suggest that Merleau-Ponty should not be ignored. For most of their lives, the two companions contested each other's views and argued constantly (as did many of their compatriots[5]) over the issue of commitment. Jointly engaged in wartime Resistance work in France, jointly involved in the 1945 founding of the influential journal *Les Temps modernes*, jointly developing the relations between phenomenology, existentialism, and Marxism, constantly supporting and criticizing every aspect of each other's works and activities – it is odd to say the least to treat Sartre in isolation.

Yet had one not read the recent, extensive collection of essays titled *The Debate between Sartre and Merleau-Ponty*,[6] one would find Sartre being so treated. One would not, and could not, however, find the same to be true of Merleau-Ponty, because, regarding most issues, and especially that of commitment, he usually has Sartre in mind. I think Sartre also often has Merleau-Ponty in mind, but there is a difference. With the focus on Merleau-Ponty, this essay begins by describing what that difference is.

II. PHILOSOPHY AND POLITICS

Sartre was a more public intellectual than Merleau-Ponty, or, better, a more public, even "scandalous," figure. Temperamentally, he was the less private man and asserted himself as the more independent and active thinker. One might even say that had Sartre not been so public a figure, then Merleau-Ponty would have been content to work in the private and scholarly confines of the French academy. Certainly he was the more reactive thinker – a "counter-thinker" Anne Boschetti almost calls him, although without wanting to undermine the independent import of his thought.[7] The difference runs deep, as can be seen in their different philosophical styles. Merleau-Ponty articulates his views, as Sartre does far less, against views already in place or against the extremes to which he fears certain views can go. Correct views turned into incorrect views: situated freedom turned into absolute freedom; existential projects turned into intellectual projects; provisional and motivated commitments turned into absolute commitments; humanistic Marxism turned into reified Stalinism. Finding a space away from, or between, extremes is how Merleau-Ponty avoids false "dilemmas" (*HT* 25–6/23–4). It is a "fragile"[8] and serious philosophical enterprise, he says, not suited to too much public hyperbole or liberal compromise. It is a reflective project of intellectual engagement that allows the philosopher to step back and watch "the forms of transcendence fly up like sparks" (*PP* viii/xiii/xv).

However, this picture misleads if it suggests that Merleau-Ponty is interested in engagement only as an academic problem. On the contrary, he is deeply concerned with the engagement of himself as philosopher in contemporary times. "Contemporary politics," he writes,

is truly an arena in which questions are badly put, or put in such a way that one cannot side with either of the two present contestants [America and the Soviet Union]. We are called to choose between them. Our duty is to do no such thing, to demand enlightenment from this side and that side, to explain the maneuvers, to dissipate the myths. (*HT* xxv/xxix)

In dissipating the myths, Merleau-Ponty sometimes becomes very outspoken. Now he seems to engage in politics with all the hyperbole and immediacy of Sartre's commitment. Still, he tries to remain true to philosophy. Even his book *Humanism and Terror* of 1947 is focused, despite its highly polemical tone, on a rather abstract philosophical argument about the engagement of the intellectual. At the time, the book was not read this way; it was read as a politically

committed text and an angry one, yet not by its critics as a successful one. It was appreciated neither for its reading of the Nikolai
Bukharin "show trial" of 1937, nor for its Marxist defense of revolutionary violence, nor for its apparent support of Stalinism, nor for
its critique of liberalism. "A regime which is nominally liberal can
be oppressive in reality," Merleau-Ponty writes. "A regime which
acknowledges its violence *might* have more genuine humanity" (*HT*
x/xv).[9] Even Sartre reads it with the immediacy of a political text.
He likes it more. He notes that it "cause[s him] to make an important decision" regarding his attitude toward communism.[10] Yet
the change in his attitude depends also on his having come to accept the philosophical argument. For he knows that the political and
philosophical arguments in a Marxist worldview, even if distinct, are
related.

Merleau-Ponty's debate with Sartre over engagement is a debate
between two temperamentally different thinkers arguing in private
and public about how best to show their engagement in contemporary politics. They carry out their debate in decidedly philosophical
terms. Whereas they hold by and large their political views in common, they disagree about how to show this commitment. Merleau-
Ponty wants to keep the philosopher's engagement distinct and constrained; Sartre resists the constraint. Merleau-Ponty increasingly
retreats from the polemical tone of his immediately postwar writings; Sartre resists the retreat. As already indicated, however, Sartre's
views move gradually much closer to Merleau-Ponty's.

When Merleau-Ponty speaks out about politics, he stresses that
he is not relinquishing his position as philosopher or thinker at a
reflective distance. He does not regard himself as thereby becoming
a "political activist," "adventurer," or "man of action." Even so, he
does think Sartre is conflating the two positions or trying to assume
both at once. Why? Because Sartre holds incorrect views on freedom,
choice, and action (the constitutive concepts of engagement). Sartre
disagrees, and with some justification, not just because he thinks
that he himself holds correct views on freedom, choice, and action, or
because he can occupy both positions at once, but because he thinks
that Merleau-Ponty is clearly exaggerating his views to show their
differences from his own. Exaggeration is not an unfamiliar strategy
in philosophical debates and not always an unconstructive one: it

serves in their own quarrel to demonstrate the difference in their attitudes toward commitment. But it does also make for fractious friendship.

When they argue about the nature of language and writing, speech and silence, communication and expression, it often looks as if they are debating aesthetic or metaphysical issues only. However, associated with those arguments are the political implications and motivations regarding the proper role of the philosopher "to bring [things] to expression" (VI 18/4) in a world that is inescapably political. In this project, Merleau-Ponty sees a similarity between himself as philosopher and Cézanne as painter. His views on the silence of language or on the nonspeaking arts are not just about retrieving or retreating into the primordial nature and invisible dimensions of human experience; they are also about what one can and cannot articulate given the historical condition of philosophy, politics, and the arts. It is no accident that his gradual political retreat into silence coincides with his placing an extra philosophical emphasis on "indirect" expression or on the unarticulated dimensions of language's significance. Nor is it accidental in his thinking about aesthetic "retreat" or political "refusal" that he calls up Socrates, a figure torn between philosophy, politics, and the arts, a figure ultimately put on trial for his philosophical life. "These questions only sound new to those who have read nothing or have forgotten everything," Merleau-Ponty explains in *Humanism and Terror*:

The trial and death of Socrates would not have remained a subject of reflection and commentary if it had only been an incident in the struggle of evil men against good men and had one not seen in it an innocent man who accepts his sentence, a just man who obeys conscience and yet refuses to reject the world and obeys the *polis*, meaning that it belongs to man to judge the law *at the risk of being judged by it*. (HT xxxiv–xxxv/xxxviii–xxxix)

It is basic to Merleau-Ponty's view of engagement that philosophers work within the particular historical situation in which they find themselves. Philosophers are situated in an indeterminate world like everyone else. Once in a letter to Sartre he wrote, "I took care to speak of Socrates in order to show that the philosopher is not someone who simply produces books but who is in the world. I attacked those who place philosophy outside of time."[11] However, the problem is still to give the correct account of the philosopher's situation, and for Merleau-Ponty it is clearly not the same as that of the political man of action. "Whether it is a question of things or of historical situations," he writes to conclude his *Phenomenology of Perception,*

philosophy has no other function than to teach us to see them clearly once more, and it is true to say that it comes into being by destroying itself as separate philosophy. But what here is required is silence, for only the hero lives out his relation to men and the world, and it is not fitting that another speak in his name. (*PP* 520/456/530)

The historical situation in which Merleau-Ponty finds himself is the situation of "modern times." It is fraught, urgent, critical, and feels unparalleled in its horror: fascism, Stalinism, death camps, anti-Semitism, Cold War divisions, McCarthyism, colonialism, Korea, Algeria. About all these, he and Sartre write in substantial detail. But do these times justify the hyperbolic tone of some of Merleau-Ponty's texts, and how, if they do, can we reconcile this with his philosophical arguments for a retreat into silence? In part the answer lies in our taking account of his development, that is, of the fact that he moved increasingly (but sometimes noisily) toward silence. In larger part, one ought to take account of the relationship he wants to establish between philosophical engagement and humanistic Marxism, whether, most importantly, he can articulate his engagement as philosopher in a Marxist history of revolutionary consciousness so that it does not make him look as if is also or thereby committing himself to Stalinism.

III. THE QUARREL

In 1953, against the complex background of a severe disagreement over editorial policy for *Les Temps modernes,* the Korean War, their continuing theoretical allegiance to a humanist Marxism in the face of its Soviet corruption, and the demand that they respond as "public intellectuals" to concrete political situations, Merleau-Ponty and Sartre enter into a private correspondence of urgent but courteous recriminations regarding the choice between involvement and retreat (and whether in fact it is a genuine choice). Sartre starts by attacking Merleau-Ponty (early summer, 1953, from Rome).[12] "That you withdraw from politics," he writes, "(that is, what we intellectuals call politics), that you prefer to dedicate yourself to your philosophical research, is an act that is at once legitimate and unjustifiable. I mean, it is legitimate *if* you are not trying to justify it."

There is nothing wrong, Sartre continues in showing one's vocation in the books one writes. But from that position of retreat can one then make judgments about and between the attitudes of those who have not retreated and have remained in "the *objective* domain of politics"? From what point of view can philosophers who abstain judge nonphilosophers who do not? You cannot "play both games" at once. It's not so bad to say privately, "I would do better to abstain," but does it then follow that for the philosopher "*it is necessary* to abstain"? Sartre fears that such a conclusion will play into the hands of "*the right*," the "reactionaries" and "anticommunists" who might well read it as conforming to their own view that "nothing can be done."[13]

Sartre thinks the rationale for Merleau-Ponty's retreat is philosophically insecure. Can one translate the empirical recognition that one never knows the complete situation, or that one only ever knows from a particular perspective, into a philosophical principle that one can only choose from a partisan position untruthfully? Whereas Merleau-Ponty is not willing to choose untruthfully or in ignorance, Sartre believes one must, but for this reason: that when one chooses, one does not actually choose from the philosophical standpoint. Sartre thus "reproaches" him for abdicating under "circumstances when it is necessary to make a decision as a human being, a Frenchman, a citizen, and an intellectual," and for using the fact of his being a philosopher "as an alibi."

Here is the difference. Whereas Sartre's engagement is entered into from the point of view of his being a human being, a citizen of France, and so on – which allows him, in his view, to act honestly, overtly, and with immediacy – Merleau-Ponty is concerned with what follows from his arguments regarding his engagement as a philosopher. This, again, does not mean that Merleau-Ponty is less interested in the situations of the world, only that he seems to be positioning himself in what Sartre takes to be an overly circumscribed philosophical space. Why, Sartre asks, did you not intervene in the Rosenberg case? Surely that was "a matter of human reactions to immediate demands." Again, he accuses Merleau-Ponty of holding a contradictory position: "you want to destroy a certain politics" (from the standpoint of politics) "by refusing to have one oneself" (from the standpoint of philosophy). But why are you doing this, perhaps to protect yourself? (He would not have been the first to do so.)

In a lengthy reply from Paris, Merleau-Ponty reminds Sartre that he has been actively engaged throughout his life in all kinds of objective political issues, but given the recent situation, he has been led to adopt a new stand.

I decided after the Korean war...no longer to write on events as they presented themselves. I did this for reasons which belong to the nature of that period and for other reasons which are permanent.[14]...Engagement on *every* event taken on its own becomes, in a period of tension, a system of "bad faith."

Here Merleau-Ponty begins to attack, as he often has before, what he perceives to be Sartre's mistaken view, namely, that one can choose and act as if historical events occur in complete isolation from one other. He rejects Sartre's (purported) view that to each separate and detached event there is an appropriate response, where each response is somehow absolute, irrevocable, or singular in its meaning. Certainly, he writes,

There are events which permit or rather demand that one judge them immediately and even in themselves, for example, the condemnation and the execution of the Rosenbergs...But...it is artificial – and deceptive – to act as if the problems were posed one by one and to break up into a series of local questions what is historically a unity.

One needs to view events more broadly, inside or amidst the patterns and logic of history.

Merleau-Ponty argues here against the breaking down of history into isolated parts, an intellectualism he rejects in all spheres of his philosophy. He also reiterates the argument he holds throughout his life on the essential contingency and ambiguity of history – history's lack of fixed and "ready-made" meanings; history's meaning always in the process of being made; history's inability to communicate its meanings directly or transparently. The events of history – its order and disorder – are better understood from a position of "suspension," from the "wait and see" attitude given by reflective distance and "doubt." "To become engaged on every event, as if it were a test of morality, to make a politics into your own cause...[, this is

LYDIA GOEHR

to] refuse without reflection a *right of correction,* which no serious action renounces."

Merleau-Ponty believes that his method is actually "closer to politics" than Sartre's own "method of *constant engagement.*"[15] Why? Because his commitment-at-a-distance puts him in a place where he can see meanings clearly, but at not so great a distance that detaches the subject from the world entirely. Sartre, Merleau-Ponty argues, commits a Cartesian error by viewing the agent or actor as a disembodied *cogito* who chooses to act, and how to act, from an absolute or unsituated standpoint. Sartre's next mistake is then to use this standpoint to generate a false dilemma – to position the actor as having to choose from a position too far outside to act in a way that is too far inside. One cannot think both that one's act has the significance of creating the world anew and that the act is a direct response to local and immediate events. One cannot live (or philosophize) with false extremes, pitting the absolute or transcendental detachment of a disembodied *cogito* against the demand to engage immediately in partisan causes. One cannot live with both or either the absolute certainty of a detached ego or the constant skepticism of the unknowing local actor. Rather, one can only live, because one does live, in the entanglements *between the extremes,* "at the joints where the multiple entries of the world cross" (*VI* 314/260).[16]

Even if Sartre chooses to speak about situated and reflective commitment, he makes it look, according to Merleau-Ponty, like a "permanently antagonistic contradiction," between the free individual and the world. This antagonistic separation, Merleau-Ponty thinks, can only result in the impotence of nonaction. Genuine freedom, he comments,

is not to be confused with those abstract decisions of will at grips with motives or passions, for the classical conception of deliberation is relevant only to a freedom "in bad faith" which secretly harbors antagonistic motives without being prepared to act of them, and so itself manufactures the alleged proofs of its impotence. (*PP* 500/438/509)

For Merleau-Ponty, reflective engagement is neither too close nor too far. It demarcates a space in which one can engage as a thoughtful intellectual, but not in an overly active form that shows "blind" allegiance to present circumstances as they immediately present themselves. As he writes in *Phenomenology of Perception,*

True philosophy consists in relearning to look at the world, and in this sense a historical account can give meaning to the world quite as "deeply" as a philosophical treatise. We take our fate in our hands, we become responsible for our history through reflection, but equally by a decision on which we stake our life, and in both cases what is involved is a violent act which is validated by being performed. (*PP* xvi/xx/xxiii)

The "radical" nature of reflective thought and action derives from Merleau-Ponty's commitment to Marxism. It is a commitment made not as an ideologue or party member (which neither Sartre nor he was), but as a situated philosopher. What is the difference? That the philosopher works with the ambiguity and reflective doubt that constitutes the core of humanistic Marxism deliberately to counter the insupportable Stalinist reification or objectification that enables the party to impose its rule on society in a totalitarian or ideological manner. What is the totalitarian manner? The complete identification or forced collectivisation of the people's thought with party dictate, made possible through a false promise by the party to the people that their thought is divergent and free (*HT* xv–xvi/xx). It is the philosopher's duty to expose the contradiction, to dissipate the myth. This is the sort of action or engagement that genuine revolutionary consciousness requires of the engaged philosopher. It is then up to the heroes (among the people) to show how true revolutionary consciousness works itself out in practice. "Heroism [is] a thing not of words but of deeds" (*SNS* 178/146).

The reflective doubt implicit in humanistic Marxism prevents the totalitarian identification. Indeed, it hinders the imposition of rules or principles altogether, especially if they are regarded as being imposed on society from outside or above. Humanistic Marxism thus accommodates a commitment motivated neither by detached consciousnesses nor by some abstract ideal of a future state (Merleau-Ponty's anti-Kantianism) (*HT* 135/126ff). Nor is it motivated by a set of principles justified outside of history (in "monuments" or "constitutional scrolls" [*HT* x/xiv]) to be applied without consideration of the particularity of situation (his antiliberalism). Rather, it recognizes "a society already committed," a society of "human relations" in which all actions are mediated, even the philosopher's, in which actors live inside "intersubjective truth" as part of an already ongoing story in the here and now (*HT* 23/21). "When one is too frank about the future, one is precisely not frank about the present," he accordingly writes to Sartre. "I look . . . into the present and leave it undecided and open as it is . . . My relation to the times is constituted above all by the present."

Of course, whether the commitment to humanistic Marxism could really be sustained in the light of a rejection of its reified, concrete expression in Stalinism was one of the most urgent questions for all Marxist philosophers of the period. How, they asked, could Marxism with its logic of history fall off the tracks?[17] Then they had to ask, too, if the distinction between Marxism and Stalinism could not be sustained, would the distinction between mediated and partisan, or intellectual and heroic, engagement collapse in its wake? It was this last question that would prompt Marxist philosophers to wonder whether philosophy could be done at all in these purportedly most totalitarian of times.

Merleau-Ponty continues his letter to Sartre: "I . . . have no need to separate philosophy from the world in order to remain a philosopher – . . . and I have in no way made an *alibi* of it." Again he uses a philosophical principle by way of justification, namely, that "the philosophic absolute is nowhere, it doesn't ever take place anywhere, it is therefore never elsewhere, it must be defended in each particular event." Yet – and this is always the mediated position – the particular event should not as such decide it. On the contrary, a reflective "gap" has to be maintained between event and judgment, a gap that maintains "good ambiguity." Certainly there are philosophers who simply *equivocate* over the interpretation of events in such a way as to produce "bad philosophy," he explains, but "good philosophy is a healthy ambiguity because it affirms the basic agreement and disagreement de facto between the individual, others and the truth and since it is patience which makes them all work together in some way or another."

"Good ambiguity" is one of Merleau-Ponty's "antisystematic" yet necessary concepts. Its imprecision is no more worrisome, in his view, than many of his other concepts. What, for example, does he mean when he speaks of people "working together in some way or another"? His antisystematic concepts serve the "in between" character of his philosophy; they demonstrate its counterintellectualism. Still, as we shall see, they are also laden with dialectically both optimistic and pessimistic assumptions about how different kinds of action and thought – philosophical, political, and artistic – mutually interact.

Merleau-Ponty's letter to Sartre shows that he views his "retreat" into silence less as a retreat from politics and more as an embracing of philosophical engagement, a form of engagement very different from the prevalent dilemma, as he sees it, that makes commitment into an impossible choice between the "cynic" and the "knave," between freedom-with-no-action and action-with-no-freedom (SNS 187/154). Commitment-at-a-distance might make philosophy "limp," he writes, but its limping "is its virtue" – its holding back, its reserve, and its irony. "True irony is not an alibi; it is a task; and the very detachment of the philosopher assigns to him a certain kind of action among men" – the action of dissipating the myths (EP 61/61).

For both Sartre and Merleau-Ponty, the debate on commitment is a Marxist debate about praxis, about class-consciousness, about theory and action, about the relation between the intellectual and the proletariat, and, most importantly, about the proper and unique function of the intellectual and the writer in successful and failing revolution. "We argued," Merleau-Ponty once wrote in his Preface to *Humanism and Terror*, and in defense of their joint project of *Les Temps modernes*,

that the dilemma of conscience and politics – commitment or refusal, fidelity or lucidity – imposes one of those heart-rending choices which Marx had not envisaged and which introduces a crisis into Marxist dialectics . . . We showed how a conscientious Communist, such as Bukharin, can pass from revolutionary violence to today's communism – and ends by seeing that communism has denatured itself en route. (HT xxvii/xxxi)

Bukharin, in Merleau-Ponty's view, represents the intellectual against the politician (or the ideologue), and thus the hope of Marxism's survival against its present Stalinist expression:

Bukharin can and should be understood as an intellectual thrown into politics. If the role of the intellectual and his outlook is to discover in a given assembly of facts several possible meanings to be evaluated methodically, whereas the politician is one who with perhaps the fewest ideas perceives most surely the real significance and pattern in a given situation, Bukharin's instability could then be explained in terms of the intellectual's psychology. Yet, though he oscillates, it is still within the Marxist framework. (HT 68/63)

Merleau-Ponty accuses Koestler, as he accuses Sartre, of holding the wrong view of commitment. He accuses Koestler of presenting the intellectual (on trial) with a false dilemma, "oscillating between revolt and passivity" (*HT* 22/20), and thus of giving the wrong analysis of Bukharin's (or Koestler's fictional Rubashov's) acceptance of his sentence. For Merleau-Ponty, by contrast, Bukharin's acceptance of his sentence is to be interpreted through the lens of a Marxist view of history in which Bukharin's perhaps blameless *intentions* nonetheless proved culpable given their *consequences*, given, that is to say, the way the objective conditions of history work themselves out:

There is a sort of maleficence in history: it solicits men, tempts them so that they believe they are moving in its direction, and then suddenly it unmasks, and events change and prove that there was another possibility. The men whom history abandons in this way and who see themselves simply as accomplices suddenly find themselves the instigators of a crime to which history has inspired them. And *they are unable to look for excuses or to excuse themselves from even a part of the responsibility*. (*HT* 43/40)

In seeming to support Bukharin's sentence, Merleau-Ponty looks as if he is also vindicating Stalin and his show trials. His polemical tone encourages the impression. Still, however, there is a gap between consequence and intention, since his intention, as I suggested earlier, is to argue for a philosophical link between the positions of Bukharin, Socrates, and himself. All are entangled in a situated pattern of "consent and refusal" from which there is no exile or escape in their most critical of times. Merleau-Ponty is thus apparently less interested in the content of the trial than in how the accused Bukharin reasons and situates himself in relation to it. Unsurprisingly, critics have focused more on the apparent Stalinist vindication and on the "naive" misreading of the trial than on his rather abstract linkages between philosophical figures. That critics have done so is a postwar and a Cold War consequence for which, by his own account, Merleau-Ponty has to assume some responsibility.[18]

IV. PHILOSOPHY AND ART

Insofar as the debate between Sartre and Merleau-Ponty on commitment is devoted to the relation between philosophy and politics, it is indefensible to ignore their mutual interaction. Yet the debate also has another set of concerns, and in relation to these Sartre's isolated treatment finds more, even if not an ultimate, justification. For the debate is also a modernist debate on the political content or form of artworks, and in this question Merleau-Ponty is not immediately interested. In describing why not, one begins to understand something significant about his views on art, namely, that even in these he is interested in carving out a subtly demarcated space for the engagement of the philosopher.

Repeatedly the debate about engagement has been treated as a debate about art's relationship to politics. Most crudely, one asserts either that an artwork engages politically, socially, or morally with the world via its "didactic" content (or "messages") or that it does not engage in this way (although it might in another), because its content is, or should be regarded as, purely aesthetic: nonreferential, nondiscursive, nonrepresentational, or nonconceptual. In this debate, prose or literature is usually taken as the paradigm of committed art, and music or poetry as the paradigm of pure or autonomous art. In more complex terms, the debate is about the demand for artists to be engaged politically with their times without succumbing to the tendentious dictates of those in power. It is also a debate about the cultural commodification of the artwork and about its contemporary status as fetish. It is about artists battling over interests on one side and claiming a false autonomy (purity) on the other. Sartre wrote on this debate, as did Georg Lukács, Walter Benjamin, Theodor Wiesengrund Adorno, René Leibowitz, Herbert Marcuse, and Bertolt Brecht.[19]

Adorno was unimpressed with Sartre's contribution to the debate. Opening his essay "Commitment" of 1962 (in the original German, Adorno uses the French word "*engagement*") he wrote "Since Sartre's essay 'What Is Literature?' there has been less theoretical debate about committed and autonomous literature. Nevertheless, the controversy over commitment remains urgent, so far as anything that merely concerns the life of the mind can be today, as opposed to sheer survival."[20] Influenced by Adorno, musicologist Leibowitz tried to alter Sartre's view on the status on music to undercut and complicate Sartre's "false dualism" between committed (literature) and pure arts (music). He did this by transferring the burden of art's commitment away from its content to its form. I shall return to this transference shortly in terms belonging to Adorno. My point here is only to indicate that there was significant exchange between the French and German theorists in this aesthetic debate.

However, in this specifically aesthetic debate Merleau-Ponty hardly plays a role. For him, the debate about commitment or engagement is not first and foremost a debate about art per se but about how especially the philosopher thinks philosophically about, and then acts upon, his existential relationship to the world qua philosopher. In this sense, he participates in a rather more specifically French debate on the public role of the intellectual and writer traceable back to the Dreyfus case and Zola's "*J'accuse.*"

In a fascinating "East–West Encounter" of 1956, when a group of eminent thinkers debated Merleau-Ponty on the subject of engagement, one finds every participant thinking much more explicitly about the arts than Merleau-Ponty, who is concerned more with "the philosophical problem," "the intellectual formula for the Cold War," the problem of "the autonomy of culture," but not with the commitment of the arts as a unique, or even a special, case. If the arts enter into his consideration at all, they do so according to his Marxist framework, to reflect something about the general relationship between cultural and political values (*TD* 26–58).

For Merleau-Ponty, the debate about engagement is a debate about the intellectual and writer, a debate that does not pit engagement against (artistic) *purity* but against (man's) *freedom*, the freedom to think in nonpartisan ways. Yet there is a link between purity and freedom that stems back to Hegel and of which Merleau-Ponty is cognizant. If art is thought to compromise its purity by being engaged, so by the same condition man is thought to compromise his freedom. The purity of art and the freedom of man fall together under the concepts of autonomy and alienation: the problem of art's autonomy or alienation is also the problem of man's. Too much engagement renders art too tendentious and man too partisan; too much freedom renders both art and man "impotent" to do anything responsible in the world. Adorno is concerned with this problem; Merleau-Ponty is, too. Both independently articulate the problem in terms of a false dilemma founded on an "insufficiently dialectical"[21] concept of engagement, which both take Sartre to be supporting.

Merleau-Ponty seeks a mediated solution for the thinker whereby, crudely put, one can be free and engaged at the same time. Yet unlike

Sartre and most others, he does not establish direct relations between politics and art. Like Sartre, he is concerned to produce an existentialist aesthetic; unlike Sartre, however, he does not ask whether the artwork per se has political content or discloses, in some unique way, political truths. Rather, he sees in the artwork, and paradigmatically the novel, the ability to offer complex and rich descriptions of how persons are situated in the world. As he argues in "Metaphysics and the Novel," an artwork can show something metaphysical and then, by extension, something political. However, all the latter means is that insofar as a person sometimes acts politically in the world, the form of that engagement will be shown. In this sense, to engage in aesthetics, for Merleau-Ponty, is to engage in existential or phenomenological description. "The function of the novelist is not to state these [philosophical] ideas thematically but to make them exist for us in the way that things exist" (SNS 34/26).

The line between Merleau-Ponty and Sartre is here very fine. Thus, drawing on Sartre's own plays and novels (and *Dirty Hands* is exemplary), Merleau-Ponty stresses how the novel can show the dynamic conflicts with which "a man of action" is faced in a complex political world, or even the conflicts with which an intellectual who is not (or should not be) "a man of action" is faced. As I have been suggesting throughout the essay but now want to make quite explicit, Merleau-Ponty is depending once again on the more general connotations of the term "engagement," over and against the more specific demand of "commitment" (even though the terms are not distinguished in French). Whereas the former does not ask *to what* we are committed (which cause do you support?), the latter does. To highlight the difference, whereas one cannot be unengaged, one can be uncommitted. Engagement asks only *in what* we are engaged and *how* we are engaged, and for Merleau-Ponty, we are all engaged in the various projects of our lives, not all of which, obviously, are political. And yet, given his principle of all things and people "working together in some way or another," he allows that even the most apolitical of projects might still have a "political bearing."

Hence, Merleau-Ponty does not want to subsume engagement entirely under the political, to reduce it, one might say, just to commitment, but he is also not trying to depoliticize engagement altogether. In his "East–West Encounter," he argues that different historical times call for different kinds of engagement, at a certain time *pessimistic* engagement and at another *optimistic*. Pessimistic engagement demands a situation (happily now over, he quips) in which "writers must keep silent, or even lie, rather than be disloyal to the institution, to the apparatus that, in their eyes, holds the promise of the future." Optimistic engagement, by contrast, consists "in believing that there can be no alternative of the kind just mentioned [pessimistic engagement]; that if such an alternative presents itself, there is no reasonable choice for writers; they simply have nothing more to write. Nothing would justify a choice that would oblige a writer to lie." In thinking about optimistic engagement, Merleau-Ponty draws on a distinction between the values of culture and those of action, and finds between them an "immanent relation." In this engagement, he writes, the two kinds of value "converge" so that the writer does not have to choose between them, or subordinate one to the other. Optimistic engagement does not place the writer in an antagonistic paradox, because even if what he writes does not have "political content," it will have, given the convergence of values, "political bearing" – "the potential to teach those who read a certain way of situating themselves within the world, and consequently a certain political way of being" (*TD* 30–1).

Here is the core of his optimistic engagement in 1956, no longer pitting the writer or the philosopher, as he sees Sartre to be encouraging, antagonistically against the world. Here is Merleau-Ponty sounding at this moment at his most comfortably philosophical or ironically doubtful (although not exactly describing what historical situation has made this possible):

Engagement is the coming into relation with others; and engagement succeeds when, in the course of this engagement with others, we come to extract from it a formula for living with them. In saying that engagement does not put an end to autonomy, I want to emphasize that this work [writing] must be done without adhering to an exterior discipline. If Malraux's *Espoir* is an engaged book, it is to the extent that within the book we constantly sense Malraux's hesitations, what disturbs him about the political movement he's associated with. One can say this book is not effective except when it is ambiguous, and that if it ceased being ambiguous, it would at once cease being effective and engaged. (*TD* 51–2)

Thus, a philosophical text, a novel, or a film can be engaged by having "political bearing" even if has no explicit political content. Each can contribute in its own right – in its independent or autonomous way – to the single but complex process that is, as Merleau-Ponty said, "the greatness of Marxism" (*SNS* 130/107). But it is also the greatness of phenomenology, in his view, to have shown that there are "several ways for consciousness" to demonstrate and express itself (*PP* 144/124/143), and that somehow these several ways all work together. Hence, if sometimes what can be said about art can also be said about politics or about philosophy, this does not immediately establish unique or fixed connections between these different spheres. It only demonstrates the interwovenness and exchanges that exist in the multifaceted world of lived experience.

Merleau-Ponty is aware that the claims he is making on behalf of novels are historical as well as metaphysical. "Since the end of the 19th century," he duly notes, "the ties between [literature and philosophy] have been getting closer and closer." That novels are metaphysical is most evident in the present state of the novel. But that we see this *now*, he continues (following an obviously Hegelian model), only means that contemporary novels are *now* consciously or explicitly doing what "intellectual works" have always done:

Intellectual works had always been concerned with establishing a certain attitude toward the world, of which literature and philosophy, like politics, are just different expressions; but only now had this concern become explicit. One did not wait for the introduction of existential philosophy in France to define all life as latent metaphysics and all metaphysics as an "explicitation" of human life. (*SNS* 35/27)

Still, we do apparently have to wait for the introduction of this philosophy in France to hear one of its major proponents telling us that engagement in the novel or in the philosophical text or in the political act each established "a certain attitude toward the world." A not very informative claim, certainly, but it does again highlight the humanistic breadth with which Merleau-Ponty chooses to employ the term "engagement."

In recognizing the historical development of the novel, Merleau-Ponty was participating in a modernist debate concerning the relation between philosophy and literature, and in terms influenced by Lukács. Yet, unlike Lukács, he did not take much interest in the idea that what had made the novel more metaphysical, or philosophy more literary, might be found in modernist innovations of form, even if he did recognize that philosophy and literature had begun to share techniques of indirect or nontransparent writing – intimate diary, philosophical treatise, and dialogue – and even if he was, as he was, always very interested in the nature of language and writing.[22]

For Lukács, Adorno, and others, it was significantly through *form* that cultural and political values could be seen to intersect, although the intersections were not interpreted, as they were by Merleau-Ponty, as harmoniously constituting a world in which all the various spheres somehow work together. I wrote earlier that Merleau-Ponty and Adorno shared in judging Sartre "insufficiently dialectical." They did so, I can now explain, on very different grounds. Adorno found sufficient dialectics in form and dissonance. Unlike both Merleau-Ponty and Sartre, he found sufficient dialectics in the kind of form that gave to dissonant music pride or, perhaps better, guilt of place. He saw the simple "convergence" of cultural and political values to be the very worst outcome of the success of the commodification of culture. If such values intersected, they did so not by convergence but by dissonant negation, in music's ability to shatter, precisely through the discomfort it caused, our comfortable patterns of easy listening. Challenging these patterns was a specific way of challenging illusions of "happiness" or "contentment" in a society or culture that was in truth, Adorno believed, providing nothing of the sort.

As we saw earlier, Merleau-Ponty criticized Sartre for antagonistically pitting absolute freedom against partisan commitment and offered a dialectical and situated engagement as the alternative. Adorno criticized Sartre for seeing commitment to occur only in the prose content of a novel but not in music's form. Sartre erred in seeing music as pure. Adorno would have criticized Merleau-Ponty, too, for assuming a similar position. Certainly within prose content one sees evidence of conflicting, existential relations, but, for Adorno, this is not enough. If commitment-at-a-distance expresses a certain kind of attitude toward the world, it does so not just though the expression of content, but also through the distance and autonomy of form. Music's form shows how this is so. (Other arts show this, too.) Adorno thus stresses dissonance in contrast to Merleau-Ponty's harmony, conflicting values in contrast to convergent values, and challenging form in contrast to the expression of existential attitudes. Without more attention being paid to form, and to the historical dialectic of form, Adorno would likely have asked Merleau-Ponty, could situated engagement ever really be dialectical enough to dissipate the myths?

Insofar as Merleau-Ponty thinks about dissipating myths, he sees philosophy doing this, but not, to the same degree, the arts. He does not seem very concerned with how the arts specifically play a role in the development of revolutionary consciousness, even if he acknowledges that they do. It seems enough for him to show that modern techniques in the arts support the existential principles that reveal how humans are related through complex emotions and reasons to the world in which they find themselves. Here one might reasonably conclude that in his consideration of the arts he lets his existentialism overpower his Marxism, and his phenomenological description overpower his dialectics.

From another point of view, this conclusion misleads. Certainly there are critics who claim that when Merleau-Ponty writes "apolitically" about art, he writes at his best. Why not, they suggest, consider the aesthetic theory independently of the Marxism? This is not hard to do. For often when Merleau-Ponty engages in his aesthetic descriptions, no politics seem to play a role, and, moreover, he writes strikingly and with insight. He thus writes about music to say something about the intuitive silence and indirection of language or to give credence to the principles of Gestalt psychology and, later, to theories of expression. He offers marvelous descriptions of reading in *The Prose of the World*, of transitions and transformations of attention, of how absorption of attention takes the eye away from the words on the page, and of how significance comes to be understood in a text (*PM* 15/9ff). In *Phenomenology of Perception*, he writes of the bodily space of the theater, of the darkness and light, of the figure and ground of performance (*PP* 117/100/115). Most influentially, he writes about painting to support his thesis of the primacy of our visual and perceptual relation to the world. What he usually does not do, however is extend these descriptions of reading, writing, or viewing *explicitly* to meet the Marxist demand to change consciousness. But why not? Or, to make the question more probing, why does Merleau-Ponty seem here to be aestheticizing rather than politicizing his descriptions of art? The answer is telling.

In one of his last essays, "Eye and Mind," he describes how art draws upon the prearticulated or brute meaning of the world with an innocence unavailable to the philosopher, since the philosopher "is always called upon to have an opinion." The writer says too much, the musician nothing at all. Music is "too beyond the world," too "pure." "Only the painter," he argues, "is entitled to look at everything without being obliged to appraise what he sees." What is the evidence he calls upon to make this point? Interestingly, that even political regimes that denounce paintings nonetheless recognize that the paintings are not very dangerous. Although they denounce them, he notes, they rarely destroy them. "They hide them, and one senses here an element of 'one never knows' amounting almost to a recognition" (Œ 14/161/123). No one really blames painters for their escapism, he concludes, because no one really fears them. In quite some detail, mostly regarding Cézanne, he then describes the precise nature of the distance the painter's "escapism" achieves. "Painting awakens and carries to its highest pitch a delirium which is vision itself, for to see is to have at a distance; painting spreads this strange possession to all aspects of Being, which must in some fashion become visible in order to enter into the work of art" (Œ 26–7/166/127).

That painting may render "vision itself" transparent does not mean, however, that it thereby becomes philosophy, or even like the metaphysical novel, for, recall, in a painting, the painter expresses no opinion. Rather, Merleau-Ponty argues, the painter achieves something metaphysical "just in that instant when his vision becomes gesture, when in Cézanne's words, he 'thinks in painting'" (Œ 60/178/138–9). Thinking in painting is the subject matter of Merleau-Ponty's essay "Eye and Mind." It is also the subject matter of his well-known essay on Cézanne. But never does Merleau-Ponty return, however, to reconsider whether political regimes might in other terms find reason to fear this nonopinionated art.

In his view, he does not have to. His interest is only to show how painting makes our visual relation to the world transparent. In this sense, he is content to cut off, aestheticize, or "disenfranchise," as Arthur Danto has recently employed that term, painting from politics altogether.[23] Is this aestheticized interest enough? He thinks that it is, because "in the single process" and "convergence of values" of Marxism, everything ultimately works together. Painting can therefore do what it does as art; it did not have to do another thing. In the grand scheme of things in which there would be a convergence of values, however, this did not stop painting from having some sort of a "political bearing." So even if Merleau-Ponty looks as if he is disenfranchising painting, it is a disenfranchising maneuver which he takes to be perfectly compatible with a humanistic Marxism. But what, we now have to ask, is the "political bearing" of the painter's task?

Although Merleau-Ponty addresses the relation between painting and painter, novel and author, he is not interested in supporting merely intentionalist accounts, just as when he assesses political action he is not interested in merely intentionalist or consequentialist accounts. Nor does he take sides, as we would expect now, with strictly subjectivist or strictly objectivist accounts of the arts. Still, both in his philosophy of art and in his political philosophy, he is interested in biography and lives that are being, and have been, led. Like Sartre he is interested in childhood and maturity, in autobiography and psychoanalysis, in what leads people to think and to act.[24] Against this background, he is concerned with art, as he is with politics, only insofar as the study of painters and political actors reveals particular and different dimensions of their particular existential modes of engagement in the world.

Merleau-Ponty wants to stress that different actors, be they painters, playwrights, novelists, philosophers, or heroes, all engage in the world in different ways with the hope that they will all somehow work together. That, it is now clear, is the baseline of his account. What he does not want to do is confuse the different roles by subsuming one under another. Thus, as we have seen, he removes from the philosopher's commitment the requirement that he act locally or immediately as a "man of action." Then he removes the same requirement from the painter's. With the painter, however, according to Merleau-Ponty, the philosopher shares much. Here is the key to the painter's "political bearing," namely, in the dialectical relation of sameness and difference in which he stands to the philosopher.

If Cézanne proves exemplary as a painter, according to Merleau-Ponty, for the metaphysical or existential "doubt" he reveals in his paintings, so comparably can a philosopher (like himself) try to situate himself as a philosopher. Merleau-Ponty might prove exemplary, as did Cézanne, not only because his philosophy, like Cézanne's paintings, might demonstrate the ambiguity and contingency of history and man's situation in the world, but his life, like Cézanne's, might show this, too.

Just as Cézanne wondered whether what came from his hands had any meaning and would be understood, just as the man of good will comes to doubt
that lives are compatible with each other when he considers the conflicts
of his own particular life, so today's citizen is not sure whether the human
world is possible. (*SNS* 9/5)

Expression in art, like life, Merleau-Ponty writes, does not guarantee
its meaning or have its meaning guaranteed in advance; instead it "is
like a step taken in the fog" (*SNS* 8/3). How now does the philosopher
and the painter follow different paths in the fog? By being engaged in
the philosopher's case with opinions, but in the painter's case with
none.

The painter, the philosopher, the politician: all "working
together."[25] Merleau-Ponty establishes the analogies. Yet he focuses
also on their disanalogies to demarcate the specific nature of the
philosopher's engagement. The task is of the utmost importance, for
were he to claim too strong an analogy on either side, he would either
render the philosopher *too harmless* in the painter's escapism or *too
harmful* in the political man of action's allegiance to a partisan cause.
However, in emphasizing the disanalogies, or in placing the philosopher between harmlessness and harmfulness, Merleau-Ponty, in
Sartre's eyes, runs the grave risk of emptying the philosopher's engagement of any meaning. The final section of this essay addresses
this risk directly.

V. PHILOSOPHICAL ENGAGEMENT

Merleau-Ponty seeks to articulate a space for the philosopher's engagement and investigates the space of artistic and political activity
to help him do so. This space is consistent with the space he seeks
always and everywhere in all his writing: the dynamic space, the
"interworld," the space of engagement-at-a-distance, a space, phenomenologically speaking, that holds our immediate, intuitive, com-
plicit, and active relationship to the world at a reflective distance;
a space of "slackening of our intentional threads"; a refusal of complicity, a looking "*ohne mitzumachen*" (*PP* viii/xiii/xiv). It is a space
of reciprocity and communication, connecting persons, spheres, and
dimensions of the world. It is a space that might save humanistic
Marxism from what it concretely has become.

The greatest part of action takes place in the intermediate space between the events and the pure thoughts, neither in things nor in spirits, but in the thick stratum of symbolic actions which operate less by their efficacy than by their meaning. To this zone belong books, lectures, but also meetings. And likewise one can say the same when one puts into circulation critical weapons, instruments of political consciousness, even if they cannot serve the moment and cannot adjudicate the issue among the adversaries.[26]

Under one philosophical characterization, the space "in between" is a negative space that refuses extremes: the extremes of philosophical and political dogmatism (intellectualism, scientism, Cartesianism, absolutism, Stalinism, etc.). Under another, it is a positive space of human freedom (historical situatedness, desirable contingency, and "good ambiguity"). It is a space overcoming dualisms and false dilemmas, a space of desirable incompleteness, unendingness, and openness. It is a dialectical space that nonetheless refuses easy syntheses. "Merleau-Ponty," Sartre writes, "accepts thesis and antithesis. It is synthesis which he rejects, reproaching it for changing dialectic into a building game. Spirals, on the contrary, are never allowed to conclude."[27]

Moreover, it is a space Merleau-Ponty thinks Sartre has not found, despite Sartre's increasing claims to the contrary. Sartre, he argues, is always falling into the kinds of extremes that lead him not to connect but either to isolate or to conflate his disparate activities. In isolating them, Sartre makes them ineffective. Sartre fails as committed writer because he has the wrong idea of committed philosophy. He fails to acknowledge the true nature of man's engagement in the world and thus fails to commit himself correctly as playwright, philosopher, and man of action. Merleau-Ponty believes he may thus legitimately assert himself to be more truthfully engaged – as a philosopher – than the much more outspoken and committed Sartre.

Is Merleau-Ponty walking an impossible path? Having purportedly found the right philosophy of engagement, has he not just committed himself to being an honest philosopher engaged in the pursuit of truth and the dissipation of myths? And if by definition to be a philosopher means that one is engaged in such a pursuit, has he rendered it self-contradictory for a philosopher to be uncommitted? A philosopher not doing philosophy? Once more, conflating the terms "engagement" and "commitment" (despite their identity in the French language) confuses the argument. Merleau-Ponty is concerned with how the philosopher engages with the world; Sartre is interested in commitment. Sartre thinks he is acknowledging the burden of the debate and Merleau-Ponty is ignoring it. For surely, Sartre suggests, in carving out the right place for the philosopher's *engagement with truth,* the burden is then to show that one has thereby also solved the question of the philosopher's *commitment to politics.*

In a recent essay entitled "The Lure of Syracuse,"[28] Mark Lilla articulates a dilemma relevant to our concerns. Lilla seeks to explain "philotyranny," the support by intellectuals of tyrannical systems. He describes how ill-conceived views of "commitment" served through the twentieth century to keep tyranny in place. Following Raymond Aron, he describes how Stalinism was once kept in place by the romantic overcommitment of the French intellectuals (Sartre et al.) and, following Jürgen Habermas, how Nazism was once kept in place by the disengagement of the Germans (Thomas Mann et al.). "Obviously," Lilla continues, "neither explanation makes sense for twentieth-century Europe as a whole"; perhaps they even fail to take us to "the heart of the matter," even if they have been and continue to be predominant modes of explanation.

Lilla finds the heart of the matter in Socrates, or, more specifically, in Plato's recognition that "there is some connection in the human mind between the yearning for truth and the desire to contribute to 'the right ordering of cities and households.'" When the desire to right the world becomes a reckless passion, however, it has to be harnessed. Lilla does not give much content to the idea of "harnessing" the desire to right the world. Instead, he expresses sympathy toward the intellectuals who have been forced by the extreme conditions of the twentieth century constantly to have to test themselves. He would like contemporary intellectuals to be more aware of the test but offers no more than this to guide them: that each intellectual must look "within" to find his or her own sense of justice.

How different is Lilla's solution to Merleau-Ponty's? "In morality as in art," Merleau-Ponty wrote at the end of the war,

there is no solution for the man who will not make a move without knowing where he is going and who wants to be accurate and in control at every movement. Our only resort is the spontaneous movement which binds us to others for good or ill, out of selfishness or generosity . . . [P]olitical experiences of the past thirty years oblige us to evoke the background of non-sense against which every universal undertaking is silhouetted and by which it is threatened with failure. (*SNS* 8/4)

For Merleau-Ponty, the place of "good ambiguity" is the place of "harnessing" the intellectual (Sartre) who would desire also to be a hero, the intellectual who would act out of certainty (blind courage). In Lilla's terms, under one form of explanation, this "too certain" knowledge contributes to keeping tyranny in place. In Merleau-Ponty's terms, it is precisely the difference between certainty and doubt that can be used to save humanistic Marxism from Stalinist tyranny. The analogy with Cézanne as painter has shown how this can be so. Failure, he writes, "is not absolute. Cézanne won out against chance, and men, too, can win provided they will measure the dangers and the task" (*SNS* 9/5).

Favoring "doubt" is how Merleau-Ponty avoids reducing "engagement" to what other theorists more morally or theologically call "conscience." Conscience is never enough; it promises exactly what it does not give. It promises action, but no action is performed. In *Humanism and Terror*, he accordingly rejects "the happy universe of liberalism where one knows what one is doing and where, at least, one always keeps his conscience" (*HT* xxxiii/xxxvii). Conscience is linked to "happy ends" and "guaranteed outcomes," but again, never is this enough: "the liberals did not cry out against barbarism. The troops marched past the dead bodies. The music played" (*HT* xxx/xxxiv).

Does the situated and doubting philosopher do more? Sometimes Merleau-Ponty judges the situation to demand pessimistic engagement, at another time, optimistic, but in either case, action lies in the "limping" exposure of myths, or, more, positively, in offering "opinions" that are "also always" constrained by the pursuit of truth. Even when philosophers claim entirely to have stopped walking or talking, even when they most strongly assert their distance from politics, they do so in response to the political situation in which they find themselves. "*For even this general refusal,*" Merleau-Ponty writes with emphasis at the end of his *Phenomenology of Perception,* "*is still one manner of being, and has its place in the world*" (*PP*

516/452/525). It is a manner of being or, as he also calls it, "a certain kind of action" with "political bearing," even if it does not have the immediacy of partisan political content.

Still, Sartre keeps asking, how effective can this philosophical action be? Sartre recalls a parting conversation he once had with Merleau-Ponty in 1950 on a train:

He repeated quietly: "The only thing left for us is silence."
"Who is 'us,'" I said, pretending not to understand.
"Well us. *Les Temps modernes.*"
"You mean, you want us to put the key under the door?"
"No, not that. But I don't want us to breathe another word of politics."
"But why not?"
"They're fighting"
"Well, all right, in Korea."
"Tomorrow they'll be fighting everywhere."
"And even if they were fighting here, why should we be quiet?"
"Because brute force will decide the outcome. Why speak on deaf ears?"
I leaned out of the window and waved, as one should. I saw that he waved back, but I remained in a state of shock until the journey's end.[29]

In a sense Merleau-Ponty is in shock, too. Toward the end of his life, a life that ends prematurely, he writes increasingly of philosophy and politics in crisis. He even worries that philosophy might not be possible any more (*RC* 141/167). Is his retreat into silence from politics becoming less an embracing of philosophy's engagement than an admission of philosophy's contemporary impossibility? Merleau-Ponty offers an explanation for his worry, seemingly motivated by considerations only in the history of philosophy. "With Hegel," he writes,

something comes to an end. After Hegel, there is a philosophical void. This is not to say that there has been a lack of thinkers or of geniuses, but that Marx, Kierkegaard, and Nietzsche start from a denial of philosophy. We might say that with the latter we enter an age of nonphilosophy. But perhaps such a destruction of philosophy constitutes its very realization. Perhaps it preserves the essence of philosophy, and it may be, as Husserl wrote, that philosophy is reborn from its ashes. (*RC* 141–2/168)

Merleau-Ponty argues against adopting the idea that what has followed since Hegel already constitutes philosophy's rebirth. At best, it has laid the seeds; at worst it has rendered thought obscure and equivocal. Thus, the task remains for the contemporary philosopher to think this rebirth through. We should not be surprised. When Merleau-Ponty is not thinking explicitly about politics, he sees philosophy working at its best, in the constant process of its being rethought.

Yet in thinking about philosophy, it still looks as if Merleau-Ponty is missing the point of Sartre's question. Might not the idea that philosophy has come to an end rest on a political recognition that in times of crisis it is no longer possible to do philosophy at all and that action – standing on the barricades – is the only option left? Merleau-Ponty does not think this a permanent answer, if only because it confuses permanent with temporary solutions, and, as we have seen, he is not willing to accept the confusion, not even, apparently, in times of crisis. Rather, in these times, when people "have no ears," it is preferable to retreat into silence, or into a place where one can investigate more quietly the terms of philosophy's rebirth. Moreover, when myths are most firmly in place (when society is most totalized), partisan action is not strong enough to dissipate them. Standing on the barricades is necessary in critical times but even this proves effective only when it is accompanied by reflection. In this sense philosophy is still needed, even if it speaks "in silence."

I suggested a moment ago that the debate between Merleau-Ponty and Sartre might have more genuinely been a debate about whether being a philosopher in modern times was possible at all. In this light, we might interpret Sartre as having chosen to become an artist and a man of action in recognition that these were the only exits left for the philosopher in a world that had, in Sartre's view, become "absurd" or meaningless in its totalized form. "I do not recognize" your philosopher's "dreamy presence," Sartre writes to Merleau-Ponty, as "my *being-there* (*être-là*).... It can mean that I am not a philosopher (that's what I believe), or that there are other ways of being a philosopher."[30]

Merleau-Ponty refuses Sartre's solution. If one kind of engagement is in crisis, then, by his principle of things "working together," the others are, too.[31] "All human acts and all human creations constitute a single drama, and in this sense we are all saved or lost together."[32]

Relinquishing philosophy to be an artist or a man of action is not the solution; indeed, I think Merleau-Ponty believes that precisely such a solution only further helps to keep tyranny in place.

Hence, Merleau-Ponty does not seek in art or action the possibility of doing philosophy vicariously. Instead, he sees increasingly the possibility and advantages of doing philosophy through indirect forms of expression. Now he shows himself once again to be caught by Socrates' lure. The painter, the philosopher, the politician: standing side by side, but not now generating equal interest. No, Merleau-Ponty is most interested in the philosopher, in situating him in between the others – at a distance from the politician, and close to the painter – but neither too distant nor too close. Yet, all the time, he is situating the philosopher through a dialectical strategy of indirection.

Once, at the end of his life, he proposes a direct analogy between the painter and the politician, although he quickly shows that the directness is deceptive. For between the painter and politician stands the philosopher; it is just that now he is silent, or, better, that he is now choosing to speak "indirectly." What is Merleau-Ponty's point? To say something about the painter and politician *in order to* justify the philosopher's retreat into indirect speech. Here, at the end of his life, is the key to Merleau-Ponty's dialectics: to establish by indirect means an appropriate mode for a continuing philosophical discourse.

History is the judge – not History as the Power of a moment or of a century, but history as the space of inscription and accumulation beyond the limits of countries and epochs of what we have said and done that is most true and valuable, taking into account the circumstances in which we had to speak. Others will judge what I have done, because I painted the painting to be seen, because my action committed the future of others; but neither art nor politics consists in pleasing or flattering others. What they expect of the artist or politician is that he draw them toward values in which they will only later recognize their own values. The painter or politician shapes others more often than he follows them. The *public* at whom he aims is not given; it is a public to be elicited by his work. The others of whom he thinks are not empirical "others" or even *humanity* conceived as a species; it is others once they have become such that he can live with them. The history in which the artist participates (and it is better the less he thinks about "making history" and honestly produces *his* work as he sees it) is not a power before which he must genuflect. It is the perpetual conversation woven together by all speech, all valid works and actions, each, according to its place and circumstance, contesting and conforming the other, each one recreating all the others. (*PM* 121–2/86)

In situating philosophy between politics and the arts, Merleau-Ponty does not think he can solve the problems of all three; but he does think he can reveal the philosopher's task. Certainly appearances deceive because, as we can see in this quotation, he speaks directly far more substantially about the political man of action's task and the painter's task than he does about the task that concerns him most. In this appearance, he makes it look as if he were leaving the philosopher standing much too limpingly between two far more effective extremes. Hence, Sartre's fear that philosophical engagement has been emptied of its content. The deception is deliberate, however, if we recognize that Merleau-Ponty intends more and more – with all the indirection he thinks necessary – to maintain the fragility of the philosophical pursuit in times of crisis.

With indirection, he believes he can connect the dots between his view of philosophical engagement and Sartre's demand for political commitment. In times of crisis, one feels the need to speak clearly, directly, and with immediacy: "even if we have no guarantee that [our] goals will ever be realized," he writes,

we can at least see very clearly the absurdity of an anachronistic tyranny like anti-Semitism and of a reactionary expedient like fascism. And this is enough to make us want to destroy them root and branch and to push things forward in the direction of effective liberty. This political task is not incompatible with any cultural value or literary task, if literature and culture are defined as the progressive awareness of our multiple relationships with other people and the world, rather than as extramundane techniques. *If all truths are told, none will have to be hidden.* (*SNS* 185/152)

In telling truths, he is arguing, one cannot always speak with the directness one desires. Yet indirection is not a matter of hiding the truth, but of telling it in a way that might break through the deafness of the contemporary ear. It might prove in its silence to be more effective.

At the end of his life, he writes of both philosophical and political thought as "the elucidation of a historical perception in which all our understandings, all our experiences, and all our values simultaneously come into play – and of which our theses are only the schematic formulation." He never relinquishes his optimism that all things will somehow work together, but now he stresses that these things also "advance only obliquely. They do not go straight, without hesitation, toward goals or concepts. That which one too deliberately seeks," he concludes, "one does not achieve" (*PM* 159/112).

Thus, one may conclude that it is more via indirect techniques of writing, than in his direct confrontation with Sartre, that Merleau-Ponty finally finds his connection between philosophical engagement and political commitment. Or, more strongly, to bring out the dialectical quality, Merleau-Ponty would never be content merely to distance the philosopher from the man of action if he did not find the artist on the other side providing him with techniques of indirection. This does not mean he aims to aestheticize philosophy or reduce philosophy to the purportedly "nonopinionated" status of the painter. On the contrary, he seeks to use these techniques, and the painter's "doubt," to demonstrate how the philosopher can stay deeply engaged in his critical times doing what he thinks philosophers have always done: pursuing truth and dissipating the myths – so long as the painter and the man of action are working somehow alongside him.

Like Socrates, Merleau-Ponty knows that in critical times, this tripartite companionship has to be defended most strongly. If the defense is needed, the challenge is needed too, however, and Sartre provides it. The danger is that any person not attentive to the dialectical relationship is likely simply to collapse the distinction between philosophical engagement and political commitment into a distinction between aesthetic disengagement and political commitment. Here is the real risk in the debate over commitment and intellectual responsibility – namely, that a fragile dialectical relationship between different kinds of thinkers and thought are not understood as dialectical. Philosophers have to assume some of the responsibility for that risk: that, in Merleau-Ponty's view, is Socrates' lesson.

It is Hegel's and Marx's lesson too, as it is later the lesson of the critical theorists, which is to say that resorting to indirect techniques of writing or into silence might more increase the risk than bring our attention to it. What Merleau-Ponty realizes increasingly is that a dialectics of form has always to interact dialectically with a dialectics of content, and that content is what he calls history. Philosophy might borrow its techniques from art as a way to avoid the "frontal action" of the committed Communists, but philosophical "engagement" always still has to be the continued interrogation of history in its most concrete and most abstract determinations. A revolutionary philosophy, he writes in his *Adventures of the Dialectic*, perpetually displays a "spiral movement – a reading of history which allows its philosophical meaning to appear, and a return to the present which lets philosophy appear as history" (*AD* 53/35).

History might therefore lead Merleau-Ponty into a silent retreat, but – and this is the point – the retreat is just the place in which this philosopher puts himself at a certain time. What his late and final silence is not, however, is a way out of history or engaged philosophy altogether, even if in appearance (it tries to) look that way. If, that is to say, Sartre's challenge will never go away, then at least Merleau-Ponty seems to think that his own silence might keep his antagonistic companion silent, for a while. But this desire to put a quarrel to rest for a while has little to do with Merleau-Ponty's lifelong engagement with history and truth as a philosopher of interrogation and reflection.

NOTES

1. *PP* xiv/xix/xxi.
2. Goldthorpe, "Understanding the Committed Writer."
3. In this essay, the terms "commitment" and "engagement" will sometimes be used interchangeably, the former being the more usual but not necessarily better translation of the original "*engagement*," but throughout, and increasingly, they will be distinguished. For a history of this term and background to the debate, see Schalk, *The Spectrum of Political Engagement*, and Boschetti, *The Intellectual Enterprise*.
4. Silverman and Barry, "Introduction: Philosopher at Work!" (*TD* xiii). Perhaps Merleau-Ponty is not mentioned because few with whom Sartre was actively engaged in this debate are mentioned, and most notably Paul Nizan whose 1932 *Les Chiens de garde* deeply influenced Sartre's 1948 "What Is Literature?" Merleau-Ponty is also not generally known for his contribution to the debate on commitment, but focusing on it here enables one to articulate clearly his approach to politics and the arts.
5. For example, Julian Benda, Roger Martin du Gard, André Malraux, François Mauriac, Paul Nizan, and Simone de Beauvoir.
6. This collection treats every conceivable aspect of their relationship.

7. Boschetti, *The Intellectual Enterprise*, 210. She actually only refers to his "counter thinking."

8. See the closing statement of "The Yogi and the Proletarian." His view of philosophy, "like the most fragile object of perception – a soap bubble, or a wave – or like the most simple dialogue, embraces indivisibly all the order and all the disorder of the world" (*HT* 206/189).

9. A treatment of his critique of liberalism is offered by Sonia Kruks in *The Political Philosophy of Merleau-Ponty*, chapter 4.

10. Sartre, "Merleau-Ponty," *Situations*, 174. "Merleau-Ponty *vivant*," in Stewart, *The Debate between Sartre and Merleau-Ponty*, 580.

11. See note 10 for reference and context to this letter.

12. As it turns out, the immediate cause of his distress was a university lecture given by Merleau-Ponty that had apparently attacked him. The letters first appeared in 1994 in *Magazine littéraire*. They are translated and contextualized by Jon Stewart in *The Debate between Sartre and Merleau-Ponty*, 327–54. Unmarked passages in what follows are from 331–44.

13. Sartre, like Merleau-Ponty, was most concerned with the future of communism, especially in France.

14. Merleau-Ponty offers a footnote here for the philosophical point: "To write about the event of the day when one does not belong to a party (and even if one, as a member of a party, is brought to philosophy) demands and simultaneously hinders one from elaborating the principles" (*Debate*, 338 n).

15. "Politics is never the encounter between conscience and individual happenings, nor is it ever the simple application of a philosophy of history. Politics is never able to see the whole directly. It is always aiming at the incomplete synthesis, a given cycle of time, or a group of problems. It is not pure morality nor is it a chapter in a universal history which has already been written. Rather it is an action in the process of self-invention" (*AD* 10/4).

16. Quoted by Schmidt, *Maurice Merleau-Ponty: Between Phenomenology and Structuralism*, 92.

17. This is a question discussed by James Schmidt in the context of his larger discussion of Merleau-Ponty's political philosophy and of the Marxist, Weberian, and Saussaurean elements that enter into it. See Schmidt, *Maurice Merleau-Ponty*, 122 ff.

18. Schmidt argues that Merleau-Ponty's analysis of Bukharin's trial exhibited "staggering naiveté," *Between Phenomenology and Structuralism*, 119. I have been much helped by Schmidt's presentation of how Merleau-Ponty interpreted the trial. He, however, does not stress the overarching philosophical argument as much as I do.

19. A useful collection of essays is Adorno et al., *Aesthetics and Politics*; cf. Leibowitz, *L'Artiste et sa conscience*, and Sartre's reply in *Situations*, 142–55. See also "What Is Literature?" to which Merleau-Ponty's *Prose of the World* was written as a response.
20. *Aesthetics and Politics*, 177.
21. Adorno famously used this phrase against Walter Benjamin.
22. See Boschetti, *The Intellectual Enterprise*, 22–3.
23. See Danto, *The Philosophical Disenfranchisement of Art*, specifically the essay under the same title.
24. See Sartre, *Situations*, 157; *Debate*, 566. Also Merleau-Ponty's essay "Cézanne's Doubt" on Leonardo da Vinci and childhood, and on Freud's thesis of being neither too attached nor too detached as part of an argument against pure consciousness: "There can be no consciousness that is not sustained by its primordial involvement in life and by the manner of this involvement" (*SNS* 31/24; *AR* 74).
25. For mention of the tripartite analogy, see *PM* 126/90.
26. *Debate*, 350. From the summary of Merleau-Ponty's lecture, in his letter to Sartre.
27. Sartre, *Situations*, 212; *Debate*, 613.
28. Lilla, *The Reckless Mind: Intellectuals in Politics*, Afterword.
29. Sartre, *Situations*, 189; *Debate*, 593–4, translation modified.
30. *Debate*, 333.
31. See *Debate*, 350.
32. "An Unpublished Text by Maurice Merleau-Ponty: *A Prospectus of His Work*," in *The Primacy of Perception*, 10.

13   Thinking Politics

I. THE SITUATION OF THE PHILOSOPHER

Is the philosophy of our age, Sartre asks, dead or alive? Must we culti-
vate the field or raze the moldering edifice? Yet thought rejects stark
choices of this kind. We know full well that Marx did not demol-
ish Hegel, that Kant did not leave Cartesianism in ruins. How could
a serious assessment of Marxism be captured in a simple verdict?
Consider instead what Merleau-Ponty tells us in the Introduction to
Signs:

> The history of thought does not summarily pronounce: This is true; that is
> false. Like all history, it has its veiled decisions. It dismantles or embalms
> certain doctrines, changing them into "messages" or museum pieces. There
> are others, on the contrary, which it keeps active. These do not endure be-
> cause there is some miraculous adequation or correspondence between them
> and an invariable "reality" – such an exact and fleshless truth is neither suf-
> ficient nor necessary for the greatness of a doctrine – but because, as obliga-
> tory steps for those who want to go further, they retain an expressive power
> which exceeds their statements and propositions.

Or again: "We are saying that a reexamination of Marx would be a
meditation upon a classic, and that it could not possibly terminate
in a *nihil obstat* or a listing on the Index" (*S* 16–17/10–11).

When Merleau-Ponty speaks of a *history of thought,* he suggests
that thought is not merely subordinate to "real" history, the mere
"expression" of a meaning occurring in social praxis, a truth that
could be assigned to it from without. Thought establishes a relation to being only insofar as it relates to itself, finds in its actual
operations both a logic that demonstrates the effectiveness of its formulations and an indeterminacy that forces it to *go further.* In other

352

words, thought is itself *praxis*, a movement that discovers its own meaning in the need to resume work and in exploiting the conditions handed down to it from the past. Such experimentation no doubt implies ruptures and discontinuities; it silently eliminates the rhetorical effect, the ornamental figure (while leaving open the possibility of rediscovering its meaning later), and advances only by retaining what is essential. As Merleau-Ponty says, not only is the philosopher unable to make a tabula rasa of the past, but the distance he takes from his predecessors brings him back to them once again; in some sense, he remains indebted to them for his ability to go further.

That said, one need only consider the practice of thought without succumbing to idealist or materialist prejudices, to concede, for example, that reflection on politics can never be divorced from reflection on the theory of politics. How, then, can we fail to be surprised when those most careful to uncover praxis at the level of collective action, technology, and social relations, and to discern the concrete transformation of schemes of production and communication according to rules and types of organization, are blind to the praxis of thought and want only to consider only "system," "worldview," or the "totalization of knowledge" at the level of theory? Is it not the case that looking deeper will expose a greater danger here, that the *foundation* – the foundation the Marxist is accustomed to calling the "real" – reveals itself when history is shown to be not just a perpetual exchange between the present and the past, but one that sends us hesitantly from the truth of what we have been given to think by others to the truth that our experience of the world, and it alone, compels us to think?

Let us then refrain from reclaiming the formula Sartre challenges: philosophy is not an "attitude always in our power to adopt." Perhaps we are powerless, and surely philosophizing, not unlike speaking, knowing, or acting, is not an *attitude* that the individual is free to take or leave. What is crucial is to remember that, once it exists, philosophy – and in particular, because it concerns a specific domain of reflection, political philosophy – constitutes a history and subjects thought to a necessity that no boundaries can contain. The form in which that necessity expresses itself changes. The evolution of philosophy inscribes itself in institutions responsive, we may suppose, to certain historical, social, and psychological conditions, but one and the same demand remains. It is not the demand to totalize the knowledge of an age, but to find a *point* to which each of our distinct experiences leads back, to welcome what happens in the silence and discord of human affairs into a language forever tied to the mystery of its own symbols, and to assemble it in the patient labor whose obscurity is never entirely dispelled by reason. Engaged in such inquiry, the man of thought cannot shirk it at some point and rest on what he considers the acquired knowledge of the day. He must let himself be guided toward the ultimate questions. In a sense, the demand to which he responds is, for him, as urgent as the demand to act is for the politician. To be sure, the one must decide, regardless of the state of his deliberations, while the other never ceases to hold his thoughts in suspense; the one confronts the immediate, the other has, as they say, all the time in the world. Yet their different fates should not obscure this essential point: the same rigor applies to both. One could thus say of political action and political thought what Heidegger, quoting Hölderlin, says of philosophy and poetry: that "between them a profound kinship reigns," although they "reside on the most distant peaks." From a distance, and without any bridge between them to ensure clear communication, they inscribe themselves in the same history.

That history is being made before our very eyes, and it would be pointless to infer from a comparison between our present situation and the past that the time for philosophy is past. However we interpret our experience, doing so can only enrich our inquiry. If it seems to us that sociology and political science are taking over a domain formerly inhabited by philosophy and history, with the aim of imposing strict limits on it, we still need to shed light on this retreat to the frontiers of exact knowledge; we should still to be surprised by it, to keep in our memory the movement that in the past tended toward totality. And this light toward which we are striving, this path we are beginning to forge, does not belong to the world of science. If politics itself, in its exercise, seems devoid of meaning, if turning away from politics seems advisable, still we cannot avoid reflecting on the truth of this privation. If, in the end, Marx's work, in spite of appearances, which is to say, in the absence of proletarian revolutions, remains alive only in its interpretation of capitalism, nothing can prevent us from confronting theory and event, essence and appearance, and measuring the gap between Marxist philosophy and Marxist ideology.

Not only is philosophy continually reborn the moment one would bury it, not only does it turn back on its adversaries to transform their arguments into questions, but, in the light of philosophy, a sudden kinship emerges between ideas everyone seems to conceive in opposition. Certainly, Marxist ideology seems far removed from positivist sociology. Those claiming to deal simply with facts, who seek to know only empirically discernible institutions and quantifiable social categories, are constrained simply to identify relations among defined variables, for the purpose of forging, at best, systems whose truth in the end lies only in their own coherence. For them, neither the concept of class nor even the idea of class struggle or historical dialectic makes any sense. Others, by contrast, insist reality is accessible only in the discovery of the fundamental contradiction that destroys human work and masks the visible organization of society, only in bringing to light the disorder and conflict apparent from the communist point of view. In their eyes, "analytical reason," in its incapacity to grasp in the present the truth of the future and recognize the whole in each of its parts, will only ever reproduce, on the symbolic level, the alienation that holds sway in practice.

Yet the ideologue joins the "man of science" inasmuch as he, too, relies entirely on conceptual tools whose purpose is to determine the intelligible order of phenomena once and for all. Both equate the real with the rational, an equation their interpretations tirelessly try to prove, and they converge in dismissing questions that would threaten their principles. The one convinces himself that the ultimate questions have been answered, the other that the only questions are questions of fact. In certain respects, however, the end result is the same: political reflection proceeds in deliberately limited horizons. Philosophically speaking, political science and Marxist ideology amount to two forms of contemporary conservatism, two aspects of the tradition in which thought that dismisses questions concerning the being of thought has long sought refuge. We ought not to infer from this that philosophy takes its point of departure outside their domain. After all, if we are so quick to denounce the positivism in a certain brand of sociology, this is something we owe in large part to Marxism. If Marxism seems to get itself caught up in redundancy, to remove itself from the test of events, this is in some respects because the progress of empirical research sharpens our curiosity and calls for renewed reflection. There is some truth in the Marxist critique of science and some truth in the scientific critique of ideology that philosophy must take on board. What is certain is that to express those truths, we will need a new frame of mind, new concepts, a new mental toolbox, a new notion of dialectic, a new ontology.

II. READING MERLEAU-PONTY

Isn't this a lot to ask? What's the use, one might say, of formulating so many questions one is incapable of answering? For our part, we would not demand the right to put questions so forcefully in this way had we not learned from reading Merleau-Ponty that inquiry forges its own path; that the critique of ideas and facts clears bit by bit a space in which thought finds itself at home, where experiences that were blind to one another converge and harmonize; that the ordeal of indeterminacy as well as the realization of knowledge establishes a relation to the universal.

The preface to *Adventures of the Dialectic* opens with this warning:

We need a philosophy of both history and spirit to deal with the problems we touch upon here. Yet we would be unduly rigorous if we were to wait for perfectly elaborated principles before speaking philosophically of politics. In the crucible of events we become aware of what is not acceptable to us, and it is this experience as interpreted that becomes both thesis and philosophy. (*AD* 9/3)

From the early essays collected in *Sense and Non-Sense* to the last statements of *Signs*, Merleau-Ponty's political writings repeat the same free movement that holds thesis and philosophy in suspense. This freedom is certainly disconcerting, because we are accustomed to seeking in a work some lesson we might choose to follow or not, because we wait for the moment when ideas will come to comprise a system, when thought will tear itself away from the contingent pattern that, so we suppose, forbids it from monumentalizing itself in the essential. We want to believe that the philosopher simply prepares himself to take possession of "perfectly elaborated principles," that he is fully aware of what is provisional in his research. When, moreover, we see death strike him down in the middle of his work, we cannot fail to imagine that he was on the way to the place where his questions would turn into answers. Yet nothing, neither the project of a "Treatise" Merleau-Ponty announced in *Adventures of the Dialectic* nor the death that deprives us of the work's conclusion and suddenly makes it appear as what should have been its goal and realization, can make us forget the resolution, recognizable in each of his writings, to tie reflection on the political philosophy of the day to the experience of events. Nothing can prevent us from discovering, beyond fortuitous circumstances, the necessity from which thought seems to draw its inspiration, a necessity that, by itself, bears the mark of a meaning.

Merleau-Ponty never makes the works of Marx an object of study. He never openly asks the question, What is the essence of history? or What is the essence of politics? Nor does he devote himself to developing a new account of modern society. This is because he does not bother with preliminary justifications, but always takes for granted that Marxism will be familiar to his readers, that their experience of the present will allow them to think what he himself is trying to think. His claims are born in a dialogue, which puts his readers in a position to remember the path he has already taken in connection with events privileged in his eyes, but meaningful to all – events for which the proliferation of opinions and interpretations has guaranteed diffusion in the milieu and the age and whose efficacy as historical symbols he would like to restore. In what might seem a flawed method, an intention expresses itself, namely, the avowed goal of not enclosing in signification the being of the signified, of combining the movement in which history opens to the indeterminacy of the future with a thought that, just as it reaches for the truth, embraces the principle of its own contestation.

We cannot know what final form Merleau-Ponty's philosophy would have taken in the domain that concerns us here, but we can at least be sure that, in the context of a treatise, this singular relationship with others and with things, this singular relation to which his various essays on politics testify, would have been preserved. For it is of the essence of his thought to eschew truths articulated in positive terms, to resist the direction the work pushes his thought, to have indefinite recourse to a new beginning, and ultimately to question what thought is, because the distance his thought takes from certain received ideas does not hide the fact that it springs from their source.

It is worth recalling the road traveled since the first articles of 1945 and 1946. The enthusiasm born of the Liberation had at first awakened the hopes that followed the end of the First World War, the success of the Russian Revolution, and the rise of communist parties all over the world. Yet from one era to another, the difference only became clearer. Nowhere did the conflict between states degenerate into civil war. In Merleau-Ponty's words, "class struggle today has been masked over." One certainly cannot say that it has disappeared, since fascism is an obvious consequence of it and shows into what kind of regression capitalism in crisis can drag humanity. But the fact that fascism was able to establish itself and that, to combat it, the regime born of the socialist revolution bound itself so closely with Western bourgeoisies, while communist parties devoted themselves where necessary to the defense of the country, reveals the equivocation of the age. From now on, "neither capitalism nor the proletariat can fight unmasked."

The first question, then, is to know what credit can still be given to a Marxist philosophy of history. Confining ourselves to the facts, nothing warrants our taking its views concerning revolution as legitimate. "We still do not know whether effective history is going to consist of a series of *diversions* – of which fascism was the first and of which Americanism or the Western bloc could be other examples – for as long as we live and perhaps even for centuries." More explicitly, "It no longer makes any sense to treat the class struggle as an *essential* fact if we are not sure that effective history will remain true to its 'essence' and that its texture will not be the product of accidents for a long time or forever" (SNS 147/121). At another point, he notes, "The proletariat is too weakened as a class to remain an autonomous factor of history at present." He adds in the same passage, however, "We are not saying that this fact refutes Marxism, since Marx himself pointed out that chaos and absurdity were one of the possible ways for history to end" (SNS 197/162–3). Indeed, this reserve clarifies all his analyses of the period. One can get rid of Marxism, he thinks, only by reducing it to a materialist and mechanistic view of history. This is the image its adversaries draw for themselves in order to refute it more easily: it calls attention to the role played by ideologies in the recent past and the submission of the proletariat to propaganda that is no longer even remotely internationalist. It is also, paradoxically, the image of official communism, stubbornly determined to reduce everything to economic determinism and to justify maneuvers, compromises, and patriotic slogans in the name of an alleged historical necessity.

This representation distorts Marx's thought. For him, material-ism was simply "the idea that all the ideological formations of a given society are synonymous with or complementary to a certain type of praxis, i.e. the way this society has set up its basic relation-ship with nature" (*SNS* 159/130). One could thus hardly say that the order of the economy is, in his eyes, that of reality, and the order of ideology that of appearance. "The bourgeois ideologies which con-taminate all of bourgeois society, including its proletariat, are not *appearances*; they mystify bourgeois society and present themselves to it in the guise of a stable world" (*SNS* 160/132). Marxism is thus in a position to recognize the full force of fascist mystification or liberal mystification; it allows us to understand that these mystifi-cations blur the lines of the class struggle, and in particular that they conceal from the proletariat the picture of its true condition and its true task. For all that, even if he affirms that exploitation and op-pression must in the long run force them to rediscover that picture, Marx never concludes from this that communism is necessary. From the moment one forgoes any recourse to a transcendent principle to explain phenomena and makes all history rest on human praxis, on the actual communication of individuals and groups at the heart of production, on the continuity of experience, it becomes essential to admit that there is "both a logic and a contingency to history, that nothing is absolutely fortuitous but also that nothing is absolutely necessary" (*SNS* 146/120, translation modified).

In his early articles, Merleau-Ponty therefore wants to call atten-tion to the difficulties faced by Marxism in its interpretation of cur-rent events and to convince us that he is not disarmed by them, but is, on the contrary, ready to welcome them, indeed, to declare Marxism's failure himself. The equivocation of facts, he thinks, casts doubt on Marxism's validity, but not in the sense its critics imagine, because from the beginning its sense of ambiguity had prepared it to confront the indeterminacy of history.

Still, the reader of these essays is right to balk at their ultimate significance. Must we, in the end, put the blame on reality or on the-ory? Was it once legitimate to interpret the future of society from the point of view of class struggle and to prescribe the communist solu-tion? Is it the impotence of historical figures that now condemns us to doubt or to retreat? Or does our present experience demand that we rethink the fundamental concepts of Marxism? When Merleau-Ponty criticizes the idea of objective necessity, he makes this distinction:

There is always the possibility of an immense compromise, of a historical decay where the class struggle, although strong enough to destroy, would not be sufficiently powerful to construct and where the dominant lines of history, as indicated in the *Communist Manifesto,* would be erased. Are we not, to all appearances, at this point now? (*SNS* 202/166)

The first hypothesis would thus be the right one: we need only admit a kind of "derailing of history," or at least imagine its possibility. Another line of thought emerges, however. From within the uncertainty to which Marxism abandons us, Merleau-Ponty recommends "a reading of the present which is as full and as faithful as possible, which does not prejudice its meaning, which even recognizes chaos and non-sense where they exist, but which does not refuse to discern a direction and an idea in events where they appear" (*SNS* 205/169). He extols a "waiting game (*politique d'attente*) without illusions about the results to be hoped from it" and advocates playing it "without honoring it with the name of dialectic" (*SNS* 207/171).

If we can still understand and take action, is it not because the failure of Marxist views does not simply confront us with the spectacle of ruin? Must we not go beyond the choice between socialism and barbarism?* We already know socialism is not *certain,* and this idea gives Marxism its depth, but we now recognize that barbarism, too, lacks the consistency of a positive reality. Thus, we confront a new demand for reflection, which in this case we do not derive from Marxism. From this period on, then, Merleau-Ponty's approach is unique: he does not argue as a Marxist, yet he claims to summon to the truth of Marx's work those who, for opposing reasons, distort its meaning. He does not restore it in order to adopt it, nor to go beyond it. Such a project would presuppose a power he does not have, for, as he says, "To go beyond a doctrine, one must first reach its level and give a better explanation of whatever it explains" (*SNS* 207/170). In short, he inquires, but in such a way that we cannot know to what extent his questions bring him closer to or farther from Marx.

It would seem that the question simply reasserts itself in *Humanism and Terror,* this time taking its pretext from the Moscow Trials

* *Socialisme ou Barbarie* was a small group of radical intellectuals led in the late 1940s by Cornelius Castoriadis and Claude Lefort; it was also the name of the magazine they published from 1949 to 1965. Critical of the bureaucratization in revolutionary social movements, the group influenced the younger generation of political activists involved in the strikes and demonstrations of May 1968. – Eds.

and from Koestler's analysis of them. Yet if it is true that the political conclusions remain the same and derive from what Merleau-Ponty will later call a "Marxist wait-and-see" (*attentisme marxiste*), their allure conceals the decisive change that occurs on the level of philosophical reflection and anticipates the final critiques of *Adventures of the Dialectic* and *Signs*. To gauge their significance, we must return for a moment to the central argument of the work. The author, you will recall, immediately excludes two interpretations of the trials: it cannot be said that the accused were traitors in the sense that the Communists were trying to establish in public opinion, nor that their confessions had been extorted by violence, because they never ceased to reply to the accusation and to refute some of its charges. Their attitude, and Bukharin's in particular, is intelligible only on the condition of recognizing that they are bound to their judges through a common attachment to the idea of revolutionary politics. Such a politics supposes in effect that at any given time, there is one, and only one, alternative and that any project that does not work directly against its adversary turns to his advantage. Not only does it teach that we are responsible for our actions, that the intentions directing them and the values they claim for themselves count only in their visible effects in history; it also transforms every situation into a limit situation, calls for immediate sanction, success or ruin. Once he fails, then, Bukharin cannot complain that treachery was driving the opposition. If he wants to persuade us that his action proceeded originally from an error in judgment, we must see that it became in reality counterrevolutionary, or, in other words, that it burdens itself with the weight of its consequences, weakens the regime while reinforcing its adversaries, threatens the very life of socialism. We should therefore not be surprised that the accused Marxists were in agreement on the principle of their responsibility, that they became their own accusers. As Merleau-Ponty once said, we must "discover their subjective honesty . . . through their own declarations as well as the summons" (*HT* 47/44).

It is on the definition of historical objectivity, however, that Merleau-Ponty resolutely distances himself from Koestler's interpretation and invites us to confront the ambiguities of Marxist philosophy, which are also those of history. In *Darkness at Noon* there was in the final analysis just one dilemma: that of the for-itself and the in-itself; of a history that requires men to act, but then merely uses them in the accomplishment of its plan, and the solitary conscience that finds in itself the enigmatic certainty of its own worth; of the pure exteriority into which each of our projects puts us, destined as it is to inscribe itself in a chain of causes and effects and to assume an independent form, and the pure interiority we are inevitably led back to once the meaning of what we have done escapes us. According to Koestler, if Rubashov accuses himself, it is because he has always subordinated his action to the idea of historical necessity. Because his failure can only seem contingent to him, he displaces it from truth to treason.

There is nothing Marxist about this view of history, however, and in reality, Merleau-Ponty observes, Bukharin behaves completely differently from Rubashov. Not only does he not recognize his guilt, but he insists on publicly demonstrating that his errors have *become* treason and on maintaining a distinction between subjective treason and objective treason. His failure does not reduce him to silence because it does not erase but rather reawakens the central question of politics: the question of the foresight, the choice, the commitment that reveals the irreducible contingency of action.

Thus there is a drama in the Moscow Trials but one which Koestler is far from giving a true presentation. It is not the Yogi at grips with the Commissar – moral conscience at grips with political ruthlessness, the oceanic feeling at grips with action, the heart at grips with logic, the man without roots at grips with tradition: between these antagonists there is no common ground and consequently no possibility of an encounter. (HT 67/62)

In other words, Bukharin was never unaware that history moves through men, that the truth of the future depends on the idea men have of it in the present, that what appears in the end to be a necessary decision was initially improvised, in confrontation or in struggle, in the absence of any objective guarantee, under threat of error, and moreover in response to so many and varied contingencies that what was truly at stake was not even obvious. Because he is a Marxist and has the experience of a political figure, he also knows that agreement on final ends does not obscure the conflict but radicalizes it, that we can maintain its sense only by making it apparent to others at each moment prior to the event and by channeling all energies into the same enterprise.

To be sure, the reasons his action is subject to the condemnation of the Revolutionary Tribunal are the same as those that forbid one to call it criminal. It is condemnable because it failed and therefore had the effect only of weakening the regime.[1] It is not criminal because it would have succeeded had it been supported by enough partisans to render it the expression of the collective will. No doubt these "ifs" cannot be formulated without reservation. To accept the hypothesis entirely would be to renounce the idea of a rational history, to assume that at any given moment in time several different policies were equally possible, as if chance alone decided their fate. It remains certain, despite all attempts to restore a past situation to its initial indeterminacy, that the present bears the truth of history. The consideration of accumulated results does not entirely dispel the ambiguity of action, however. The policies of the leaders cannot present themselves as just, simply by claiming to be confirmed by their consequences, for they also effect a back-and-forth between past and present and invoke necessity only to legitimate the decision.

The paradox of history is thus insurmountable, and it is this that breeds the tragedy of the revolutionary situation. We cannot avoid it except by surrendering either to pragmatism or to fatalism, which is to say, in both cases, by losing sight of the idea that history comprises a task and that *truth* exists only in the action of men.

One can see, then, why the Moscow Trials captured Merleau-Ponty's attention so forcefully. In the drama of Bukharin, he rediscovers the idea that was at the center of his early writings, namely, that the connection between logic and contingency cannot be undone. This connection is woven ineluctably into all human action, but reflection on revolutionary action now calls for thought concerning that connection in its own right. It is no longer enough to assert in a general way that Marxism subordinates the establishment of communism to the initiatives of men, that the future depends on our power to understand the meaning of the situation to which we consecrate the social ties created by the past, that this initiative, this power, deprived of any absolute guarantor in things, can lose itself momentarily or forever. He discovers in the ambiguity of Marxist politics a *historicity* of agents, the meaning of which is given only by a singular historical entity, the proletariat.

When we said that Bukharin's goal excluded both the demand for subjective truth and blind faith in an "object-like history" (*histoire-objet*), we stated what is in effect a merely negative conclusion. If he impugns and at once "defends his revolutionary honor," it is because in both cases he judges himself responsible for his actions before others; he knows they were born in the milieu of the revolutionary class and were aborted there as well. It is not that failure in itself condemns him, any more than success justifies the policies of the winner. Rather, his endeavor *became* treason because it wasn't able to take root in the life of the party and, through the party, in the proletariat. From the moment his ideas failed to inscribe themselves in collective praxis, from the moment they were not taken up, expanded, transformed into demands, and failed to take on a social dimension, they were destined either to perish or to turn into opposition from the *outside*.

Conversely, just policies are not those that translate a putative objective necessity; they are the those in which the proletariat recognizes the expression of its interests and its aspiration, from which it derives greater consciousness and strength. In other words, the proletariat constitutes the positive and concrete milieu in which economic conditions and the power relations they effect are transformed into a movement toward an end, an experience aware of itself. If, as Merleau-Ponty says, "the same man tries to realize himself in ... two dimensions," it is because the proletariat proves by its very existence that the two dimensions are identical. If, "between interior and exterior, subjectivity and objectivity, judgment and instrument," a dialectical relationship is established, "a contradiction founded in truth," it is because, at the heart of the revolutionary class, these opposites blend into one another, because the revolutionary class itself is indivisibly subject–object.

So, we are now in a position to posit, along with the positivity of the proletariat, the paradox of history, though certainly not to diminish it, because the positive principle reveals itself to us only in the form of a *becoming* of truth. Historical reason lies in the experience of class, but that experience is never in full possession of its own sense. It calls for and makes possible a clarification of present conditions, and an anticipation, but subordinates them to the movement in which the sum of its relations to the natural and social milieu continually inscribes itself, manifesting its effective power to master irrationality.

The decision, we said, will not be just unless it is borne out, but this prescription remains abstract as long as we fail to understand that political reflection is caught up in collective praxis, that it is one of its moments, and as a result cannot transform it into an object of representation. The reasons invoked by the revolutionary leader to explain his action can never suffice; they give, at best, the general equivalent of a truth that necessarily resists any rigorous formulation. Just as it is impossible to forgo interpretation and a rational construal of history, so, too, are we barred from giving a final criterion of truth and falsity because truth appears only at the site of proletarian practice, the action of the party, and the decisions of its leaders. Yet in the absence of such a criterion, how can there not be interminable debate about what policies to follow? Wouldn't all positions simply cancel each other out? In trying to disentangle them, how could we avoid subjecting them to the judgment of militants, given that, more often than not, questions are interconnected? Wouldn't enduring factions become entrenched, at the very least a majority and a minority, a direction and an opposition? The revolutionary party can only acknowledge the principle of democracy: the opposition has a right to its view.

The fact remains that the fierce struggle among factions has the effect of stifling opposition, or expelling it from the party. This is more to invoke than to explain the logic of class struggle. It is true that revolution tends to transform every situation into a limit situation, to infuse all conflicts with a choice between capitalism and socialism, so that weakening one reinforces the other. But this truth is still only partial, for it allows us to forget that, for Marxism, the two are not comparable; we are not in the presence of two equally determinate forces. Unlike the bourgeoisie, the proletariat is not defined by a set of interests the effect of which would inscribe itself objectively in a policy; rather, it discovers its historical task through an experience that strips it of any particular interest, opens it to self-consciousness, through a movement that comprises reflection and critique at every step. When critique occurs, it does not weaken the proletariat; indeed, Merleau-Ponty recalls, there was a time, the age of Leninism, when, at least in certain circumstances, the leaders didn't hesitate to acknowledge their errors publicly.

The real question is whether this exercise approaches a limit that necessarily restricts its scope. The gap between the present and the future is not in effect that between hypothesis and confirmation. Every decision alters the givens of the class struggle; it inscribes itself in history in such a way that we can no longer, at a later stage, put it to one side to gauge its effects, and so assess the new situation in the terms of the old one. The praxis we wanted to make our judge, in the last resort to the policies of the party, is now imposed by those policies, in such a way that it becomes necessary to try to read the truth of the future and give up discovering that of the past.

This difficulty is no doubt bound up with all human action, yet it subjects revolutionary politics to a decisive test. Not only can no crucial experience ever decide between the opposition and the party leadership, but inasmuch as the leadership holds power and, by the measures it demands, shapes the experience of men, its past positions will naturally be confirmed in the behavior and attitudes of the workers. It remains true, one might say, that the opposition would carry the day if a mass movement formed in its favor. Probably, but such movements, the strength of which dispels all doubt, occur only in exceptional circumstances. Otherwise, the competition does not offer its adversaries an equal chance. The party leadership, apart from the advantages it has, which we intentionally pass over in silence, can always find in present conditions a reflection of its own policies, which suffices to maintain them in order to avoid a split between the party and the masses. As for the opposition, its winning would require nothing less than a new revolution.

The same logic works in the consolidation of power and the elimination of the opposition. Each is defined as a function of the interests of the proletariat and calls on the proletariat to end the conflict, or at least expects its actions to constitute a destiny. To the extent that the masses fail to make their desires clear, it is necessary to interpret their interests, to decipher the meaning of praxis. The certainty that from where one stands there is truth in history is of a piece with the failure to locate the foundation of action in practice. The combination of absolute knowledge and doubt always makes argument less tolerable. Self-criticism and the open confrontation of ideas now give way to a fight to the death in which the vanquished can only resign himself to condemnation because he cannot abandon the party that abandons him and can only defend his honor because he cannot renounce his right of opposition.

Granted, the conditions in which conflicts developed within the party after the death of Lenin can seem exceptional: the weakness in numbers of the working class, the disarray of the economy, and the isolation of the USSR in the world all made for a situation as unfavorable as possible to the exercise of a proletarian democracy. Those difficulties merely reveal a contradiction that Marxist thought continually confronts. Marxism sees its truth in the idea of a universal class that embodies the future of humanity, but it deals only with an empirical, heterogeneous proletariat, condemned to division by the mode of production and blinded to its historical role by bourgeois ideology. In principle, proletarian praxis offers a solid foundation for revolutionary politics; in reality, it evinces nothing, sometimes manifesting, sometimes concealing itself. When it manifests itself, nothing guarantees that it won't vanish again; when it conceals itself, hope remains that it will reappear. In the party, the leadership and the opposition share the same expectation that imagination will supplant knowledge and terror will dissolve contradiction.

Let us return to the interpretation of the trials and to Bukharin. Merleau-Ponty seems to admit that Bukharin's positions were in error. But it is no accident that he gives no account of them, denying only that they might have been just in the absence of a social upheaval that would have guaranteed their diffusion and caused a reversal of the majorities in the party or the creation of new proletarian organs. At the same time, he is careful not to present Stalinist positions as true, for this would be to suppose that there was in 1929, for example, only one way to go and to base one's argument on a situation created, at least in part, by the party leaders to justify them. When he finally comes to consider the case of Trotsky, it is not to demonstrate that he had been wrong about Stalin. His error was only to have condemned without reservation, from exile, the Stalinist deviation, having refused, while he remained in Russia, to break with the party and engage in a power struggle he knew was doomed to fail and that would most certainly have been exploited by the enemies of the revolutionary class (HT 81/75–6). Trotsky's position on the unconditional defense of the USSR during wartime reveals more of the ambivalence in his critique because it insists that in extreme circumstances the opposition must efface itself and support the regime. These arguments show that, despite appearances, Trotsky's position is not far from that of Bukharin and that, for the one as for the other, there is a moment when radicalism becomes counterrevolutionary.

Is the prudence of Merleau-Ponty's judgment that of the philosopher stuck in the position of a spectator? Yet he was the first to recognize the dangerousness of such a position and the first to warn us away from it:

The philosopher who abstractly takes up one opinion after another can find nothing in them to separate them radically and concludes that history is terror. He then adopts a spectator standpoint which employs terror merely as a literary device. He thus fails to notice that this outlook is related to the precise circumstances of being a mind in isolation and to the quite particular prejudice of trotting from one perspective to another and never settling on any one. In this manner such an historian himself acquires an historical outlook and understands everything except that others as well as himself can have an historical *perspective*.

We must therefore acknowledge once again that there is a truth of engagement that resists reflection. "Stalin, Trotsky, and even Bukharin," Merleau-Ponty adds, "each had a perspective within the ambiguity of history and each staked his life upon it" (*HT* 101–2/95). His concern is to show that one can suppress neither the idea of contingency nor that of truth, that this double obligation founds terror and that every Marxist necessarily recognizes its principle. He notes, "The Terror of History culminates in Revolution and History is Terror because there is contingency" (*HT* 98/91). Further, "the common assumption of all revolutionaries is that the contingency of the future and the role of human decisions in history makes political divergences irreducible and cunning, deceit and violence inevitable" (*HT* 103/96).

This analysis raises again the question we asked in our reading of *Sense and Non-Sense*. Does Merleau-Ponty speak from inside or outside Marxism? If he does not embrace any party and yet decries the position of the spectator, is it to define a new perspective that would supplant earlier ones and presuppose a new way of being in society? The problem has grown considerably, however, because with the theory of the proletariat Marxism has proved to be the philosophy of history par excellence. "The Marxist theory of the proletariat," he writes at the beginning of Part Two of *Humanism and Terror*, "is not an appendix or an addendum. It is truly the core of the doctrine because it is in the condition of the proletariat that abstract concepts come to life and life itself becomes awareness" (*HT* 121–2/113).

There is a sense in which Marxism gave him what he was looking for, what his research on the body and perception had already given him to think about: a relation to being that attests to our participation in being, in this case, a philosophy of history that reveals our historicity. The proletariat is precisely this singular being in which we find the genesis of history, in which the past survives in its meaning, in which the truth of what is to come is announced. It is the universal class, stripped of any particular interest, in which "the dissolution of every class" is henceforth effected, and in which the particularities of provincialism and chauvinism disappear (*HT* 125/116–17). It is the class that concentrates in itself all human alienation and that alone can know its origin and overcome it. Both in its essence and, as we have said, as a particular historical formation, this universal class is the one whose empirical features are drawn by capitalism, whose situation is always tied to a certain state of technology and to power relations among states and nations.

At the same time, it embodies the rationality of history and finds itself a product of history. More precisely, it is history: an experience is inscribed in it that, like every experience, is at once trial and action, but turns out to be privileged inasmuch as it "changes life into awareness," every particular determination into a mode of the universal. To the extent that Marxist politics finds an *anchoring* in proletarian existence, it gains rightful access to the truth; it attains a view of society at large that authorizes it to analyze society's structure, as Marx did in *Capital* and, at the same time, admits the limits of its knowledge, clarifying the horizons that constitute the milieu of the working class of its time. Finally, the truth of Marxist dialectic appears in full in the theory of the proletariat. This theory forces us to think the dialectic through to the end: it shows us our implication in the history we have to know and transform, and so, too, the relativity of our knowledge in politics. It forces us to go beyond any argument that would claim to fix the meaning of history, to subordinate our idea of the dialectic to the de facto dialectic proletarian praxis describes.

It is thus no longer a question of abandoning ourselves to "a Marxism without illusions, completely experimental and voluntary" (*SNS* 151/124), as he argued in his early essay "Concerning Marxism," nor of resorting to a "wait-and-see" politics while refusing to "honor it with the name of dialectic." We no longer have the liberty to take or leave dialectics, to foster our illusions or give them up. Marxism cannot retreat to empiricism or allow the party's decisions to take the place of a provisional morality in the absence of a revolutionary uprising. Going to the heart of the doctrine, one must acknowledge that it derives its truth wholly from the existence of the proletariat and from the force that drives it in practice to take on for itself the meaning of human history. We must interpret every situation in terms of it; on it we must bring to bear our ideas of the future, and our doubts. With the theory of the proletariat we are at last embarked on the truth, continually facing the same task. To turn away from it would be to surrender to irrationality, and doubly so: by admitting that the human drama is meaningless and by surrendering to the obscurity of value judgments or the sheer contingency of representation without regard to our connection to a milieu and an age; to do so would be to return to subjectivism or objectivism or to vacillate between the two.

Yet we are so well embarked on the truth that the Marxist position becomes, in principle, invulnerable. Whatever happens, events will never undermine it. If, to be sure, class struggle is no longer apparent, we cannot conclude that the proletariat no longer embodies historical reason simply because we have agreed once and for all on its ambiguity, on its factual submission to bourgeois society, as well as its essential disposition to revolution. To the extent that it grants itself the right to uncertainty, the theory resists any critique that would challenge it with what is uncertain by way of calling its principles into question, and it ignores any disavowal of experience. To the extent that it succeeds in internalizing reality, what seems to come from outside immediately loses its externality and ceases to be a threat to the truth of what has already been thought. To be sure, Marxism explains everything, even its own contradiction, that of a bourgeois proletariat or, in the case of the USSR, that of a bureaucratic socialism. That contradiction is mere appearance, the shadow destined to be reabsorbed in the light of the revolution.

To be sure, these strange consequences are not clearly spelled out in *Humanism and Terror,* but while remaining implicit, they nonetheless command the author's attention in the second part of the book. Merleau-Ponty does not avoid confronting the facts that trouble the Marxist interpretation of the present age, particularly when it comes to the evolution of the USSR. On the contrary, he ruminates on them at length. We are witnessing, he says in effect, a collectivized economy in the process of constructing itself, but the working class is reduced to silence, confined to tasks of execution.

The decisions made in its name are out of its control. Proletarian internationalism no longer inspires communist policies. Perhaps we must conclude that "the revolutionary significance of the present policy is hidden beneath the 'economic infrastructure' of the regime and will only appear later, like those seeds deep in the earth which germinate after centuries" (*HT* 146–7/136). Yet how can we interpret the present from the point of view of communism when we no longer have any clear indication of its coming to pass? The relation between the present and the future is now "on the order of the occult." Reality is always far removed from the image ideology offers of it, but if we judge with Marx that "men of honest intentions carry little weight in history where only deeds and their internal logic count for anything" (*HT* 152/141), we have a right to wonder if this logic might unleash its consequences, if, for example, the reestablishment of hierarchy might consolidate a stratum of privilege and give society its final form.

Alongside these facts, which have to do with the structure of the USSR, are other no less disconcerting ones bearing on the evolution of theory. Marxism as it is now taught loses itself in materialism and pragmatism and no longer has anything in common with the philosophical dialectic that constituted its originality. For Merleau-Ponty, however, these developments remain ambiguous and cannot decide the truth of Marxism because as we have seen, the latter sees in the existence of the proletariat only the promise of a rational history and, in principle, accepts contradictions in the present. Renouncing that hope is that much more difficult because we would then no longer be able to understand our society and reject what seems unacceptable to us.

There is another fact, however, that Marxism never ceases to explain, even as it fails to convince us entirely of its truth. Merleau-Ponty writes,

The decline of proletarian humanism is not a crucial experience which invalidates the whole of Marxism. It is still valid as a critique of the present world and alternative humanisms. In this respect, at least, *it cannot be surpassed*. Even if it is incapable of shaping world history, it remains powerful enough to discredit other solutions. (*HT* 165/153)

Yet it is not easy to embrace this conclusion. How can we understand Marxism to have merely critical value? Aren't the categories that inform its critique of capitalism those that figure in the shaping of the future? Don't the contradictions of capitalism reveal themselves from the perspective of a conception of social labor that only the idea of communism, already latent in the present society, can teach us? One might well wonder whether class struggle culminates in a positive outcome, for that does not spoil Marx's philosophy, but not whether that philosophy is both true and untrue in the same time. Because he is aware of this difficulty, Merleau-Ponty finds himself obliged, despite the misgivings he has expressed, to take a further step in the justification of Marxism. Recognizing that it remains critically fertile, he ultimately grants it a positive power of explication:

a number of facts... show it to be still alive at least in the background if not the foreground of history. Present-day history is not led by a world proletariat, but from time to time it threatens to make its voice heard again.... This is enough for us to regard the Marxist attitude as still attractive, not only as moral criticism but also as an historical hypothesis. (HT 169/156–7)

Maintaining such a hypothesis, however, does not absolve us of the difficulty, for as we have seen, this hypothesis is not just one among others; it is decisive.

On close consideration, Marxism is not just any hypothesis that might be replaced tomorrow by some other. It is the simple statement of those conditions without which there would be neither any humanism, in the sense of a mutual relation between men, nor any rationality in history. In this sense Marxism is not a philosophy of history; it is *the* philosophy of history and to renounce it is to dig the grave of Reason in history. (HT 165/153)

Thus, the "no" suggested by experience dissolves before a new "perhaps." Better yet, certainty is not reinstated, but, rather, doubt confronts doubt and so builds a future for Marxism.

What are we now left with but vague indeterminacy? What Merleau-Ponty sought in Marxism was the idea of a logic composed of contingency, the principle of a *determinate indeterminacy* that he believed could be found in the proletariat, the inscription within history of a fertile ambiguity that opened onto the truth. Yet to conclude that the Marxist interpretation of history may be true simply because it is not definitely false – is this again merely to think what one wanted to think? Is it mere thought?

Later, *Adventures of the Dialectic* and *Signs* will resolutely condemn this retreat into a domain of pure uncertainty, but we must remember that the urge to question is anticipated in *Humanism and Terror*, for it is in this work that Merleau-Ponty goes to the heart of Marxism. It is there that he genuinely questions the possibility of going further, and the possibility of remaining in the same place. The more he looks for an origin in thought (*pensée-origine*) in Marx's philosophy, the idea of a radical dialectic that would resist conversion into a thesis of the world and a retreat from the critique of our own principles, the more he appreciates the difficulty of stopping at the distinction between sense and non-sense and reducing all questions that emerge in our historical experience to it. That distinction grips him, but it offers only an abstract formula of an enigma, rather than opening a path to inquiry.

Such a path is only glimpsed in the last pages of *Humanism and Terror*. Returning to the hypothesis of irrationality of history, Merleau-Ponty abruptly asks if we can ever escape the demand to think through our situation, and if that demand indicates a relation to the truth that it is not in our power to sever. No doubt, there are

periods in which intellectuals are not tolerable and enlightenment is forbidden. While they have the platform one cannot ask them to say anything other than what they see. Their golden rule is that human life and history in particular are compatible with truth *provided only that all its aspects are clarified.* (HT 202/185)

To claim the right to regard experience under all its aspects is to give up the idea that one and only one perspective, the one that initiates our participation in the revolutionary class, affords access to the meaning of history. It is also to bring inquiry to bear on what has formerly been called the "meaning of history," to make clear that events don't necessarily order themselves as the givens of a single problem, as the function of a single hypothesis, and that a truth nonetheless reveals itself in the movement of thought which enables us to see what is there without settling on a determinate representation. It is, indeed, to maintain that the being of history is irreducible to any definition of knowledge and that a *solution* cannot be expected in the future.

When people demand a "solution," they imply that the world and human coexistence are comparable to a geometry problem in which there is an unknown but not an indeterminate factor and where what one is looking for is related to the data and their possible relationships in terms of a rule.

But the question that we face today is precisely that of knowing whether humanity is simply a *problem* of that sort. (*HT* 203/186)

This question goes beyond a "Marxist wait-and-see" politics. When Merleau-Ponty wrote, "we cannot indefinitely defer the moment of deciding whether the philosophy of history is or is not accepted by history itself," or when he recalled that Trotsky himself finally set Marxism a deadline, he was dealing again with questions of fact. The conclusion of *Humanism and Terror*, however, leads directly to *Adventures of the Dialectic*, that is, to a reflection that will bear on the very principles of Marxism.

Such reflection admittedly follows a unique path in the later work, for Merleau-Ponty apparently only wants to draw our attention to changes in theory in the past thirty years and force us to gauge the distance between the dialectical interpretation of Lukács and the resolutely antidialectical views of Sartre. We must understand, however, that that factual evolution is significant, that the Marxist dialectic could only unravel in the antidialectic if it insisted on maintaining the idea of the proletariat as a universal class, of revolution as realizing negation, of communism as the solution to the problem of humanity.

The essential argument is developed in Merleau-Ponty's discussion of Sartre's "ultrabolshevism," which has the merit of offering a philosophical formulation of the new communist politics, thereby bringing about the reversal that has occurred in theory. Marx, we said, claimed to read the truth of human history in the actual future of the proletariat. As a class bound both to the contingency of its condition and to the universal, it was at once subject and object, a singular entity that bore the project of socialism inasmuch as it already realized a true community in the experience of production. In it, both human alienation and human productivity reemerge. The relations between the party and the class, between theory and praxis, between present life and the representation of the future were merely clarified by this fertile ambiguity. Sartre, by contrast, "founds communist action precisely by refusing any productivity to history and by making history, insofar as it is intelligible, the immediate result of our volitions. As for the rest, it is an impenetrable opacity" (*AD* 139/97–8). The social drama is reduced to the antagonism between bourgeois and proletarian, the former conceived as one who possesses, the latter as one utterly dispossessed. As long as it is unresolved, this antagonism remains the same, and the problem is to know at each moment if, by an awareness that is at once an act of will, the exploited class will manage to liberate itself from the condition capitalism creates for it and posit itself as subject. As Merleau-Ponty again writes, revolutionary politics from now on depends "on the nonbeing of the proletariat and on the decision which, out of nothing, creates the proletariat as the subject of history" (*AD* 140/98).

This absolute negativism indeed calls for an absolute positivism because the power of the proletariat in principle thrusts humanity into being, but the internal relation of the one to the other that Marxism tried to clarify is no longer conceivable: the existence of the proletariat no longer anticipates socialism, for it is in the present – precisely where *it is not* – that the proletariat is capable of converting society to the positivity of being. What is more, the same considerations that dissuade us from looking for meaning in the history of the proletariat render equally vain any question concerning the relations between the masses and the revolutionary party, or, within the party, between leaders and activists, or between the majority and the opposition. From the moment the class exists just by positing itself over against the other as subject, the only thing that counts, the only historical truth, is the decision of the leaders that gives it its ideal unity. In short, Sartre reduces to an identity of terms – class, party, leaders – what were for Marx moments of a dialectical relation, and he reduces to a contradiction of opposites – the empirical proletariat and the ideal proletariat, or the proletariat in capitalist society and in postrevolutionary society – a dialectical relation that implied both continuity and discontinuity, which is to say a bond in history.

Yet the critique of Sartre can hardly proceed from within Marxism. For once we have rejected his interpretation as an inadmissible schematization of Marx's thought, we must still recognize that its principle was introduced at the outset, along with the very categories governing the dialectic. However great Marx's effort was to think the dialectic through to the end, he ran up against an impossibility as soon as he sought to find a *place* for it in history, to embody it in a particular class. No doubt this class had a history of its own in which Marx should have discovered a principle of indeterminacy, but he relied instead on an absolute foundation that from then on exempted him from having to think anything unrelated to it. Marx sought in the idea of a singular and universal class the bond between positivity and negativity in history, the very bond Sartre's philosophy breaks, but he did not question the meaning of what was called *positivity* and *negativity*, and so he forgot that such principles cannot appear as "contents" in sensible experience. In the proletarian revolution, he believed he had discovered the particular and decisive moment of a destruction–realization, but in truth he merely opened himself to the myth of the end of history and, to evade the consequences, left vague what we were to understand by *realization*. "The illusion," writes Merleau-Ponty, "was only to precipitate into a historical fact – the proletariat's birth and growth – history's total meaning, to believe that history itself organized its own recovery, that the proletariat's power would be its own suppression, the negation of the negation" (*AD* 284/205).

It thus no longer makes sense to wonder, as *Humanism and Terror* did, whether, having renounced the theory of the proletariat, it is still possible to think history. Any new philosophical reflection would have to dispel the illusion that comes from viewing all human history from the perspective of a single historical fact. Despite its attempt to think history from within history, Marxist thought does not break with idealist philosophy of history because it claims to have found the constitutive principle of the totality or, indeed, because it only conceives of being in the form of totality. We cannot think history without thinking ourselves situated in history, and without preserving a memory of the mystery of our situation. In that situation we find an experience that is necessarily circumscribed: we can think only what others, and those closest to us, have given us to think; we can act only within limits imposed by conditions we have inherited from the past. Society cannot become an object of representation or a thing for us to transform because we are rooted in it and discover in the particular form of our "sociality" the meaning of our undertakings and tasks. It is true that belonging to a milieu and an age ties us to every milieu and every age, and it is the greatness of Marxism to have shown this. Yet the past reveals itself only in the symbolic context constituted by the structure of present society, so that we can exhaust its meaning neither in practice nor in thought. Our symbolic milieu opens us to other milieus, but communication does not abolish distance. For the same reason, we can never think the future by supposing the present institutions we criticize are wholly contingent, as if overcoming them could finally bring about the relation of man to man that man is in essence. Society clings to its own past just as future society clings to the present: this does not mean there are no ruptures or ventures or new tasks in history; we must simply acknowledge that even if institutions change, the symbolism remains; that there is, as Merleau-Ponty says, "a flesh of history," a principle of conservation in becoming, something like a static time superimposed on historical duration.

III. RADICALIZING A RADICAL PHILOSOPHY

The critique of Marx sketched out by Merleau-Ponty does not yield a new political theory. What is clear is that it in no way attempts to restore a pre-Marxist conception of history but aims instead to radicalize a philosophy that already called itself radical, announced the death of philosophy and its realization in the lives of men, and insisted that any reflection on its principles was the sign of a second fall into vulgar idealism or empiricism. Marxist radicalism was the radicalism of a thinking that has its roots in human praxis – and essentially in the praxis of a class – and it was the radicalism of a politics with the agenda of permanent revolution and the reorganization of society on entirely new foundations. We must now ask whether thought and action can ever find their origin and their end in this way or, better yet, whether it would ever be possible to give positive "content" to that origin or that end.

It remains true that our thoughts are born at a given time in a given society and that philosophy has its roots in the milieu of history. The question, however, is whether this milieu is determined or contains an indeterminacy in its very structure, if philosophy's relation to it can be conceived as a relation of expression, or if the task of expression is not precisely to restore that indeterminacy in the context of its own symbolism by abandoning it to free inquiry. It is true that the class struggle has not vanished, even if it is evolving at present in unexpected ways. It is also true that the expansion of bureaucracies and industrial rationalization tend to multiply divisions among different sectors of human activity, reestablish social hierarchy on new foundations, concentrate information and decision making in small groups of directors, and deprive as many as possible of the power to intervene in matters in which their own fate is at stake. Resistance to the alleged necessities of capitalism thus retains its significance.

There is also the question, however, of whether such resistance could inspire a politics aimed at establishing a regime free of the exploitation of man by man, one that would translate itself into the program of a party demanding power. We would believe that only if we imagined that the institutions we attack contain nothing but the effects of certain human actions, the embodied power of certain groups, and that changing their meaning completely merely requires another action and another power. On the other hand, if we agree that it is impossible to separate at the structural level the role of individuals and the conditions in which our relation to nature is inscribed, no political opposition will be able to forget the actual horizons of its own development and pretend to offer a solution to the "social problem." The opposition will be revolutionary only relative to conservatism or conformism, both of which mask antagonisms and attempt to obscure the depth at which they take root in human history. The opposition will be revolutionary not in awaiting some decisive event that might guarantee passage from the negative to the positive, but in the demand for a permanent and realistic debate, one aware of its own limits.

The idea of thought committed to indeterminacy and politics committed to debate is not alien to the spirit of Marxism. It was Marx who taught us to see in the advent of modern society the collapse of ancient communities, the destruction of traditional means of production and communication, of rules, models, and ideologies promising men both a definite role in society and a rootedness in nature. In the image he draws of the proletariat, we recognize the symbol of a blossoming social unity and a calling into question, in the very movement of history, man's relation to being. If these intuitions have been buried in the myth of the universal class and a human community expanding to the limits of the earth, it is perhaps, in the final analysis, because Marx was more influenced than he realized by the rationalism of Western political philosophy. And if we now question his radicalism, it is perhaps because it was, appearances notwithstanding, the last expression of a tradition in which modern thought can no longer recognize itself.[†]

[†] This essay is excerpted from "La Politique et le pensée de la politique," in *Sur une colonne absente: Écrits autour de Merleau-Ponty*. Alexander Hickox assisted with the translation. – Eds.

NOTE

1. Here we remain close to the central argument of *Humanism and Terror*.
   If we were to return to it in detail, our critique would touch on at least
   two points. First, I accept without further ado a thesis widely dissemi-
   nated in communist circles, namely, that German aggression against the
   Soviet Union justified a posteriori the condemnation of the opposition
   that threatened the stability of the regime or rendered it more vulner-
   able in the face of a foreign attack. From 1947 on, one could wonder
   whether Stalinist terror and the famous trial made possible a consolidation of the regime or, on the contrary, weakened it. Trotsky's analyses of
   the disorganization in the administration and the army should be taken
   into consideration. Since then they have been completely confirmed
   by the revelations that Khrushchev made at the Twentieth Congress
   [of the Communist Party of the Soviet Union, February 1956 – Eds.].
   Second, and this goes to the heart of the matter, if it was fruitful to
   base an argument on the statements of the accused and of the prose-
   cutor and to reveal the logic that governed their dialogue, the question
   arises nonetheless where language reveals and where it masks reality
   and to what extent the constant references to revolution and socialism were *expressions* or *rationalizations*. At one point, Merleau-Ponty
   briefly notes that one can hardly explain the conduct of the leaders in
   terms of a thirst for power or the interests of the state apparatus. That
   interpretation is surely too simple. But is it necessary to adopt the opposite thesis – namely, that everyone was reasoning wholly in the service
   of the interests of the revolution? If it is true, as *Adventures of the Dialectic* will say, that to create a new mechanism of production Soviet
   society had to put in place a mechanism of constraint and organize the
   privileges that little by little constituted the true shape of its history, is
   it not also true that those at the head of state altered their aspect and
   could only conceal their new features behind the revolutionary mask?

REFERENCES

ABBREVIATIONS OF CITED WORKS BY MERLEAU-PONTY

AD   *Les Aventures de la dialectique*. Paris: Gallimard, 1955 (folio essais). *Adventures of the Dialectic*. J. Bien, trans. Evanston: Northwestern University Press, 1973.

AR   *The Merleau-Ponty Aesthetics Reader: Philosophy and Painting*. G. A. Johnson and M. B. Smith, eds. Evanston: Northwestern University Press, 1993.

EP   *Éloge de la philosophie*. Paris: Gallimard, 1953. *Éloge de la philosophie et autres essais*. Paris: Gallimard, 1960 (folio essais). / *In Praise of Philosophy and Other Essays*. J. Wild, J. Edie, and J. O'Neill, trans. Evanston: Northwestern University Press, 1988.

HLP   *Husserl at the Limits of Phenomenology*. L. Lawlor and B. Bergo, eds. Evanston: Northwestern University Press, 2002.

HT   *Humanisme et terreur, Essai sur le problème communiste*. Paris: Gallimard, 1947. / *Humanism and Terror: An Essay on the Communist Problem*. J. O'Neill, trans. Boston: Beacon Press, 1969.

Œ   *L'Œil et l'esprit*. Paris: Gallimard, 1964 (folio essais). / "Eye and Mind." *The Primacy of Perception and Other Essays on Phenomenological Psychology, the Philosophy of Art, History and Politics*. J. M. Edie, ed. Evanston: Northwestern University Press, 1964. / "Eye and Mind." *The Merleau-Ponty Aesthetics Reader: Philosophy and Painting*. G. A. Johnson and M. B. Smith, eds. Evanston: Northwestern University Press, 1993.

N   *La Nature: Notes, Cours du Collège de France*. D. Séglard, ed. Paris: Seuil, 1994. / *Nature*. D. Séglard, ed. R. Vallier, trans. Evanston: Northwestern University Press, 2003.

NC   *Notes des Cours au Collège de France: 1958–1959 et 1960–1961*. Paris: Gallimard, 1996.

PM   *La Prose du monde.* C. Lefort, ed. Paris: Gallimard, 1969. / *The Prose of the World.* J. O'Neill, trans. Evanston: Northwestern University Press, 1973.

PP   *Phénoménologie de la perception.* Paris: Gallimard, 1945. / *Phenomenology of Perception.* C. Smith, trans. London: Routledge & Kegan Paul, 1962. / London and New York: Routledge, 2002.

PrP   *Le Primat de la perception et ses conséquences philosophiques.* Verdier, 1996. / *The Primacy of Perception and Other Essays on Phenomenological Psychology, the Philosophy of Art, History and Politics.* J. M. Edie, ed. Evanston: Northwestern University Press, 1964.

RC   *Résumés de cours, Collège de France 1952–1960.* Paris: Gallimard, 1968. / "Themes from the Lectures at the Collège de France, 1952–1960." *In Praise of Philosophy and Other Essays.* J. Wild, J. Edie, and J. O'Neill, trans. Evanston: Northwestern University Press, 1988.

S   *Signes.* Paris: Gallimard, 1960. / *Signs.* R. McCleary, trans. Evanston: Northwestern University Press, 1964.

SC   *La Structure du comportement.* Paris: Presses Universitaires de France, 1942. / *The Structure of Behavior.* A. Fisher, trans. Boston: Beacon Press, 1963.

SNS   *Sens et non-sens.* Paris: Nagel, 1948. / *Sense and Non-Sense.* H. L. Dreyfus and P. Dreyfus, trans. Evanston: Northwestern University Press, 1964.

TD   *Texts and Dialogues.* H. J. Silverman and J. Barry, Jr., eds. M. B. Smith, et al., trans. Atlantic Highlands, N.J.: Humanities Press International, 1992.

U   *L'Union de l'âme et du corps chez Malebranche, Biran et Bergson.* 2d ed. J. Deprun, ed. Paris: Vrin, 2002. First edition pagination. / *The Incarnate Subject: Malebranche, Biran, and Bergson on the Union of Body and Soul.* A. G. Bjelland and P. Burke, eds. P. B. Milan, trans. Amherst, N.Y.: Humanities Books, 2001.

VI   *Le Visible et l'invisible.* C. Lefort, ed. Paris: Gallimard, 1964. / *The Visible and the Invisible.* A. Lingis, trans. Evanston: Northwestern University Press, 1968.

OTHER WORKS BY MERLEAU-PONTY

Parcours, 1935–1951. J. Prunair, ed. Paris: Verdier, 1997. Short critical pieces on such figures as Kafka, Levinas, Marcel, Marx, Sartre, and Scheler.

Parcours deux, 1951–1961. J. Prunair, ed. Paris: Verdier, 2001. Short pieces on Husserl, Malebranche, and a variety of subjects; correspondence with Sartre.

Psychologie et pédagogie de l'enfant. Cours de Sorbonne 1949–1952. J. Prunair, ed. Paris: Verdier, 2001. Includes "La Conscience et l'acquisition du langage" of 1949–50, translated as *Consciousness and the Acquisition of Language.* H. J. Silverman, trans. Evanston: Northwestern University Press, 1973.

Causeries 1948. S. Ménasé, ed. Paris: Seuil, 2002.

L'Institution dans l'histoire personnelle et publique. Le Problème de la passivité: Le Sommeil, l'inconscient, la mémoire. Notes de cours au Collège de France (1954–1955). D. Darmaillacq, C. Lefort, S. Ménasé, eds. Paris: Belin, 2003.

WORKS BY OTHER AUTHORS

Adorno, T., W. Benjamin, E. Bloch, B. Brecht, G. Lukács. *Aesthetics and Politics* (with and afterword by Frederic Jameson). London and New York: Verso, 1977.

Alexander, F. M. *Man's Supreme Inheritance.* New York: Dutton, 1918.
Constructive Conscious Control of the Individual. New York: Dutton, 1924.
The Use of the Self. New York: Dutton, 1932.

Amidzic, O., H. J. Riehle, T. Fehr, C. Weinbruch, T. Elbert. "Patterns of Focal γ-Bursts in Chess Players: Grandmasters Call on Regions of the Brain Not Used So Much by Less Skilled Amateurs." *Nature* 412 (9 August 2001): 603.

Barbaras, R. *Le Tournant de l'experience: Recherches sur la philosophie de Merleau-Ponty.* Paris: Vrin, 1998.

Beauvoir, S. de. *Memoirs of a Dutiful Daughter.* J. Kirkup, trans. New York: Harper & Row, 1974.

Benner, P. *From Novice to Expert: Excellence and Power in Clinical Nursing Practice.* Menlo Park, Calif.: Addison–Wesley, 1984.

Blackmore, S. J., G. Brelstaff, K. Nelson, and T. Troscianko. "Is the Richness of Our Visual World an Illusion? Transsaccadic Memory for Complex Scenes." *Perception* 24 (1995): 1075–81.

Boschetti, A. *The Intellectual Enterprise: Sartre and Les Temps Modernes.* R. M. McCleary, trans. Evanston: Northwestern University Press, 1988.

Boyd, R. "The Current Status of Scientific Realism." *Scientific Realism*, J. Leplin, ed. Berkeley: University of California Press, 1984.

Brandom, R. *Articulating Reasons: An Introduction to Inferentialism.* Cambridge: Harvard University Press, 2000.
ed. *Rorty and His Critics.* Oxford: Basil Blackwell, 2000.

Burnyeat, M. "Idealism and Greek Philosophy: What Descartes Saw and Berkeley Missed." *Philosophical Review* 91 (1982): 3–40.

Butler, J. "Sexual Ideology and Phenomenological Description: A Feminist Critique of Merleau-Ponty's Phenomenology of Perception." *The Thinking Muse: Feminism and Modern French Philosophy*, J. Allen and I. M. Young, eds. Bloomington: Indiana University Press, 1989.

Canguilhem, G. *The Normal and the Pathological* (with an introduction by Michel Foucault). C. R. Fawcett and R. S. Cohen, trans. New York: Zone Books, 1991.

Carman, T. "The Body in Husserl and Merleau-Ponty." *Philosophcial Topics* 27 (1999): 205–26.

Heidegger's Analytic: Interpretation, Discourse, and Authenticity in "Being and Time." Cambridge: Cambridge University Press, 2003.

Chipp, H. B. *Theories of Modern Art: A Source Book by Artists and Critics.* Berkeley: University of California Press, 1968.

Coghill, G. E. *Anatomy and the Problem of Behavior.* New York: Macmillan, 1929.

Danto, A. "The Artworld." *The Journal of Philosophy* 61 (1964): 571–84.

The Philosophical Disenfranchisement of Art. New York: Columbia University Press, 1986.

Das, R., and S. Das. "Catching a Baseball: A Reinforcement Learning Perspective Using a Neural Network." *Proceedings of 11th National Conference on Artificial Intelligence (AAAI-94).* Seattle, Washington, 1994.

Davidson, D. "Actions, Reasons, and Causes." *Actions and Events.* Oxford: Oxford University Press, 1980.

"On the Very Idea of a Conceptual Scheme." *Inquiries into Truth and Interpretation.* Oxford: Oxford University Press, 1984.

"Replies to Seventeen Essays." *Reflecting Davidson: Donald Davidson Responding to an International Forum of Philosophers.* R. Stoecker, ed. Berlin: Walter de Gruyter, 1993.

"Laws and Cause." *Dialectica* 49 (1995): 263–78.

"Seeing through Language." *Thought and Language*, J. M. Preston, ed. Cambridge: Cambridge University Press, 1997.

"A Coherence Theory of Truth and Knowledge." *Subjective, Intersubjective, Objective.* Oxford: Clarendon Press, 2001.

Deleuze, G., and F. Guattari. *What Is Philosophy?* H. Tomlinson and G. Burchell, trans. New York: Columbia University Press, 1994.

Dennett, D. C. *Content and Consciousness.* London and Boston: Routledge & Kegan Paul, 1969; 2d ed. 1986.

"Conditions of Personhood." *The Identities of Persons.* A. Rorty, ed. Berkeley: University of California Press, 1976.

"On the Absence of Phenomenology." *Body, Mind and Method: Essays in Honor of Virgil Aldrich*, D. Gustafson and B. Tapscott, eds. Dordrecht: Reidel, 1979.

The Intentional Stance. Cambridge: MIT Press, 1987.

Consciousness Explained. Boston: Little, Brown, 1991.

Darwin's Dangerous Idea: Evolution and the Meanings of Life. New York: Simon & Schuster, 1995.

Kinds of Minds: Toward an Understanding of Consciousness. New York: Basic Books, 1996.

Brainchildren: Essays on Designing Minds. Cambridge: MIT Press, 1998.

Derrida, J. *Speech and Phenomena and Other Essays on Husserl's Theory of Signs.* D. B. Allison, trans. Evanston: Northwestern University Press, 1973.

Edmund Husserl's "Origin of Geometry": An Introduction. J. P. Leavey, trans. Lincoln: University of Nebraska Press, 1989.

Descartes, R. *The Philosophical Writings of Descartes.* 3 vols. J. Cottingham, R. Stoothoff, and D. Murdoch, trans. Cambridge: Cambridge University Press, 1985. References are to the volume and page numbers of the Adam and Tannery edition (AT).

Descombes, V. *Modern French Philosophy.* Cambridge: Cambridge University Press, 1980.

Dewey, J. *Experience and Nature.* Carbondale: Southern Illinois University Press, 1981.

Dosse, F. *History of Structuralism, Volume 1: The Rising Sign, 1945–1966; Volume 2: The Sign Sets, 1967–Present.* D. Glassman, trans. Minneapolis: University of Minnesota Press, 1997.

Dreyfus, H. L. Review of F. J. Varela, E. Thompson, and E. Rosch, *The Embodied Mind: Cognitive Science and Human Experience. Mind* 102 (July 1993): 542–6.

"The Primacy of Phenomenology over Logical Analysis." *Philosophcial Topics* 27 (1999): 3–24.

Dreyfus, H. L., and S. E. Dreyfus. *Mind over Machine.* New York: Free Press, 1986; paperback ed. 1988.

Dreyfus, H. L., and H. Hall, eds. *Husserl, Intentionality, and Cognitive Science.* Cambridge: MIT Press, 1982.

Dreyfus, H. L., and S. Todes. "The Three Worlds of Merleau-Ponty." *Philosophy and Phenomenological Research* 22 (1962): 559–65.

Evans, G. *Varieties of Reference.* J. McDowell, ed. Oxford: Clarendon Press, 1982.

Fleck, L. *Genesis and Development of Scientific Fact.* F. Bradley and T. Trenn, trans. Chicago: University of Chicago Press, 1979.

Florenne, Y., ed. *Écrits sur l'art.* 2 vols. Paris: Livre de poche classique, 1971.

Focillon, H. *The Life of Forms in Art.* C. B. Hogan and G. Kubler, trans. New York: Zone Books, 1992.

Føllesdal, D. "Husserl's Notion of *Noema.*" *Journal of Philosophy* 66 (1969): 680–7. Reprinted in *Husserl, Intentionality, and Cognitive Science.* H. L. Dreyfus and H. Hall, eds. Cambridge: MIT Press, 1982.

Foucault, M. *The Order of Things: An Archaeology of the Human Sciences.* New York: Random House, 1970.

  Aesthetics, Method, and Epistemology: Essential Works of Foucault 1954–1984, Vol. 2. J. D. Faubion, ed. New York: The New Press, 1998.

Freeman, W. J. "The Physiology of Perception." *Scientific American* 264 (1991): 78–85.

Fried, M. *Courbet's Realism.* Chicago: University of Chicago Press, 1992.

  Art and Objecthood. Chicago: University of Chicago Press, 1998.

Gibson, J. J. *The Ecological Approach to Visual Perception.* Boston: Houghton Mifflin, 1979.

Goldstein, K. *The Organism: A Holistic Approach to Biology Derived from Pathological Data in Man.* New York: Zone Books, 2000.

Goldthorpe, R. "Understanding the Committed Writer." *The Cambridge Companion to Sartre.* C. Howells, ed. Cambridge: Cambridge University Press, 1992.

Gorman, R. P., and T. J. Sejnowski. "Learned Classification of Sonar Targets Using a Massively-Parallel Network." *IEEE Transactions on Acoustics, Speech, and Signal Processing* 36 (1988): 1135–40.

Gunther, Y., ed. *Essays on Nonconceptual Content.* Cambridge: MIT Press, 2003.

Gurwitsch, A. *Studies in Phenomenology and Psychology.* Evanston: Northwestern University Press, 1966.

Hacking, I. *Representing and Intervening: Introductory Topics in the Philosophy of Natural Science.* Cambridge: Cambridge University Press, 1983.

Harman, K. L., G. K. Humphrey, and M. A. Goodale, "Active Manual Control of Object Views Facilitates Visual Recognition." *Current Biology* 22 (1999): 1315–18.

Heidegger, M. *History of the Concept of Time: Prolegomena.* T. Kisiel, trans. Bloomington: Indiana University Press, 1985. Page references to the German edition.

  Sein und Zeit. Tübingen: Max Niemeyer Verlag, 1927; 15th ed. 1979. *Being and Time.* Macquarrie and Robinson, trans. New York: Harper & Row, 1962. Page references to the German edition.

  "The Origin of the Work of Art." *Off the Beaten Track.* J. Young and K. Haynes, eds. and trans. Cambridge: Cambridge University Press, 2002.

  The Principle of Reason. R. Lilly, trans. Bloomington: Indiana University Press, 1991.

Husserl, E. *Logical Investigations*. 2 vols. J. N. Findlay, trans. London: Routledge, 1970.

    Thing and Space: Lectures of 1907. R. Rojcewicz, ed. Dordrecht and
Boston: Kluwer Academic, 1997. Page references are to the German edition.

    *Ideas Pertaining to a Pure Phenomenology and to a Phenomenological
Philosophy, First Book*. F. Kersten, trans. The Hague: Martinus Nijhoff,
1983. Page references are to the German edition.

    *Ideas Pertaining to a Pure Phenomenology and to a Phenomenologi-
cal Philosophy, Second Book*. R. Rojcewicz and A. Schuwer, trans.
Dordrecht: Kluwer Academic, 1989. Page references are to the German
edition.

    Experience and Judgment: Investigations in a Genealogy of Logic. J. S.
Churchill and K. Ameriks, trans. Evanston: Northwestern Univeristy
Press, 1973.

    The Crisis of European Sciences and Transcendental Phenomenology, D.
Carr, trans. Evanston: Northwestern University Press, 1970.

    Cartesian Meditations. D. Cairns, trans. The Hague: Martinus Nihjoff,
1960.

    *Psychological and Transcendental Phenomenology and the Confronta-
tion with Heidegger (1927–1931)*. T. Sheehan and R. E. Palmer, eds. and
trans. Dordrecht: Kluwer Academic, 1997.

James, W. *The Principles of Pscyhology*. 2 vols. Henry Holt, 1890; Dover,
1950.

Johnson, G. A., and M. B. Smith, eds. *The Merleau-Ponty Aesthetics Reader:
Philosophy and Painting*. Evanston: Northwestern University Press,
1993.

Jones, F. P. *Body Awareness in Action: A Study of the Alexander Technique*.
New York: Schocken, 1979.

Kant, I. *Kritik der reinen Vernunft*. R. Schmidt, ed. Hamburg: Felix Meiner,
1956. *Critique of Pure Reason*. P. Guyer and A. W. Wood, eds. and trans.
Cambridge: Cambridge University Press, 1997. Page references are to
the original A and B editions.

Kelly, S. D. "Grasping at Straws: Motor Intentionality and the Cognitive Science of Skilled Behavior." *Heidegger, Coping, and Cognitive Science*. M. Wrathall and J. Malpas, eds. Cambridge: MIT Press,
2000.

    "The Nonconceptual Content of Perceptual Experience: Situation Depen-
dence and Fineness of Grain" (response by Christopher Peacocke). *Philosophy and Phenomenological Research* 62 (2001): 601–8. Reprinted
in *Essays on Nonconceptual Content*, Y. Gunther, ed. Cambridge: MIT
Press, 2003.

"Husserl and Phenomenology." *Blackwell Guide to Continental Philoso-phy*, R. C. Solomon, ed. Oxford: Blackwell, 2003.

"Logic of Motor Intentional Activity." Unpublished manuscript.

Koffka, K. *Principles of Gestalt Psychology*. New York: Harcourt, Brace, 1935.

Köhler, W. *The Selected Papers of Wolfgang Köhler*. M. Henle, ed. New York: Liveright, 1971.

Krauss, R. *Passages in Modern Sculpture*. Cambridge: MIT Press, 1981.

Richard Serra/Sculpture. New York: Museum of Modern Art, 1986.

Kruks, S. *The Political Philosophy of Merleau-Ponty*. Brighton, Sussex: Har-vester Press, 1981.

Kuhn, T. *The Structure of Scientific Revolutions*. 2d ed. Chicago: University of Chicago Press, 1970.

Kukla, A. *Social Constructivism and the Philosophy of Science*. New York: Routledge, 2000.

Kwan, H. C., T. H. Yeap, D. Borrett, and B. C. Jiang. "Network Relaxation as Biological Computation." *Behavioral and Brain Sciences* 14 (1991): 354–6.

Lacan, J. *The Four Fundamental Concepts of Psychoanalysis: The Seminar of Jacques Lacan, Book XI*. Miller, J.-A. ed. A. Sheridan, trans. New York: Norton, 1998.

Latour, B., and S. Woolgar. *Laboratory Life: The Construction of Scientific Facts*. 2d ed. Beverly Hills, Calif.: Sage, 1986.

Lefort, C. *Sur une colonne absente: Écrits autour de Merleau-Ponty*. Paris: Gallimard, 1978.

Leibowitz, R. *L'Artiste et sa conscience*. Paris: Arche, 1950.

Les Philosophes célèbres. Paris: Éditions Lucien Mazenod, 1956.

Lévi-Strauss, C. *The Savage Mind*. Chicago: The University of Chicago Press, 1966.

Lilla, M. *The Reckless Mind: Intellectuals in Politics*. New York: New York Review of Books, 2001.

Malebranche, N. *Treatise on Nature and Grace*. P. Riley, trans. Oxford: Clarendon Press, 1992.

Treatise on Ethics (1684). C. Walton, ed. Dordrecht: Kluwer Academic, 1993.

The Search after Truth. T. M. Lennon and P. J. Olscamp, eds. Cambridge: Cambridge University Press, 1997.

Malraux, A. *The Voices of Silence: Man and His Art*. S. Gilbert, trans. Garden City, N.Y.: Doubleday, 1953.

Maturana, H. R., and F. J. Varela. *Autopoiesis and Cognition: The Realization of the Living*. Dordrecht and Boston: Reidel, 1980.

The Tree of Knowledge: The Biological Roots of Human Understanding. Boston: New Science Library, 1987.

McDowell, J. Mind and World. Cambridge: Harvard University Press, 1993.

Mead, G. H. Mind, Self, and Society. Chicago: University of Chicago Press, 1962.

Melville, S. "Phenomenology and the Limits of Hermeneutics." The Subjects of Art History: Historical Objects in Contemporary Perspectives, M. Cheetham, M. A. Holly, and K. Moxey, eds. Cambridge: Cambridge University Press, 1998.

Milner, D., and M. Goodale. The Visual Brain in Action. Oxford: Oxford University Press, 1995.

Mulligan, K. "Perception." The Cambridge Companion to Husserl, B. Smith and D. W. Smith, eds. Cambridge: Cambridge University Press, 1995.

Novotny, F. "Cézanne and the End of Perspective." Cézanne in Perspective. J. Wechsler, ed. Englewood Cliffs, N.J.: Prentice Hall, 1975.

O'Regan, J. K., R. A. Rensink, and J. J. Clark. "Change-Blindness as a Result of 'Mudsplashes.'" Nature 398 (1999):34.

Panofsky, E. Perspective as Symbolic Form. C. S. Wood, trans. New York: Zone Books, 1991.

Peacocke, C. "Perceptual Content." Themes from Kaplan. J. Almog, J. Perry, and H. Wettstein, eds. New York: Oxford University Press, 1989.

Putnam, H. Meaning and the Moral Sciences. London: Routledge & Kegan Paul, 1978.

Quine, W. V. O. "Two Dogmas of Empiricism." From a Logical Point of View: Nine Logico-Philosophical Essays. 2d ed., rev. Cambridge: Harvard University Press, 1961.

"Epistemology Naturalized."Ontological Relativity and Other Essays. New York: Columbia University Press, 1969.

From Stimulus to Science. Cambridge, MA: Harvard University Press, 1995.

Ravetz, J. Scientific Knowledge and Its Social Problems. Oxford: Oxford University Press, 1971.

Rheinberger, H.-J. "From Microsomes to Ribosomes: 'Strategies' of 'Representation.'" Journal of the History of Biology 28 (1995): 49–89.

Riegl, A. Late Roman Art Industry. R. Winkes, trans. Rome: Giorgio Bretschneider, 1985.

Rock, I. Indirect Perception. Cambridge: MIT Press, 1997.

Rorty, R. Philosophy and the Mirror of Nature. Princeton: Princeton University Press, 1979.

Rotonchamp, J. de. Paul Gauguin, 1848–1903. Weimar-Kessler, 1906.

Rumelhart, D. E., and J. L. McClelland. *Parallel Distributed Processing,*
Vol. 1. Cambridge: MIT Press, 1986.

Russell, B. *The Problems of Philosophy.* Oxford: Oxford University Press,
1912.

Sartre, J.-P. *L'Imaginaire: Psychologie phénoménologique de l'imagination.*
A. Elkaïm Sartre, ed. Paris: Gallimard, 1940, 1986 (folio essais). / *The*
Imaginary. J. Webber, trans. London and New York: Routledge, 2004.

L'Etre et le néant: Essai d'ontologie phénoménologique. Paris: Gallimard,
1943. / *Being and Nothingness: An Essay on Phenomenological Ontol-*
ogy. H. E. Barnes, trans. New York: Washington Square Press, 1966. /
London and New York: Routledge, 2003.

Situations. B. Eisler, trans. Greenwich: Fawcett, 1966.

"What Is Literature?" And Other Essays. S. Ungar, ed. Cambridge, MA:
Harvard University Press, 1988.

Schalk, D. L. *The Spectrum of Political Engagement. Mounier, Benda, Nizan,*
Brasillach, Sartre. Princeton: Princeton University Press, 1979.

Schank, R. C. *What We Learn When We Learn by Doing.* Technical Report
No. 60. Evanston, IL: Institute for Learning Sciences, Northwestern University, 1994.

Schmidt, J. *Maurice Merleau-Ponty: Between Phenomenology and Struc-*
turalism. New York: St. Martin's Press, 1985.

Searle, J. *Intertionality: An Essay in the Philosophy of Mind.* Cambridge:
Cambridge University Press, 1983.

Sellars, W. *Science, Perception and Reality.* New York: Humanities Press,
1963.

Shusterman, R. *Practicing Philosophy: Pragmatism and the Philosophical*
Life. New York: Routledge, 1997.

Performing Live: Aesthetic Alternatives for the Ends of Art. Ithaca: Cornell University Press, 2000.

"Wittgenstein on Bodily Feelings: Explanation and Melioration in Mind,
Art, and Politics." *The Grammar of Politics: Wittgenstein and Political*
Philosophy. C. J. Heyes, ed. Ithaca: Cornell University Press, 2003.

Silverman, H. J., and J. Barry, Jr. "Introduction: Philosopher at Work!" In
Merleau-Ponty, *TD.*

Simon, H. A. *Models of Thought.* 2 vols. New Haven: Yale University Press,
1979; 1989.

Stein, E. "Beiträge zur philosophischen Begründung der Psychologie
und der Geisteswissenschaften." *Jahrbuch für Philosophie und*
phänomenologische Forschung, vol. V., E. Husserl, ed. Halle: Max
Niemeyer, 1922.

Stewart, J. ed. *The Debate between Sartre and Merleau-Ponty.* Evanston, IL:
Northwestern University Press, 1998.

Sutton, R. S., and A. G. Barto. *Reinforcement Learning*. Cambridge: MIT Press, 1998.

Taylor, C. "The Validity of Transcendental Arguments." *Philosophical Arguments*. Cambridge: Harvard University Press, 1995.

Tesauro, G. J. "TD-Gammon, a Self-Teaching Backgammon Program, Achieves Master-Level Play." *Neural Computation* 6 (1994): 215–19.

Todes, S. "Comparative Phenomenology of Perception and Imagination, Part I: Perception." *Journal of Existentialism* 6 (1966): 253–68.

Body and World. Cambridge: MIT Press, 2001.

Varela, F. J. "Organism: A Meshwork of Selfless Selves." *Organism and the Origins of Self*, A. Tauber, ed. Dordrecht: Kluwer Academic, 1991.

Varela, F. J., E. Thompson, and E. Rosch. *The Embodied Mind: Cognitive Science and Human Experience*. Cambridge: MIT Press, 1991.

White, M. "The Effect of the Nature of the Surround on the Perceived Lightness of Grey Bars within Square-Wave Test Gratings." *Perception* 10 (1981): 215–30.

Wittgenstein, L. *Philosophical Investigations*. 3d ed. G. E. M. Anscombe, trans. New York: Macmillan, 1953.

Zettel. G. E. M. Anscombe and G. H. von Wright, eds., G. E. M. Anscombe, trans. Berkeley and Los Angeles: University of California Press, 1970.

On Certainty. G. E. M. Anscombe and G. H. von Wright, eds., D. Paul and G. E. M. Anscombe, trans. New York: Harper & Row, 1972.

INDEX